For Jane, photographer and naturalist, my constant and observant companion on these walks.

Published by Times Books
An imprint of HarperCollins Publishers
Robroyston Gate,
Glasgow
G33 1JN

www.harpercollins.co.uk
HarperCollins Publisher
Macken House
39/40 Mayor Street Upper
Dublin 1
D01 C9W8
Ireland

1st edition 2016
2nd edition 2025
© HarperCollins Publishers 2025
Text © Christopher Somerville 2025

Thanks and acknowledgements go to Joanne Lovey and Robin Ashton
at News Licensing and, in particular, at The Times, Ian Brunskill and,
at HarperCollins, Harley Griffiths, Lauren Murray, Kevin Robbins
and Rachel Weaver.

A catalogue record for this book is
available from the British Library.

ISBN 978-0-00-874518-9

10 9 8 7 6 5 4 3 2 1

If you would like to comment on any aspect
of this publication, please contact the
Publishers at the above address or online.

e-mail: times.books@harpercollins.co.uk
www.timesbooks.co.uk

Printed in Bosnia and Herzegovina

MIX
Paper | Supporting
responsible forestry
FSC™ C007454

This book contains FSC™ certified paper and other controlled
sources to ensure responsible forest management.

For more information visit: www.harpercollins.co.uk/green

THE TIMES

BRITAIN'S BEST WALKS

200 CLASSIC WALKS FROM THE TIMES

CHRISTOPHER SOMERVILLE

LOCATOR MAP

CONTENTS

INTRODUCTION

Since *Britain's Best Walks* was first published in 2016, a lot has changed across these islands. The restrictions of the Covid pandemic opened many eyes to the solace and renewal that lie among the green fields and open spaces. On one hand you'll find more buildings in the countryside, more dogs on (and off) the paths; fewer village pubs and rural buses. On the other, there's better coverage for mobile phones and GPS, and more people than ever are going out walking for fitness and for the sheer pleasure of it.

Throughout these years The Times has continued to feature my weekly column, 'A Good Walk'. With more than 700 of these walks to choose from for this new 2025 edition of *Britain's Best Walks*, I have cast my net as widely as possible from tip to toe of Britain. Among the 200 walks I've included there's a selection of classics from the first edition, but most of the walks here have never yet been published between covers.

I can truly say I have loved doing every one of these excursions on foot. They range from short strolls in easy country to tough mountain hikes. Wherever a decent pub has survived the pandemic, I've tried to include it. The walk directions are designed to enable you – whether you're an experienced hiker or an absolute beginner – to complete the expedition without getting lost. Having said that, you'll find the recommended Ordnance Survey Explorer map at a scale of 1:25,000 (online at www.osmaps.com) a great help. A good GPS takes the worry out of wayfinding, too. My website (see below) contains more details of many of these walks.

Whichever walks you follow, you are in for a treat. The coastal walks will introduce you to the great chalk cliffs of the south, the moody shores of the Thames and the pebbly strands and saltmarshes of Suffolk and Norfolk. Here are the vast sands and estuaries of the Lancashire coast, the flowery dunes of Scotland's east coast, and the beautiful islands out west and north.

Inland there are ancient trackways and level canal towpaths where the walking is slow and easy. If you like your walking with a spice of wildness, try the moorland routes in the Forest of Bowland, the North York Moors or the mountain lochs and lonely island bays of Scotland. Upland walks include the Lake District fells and the rolling Cheviot Hills of Northumberland. Go wild swimming in Loch Neldricken, and climb to the peaks of Mellbreak and Arenig Fawr and Little Wyvis for the satisfaction and the tremendous views.

Lesser-known pleasures are here for discovery, too – the Lincolnshire Wolds and the Yorkshire Wolds hide secret valleys, and Northern Ireland offers wild uplands, enormous sands and volcanic mountains with hundred-mile views. And of course these walks are rich in wildlife wonders – lady's bedstraw, centaury and viper's bugloss on the former USAF airfield of Greenham Common, portions of wild Cambridgeshire fenland carefully preserved with their orchids, hobbies and dragonflies, and the dazzling springtime display of delicate Ice Age flora in Upper Teesdale where the air is full of the piping of nesting redshank and lapwings.

There are 140,000 miles of public paths in Britain, a network of rights of way that's the envy of the walking world. Stiles and gates make the paths accessible, waymarks indicate the route. But all that is under threat from financial cutbacks. There's no such thing as the Path Fairy; it takes money and effort to maintain our rights of way. You can help preserve these wonderful paths by walking them, by knocking aside nettles and brambles, and by reporting obstructions and missing signs to the Ramblers at paths@ramblers.zendesk.com.

I have walked every step of these 200 walks, but things change from day to day in the countryside. Please let me know if you meet any problems.

Website: www.christophersomerville.co.uk
Twitter/X: @somerville_c

Enjoy these walks, to the hilt!

Christopher Somerville
Bristol, 2025

KEY

Key to text pages

Walk title

Walk map

Walk description

Page number

Region

Walk information

Key to maps

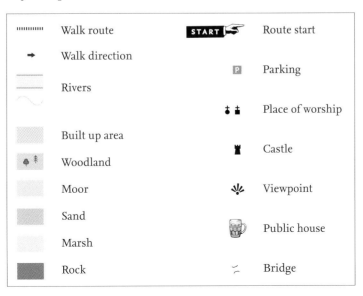

....	Walk route	**START**	Route start
→	Walk direction		
	Rivers	🅿	Parking
		♟ ♟	Place of worship
	Built up area		
🌲	Woodland	♜	Castle
	Moor	✻	Viewpoint
	Sand		
	Marsh	🍺	Public house
	Rock	⌣	Bridge

THE SOUTH WEST

Lulworth Cove, Dorset

On Bodmin Moor stand 60 or so stout lads, all turned to stone, as the legend goes, for daring to play at hurling on a Sunday. As for an impious pair of music-makers who blew their bagpipes on the sacred day – why, there they are alongside, struck to stone for ever more.

Cornwall is full of Neolithic monuments and hoary legends, but the Hurlers and their attendant Pipers are tremendously impressive in their flattish moorland setting at the edge of the old tin-mining and granite-quarrying village of Minions.

From the Hurlers we made north across the moor to scramble among a clitter of boulders to the top of Stowe's Hill, an abrupt bump in this wild landscape. Up at the summit the winds and frosts of millennia have weathered the granite into tors or piles of slabs, so smoothed and shaped that they seem more like artistic installations than natural features. Most photogenic of all is the Cheesewring, a stack of wedges piled up as the result of a boulder-chucking contest between St Tue and Giant Uther – so some say.

We skeltered down the hillside through a quarry of black cliffs where jackdaws glided in and out of the cracks that held their nests. From the quarry mouth a wriggle of former tramways led away. We followed one past a pair of ominous pit shafts, chuting straight down and away from the upper world.

We dropped down into the valley and up a scrubby hillside to join the trackbed of another old industrial railway. It was a 3-mile walk back to Minions, trudging a circle round the waist of Caradon Hill past massive mine ruins, quarry canyons and unexpected corners of green leaves and trickling streams.

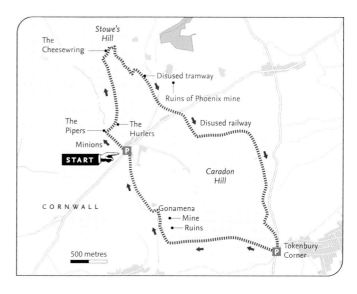

Start & finish Hurlers car park, Minions, Liskeard PL14 5LE (OS ref SX 260711)

Walk (6½ miles; moderate; OS Explorer 109): From car park follow track to the Pipers twin stones (257713), then Hurlers stone circles (258714). Head north to climb Stowe's Hill to the Cheesewring granite tor (258724). Descend right (east) side to track through quarry (259723) and on. Pass two fenced mine shafts (260722); in 50m, left down to old tramway (262722). Right; in ¼ mile, fork left at granite marker post (264719) to cross road (265717). Stiles, yellow arrows (YAs) to road (267716). Left; in 100m, right (gate) down to cross stream (268715). Don't turn left (YA), but climb slope to disused railway (269712); left. In 1¼ miles, just past spoil heap (279701), bear left on track to Tokenbury Corner car park (280697). Right on old railway. In ¾ mile, pass engine house and chimney; through arch (269698). In ½ mile, just past reservoir in a dip on right, fork left (264701) into dip. At "Private" gate, left across granite stile (263703); right on green track to Minions.

Lunch Picnic

More information Liskeard Tourist Information Centre (01579 349148)

LUXULYAN VALLEY AND THE SAINTS' WAY

Birdsong was loud in the trees of the Luxulyan Valley on a morning of brilliant sunshine. Among the mossy trunks of oak and beech the giant legs of an aqueduct stepped across the ravine, a scene from a post-apocalyptic dream.

All over Cornwall, the landscape goes hand-in-hand with the architecture of long-dead industries, most notably here in the twisting valley that winds down towards the china clay port of Par. When Joseph Treffry built the structure that served as aqueduct and viaduct across the Luxulyan Valley in 1839–42, it was one piece in a great jigsaw of tramroads, watercourses and railways this powerful engineer and industrialist created to link up his copper and tin mines and granite quarries with the ships and quays he operated down on the coast.

From the eastern end of the viaduct we followed the granite setts and rusted rails of the Higher Tramway beside the ferny channel of Carmears Leat, then down a long steep incline.

At the foot of the incline a chalky grey lane shadowed a tangle of railway lines along the flat valley bottom where glossy horses grazed and the stream beds sparkled with chips of mica. A swift blast of traffic fumes and noise at the level crossing in St Blazey, and we were heading away and up through quiet beechwoods on the Saints' Way path. Dark Ages pilgrims and holy wanderers used this ancient route across the Cornish peninsula to shorten the perilous sea journey from Ireland to the Continent.

Soon a run of stone arches, pale grey and ghostly, floated into view above the trees of the Luxulyan Valley, and we dropped down to cross the Treffry Viaduct in woodland now hushed with the approach of nightfall.

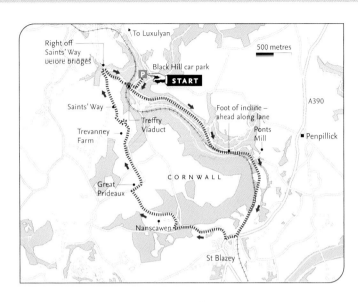

Start & finish Black Hill car park, Luxulyan PL24 2SS approx. (OS ref SX 059572)

Walk (5 miles; easy; OS Explorer 107): Up steps by information boards; right along leat; in 30m, left up woodland path to Treffry Viaduct (057571). Left; in nearly 1 mile, at foot of incline (070563), ahead along lane. Follow lane; then from Ponts Mill (073561) follow old railway track south to A390 in St Blazey (071551). Right; in 100m, right ("Luxulyan"). In half a mile, right (062553, "Saints Way"/SW) up woodland path. In 100m bend right along edge of woodland. Follow SW (cross logo, yellow arrows/YA) past Nanscawen (060554), Great Prideaux (058558), Trevanney Farm (056566) and on across fields for 1½ miles. Descend into valley. Just before bridges, right off SW (053574, YA). In 50m cross stile into field; in 100m, left at cross-paths to gate onto old tramway (055573). Right across Treffry Viaduct and retrace outward route to car park.

Lunch King's Arms, Bridges PL30 5EF (01726 850202)

More information The Friends of Luxulyan Valley, interactive map luxulyanvalley.co.uk

On a breezy, blustery day on the North Cornwall coast, a Sunday morning hush hung over Padstow.

Up on the coast path to Stepper Point the westerly wind pushed and smacked, shoving roughly, tossing the yellow heads of alexanders vigorously enough to make a hiss that almost drowned the sulky roar of the incoming tide in the mouth of the Camel Estuary.

Up on Stepper Point the old daymark tower whistled quietly to itself. Here, stories said, the women of Padstow had paraded in their red cloaks to frighten off the French. What a sight they'd have made on a morning like this, billowing scarlet before the gale sailed them all away over the estuary.

Picturing that, I leant on the wind and plodded west down the black line of the coast, looking ahead along many miles of foam-battered cliff. The rabbit-nibbled turf was spattered with thousands of pale blue stars, the petals of late-flowering spring squill.

Skirting an enormous blowhole in the cliffs near Trevone, I pushed on to Harlyn, where the thought of breakfast suddenly occurred. Well, brunch, then – a cheeseburger with relish and mustard from the Food for Thought kiosk overlooking Harlyn Bay.

Completely delicious, but just what the doctor wouldn't have ordered. "You say that," observed the lady of the van, "but we have a doctor who's a regular customer – and he tells his patients to eat here too!"

I was tired of fighting the wind, and just as well; I had it at my back now. I sauntered like a man in no sort of hurry past sleepy Trevone, through a hamlet too small to have a name, and on among the clucking bantams and stolidly chewing lambs of Trethillick.

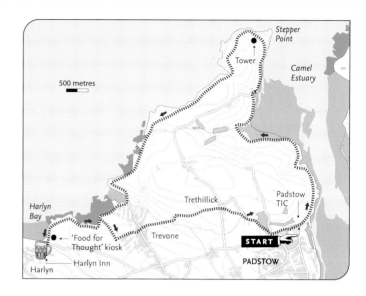

Start & finish Padstow Tourist Information Centre, The Red Brick Building, North Quay, Padstow, Cornwall PL28 8AF (OS ref SW920755)

Walk (9 miles; moderate; OS Explorer 106): Pass Shipwright's Arms; up path ("Coast Path, Hawker's Cove"); follow Coast Path arrows/acorns for 6¾ miles to Harlyn, and nearly back to Trevone. At kissing gate (887757, marked "Playing Field" on Explorer map), right (footpath sign) up field edge. Dogleg left/right; left along upper field edge to road (893755); left to road in Trevone. Left for 50m; right at left bend (fingerpost) by Hursley house; through gateway, across two fields. In third field, left across stream; on past buildings, over stile at bend of lane; on across fields to lane (905758); right to Trethillick. Right, then left; over stile; cross two fields to road (910757). Right to Padstow.

Lunch Food for Thought kiosk, Harlyn Bay; Harlyn Inn, Harlyn Bay PL28 8SB (01841 520207; www.harlyn-inn.com)

More information Padstow Tourist Information Centre (01841 533449; padstowlive.com); visitcornwall.com; ramblers.org.uk

God, what a miserable summer! Rain, rain and … yes, more rain, drenching the Cornish beaches, making rivers of the Cornish lanes. Today, for a miracle, it wasn't forecast to rain until, ooh, 10am at least. So I was up with the lark (there were no larks to be heard; they were probably cowering in the nest) and down on Polkerris beach by 6 o'clock.

"Mackerel sky, mackerel sky, neither wet, neither dry," we said as kids, and here was a sky as blue and silver as a mackerel's belly, together with a soft mist rolling in with the south-west wind. I climbed the old cliff road to Tregaminion Farm with ferns and wet grasses pearling my rain trousers. Never a dog barked as I crossed the neck of the Gribbin Head peninsula, a ghost slipping through a rain-soaked landscape now glinting brilliantly in the early sunshine. In the hamlet of Lankelly the herringbone walls were smothered in foxgloves and wall pennywort. I found the flowery, high-banked hollow of Love Lane, and followed it down through Covington Woods to the shattered old stub of St Catherine's Castle, high on a cliff knoll on the south flank of Fowey.

It was a beautiful hike back along the cliffs, across the lake outfall at impossibly picturesque Polridmouth, up on the nape of Gribbin Head under the soaring, candy-striped lookout tower. As always in such places, I longed for a six-year-old companion to play at Rapunzel. Rain began to freckle in from the sea as I skirted the sea buckthorn thickets beyond Gribbin Tower, but I beat the serious stuff into Polkerris by a short head. Now for a bacon sandwich and a good solid cup of bo'sun's tea. Proper job, that'd be.

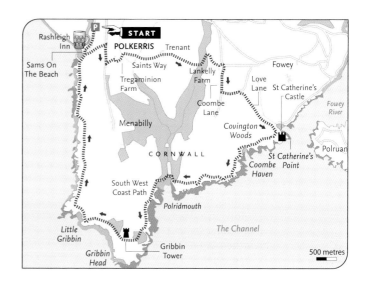

Start & finish Polkerris car park, PL24 2TL (OS ref SX094523)

Walks (6 miles; moderate; OS Explorer 107): From Polkerris car park (pay), walk down lane, past Rashleigh Inn, down ramp to beach. Left up ramp past Polkadot Café/Polkerris Beach Watersport shop. At "Toilets" sign, right up path ("South West Coast Path/CP"). In 20m, CP goes right up steps, but you keep ahead up sunken lane to road (096522). Right for 250m; left ("Saints Way/SW"). Skirt right round Tregaminion Farm (yellow arrows) and on along field paths for ⅓ mile to Trenant Cottage. Cross driveway; on along hedged path, then through fields, across stream valley, up to Lankelly Farm. Right along Coombe Lane; in 300m, left (SW); in another 300m, right (115515; SW) along Love Lane, descending towards sea for ⅓ mile. Just before houses, leave SW (117511) and follow CP past NT Covington Woods sign (acorn waymark, yellow arrow). Follow CP for 3¾ miles, via Coombe Haven, Polridmouth and Gribbin Tower, back to Polkerris.

Lunch Rashleigh Inn, Polkerris PL24 2TL (01726 814685; therashleighinnpolkerris.co.uk); Sam's on the Beach (01726 812255; samscornwall.co.uk/on-the-beach/on-the-beach-about)

More information Fowey Tourist information Centre (01726 833616; fowey.co.uk); ramblers.org.uk

TINTAGEL TO BOSCASTLE

I crossed the footbridge slung over the chasm that separates the mainland part of Tintagel Castle from the section that stands on a massive, rock-like promontory, known as Tintagel Island. Here, if the ancient chroniclers and poets can be believed, Arthur the Once and Future King was conceived.

Was Arthur born at Tintagel? Or was he washed up there on a tempest driven wave, to be raised by Merlin in the cave that still underpins Tintagel Island? And what of the ancient stone inscribed "Artognou" (which is similar to the Welsh name *Arthneu*), unearthed at Tintagel in 1998? I pondered these signs and wonders as I explored the tiny Dark Ages dwellings. Then I set out north along the coast path with the sun on my back and the wind in my face.

In the gorse banks at the top of Smith's Cliff, tiny Dartmoor ponies galloped skittishly to and fro. I walked out to the spectacular sheer-sided promontory of Willapark. Beyond Benoath Cove's perfect stretch of dull-gold sand lay Rocky Valley, where the Trevillett River jumps down towards the sea over a series of rock steps. I crossed a little grassy saddle near Firebeacon Hill, brilliant with violets and shiny yellow stars of celandine.

Under the white tower of a coastguard lookout, the coal-black cliffs of Western Blackapit stood twisted, contorted and streaked with splashes of quartzite, as though a painter had flicked his brush across them. Beyond the promontory, the white houses of Boscastle lay hidden in their deep narrow cleft, appearing in sight only at the last moment as I turned the corner by the harbour wall – a magical revelation of which Merlin himself might have been proud.

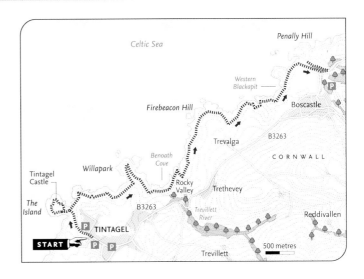

Start Tintagel Castle, near Camelford, Cornwall PL34 0HE
(OS ref SX052889)

Finish Boscastle

Walk (6 miles; strenuous; OS Explorer 111): Follow South West Coast Path to Boscastle.

Lunch Harbour Light Tea Garden, Boscastle PL35 0HD
(01840 250953)

More information Boscastle Visitor Centre (01840 250010; visitboscastleandtintagel.com); visitengland.com; ramblers.org.uk; Tintagel Castle (English Heritage 01840 770328; english-heritage.org.uk)

BEER, BRANSCOMBE AND HOOKEN UNDERCLIFF

The seaside village of Beer was looking particularly good this sunny afternoon from our viewpoint on Beer Head cliffs. The houses huddled close behind their pebbly beach, set between cliffs spectacularly coloured in red, grey and white.

Its isolated position and handy nearby caves made Beer a natural haven for smugglers. King of them all was Jack Rattenbury, the "Rob Roy of the West". Jack was captured again and again, by the French, by the Spanish, by the excisemen and the press gang. Somehow he managed to return like a bad penny to his native harbour at Beer, usually richer and never the wiser.

Just inland, the village of Branscombe curled along its road towards the fortress-like tower of St Winifred's Church. In the cool interior we found a beautifully carved Elizabethan west gallery, and on the wall nearby a painting made perhaps a hundred years earlier. Only one of the Seven Deadly Sins depicted has survived – Lust, portrayed by a man with flowing hair under a green cap, and a woman *en décolleté* with a saucy pillbox hat.

A fluffy cat came to help us with our picnic on the bench outside. Then we climbed a steep path, through woods scented with wild garlic, to reach the coast path and a steep descent to Branscombe Mouth once more.

In March 1790 a mighty landslip caused Hooken Cliff, just east of Branscombe Mouth, to crash seaward. The homeward path led through the undercliff created by the slip, a tremendously lush, ferny "lost world". Looking back from the top of the climb we had a last glimpse of the westward coast, the sea sparkling in the late sun, the cliffs marching away in red sandstone slopes to be lost in the evening sea fog along the distant shores of Tor Bay.

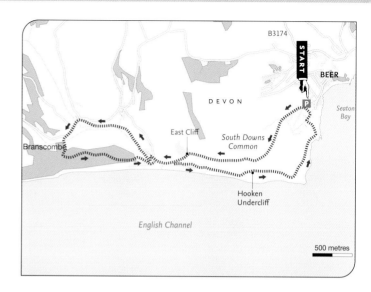

Start & finish Cliff Top car park, Common Hill, Beer EX12 3AQ (OS ref SY 227888)

Walk (6 miles; strenuous; OS Explorers 115, 116): Left up road. In 400m fork left (224887, bridleway). Follow Coast Path to Branscombe Mouth. Many steps down East Cliff. At foot of West Cliff, right (207881, "Branscombe Village") to Branscombe. Left at road (198887) to church (196885). Left through churchyard, down to cross stile on south boundary (yellow arrow). Steeply up steps to Coast Path (196882). Left to Branscombe Mouth. Up first field of East Cliff; keep ahead at fingerpost (210881, "Coast Path Beer") between chalets and on through undercliff (narrow path, slippery in places, unguarded edges, many steps). In 1 mile climb to clifftop path (222880); right to car park.

Lunch Smugglers Kitchen, Fore Street, Beer EX12 3JF (01297 22104, thesmugglerskitchen.co.uk)

More information beer-devon.co.uk

It was a brilliantly sunny winter's afternoon on the hillside above Clovelly. The eternal sea wind has streamlined the clifftop woods into a smooth curve that bends inland, with hardly a twig breaking the continuous line of the treetops. In the woods the wind blew softly, and as we walked the coast path westward we had glimpses between the leafless oaks of the sea whipping itself into cream on the pebbly beaches far below.

The view back from Gallantry Bower showed the eastward run of the coast to the estuary of the Taw and the Torridge, then on towards the ghost of Baggy Point in a haze of spray.

We dropped steeply down to lonely Mouthmill Beach, with its abandoned lime kiln. In Victorian times the Welsh limestone boats would dump great stone blocks here to be burnt to quicklime and spread as fertiliser on the acid local land.

Steeply up again to Brownsham Cliff, where we left the coast path to follow the fields to the ancient farming community of Brownsham. Then up and on through the parkland of Clovelly Court, and a steep descent on a path of cobbled steps into Clovelly.

The early 20th-century chatelaine of Clovelly Court, Christine Hamlyn, ran an extremely tight ship. Everything in Clovelly had to be kept just so. What she left for posterity is a village about as perfect as you could wish for, a photogenic tumble of cottages down a ludicrously steep cobbled street. As we climbed the roadway back to the car park, a full moon sailed across the bay and spread a sheen of silver across the restless sea, a scene so beautiful it was hard to believe it was real.

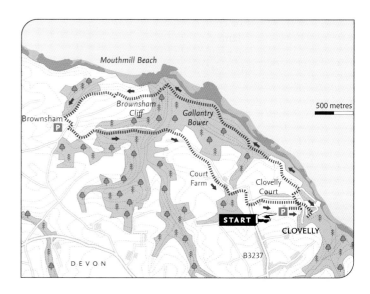

Start & finish Clovelly car park, North Devon EX39 5TL (OS ref SS 315249)

Walk (6 miles; moderate; OS Explorer 126): Through visitor centre to roadway; left on Coast Path/CP ("Brownsham") for 2¼ miles. On Brownsham Cliff, where CP turns right down steps, ahead (290264, "Brownsham"); follow red arrows/"Brownsham" to Brownsham car park (286260). Right through car park; left down steps; left (CP) past shed; right ("Mouth Mill") on bridleway through woods. At fork in ¾ mile, keep right (ahead) across stream (297259). Left at junction; in 50m, right (blue arrow/BA) up track. Continue across fields (BA) to farm track at corner of wood (302256, arrow post). Left to Clovelly Court; right by church (309251) to road. Left; follow road for 700m to junction (316250). Right; in 50m, left down path, then cobbled steps into Clovelly. Right up village street to car park.

Lunch Red Lion, The Quay EX39 5TF (01237 431237); New Inn, High Street EX39 5TQ (01237 431303)

More information Clovelly Visitor Centre (01237 431781); clovelly.co.uk; visitengland.com; ramblers.org.uk

KINGSTON AND BIGBURY-ON-SEA

Crockers and Terrys lie companionably in the churchyard of St James the Less at Kingston, our starting point for a walk along the coast of this isolated region of south Devon.

Between the leafless, wind-streamed trees of Furzedown Wood we caught glimpses of the tide-ribbed, dull gold sandflats and milky turquoise water of the Erme estuary, a snaking channel that reached its mouth between wooded headlands of black rock.

It was heady walking, with the sea-monster shape of tidal Burgh Island as an aiming point ahead. The island's Art Deco hotel gleamed in the muted winter light, an exotic morsel much picked over by guests both actual and apocryphal – Noel Coward, Winston Churchill, The Beatles and M. Hercule Poirot among them. We descended to the shore in Bigbury-on-Sea opposite Burgh Island's other hostelry, the tiny old Pilchard Inn. Jane opted to cross the sandy causeway for a bowl of soup and a bit of a sit-down there, while I set off back to Kingston through the switchback fields and stream valleys of the hinterland.

By the time I'd fetched the car and negotiated the narrow lanes back to Bigbury-on-Sea, the tide had risen to cover the causeway. I watched as Jane came ashore on Burgh Island's tall blue sea tractor, riding in state like Queen Suriyothai on her war elephant.

The Dolphin in Kingston is one of those pubs that draws you in on a cold winter's night – a combination of lamp-lit windows, the promise of a pint and a plate of food, a cosy setting and the flicker of a real good fire. It was great to settle down there with the wind and rain shut out, the map spread on the table and a great day's walking to chew over at leisure.

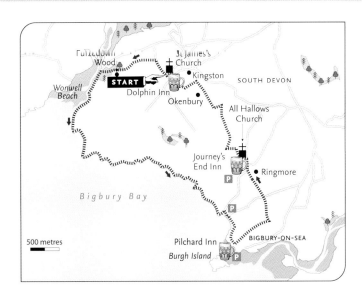

Start & finish Dolphin Inn, Kingston, Devon TQ7 4QE (OS ref SX 636478)

Walk (9 miles; strenuous; OS Explorer OL20): From Dolphin Inn, left past church. At crossroads, right ("Wonwell Beach"). In ¼ mile, just past dogleg, left (632481; "Wonwell Beach"); follow fingerposts and yellow arrows/YAs over fields for ¾ mile, down through Furzedown Wood to road by Erme estuary (620478). Left for 150m; left up steps ("Coast Path, Bigbury-on-Sea"). Follow coast path for 5 miles to Bigbury-on-Sea (if tide allows, cross sands causeway 651442, to Pilchard Inn 648440). Climb Parker Road; at top, through gate (653446; arrow, fingerpost/FP). On across fields; at end of 3rd field (658448), left downhill with fence on right (FP, "Ringmore"). Follow YAs, crossing lane at 656453, to Ringmore. At road, ahead to T-junction by church (653460). Right, then left up side of church. In 150m, left through kissing gate (653461; "Kingston" FP). Diagonally right across field and through gate; follow YAs through gates and fields, turning left (650463) to descend to stream in valley. Bear right (648463) along stream, crossing it at ruined Noddonmill (649465); on (YA) along left bank of stream, into wood (very muddy!). In ¼ mile, steeply uphill out of trees; anti-clockwise round field to far right corner (645471; FP). Right along farm track. Round left bend, and turn right (644473; FP) across field to lane (643474). Left (YA) for 50m; right (FP) and follow YAs along field edges and through woodland to road (637476). Right to T-junction in Kingston (636477); right, then left to Dolphin Inn.

Lunch Pilchard Inn, Burgh Island (01548 810514; soup and baguettes only; if marooned by high tide, return ashore on Sea Tractor, £2, check times/tides in advance); Journey's End Inn, Ringmore (01548 810205)

MOLLAND AND ANSTEY MOORS

It's just as well that the Courtenay family, stout recusants and traditionalists, held such sway in the countryside around Molland in the 19th century. They didn't see why Victorian "improvers" should be allowed to lay a finger on the tiny moorland village's church of St Mary. So no one did. What has survived here is the most perfect Georgian interior, a rare treasure.

We opened the church door on a maze of shining box pews, a fine three-decker pulpit, and the Ten Commandments sternly admonishing us from their place above the low chancel screen. The north arcade leans so dramatically out of kilter that it had to be braced with wooden beams. And the elaborate, faded Courtenay wall monuments are a-bulge with cherubim, swags, scrolls and elaborate encomia.

Although Exmoor still lay in the chilly clutch of winter, there were signs that spring might not be too far off. Daffodils and primroses were beginning to open pale yellow eyes in the churchyard.

The bare hedges whistled along deep-sunk lanes whipped by a cold south wind. We put our backs to it and went trudging up a stony bridleway over the moors that rose to the north in waves of creamy grass and black heather.

Up here it's all airy, bleak and open, proper Exmoor upland where the weather comes hard across you. The views are enormous over the winter-dried moors to lush pasturelands lower down. Below Guphill Common we turned back along a moor road, skirting its winter potholes and dipping into muddy hollows. A bridleway brought us down into lower country of steep green pastures, where heavily pregnant ewes lumbered off and starlings whistled their jaunty vespers from the bare oak tops far below.

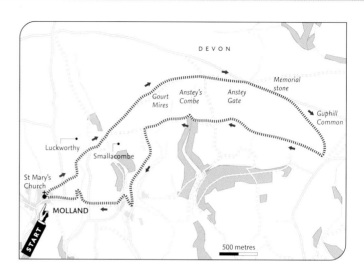

Start & finish Church car park, Molland, South Molton EX36 3NG (OS ref SS 807284)

Walk (6½ miles; moderate; OS Explorer OL9): Pass London Inn; right up laneway beside inn; right on footpath (fingerposts, yellow arrows/YAs) NE across fields to Smallacombe, crossing Moor Lane (810286), then lane to Luckworthy (814290). Bridleway from Smallacombe across ford (816291); follow it NE, then east for 1½ miles across the moor via Gourt Mires and top of Anstey's Combe (828299) to Anstey Gate (835298). Right along road. In 500m, pass memorial stone; in 100m, opposite boundary stone, right between posts (840296) on faint track SE over Guphill Common, aiming for line of trees, then their right-hand end. At road, right (845288); in 1¼ miles, cross Anstey's Combe (827294); in another 700m, bear right, through gate (821291). Follow bridleway down to road (819282). Right ("Molland"), cross stream; right (817283, steps, stile); climb to YA, then stile (YA); footpath to road (813283), follow "Molland".

Lunch London Inn, Molland EX36 3NG (01769 550269, londoninnmolland.co.uk)

More information South Molton Tourist Information Centre (01769 572501); ramblers.org.uk

POSTBRIDGE, BELLEVER TOR AND LAKEHEAD HILL, DARTMOOR

Postbridge lies more or less in the middle of Dartmoor. Its main attraction is the medieval clapper bridge that crosses the East Dart River. Early on this brisk morning I had the bridge with its great granite slabs and piled supports to myself.

Out on the open moor a broad grassy bridlepath ran south through pale wiry grass. All round the long skyline of the moor swelled, its smooth undulations broken by the hard outlines of granite tors.

Down in a sheltered hollow lay the white cottages of Bellever. The village has its own clapper bridge but the central slab is missing and it would be a brave leaper who dared the jump.

Beyond silent and derelict Laughter Hole Farm, I turned off along a green track to pass the Laughter Man, an 8-ft (2.4-m) tall standing stone on the slope of Laughter Tor. From here Bellever Tor stood tall on the western skyline, a jumble of granite that resolved itself as I got nearer into piles of flat wind-sculpted rocks stacked like grey pancakes.

It might have been the arresting profile of Bellever Tor that caused our ancient ancestors to construct their sacred sites across the slopes of Lakehead Hill. I followed a rough path through the tussocks, stumbling upon stone circles, a cist burial under a flat capstone, and a row of 12 tooth-like stones carefully aligned with the rising and setting of the sun.

There was something about these obscure monuments half buried in the moor grass that made me linger in their presence. Walking on at last, I thought of Tom White of Postbridge, a lovelorn suitor who dallied too long with his girlfriend. The pixies of Bellever Tor taught him a lesson by making him dance from midnight till dawn.

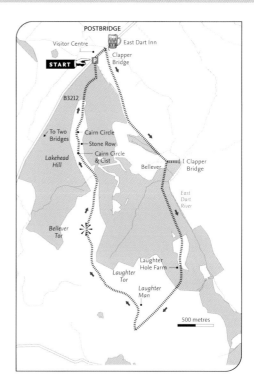

Start & finish Bellever Forest car park, Postbridge PL20 6TH (OS ref SX 647786)

Walk (5¾ miles; moderate; OS Explorer OL28): From car park, follow signs to clapper bridge (649788). Just before bridge, turn south off road ("Bridleway"); up steps onto moor. In ⅔ mile at gate (652778) cross track; bridleway descends into Bellever. At road, left (656773) to clapper bridge (659773). Return along road; left through forest car park; follow track past Laughter Hole Farm (659759). On up hill ("Country Road B3157" fingerpost). At gate leave trees (658755); ahead ("Dunnabridge Pound"). In 500m at cross-tracks (654752), right past Laughter Man standing stone (653753); on towards Bellever Tor. In ½ mile through/over gate (646758); right on grassy track to Bellever Tor summit (645764). Down broad path towards forest; in 400m, fork left (646767) on path up right flank of tussocky Lakehead Hill between forestry blocks. Follow it for 1 mile past cairn circle and cist (644774), stone row (644776) and stone circle (644777) to Kraps Ring settlement (645781). Path through trees beyond (post "5A"); in 200m, right on track, then left to Postbridge.

Lunch East Dart Inn, Postbridge PL20 6TJ (01822 880213)

More information Visitor Centre, Postbridge (01822 880272, dartmoor.gov.uk)

Under a clearing sky and a brisk wind we set out among the cottages of Abbotsbury with their walls of deep golden stone under grey-green thatch.

Stony, sunken Blind Lane led away uphill between horse pastures. From here we looked back over Abbotsbury and its steep guardian hill topped by St Catherine's Chapel, the shingle bar of Chesil Beach enclosing the long inlet of the Fleet, and the leonine form of the Isle of Portland with its long back and tail sloping down into the dull sea.

Up over the corrugations of medieval strip lynchets to the ridge, where the South Dorset Ridgeway ran out west along a bracken-brown bar of downland parallel to the sea. The tribal leaders of 3,000 years ago were laid to rest on this high eminence overlooking land and sea.

On the ramparts of Abbotsbury Hillfort, we had a grand prospect of the Jurassic Coast round the great curve of Lyme Bay, with the crumbling cliffs of Golden Cap shining a rich gold in the muted late-year light.

A cobbled green lane descended to West Bexington between hedges bright with fruit – hard red blackberries, shiny black dogwood berries, the burnished scarlet of hawthorn peggles, and old man's beard draped over the stone walls.

The single street of West Bexington sloped down to the seafront. We turned east into the wind and crunched along a beach of pebbles almost as small as sand.

On the seaward side of Abbotsbury we climbed steeply across strip lynchets to reach St Catherine's Chapel. In medieval times the maturer maidens of Abbotsbury would make an annual pilgrimage to offer a fervent prayer in the chapel on the hill, finishing with "Arn-a-one's better than narn-a-one, St Catherine!"

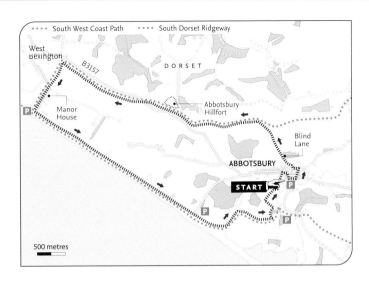

Start & finish Abbotsbury car park, Rodden Row, Abbotsbury DT3 4JL (OS ref SY 578852), £1 an hour, signposted in village

Walk (8½ miles; moderate; OS Explorer OL15): Cross B3157; up Rosemary Lane; left on Back Street. In 150m, right beside Spar House up Blind Lane (578854, "Hillfort"). In 600m, through gate (574859, yellow arrow), then another (blue horse). At ridge, left (571863, gate, "West Bexington"). Follow "South Dorset Ridgeway" and "Bexington" signs for 2¾ miles to West Bexington seafront (531864). Left along shore path, then road for 2¼ miles to road end (560846). Ahead along lower edge of car park. Follow "Coast Path" signs for ⅔ mile to 3-finger post; right (568847, "Swannery"). In ½ mile, left at stone marker (575845, "St Catherine's Church"). Steeply uphill to chapel (572848); downhill into Abbotsbury.

Lunch Manor House, West Bexington, Dorset DT2 9DF (01308 897660, manorhoteldorset.com)

More information Bridport Tourist Information Centre (01308 424901)

A gorgeous afternoon of sun and blue sky over the Dorset coast – exactly the sort of day to be walking the sandy paths of Arne Nature Reserve, a rare and precious example of conservation triumphant.

Almost all of Dorset's lowland heaths, the landscapes that Thomas Hardy immortalised, have been lost to farming and housing encroachment. If the RSPB hadn't got hold of Arne's 1,000-odd acres of lowland heath on the western shore of Poole Harbour the chances are it would all have been ploughed up or built over. That would have been the end of the Dartford warblers, the nightjars, the marsh harriers and raft spiders, lizards and slow worms that inhabit this highly specialised marsh and seashore.

We followed the Red Trail through quiet woods of oak and beech between hay meadows streaked yellow with buttercups. Soon the pastoral scene had given way to gorsy heath of tall pine trees.

Stout southern marsh orchids grew in a rank beside the path, now dull red with fallen pine needles, that led to a sandy little beach at Shipstal Point. From the viewpoint hillock behind the beach we got a fine view over Poole Harbour, the thick wooded hump of Brownsea Island prominent among a flotilla of little islets.

Back at the car park we set out on the second half of the walk, the Coombe Heath Trail across a windy, sombre-coloured heather upland.

Down in the inaccessible marshland beyond the tip of the heath, a tall pole held a sturdy platform. A large white bird of prey sat there, and looking through binoculars we realised with a thrill it was an osprey. As though intuiting it had been spotted, it slowly rose and flapped away.

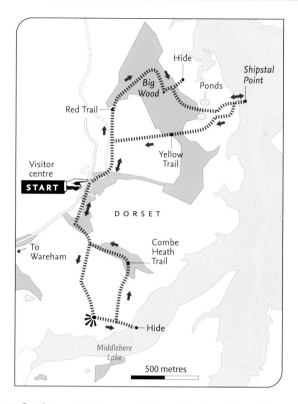

Start & finish Arne RSPB car park, Arne, Wareham BH20 5BJ (OS ref SY 971876)

Walk (4½ miles; easy; OS Explorer OL15): From Visitor Centre follow "Shipstal Trails". Red Trail for 1½ miles to 4-finger post (982884). Left to Shipstal Point beach. Returning, left up steps to viewpoint. Right down steps to 4-finger post. Left ("Car Park") back to car park. Through gate at far end; follow "Coombe Heath Trail" (white arrows) anticlockwise via viewpoint (975868) back to car park.

Lunch Arne RSPB café (01929 557828; closes 4pm)

More information rspb.org.uk/arne 01929 553360; downloadable trail map available

Sunk deep in the green downland valley of the River Frome lies the sprawling village of Maiden Newton. William Barnes, the Dorset dialect poet, caught the scene in 'The Fancy Feäir': "The Frome, wi' ever-water'd brink/Do run where sholvèn hills do zink/Wi' housen all a'cluster'd roun'/ The parish tow'rs below the down."

We found the brink of the shallow, gravel-bottomed River Frome well-watered, and well-muddied too. It was a squelch and a splosh up the riverside path to Cattistock. Sir George Gilbert Scott designed Cattistock's church with a remarkable tall tower. It beckons you into the crooked street of the village that William Barnes called "elbow-streeted Catt'stock".

Cattistock has kept its village amenities intact – church, post office, cricket field, Fox & Hounds inn, and an active pack of fox hounds. We heard them give tongue from their kennels as we headed east up the chalk grassland slopes of Lankham Bottom.

Up at Stagg's Folly we braved the rushing traffic tide of the A37, then sauntered along a forgotten old strip of road where moss grew through the tarmac and down across the pastures to where Sydling St Nicholas unravelled along its watercress stream.

Ancient Court House Farm and tithe barn lay together alongside a church guarded by fat-cheeked gargoyles choking on their waterspouts.

The Wessex Ridgeway hurdled us back across the downs, a broad and muddy old track in a sunny green tunnel of trees that rose to the ridge and fell away west towards Maiden Newton. The western sun turned all the clipped hedges to gold, and over the invisible sea beyond the hills to the south a strong clear coastal light silvered the base of clouds slowly building out there.

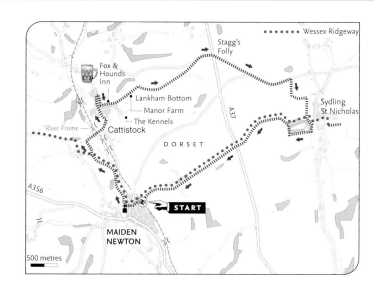

Start & finish Maiden Newton railway station, Dorchester DT2 0AE (SY 598979)

Walk (8½ miles; easy; OS Explorer 117): Down Station Road; left at junction. In 100m, right past church; left (597979, "Wessex Ridgeway"/WR, "Frome Valley Trail" fish arrow waymark). In ¾ mile, right at road (590988); in 650m, under railway; left at junction (592993). In 100m, left ("Macmillan Way"); fork left in Cattistock churchyard; ahead up street. Just beyond post office, right by Rose Cottage (591998, "Stagg's Folly"); follow bridleway to pass Manor Farm. On up Lankham Bottom; in 700m, by metal gate on right, half left (604000) past post, up slope to gate (606002). On to gate onto road (612005); right to cross A37 (613004). Follow old road; left at junction (620002); in 600m, right (626001, gate with shackle) across two fields; left along farm track (628998). In 200m, right (630998, stile) to junction (630994); keep ahead; in 100m, right (kissing gate, "Breakheart Hill"). Left down east end of church; cross stile; right on track for 550m to meet Wessex Ridgeway (627993). Left; follow WR for 2 miles back to Maiden Newton.

Lunch Fox & Hounds, Cattistock DT2 0JH (01300 320444, palmersbrewery.com/pubs/fox-and-hounds)

More information visit-dorset.com

POWERSTOCK AND EGGARDON HILL

A sunny autumn morning over the Dorset hills, the grass in the pastures wet with dew. The stone-built cottages and church tower of Powerstock looked across a shadowed valley to Nettlecombe, sunlit on the ridge opposite.

From the fields beyond, we looked ahead to see Eggardon Hill rising on the south-west skyline. We crossed the old railway line below Nettlecombe, where a cheerful man with a car boot full of yapping terriers was whistling for a stray. It scampered up, frisking and unrepentant. "Getting his own back," his owner said, fondly, "because he didn't get a walk yesterday."

Down on Spyway Road we turned past a thatched longhouse and the lonely Spyway Inn before following a bridleway past South Eggardon Farm. Back in the 18th century Isaac Gulliver, king of the Dorset smugglers, owned the farm. He planted a clump of pine trees on Eggardon Hill as a landmark for his fleet of 15 luggers bringing silk, lace, tea and gin untaxed from the Continent. The trees were felled by order of the authorities, and Gulliver himself became a respectable citizen.

Now the crumpled ramparts of the Iron Age hillfort on Eggardon Hill stood in full view, a little line of limestone outcrops at one end.

A fenced path led to the hilltop, its smooth flanks hollowed and velvety, seamed like corduroy with hundreds of erosion terraces. Handsome bronze and white cattle moved slowly off in front of us, as a superb prospect opened southward, the sea showing grey-blue in the dips of the cliffs.

A succession of green lanes brought us back to Powerstock, from where Eggardon Hill resumed its modest status as one bump among many in this steep green country.

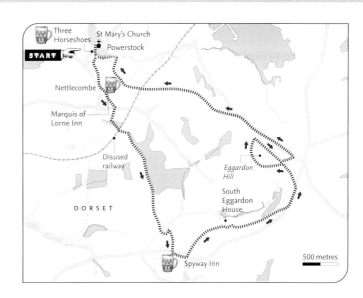

Start & finish St Mary The Virgin Church, Powerstock, Bridport DT6 3TD (OS ref SY517961)

Walk (7 miles; moderate; OS Explorer 117): Pass Three Horseshoes pub. In 100m, right downhill ("Nettlecombe"); path to road (517956). Left past inn; in 100m, right past No 3; in 50m, left across playing field. Cross road (520953); cross field to bench; down woodland path; cross old railway (520950). Field track for 1¼ miles to road (528933). Left past Spyway Inn. Left (530932) up drive. At South Eggardon House, right on bridleway up to road (545939). Left; in 350m left (546942) for circuit of Eggardon Hill. Back at "National Trust" gate (544945), left (gate) across field to lane (546946); left. In ¾ mile, lane bends right (536952); ahead here (green lane). In ½ mile track bends left (529955); ahead (yellow arrow/YA) to cross old railway (523956). In 200m, right (522956, stile) downhill. At bottom dogleg left/right (521956) over footbridge. Streamside path, then lane up to road (520960). Left to Powerstock.

Lunch Marquis of Lorne, Nettlecombe DT6 3SY (01308 485236, themarquisoflorne.co.uk); Three Horseshoes, Powerstock DT6 3TD (01308 485328, palmersbrewery.com)

More information visit-dorset.com

"Please treat the church and houses with care," said the handwritten plea left pinned by the villagers of Tyneham to their church door in the dark days of the Second World War. "We have given up our homes where many of us lived for generations to help win the war to keep men free. We shall return one day," the note ended, poignantly, "and thank you for treating the village kindly."

That return was to remain forever a dream. Evicted by the Army in 1943 so that their homes and lands could be used for training soldiers, the villagers of Tyneham never returned to the lonely valley in the Dorset downs.

We wandered around the skeleton village with the ghosts of dairyman Walter Candy, shepherd James Lucas and a host of pinafored children and hobnailed farmworkers at our elbow, then made for the grassy track along the crest of Whiteway Hill. We teetered down the steep slope below the ramparts of Flower's Barrow hillfort, and had a quick, ecstatic plunge in the semicircle of sea under the sloping cliffs of Worbarrow Bay. A stiff climb out of the cove and we were looking down on the Tyneham valley, its green slopes untouched by the intensive agriculture of the past 70 years.

The submerged rock ledges far below off Brandy Bay shimmered orange, black and jade green. In the sea haze the long wedge of Portland seemed not so much a peninsula as an island detached from the shore. A last look east to the much-quarried freestone cliffs under St Alban's Head, and we were bowling back to Tyneham along the ridge of Tyneham Cap where sparrowhawks hovered on quivering wings, and a croaky old raven was teaching formation flying to this year's youngsters.

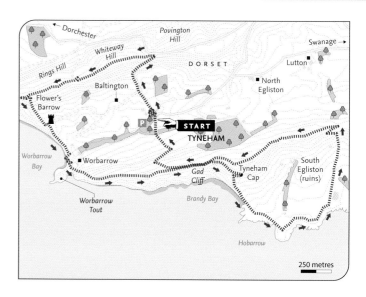

Start & finish Tyneham car park, near East Lulworth, Dorset (OS ref SY882802)

Walk (8 miles, moderate/strenuous; OS Explorer OL15): From Tyneham Church, track north (yellow markers/YM) to top of down (882810). Left along crest of down (YM) for 1 mile to Flower's Barrow hillfort. At South West Coast Path marker stone, hairpin left (866805); follow Coast Path east for 3 miles via Worbarrow Bay and Brandy Bay to Kimmeridge Bay. At "Kimmeridge View Point" board and flagpole on right, turn left (904792), following YMs to top of down (905802); left/west for 1¼ miles. Opposite Tyneham, fork right (883797) and follow YMs back to car park.

Lunch Picnic

More information Lulworth Range walks and Tyneham are open most weekends and some school holidays/bank holidays (01929 404819; tynehamopc.org.uk); Dorchester Tourist Information Centre (01305 267992; visit-dorset.com); visitengland.com; ramblers.org.uk; tynehamvillage.org

It was a glorious day of sun and wind, with cotton-wool clouds chasing each other across the deep-blue sky over Corton Denham.

We headed north along the Monarch's Way with an enormous prospect spread on our left hand, a wooded vale leading to Glastonbury Tor, the summit tower a tiny pimple at the apex of its steadily rising, beast-like back.

On the slopes under Parrock Hill a flock of sheep ran frantically bleating after the farmer as she puttered by on her quad bike to refill the feeder. One of the ewes came cautiously up to sniff my fingers, her lamb peeping out shyly from the shelter of its mother's flank.

From the mellow stone houses of Sutton Montis the old greenway of Folly Lane brought us across the medieval ridge and furrow to South Cadbury, tucked in the lee of Cadbury Castle's great ramparted hillfort. A look round the excellent archaeological display in the Camelot inn, a glance at the 700-year-old figure of Thomas à Becket painted on a window arch in the village church, and we were climbing a stony track through the Iron Age ramparts to the wide, sloping summit of the hill.

Did King Arthur ever feast here with his warriors and treacherous queen? Undoubtedly not as Tennyson and Hollywood depict him, all in shining armour in many-towered Camelot. However, an excavation in 1966–70 brought to light the foundations of a great aisled feasting hall, built in the early Dark Ages at the crown of Cadbury Castle. And spectral riders still sally forth from the fort at midnight, according to local stories, their horses shod with silver that flashes in the starlight.

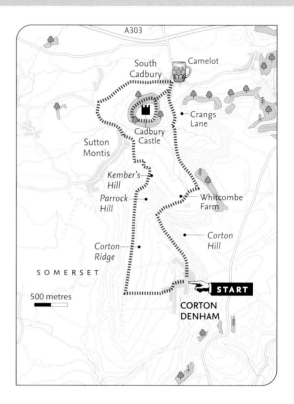

Start & finish The Queen's Arms, Corton Denham, Somerset DT9 4LR (OS ref ST 635225)

Walk (7½ miles; easy; OS Explorer 129): From Queen's Arms, left; left along Middle Ridge Lane; 30m beyond left bend, right (633224, "Woodhouse") up lane. Over stile, west across 3 fields, then north on Monarch's Way for 1 mile to road at Kember's Hill (629241). Up road opposite; in 150m, left along lane to road (626246). Left to T-junction; right along road for ½ mile. On left bend (620252), right on Leland Trail to South Cadbury. At Camelot pub, right (632256); 100m beyond church, right ("Cadbury Camelot") to Cadbury Castle. Return to road; right; in 500m, pass Crangs Lane; in 100m, left (633249, yellow arrow/YA) southwards across fields. In ⅔ mile, right (637240, YA) past Whitcombe Farm to road (631237). Left; pass road on left; in 100m, left up steps, over stile ("Corton Denham"). Path SE for ⅔ mile to road (635228); left to Queen's Arms.

Lunch The Camelot, South Cadbury, Yeovil BA22 7EX (01963 441685, camelotpub.co.uk), features Cadbury Castle exhibition

More information Yeovil Tourist Information Centre (01935 462781); Wyndham Museum (01935 845946); visitengland.com; ramblers.org.uk

THE QUANTOCK HILLS

A good friend came up with this tempting route through the Quantock Hills. A sight of the sea, a proper draught of moorland air: it was just what we wanted. Nine of us set off from Beacon Hill, dropping steeply under sweet chestnut trees to Weacombe. The combe sides rose steeply, flushed purple by thousands of foxgloves.

Up on Black Ball Hill the wind carried a faint sharp hooting. A steam train on the West Somerset Railway was panting its way down the valley towards Minehead, but locomotive and carriages stayed hidden from sight. We sat on the heather among Bronze Age burial mounds to eat our picnic with an imperial view all round, north over the Severn Sea to Wales, east to the camel hump of Brent Knoll, west into Exmoor's heights.

By the time we'd serenaded the skylarks with mouth organ tunes and descended among the trees of Slaughterhouse Combe, the sun was backlighting oak leaves and pooling on bracken banks where bilberries and star mosses winked with raindrops. Thunder ripped across the sky, a last sulk of the weather gods, as we walked west up Sheppard's Combe. A bank of sundews lay pearled with rain, their tiny pale flowers upraised on long stalks above sticky scarlet leaves.

We climbed to Bicknoller Post on its wide upland with a wonderful prospect north-west to the stepped flank of Porlock Hill and a sea full of shadows and streaks of light. Our steps quickened along the homeward path – not to unload nine souls full of immortal verse, but to beat the clock into Holford by car for the cream tea we suddenly knew we'd earned.

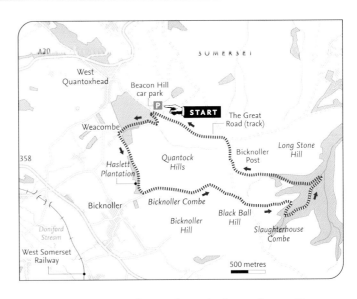

Start & finish Beacon Hill car park, Staple Plain, Hill Lane, West Quantoxhead, Somerset TA4 4DQ approx. (OS ref ST117411)

Walk (5½ miles; moderate; OS Explorer 140): From SW corner of car park, left downhill (green NT arrow) through trees. At bottom (117408), right to cottage at Weacombe (111408). Left ("Quantock Greenway") through gate; south past Haslett Plantation. In ½ mile, arrow points right at junction (115399) but go left here up Bicknoller Combe for 1 mile, climbing to junction of tracks (130398). Ahead on stony track; in 200m, fork left along grass track over Black Ball Hill and descend to bottom of Slaughterhouse Combe (143401). Left (west) for 1 mile to Bicknoller Post (128403). Right (north) for 300m to Great Road track; left to car park.

Lunch Picnic. Tea Combe House Hotel, Holford TA5 1RZ (01278 741382; combehouse.co.uk)

More information Taunton Visitor Centre (01823 340470; visitsomerset.co.uk); visitengland.com; ramblers.org.uk

On a lovely afternoon of early spring, a bit cloudy, a bit sunny, we set out from the Avalon Marshes Centre to explore Shapwick Heath National Nature Reserve, one of several bird-haunted national nature reserves in these watery West Country moors.

The main spine of the Shapwick Heath Reserve is the old branch railway line across the moors to Burnham-on-Sea. The path we followed led through lush carr woodland of birch, alder and pussy willow stubbled with silky catkins. Pollarded willows bristly with stems stood above their reflections in black mirrors of shallow, peat-stained water. A lush, marshy, ferny place of luminous green mosses, the surfaced paths springy underfoot, everything permeated by water.

Our ancestors built cunning wooden trackways to get them safely over this treacherous ground. We came across two replicas of these early thoroughfares deep in the carr woods. The Meare Heath trackway of the late Bronze Age had planks laid lengthways in pairs, held in place with wooden pegs. Further into the marsh lay a wobbly section of single planks about 8in (20cm) wide, laid end to end, held with pegs and cross ribs – a replica of the Sweet Track that was built over these marshes 6,000 years ago.

We teetered along the bouncy planks with arms outstretched for balance, conscious of the black water just one clumsy step away, before reaching firmer footing and the path to Decoy Hide.

Back on the railway path we followed the old track east past huge reedbeds and lagoons, former peat diggings now flooded and packed with wintering ducks. As we turned for home, a Cetti's warbler suddenly emitted a burst of chatter from the scrub, loud enough to make us jump.

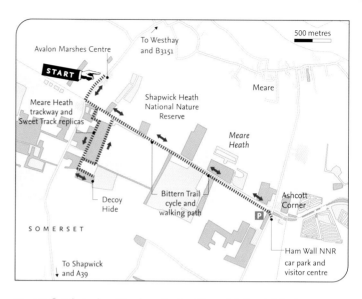

Start & finish Avalon Marshes Centre, Shapwick Road, Westhay, Glastonbury BA6 9TT (OS ref ST 426416)

Walk (6½ miles; easy; OS Explorer 141): Left along Shapwick Road; just after bridge, left (423411) along old railway track ("Bittern Trail"). In 200m, right, following "Sweet Track", then "Decoy Hide" for ¾ mile to Decoy Hide (closed at present, but still a great birdwatching spot). Return, following "Reserve Entrance" to old railway (427409). Right for 1¾ miles to Ham Wall Reserve car park (450396); return along old railway to Avalon Marshes Centre.

Lunch Marshes Hub Tea Stop café

More information Avalon Marshes Centre (01458 860120, avalonmarshes.org, leaflet maps/trail guides available at the centre or online)

There was a feeling of eternal spring on this glorious sunny morning in the Arts & Crafts village of Mells. Toddlers played in the stream. We followed a bridleway eastward through Wadbury Valley and the remnants of the once-mighty Fussells ironworks that brought prosperity and industrial clatter to the green valley from the 1740s onwards.

A baby chaffinch squatted on a hazel branch, its parent hovering in mid-air, cramming insect morsels into its open beak. At Bedlam a boy showed us his catch – two big crayfish six inches long. Beyond Bedlam the river swung off into Vallis Vale, past caves with twisted rock strata.

We were lucky to stumble upon the De la Beche Unconformity, one of 19th-century UK geology's landmark sites, a lightbulb moment of understanding about how the world was really made. A thick layer of yellow Jurassic inferior oolitic limestone lies horizontally on top of a steeply inclined grey mass of carboniferous limestone. Yet there's a gap of 170 million years between the two depositions. Unconformities like this helped pioneering geologists such as Henry De la Beche understand that the material that composes rocks was not laid down in one slow process, but by a series of upheavals and collisions.

We wandered back along the East Mendip Way to Bedlam. Here we climbed out of the valley and over a ridge to find the long track of the old Frome–Radstock railway line, now the Collier's Way cycle path. We followed it west on a high embankment where the rusty old rails accompanied us.

A short road section along Conduit Hill and we were walking a wheat field path toward the tower of Mells Church, seemingly adrift in a sea of corn and newly mown grass.

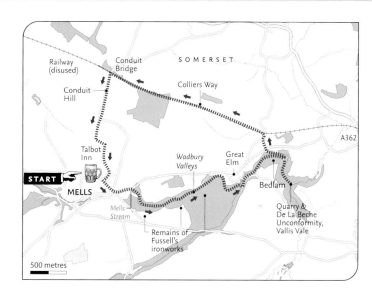

Start & finish The Talbot Inn, Mells, Frome BA11 3PN (OS ref ST 728492)

Walk (8 miles; easy; OS Explorer 142): Left along street past shop. Left (730490, "Great Elm"). In 250m right (733490, bridleway) along Wadbury Valley beside Mells Stream. In ⅔ mile fork right (743491, "Wyvern Way"). In ⅓ mile join East Mendip Way/EMW (748491); follow past Bedlam for ⅔ mile. Where EMW turns right over bridge (755491), turn left; in 50m cross open space; keep ahead (narrow, unsigned path) through bushes to old quarry/De la Beche Unconformity (756492). Return along EMW; in ¼ mile, right across river in Bedlam (754495); up roadway to road (752495). Dogleg right/left across; stile (fingerpost), field path, then road; left along Colliers Way cycle path (751498). In 1½ miles, left at Conduit Bridge (730506) along road. In 650m on left bend, ahead (728500); field paths to Mells.

Lunch The Talbot Inn, Mells (01373 812254, talbotinn.com)

More information mellsvillage.co.uk

WEST MENDIP WAY

A brisk wind over the Mendip Hills scoured the sky to a delicate China blue as we set out from Rodney Stoke on the valley road to Cheddar. The tips of the silver birches were beginning to flush a milky pink, but otherwise the woods were still caught fast in their long hibernation.

At the top of the ridge we found craggy outcrops of limestone, very pale in the late winter sun, and one of those giant West Mendip views over the Somerset Levels that took in the low ridge of the Polden Hills, the Blackdowns beyond, the Quantocks further west, Exmoor in ghostly grey, and the Welsh hills beyond a broad chink of sea in the Bristol Channel. The long, canted back of Glastonbury Tor with its pimple of a tower lay at the heart of this truly remarkable prospect.

The West Mendip Way led east, an upland path through big square fields enclosed by drystone walls. Each wall contained its stile, a solid slab of limestone with steps up and down, some of the stiles 3–4ft (1–1.2m) tall.

On the outskirts of Priddy, the only settlement on Mendip's broad plateau, we turned back on a path slanting south-west down the long slope of the escarpment.

In Cook's Fields Nature Reserve the path ran over limestone sheathed in aeolian soil, a pleasing name for the soil that blew down here 10,000 years ago on Arctic winds from the retreating glaciers to the north.

We descended over strip lynchets made by ox ploughs 1,000 years ago. Lambs sprang and bleated at Kites Croft, and six jolly pigs looked over their sty wall and grunted us back to civilisation down at Old Ditch.

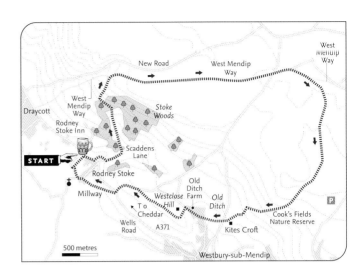

Start & finish Rodney Stoke Inn, near Cheddar, Somerset BS27 3XB (OS ref 484502)

Walk (7 miles; moderate; OS Explorer 141): From Rodney Stoke Inn, right along A372. In 250m, left (486501) up Scaddens Lane. In 400m, left (490502) on path climbing north up field, through Stoke Woods (yellow arrows/YA). At top, over stile (487510, YA). Half right; cross stile at left end of hedge on skyline (489513). East along West Mendip Way/WMW for 1½ miles to road (512513). Lane opposite; in 250m (514514), right on WMW. Just before Coxton End Lane, right on path for 1¾ miles, south, then SW over Cook's Fields Nature Reserve to gate below barn (506493). Track to Stancombe Lane; left; in 50m, right down field to stile into lane; fork right to road (502493). Right; in 200m pass "Martins" house on right; in 150m, left (499495, fingerpost) up Westclose Hill. At top, right for 700m to road (492497). Left to cross A371 (489497); Millway to T-junction (483499). Left; in 100m, right up Butts Lane to A371; right to inn.

Lunch Rodney Stoke Inn (01749 673091 rodneystokeinn.co.uk); a cheerful, bustling pub

More information Wells Tourist Information Centre (01749 671770); visitengland.com; ramblers.org.uk

BISHOPSTONE AND THE RIDGEWAY

It was scarf and frozen fingers weather over the Wiltshire Downs on a murky, muted morning. As we left Bishopstone the village children were prancing to school past the thatched houses with their walls of clunch or chalk blocks.

Chaffinches sang us off along an ivy-tangled lane that led to a valley with medieval strip lynchets lying in parallel ledges along the slopes. We threaded our way among a flock of recumbent sheep, the gently rising track turning from grass green to chalky white as it reached the Ridgeway on the crest ahead.

The ancient ridge track, a dozen paces wide, was potholed and puddled. A blackbird sang with piercing sweetness from a hawthorn twig, so close and unafraid that we could see the working of its throat and the trembling of its bright orange beak with every phrase.

A line of leafless beech trees kept the wind from the sheds at Ridgeway Farm. Here we turned south past a pig farm, the pink incumbents scampering away as though stung simultaneously into flight.

At the top of the track we turned east with red kites cutting circles overhead. There were big views to far ridges north and south, and as we descended the slope of Idstone Down a fine prospect ahead to the tall white shape of Ashdown House, a grand hunting lodge built in the 17th century for Elizabeth Stuart, elder sister of Charles I and Queen of Bohemia.

We passed the clamorous rookery in Swinley Copse and followed a wide valley track up to turn for home along the Ridgeway. A path led us aside down a steep, twisting valley, quiet and beautiful, and we beat the rain into Bishopstone by a very short head.

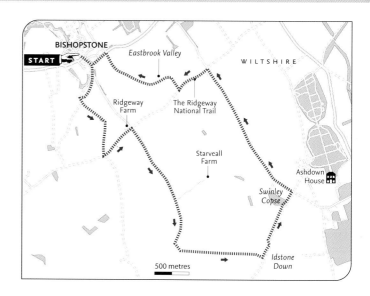

Start & finish Royal Oak, Bishopstone, Swindon SN6 8PP (OS ref SU 247837)

Walk (7¼ miles; easy; OS Explorer 170): Between Bishopstone Stores and Village Hall, take pathway ("Ridgeway") to road (247836). Right; right up Nell Hill. In 150m fork right ("Ridgeway"). Follow "Ridgeway" signs up valley to the Ridgeway (249823). Left; in ⅓ mile at Ridgeway Farm, right (253827, "Public Right of Way") along track. In ¾ mile climb slope; at top, left at track crossing (259810); in 100m, fork left (260809, arrows). In ¼ mile through gate (265809, blue arrow); on along fence. In ½ mile bear half left (273810, "Ashdown") to cross stile. Keep same direction downhill, pass Swinley Copse (276816); in 100m in valley bottom, left on grassy track (277818). In 1⅓ mile, left along the Ridgeway (264835). In ⅓ mile, right over stile (260832, "Permissive Path"). After next stile, bear left down Eastbrook Valley. At bottom, through squeeze stile (251834); down track to road (249837); left (take care) into Bishopstone.

Lunch Royal Oak, Cues Lane, Bishopstone SN6 8PP (01793 790481), helenbrowningsorganic.co.uk

More information bishopstoneandhintonparva.org

Some call it Shroton, others Iwerne Courtney. Whatever the name, it's a pretty little village of chalk, flint and thatch that lies among the undulating downland of Blackmore Vale.

A yellowhammer with a sulphurous head was practising his spring flirting with a drab female in a bramble bush, and larks went up singing from the sheep pastures. There was a hint of spring in the air, though not in the wind, still wintry enough to bring tears to our eyes.

Soon the massive ramparts of Hambledon Hill came over the skyline. Neolithic people mounded them round the long L-shaped crest of the hill and crossed them with linking causeways, a vast undertaking 5,000 years ago. Human skulls were ceremonially laid at the bottom of the ditches.

A hailstorm came pattering across as we turned south along a field track, the ice pellets bouncing off the grass and piling up in the ruts. We ducked into a barn and waited out the shower among bales of straw, then followed a rollercoaster path steeply down and sharply up again to the heights of Hod Hill. It was the Durotriges tribe that walled in this hilltop. The invading Romans chased the Durotriges away in AD43 after a brief bombardment with ballistae – several of these iron catapult bolts have been found up here.

We crossed the plateau through Roman and British ramparts, both sets of fortifications still prominent on the ground.

Down in the valley below we turned for home along a rutted track, walled with brick, flint and hard chalky clunch. A buzzard wheeled overhead, the edges of its wings silvered by a sun already sunk behind the rim of the western hills.

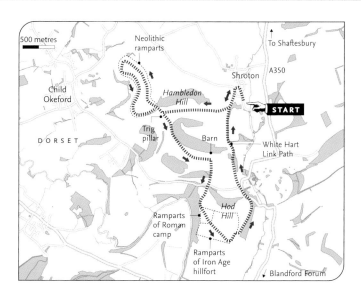

Start & finish St Mary's Church car park, Shroton, near Blandford Forum, Dorset DT11 8RF (OS ref ST 860124); £1 honesty box for parking

Walk (6 miles; moderate; OS Explorer 118): Right along road; left ("Child Okeford"); in 100m, left (859126, stile, "White Hart Link"/ WHL, "Wessex Ridgeway"/WR). Track uphill; at gate, right (WR). In just over ½ mile at trig pillar, right (848123), anticlockwise round Hambledon Hill ramparts. Back at trig pillar, ahead; in 250m, ahead at fingerpost (849120, "Steepleton Iwerne"). In 900m right at barn (855116); down to cross road (855112). Through gates opposite; up track; in 150m fork right (855111) up to gate (National Trust/NT "Hod Hill"), half left across Hod Hill for 700m. Through outer ramparts (858103); left on lower path. In 250m, right through gate (860105, NT); left on track down to road (861111). Follow WHL for a mile back to Shroton.

Lunch The Cricketers, Shroton DT11 8QD (01258 268107, thecricketersshroton.co.uk)

More information shroton.org; visit-dorset.com

DEVIL'S DEN, FYFIELD DOWN AND THE GREY WETHERS

The sun had broken through at last, rolling away a cold blanket of mist to reveal the Wiltshire downs and their subtle undulations.

This wide open downland is horse and cattle country, the gallops tending to stretch along the tops, the cattle grazing the dry valleys below. A very fine Charolais bull, contentedly recumbent, kept a lazy eye on us as we passed on our way to the Devil's Den.

Neolithic men raised the huge stones that form the structure of this passage grave. After the end of the last glaciation, these sarsens – "saracens" or foreign stones – lay scattered all across the downs, easy pickings for the builders of Stonehenge and other ancient monuments.

We followed a wide path west through a shallow valley where a great congregation of lichen-stained sarsens delineated the curve of the hollow. Local people, seeing their resemblance to an enormous flock of sheep in bedraggled fleeces, named these clustered stones the Grey Wethers.

We shadowed the river of stones up the valley, then took to the ancient downland tracks that are the pride and joy of Wiltshire's walkers. The Herepath (a Saxon word for warpath) led to the Ridgeway, a high road of braided ruts with a stunning view westward over many miles of downs and wooded valleys gilded by the afternoon sun.

Sarsens lay alongside the Ridgeway, and sarsens bounded the White Horse Trail, another venerable downland track that led us homeward between leafless hedges. A yellowhammer perched high on a bush, its breast sulphurous in the sunlight, and fieldfares flew over with vigorous wing thrusts, flocking together for protection and company in obedience to an age-old winter instinct.

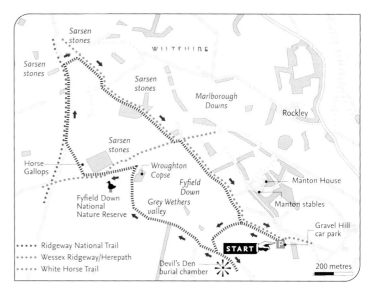

Start & finish Gravel Hill car park, Downs Lane, near Fyfield, Wilts SN8 1PL (OS ref SU 159700)

Walk (7½ miles; easy; OS Explorer 157): Follow gravelled trackway west. In 700m go left through gate (153703); on through field, with fence on left. In 500m, left (149701) down slope beside fence; left through gate (150698) to Devil's Den stones (152697). Return to gate; on along grass track through Grey Wethers valley. In 1 mile path curves right to metal gate (137706). On with fence on right to corner of Wroughton Copse (138711); left down slope; left along Wessex Ridgeway/Herepath (133710). In 300m cross gallop (130709); bear right for 550m to stile on to Ridgeway National Trail (127714). Right for 1 mile; right on to White Horse Trail/WHT (125729). In ⅔ mile fork right at copse (132723), cross track and on (WHT). Through wood (135720), then grassy track (WHT). In 600m, left on Wessex Ridgeway/Herepath (143714); in 100m right ("Byway") to car park.

Lunch Knife and Cleaver, The Grove, Houghton Conquest MK45 3LA (01234-930789, knifeandcleaver.co.uk)

More information uksouthwest.net

The infant River Thames links Gloucestershire to Wiltshire at the outer edge of the Cotswolds, in low-lying gravelly country. Setting off along the towpath of the reed-choked old Thames and Severn Canal, we marvelled at how dozens of unsightly old gravel pits have been transformed into the wide, tree-hung lakes of the Cotswold Water Park. This is a fine example of a conservation landscape; and down beyond the hamlet of Cerney Wick there's another in the lush 100-acre grassland of North Meadow.

Entering the meadow from the old canal, we walked among spatters of wild flowers – golden buttons of dandelions and buttercups, creamy yellow cowslips, the pale blues and pinks of milkmaids. And everywhere the large drooping heads of snake's head fritillaries bobbing and trembling in the wind on their dark red stems. We got down on our knees, as though in obeisance, to enjoy a close-up look at one of Britain's rarest and most spectacular plants. Some of the downward-hanging flowers were white with green spots inside; the majority were a dusky, deep rose-pink, speckled within in pale pink and rich purple, like stained-glass bells filtering the sunlight.

Snake's head fritillaries are particularly choosy about where they colonise. They are nationally scarce – but not here. North Meadow, meticulously managed by Natural England, is home to 80 per cent of the entire British population of these remarkable flowers. The Thames, no wider than a stream, dimples through the meadow, its waters slow and thick with nutritious earth particles, which are spread across the land by winter floods. The silt-enriched grass is left uncut until midsummer or later, by which time the fritillaries and all the other plants have had time to set the seeds of the next generation.

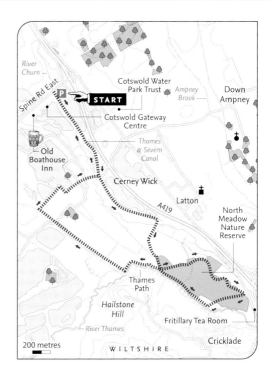

Start & finish Cotswold Gateway Centre car park, Spine Road, South Cerney, Glos GL7 5TL (OS ref SU072971)

Walk (6½ miles; easy; OS Explorer 169): Past Cotswold Gateway centre to canal; right on towpath for 1½ miles to Latton Basin (088954). Right down road; right along track past lock keeper's cottage; on south along disused canal for 650m. Through gate (087948); left through kissing gate/KG; clockwise circuit of North Meadow, returning to KG. Thames Path on left bank of Thames; in 500m, right along old railway. In ¾ mile, pass under viaduct; in another 250m, right (070956, KG) through fields, crossing two roads. At 2nd road, ahead past Crown Inn to canal (079960); left to car park.

Lunch Old Boathouse Inn, Cotswold Gateway GL7 5FP (01285 864111; phcompany.com/de-vere/cotswold-water-park-hotel/dining/old-boathouse); Fritillary Tea Room, Thames Bridge, Cricklade (some weekends in April and May; crickladeinbloom.co.uk)

More information Cotswold Water Park (01793 752413; waterpark.org); North Meadow Natural England (01452 813982; naturalengland.org.uk); visitengland.com; ramblers.org.uk, fritillary updates crickladecourtleet.org.uk/category/fritillary-watch/

WOOTTON RIVERS

I am sure Mary Poppins would declare Wootton Rivers "practically perfect". The little Wiltshire village lies snug under the downs on the edge of the Vale of Pewsey, all thatched roofs and red brick. Sparrows chittered as we walked out under a milky blue sky and up along a green lane to the roof of the downs. Up there runs the ancient trackway known as Mud Lane.

I became aware of a staring pair of eyes in the shadows of an oak, and made out the leafy face of the Green Man, venerable spirit of the greenwood, carved with wonderful skill from the stump of a branch. The artist had resisted the temptation to give him a jolly grinning countenance; instead he had an expression appropriate to his status as a woodland god, thoughtful, solemn and crafty.

Mud Lane ran out of the trees and over the nape of Martinsell Hill. The promontory down curled away like the flank of a great beast, dimpled with old pits that might have been medieval rabbit warrens, or the clay delvings of the British potters who lived up here 2,000 years ago. Nowadays, walkers stop to stare across the Vale of Pewsey to the far hills, one of southern England's most breathtaking views.

Below Martinsell Hill we followed a track across the high ramparts of the Giant's Grave, an Iron Age hillfort where autumn gentians trembled in the wind. Here there was a view to challenge the Vale of Pewsey, down into the secret cleft of Rainscombe, where a fine Georgian house lay among gold, scarlet and green trees. A slippery clay path brought us down into the Vale, and we followed the towpath of the Kennet and Avon Canal back to Wootton Rivers.

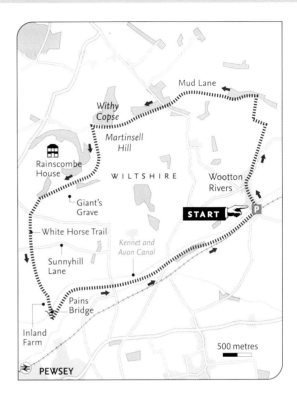

Start & finish Wootton Rivers village hall car park, near Marlborough, Wilts SN8 4NQ (SU197631)

Walk (8½ miles; moderate; OS Explorer 157): From car park, left past Royal Oak pub. In 200m, pass "Tregarthen"; keep ahead (197634) up green lane. At top of rise (200642), left, then right ("Mid Wilts Way"/ MWW) to Mud Lane trackway (198646). Right for about 50m to see Green Man; return along Mud Lane. Follow MWW for 4¼ miles via road crossing (183645), Martinsell Hill (177642), left turn off Mud Lane by Withy Copse (171642), Giant's Grave (166632); cross Sunnyhill Lane (161623); follow green lane near Inlands Farm (164616) to Pains Bridge on Kennet & Avon Canal (165612). East along canal for 2½ miles to Bridge 108/lock (198629); cross canal to car park.

Lunch Royal Oak pub, Wootton Rivers SN8 4NQ (01672 810322; wiltshire-pubs.co.uk), friendly local

More information Devizes Tourist Information Centre (01380 800400; devizes.org.uk); visitengland.com; ramblers.org.uk

Seven Sisters, East Sussex

CHARLESTON AND FIRLE BEACON

In 1916 Vanessa Bell and Duncan Grant came to live at Charleston Farmhouse in the shadow of the Sussex downs. This bohemian London couple decorated the farmhouse walls and furniture with primitive designs. Charleston soon became a magnet for such Bloomsbury Group illuminati as Virginia Woolf, David Garnett, John Maynard Keynes and E.M. Forster.

Walking over to Charleston, I was expecting a chocolate-box house in a picture-book setting. Instead, there were grunting tractors, workaday sheds and ordure-spattered dung spreaders busy in the fields around what is still a working farm. It was strange to be guided around the little rooms, with their vividly daubed walls and tables, and then to step out into such a practical farming landscape.

What shapes the scene is the long green arm of the downs behind, enclosing the southern skyline in a simple and perfect undulation. Up on the spine of the downs a cold wind came rushing in from the north, hammering at my face and tugging my beard like an impatient child. It was quite a prospect: north for many miles over the wooded hollows of the Sussex Weald, south to the spindly arms of Newhaven harbour embracing the sea.

I pushed on into the wind to the hummock of the long barrow on Firle Beacon. A fine flint wall accompanied me back to Firle, one of those well-kept estate villages where all seems right with the world.

Peter Owen Jones, vicar of Firle, writes lyrically of his downland walks. Outside St Peter's Church I found a tree festooned in prayer ribbons; inside, a Tree of Life window by John Piper. Its vivid pinks and yellows lit the cloud-shadowed vestry more brightly than any painted room in the Bloomsbury farmhouse across the fields.

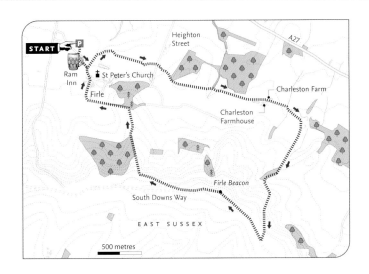

Start & finish Firle village car park, East Sussex BN8 6NS approx. (OS ref TQ469074)

Walk (5 miles; moderate; OS Explorer 123): From car park walk to Ram Inn. Left along street; left at post office (470071) down lane, through gate. Follow track across parkland. In 200m, right up roadway; in 50m, left at post, aiming for flint house halfway along edge of wood ahead. Cross road at cottage (478073); through iron gate; follow bridleway through shank of wood (480071), on over fields to pass Charleston Farm (491069). In 200m, right (493068) along concrete track. At barns (494067), bear right, following track towards downs. In 550m, cross track (492062); on in tunnel of trees; through gate (490060, BA). Bear left up track to top of downs. Right (490054) along South Downs Way to trig pillar on Firle Beacon (485059). In 300m, through gate (482059); in 150m, fork right off South Downs Way, descending path for ¾ mile to T-junction (475068); left beside wall to Firle.

Lunch Ram Inn, Firle (01273 858222, raminn.co.uk)

More information Charleston Farmhouse (charleston.org.uk, 01323 811265); visitengland.com; ramblers.org.uk

DITCHLING BEACON

The shepherd came bouncing up the long flank of Home Bottom on his quad bike, three energetic sheepdogs in attendance. We chatted a while; then he went about his business, and we walked on past circular dew ponds and Bronze Age tumuli. Up here near Ditchling Beacon, the South Downs National Park displays some of its most spectacular scenery; a great circle of East and West Sussex, north for 15 or 20 wooded miles, south through the dips of Hogtrough Bottom and Home Bottom and out across the massed roofs of Brighton to the sea.

At Ditchling Beacon Nature Reserve the wildflowers provided us with a spectacle as dramatic as the view – harebells thickly sprinkled, mauve feathery bartsia, purple knapweed and sky-blue chicory, bright yellow froths of lady's bedstraw and fragrant pink thickets of wild marjoram.

The Clayton Windmills stood breasting the north wind on their ridge. Here we left the South Downs Way and the panoramic ridge, plunging south into the sheltered bottoms or steep dry valleys that seam these chalk downs. Beyond deep-sunk Lower Standean farm we found another shepherd working his sheep in the pastures of North Bottom, flying up and down the slopes on his puttering quad, the dogs racing round behind the flock, the sheep on the canter, every lamb and ewe bleating so that their panicky voices filled the valley, high and low. When all were corralled and their wobbly laments stilled, the three dogs took a leap into a drinking trough and splashed about there luxuriously.

We swung north for the homeward stretch up a nameless bottom, opening on a far view of brilliant white cliffs, the scuff of our boots in the chalk and flint of the path the only sound in this secluded and now silent hollow of the downs.

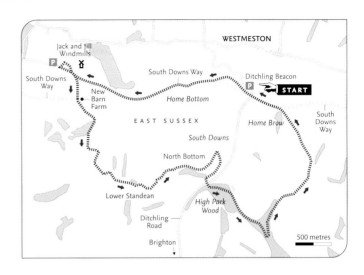

Start & finish Ditchling Beacon car park, near Brighton, East Sussex BN6 8RJ (OS ref TQ 333130) – £2 a day (National Trust members free)

Walk (8½ miles; easy/moderate; OS Explorer 122): From car park, west along South Downs Way (SDW) for 2 miles to Jack and Jill Windmills (303133). Just before mills, left (305132, "Devil's Dyke"). Beyond New Barn Farm, SDW turns right; ahead here (306129, "Chattri War Memorial", blue arrow). In ½ mile, left at 3-finger post (307121), crossing Sussex Border Path (309117), to Lower Standean. Just before house, left (316115) past pond; right along edge of trees to meet gravel track (318116). Bridleway along North Bottom for ¾ mile; just before gate (328121), right; cross Ditchling Road (327116). SE through High Park Wood for 1 mile; left under power lines (337108); NE for ¾ mile to bridleway crossing (343117). Bear NNW to SDW on Home Brow (339128); left to car park.

Lunch Half Moon Inn, Plumpton BN7 3AE – a well-run, characterful pub (01273 890253; halfmoonplumpton.com)

More information visitbrighton.com; nationalparks.gov.uk; visitengland.com; satmap.com; ramblers.org.uk

FRISTON FOREST AND THE SEVEN SISTERS

The immaculately kept East Sussex village of East Deanlies, just inland of the Seven Sisters cliffs at the heart of a superb coast and countryside landscape. Ramblers know they'll be welcome at the cosy old Tiger Inn and the Hiker's Rest teashop on the village green, the hub of a network of footpaths. I chose a circuit that would thread woodland, downs and cliffs together, and set out early from the Tiger into a red dawn.

Friston Forest sighed gently in the morning wind. Sunk in the woods, the medieval rectory and church at West Dean gleamed in dew-wet flint. A long flight of steps, the crest of a hill, and I was looking down over one of England's classic views – the extravagant snake bends of the Cuckmere River sinuating its way seaward through a dead flat littoral between great curves of downland. At the brink of the Cuckmere Haven cliffs, a terrace of coastguard cottages stood isolated, their tall chimneys silhouetted against a pale wintry sea.

Foxhole Farm lay tucked into a fold of the downs. Beyond the farm the South Downs Way ribboned east along the furrowed brows of the Seven Sisters cliffs. At their feet fresh falls of chalk lay scattered, staining the shallows a milky white. It was hard to tear myself away from this captivating stretch of coast, but my way lay inland, funnelling up Gap Bottom past the old farming hamlet of Crowlink. A last trudge over the downs and I was dipping down the steep slope towards East Dean with a pint of Tiger's Claw in my sights and a head full of wonders to sort through.

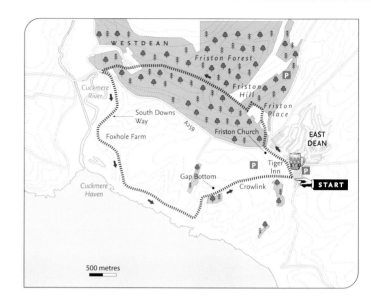

Start & finish Tiger Inn, East Dean, near Eastbourne, East Sussex BN20 0DA (OS ref TV556978)

Walk (8 miles; easy/moderate; OS Explorer 123): Footpath from East Dean (556979) to Friston Church (551982); cross A259; footpath (yellow arrow) into trees; right through trees, across field, lane and next field, to lane round Friston Place (550989). Left to corner (548990); left for 100m; right (opposite entrance) on bridleway through woods for 1½ miles to West Dean. Pass church (525997) to T-junction; left along South Downs Way/SDW. Follow SDW south and east along cliffs for 2¾ miles. By National Trust "Crowlink" sign (538968) inland to pass Crowlink hamlet. Right here (545975) on footpath east for 600m, to go through kissing gate (551976). Pass right side of triangular woodland; cross stone wall stile (554977, ahead, not right); downhill to East Dean.

Lunch Tiger Inn, East Dean; The Cuckmere Inn, Exceat Bridge, Seaford BN25 4AB (01323 892247; vintageinn.co.uk)

More information Eastbourne Tourist Information Centre (01323 415415; visiteastbourne.com); visitsussex.org; ramblers.org.uk; satmap.com

GLYNDE, MOUNT CABURN AND BIBLE BOTTOM

On a warm midday the half-moon shapes of paraglider sails were wheeling in cloudy air off Mount Caburn. Looking south from the summit of the Iron Age ceremonial enclosure, we watched the paragliders swooping this way and that against a backdrop of the silvery sinuation of the River Ouse as it carved its way seaward through the chalk rampart of the South Downs.

The diminutive brick and flint estate cottages of Glynde lay neatly stretched below. A tufted path, jumping with grasshoppers, had led us up from the village.

The 2,500-year-old ditch around the hilltop enclosure was spattered with blue flowers – scabious, harebells and viper's bugloss – among which flitted blue butterflies. The same theme of chalk grassland flowers and butterflies continued all along the path that dropped down a slope into a tangle of dry, flat-bottomed valleys.

In Oxteddle Bottom faint foundations in the grass showed where winter sheds for plough oxen stood in medieval times. Bible Bottom's enclosure was too well-camouflaged under grass and wild vegetation to make out.

We picnicked on a bank of marjoram, the bushy pink flowers exuding an oily pungency. Sheep were grazing these valleys as they have done for centuries. It was a scene straight out of an Eric Ravilious painting.

Up on the nape of the downs we turned for home as views opened up to the north over the broad-hedged lowlands of the Sussex Weald, a vista in total contrast to the billowing downs to the south. We threaded between Bronze Age burial mounds and old chalk quarries before turning off down the long path to Glynde, with the dimpled green wall of the South Downs beyond.

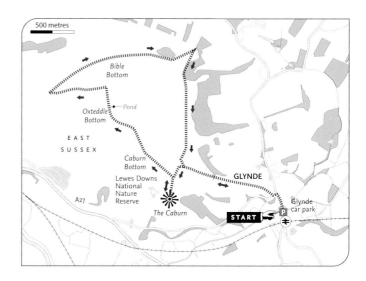

Start & finish Glynde railway station, Lewes, East Sussex BN8 6RU (SO ref TQ458087)

Walk (5½ miles; easy; OS Explorer OL25): From station, left; in 300m left (457090, Ranscombe Lane); in 40m, right (gate, yellow arrow/YA) on field path for ¾ mile to ridge. At gate in ridge fence (445093), left to The Caburn (444089). Return towards gate; 100m past outer ditch of hillfort, left (444091) on path down Caburn Bottom. At bottom, ahead (440097) along Oxteddle Bottom. At pond, right-hand gate (437099, permissive path); in 300m bear left; cross stile (437101). Follow fence on left; in 400m, chalk path (433101) up to gate (431101). Ahead (YA) to post (430100, YA); right. In ¾ mile at Southerham Farm notice, kissing gate (442105); past waymark post, then wood on left. In 200m pass dew pond; before stile, right along fence (447105). In 300m fork left (466103), up to stile; on with fence on right. In ½ mile, left at gate on right (445093); retrace steps to Glynde.

Lunch Little Cottage Tea Rooms, Ranscombe Lane, Glynde BN8 6ST (01273 858215; littlecottagetearooms.co.uk)

More information glynde.co.uk

RODMELL AND HARVEY'S CROSS

A cool, windy morning over the South Downs, with the village of Rodmell dreamlike in muted colours, its flint and weatherboarded houses lining the lane down to the River Ouse.

Looking out on the lane is Monk's House, a modest building of weatherboard and brick, bought by Leonard and Virginia Woolf in 1919 and loved by them as a country retreat for themselves and their Bloomsbury friends.

From Monk's House we followed a stony lane across a flat floodplain of rough cattle pasture to the banks of the Ouse. Here Virginia came on 28 March 1941, distraught at a recurrence of her mental illness, to drown herself in the river, having filled her coat pockets with heavy stones to weigh her down.

Melancholy overhangs the spot, but we felt it lift with the clouds and the landscape as we passed the church at Southease with its Saxon round tower and climbed into the higher countryside of the downs.

It's all "bottoms" around here, dry valleys that wriggle into the flanks of the chalk downs. Looking back from the far ridge, it was all classic downland: white chalky tracks, a twisted thorn tree, long curves of dark flinty ploughlands and green corn.

Through tiny, tucked-away Telscombe where the hedges were a-twitter with sparrows, then up and away on breezy downland tracks. Up here the lonely marble monument of Harvey's Cross marks the spot where in 1819 John Harvey of Bedfordshire was killed in a fall from his horse.

We stepped out the last blustery mile, under a blue sky scoured of clouds, to Mill Hill and the sloping lane to Rodmell.

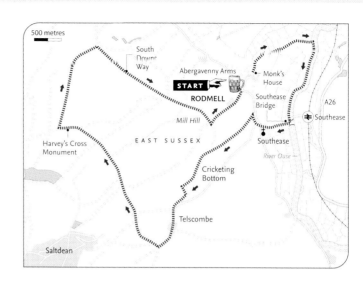

Start & finish Abergavenny Arms, Newhaven Rd, Rodmell BN7 3EZ (OS ref TQ 418060)

Walk (10½ miles; easy; OS Explorer 11): Left down lane ("Monk's House"). Beyond Monk's House (421063), follow stony lane to River Ouse (432068). Right to Southease Bridge (427053). NB For Southease railway station, left across bridge. To continue walk: Right from Southease bridge past Southease Church to road (422053). Right (South Downs Way/SDW); in 50m, cross road (take care); up Gorham's Lane. Immediately right through gate; follow SDW. At foot of slope, left (421055, SDW). In ⅔ mile SDW turns right (413049), but keep ahead past farm. In ⅔ mile dogleg left/right across Cricketing Bottom (407042); up slope to road (406038); right through Telscombe. Where road ends at cattle grid, right on track (403031, "St Michael's Landour"). At cattle grid by fancy gate posts, right (399033); in 50m, through gate and on. In 1½ miles, pass Harvey's Cross monument (386052); in 200m fork right for 1¼ miles to SDW (391067). Right for 1½ miles to Mill Hill (413053); left ("To the Pub") to Rodmell.

Lunch Picnic above Cricketing Bottom; Monk's House: 01273 474760, nationaltrust.org.uk (phone for opening hours)

More information Lewes Tourist Information Centre (01273 483448); satmap.com; ramblers.org.uk

Rye Harbour is a strange old place. The ivy-strangled Martello tower and the Second World War bunkers tell you that this is a coast that has been under constant threat of invasion. And the enormous expanse of flint pebbles, spreading inland for more than a mile, betokens the incursions of thousands of tons of shingle, dumped by the restless sea.

It is moody country on a cold morning. A whistling east wind drove us along the beach. Lesser black-backed gulls sulked on the sandbanks and redshanks foraged with jerky steps in the pools of the harbour nature reserve, on the inland side of the seabank.

King Henry VIII built Camber Castle as a coastal stronghold to keep the French at bay. Now, five centuries later, the stark fortress stands more than a mile inland among wide fields where a thin skin of grass overlies a wilderness of pebbles. We walked a circuit of the eroded bastion walls, then made for a hide on the shores of Castle Water, where green-headed shoveller drakes swept for food with heavy spatulate bills. Elegant terns hung over the water on crooked wings and the big black outline of a marsh harrier ghosted quietly across the reedbeds.

Back on the shore we found the gaunt blocky shed from which a crew of Rye Harbour men launched the lifeboat *Mary Stanford* on a bitter November morning in 1928. She was lost with all hands, seventeen men from one village. The lifeboat house has remained locked and unused since – a memorial to bravery and death on an unforgiving shore.

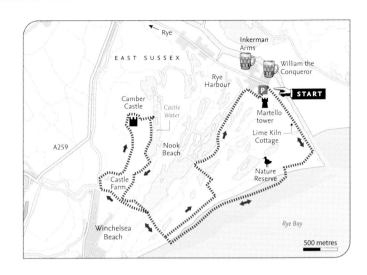

Start & finish Rye Harbour car park, Rye, East Sussex TN31 7TU (OS ref TQ 942190)

Walk (8¼ miles; easy; OS Explorer 125): From car park follow seawall past Lime Kiln Cottage information centre (946186) to river mouth (949181). Right along beach or coast road. In 1 mile, pass old lifeboat shed (932172); in another 650m, right inland on path past info board (928168) over two crossings (925171, 921173) for ¾ mile to road (917175). Right; just past Castle Farm, fork left (920176) to Camber Castle (922185). Clockwise round castle; on east side, path along fence to wooden gate (924185) leading to bird hide. Return to gate; left through metal gate; field edge south. Left across end of Castle Water to junction (925179); right; in 400m, left through gate No 9 (923177). On past Camber Cottage (921174); through gate, then left for ½ mile to shore road (928168). Left to lifeboat house; in 300m, left on gravel track (934174). In 300m, through left of two gates (934176); ahead to junction (931178); right on gravel track for 1 mile to road; right to car park.

Lunch Inkerman Arms (01797 222464) or William the Conqueror pub (01797 223315), Rye Harbour

More information Lime Kiln Cottage information centre (wildrye.info); visitengland.com; satmap.com; ramblers.org.uk

BURLEY AND WHITTEN POND, NEW FOREST

Notwithstanding its name, the New Forest is not a monolithic block of trees. These 150 square miles of ancient royal hunting ground comprise woodland, wetland, heathland, water and farmland – a wonderful patchwork of accessible countryside from which to tease out a walk for a short winter's day.

Waymarks are thin on the ground in the New Forest, but the patch of open heath that stretches south of Burley is crisscrossed with good, clear paths.

New Forest ponies cropped the grass by the path. From Turf Hill the southern skyline was spiky with ranks of conifers. We caught a glimpse of a pale blue whaleback hill on the distant Isle of Wight. Between hill and trees rose the slender rocket shape of Sway Tower, a Victorian folly 218ft (66m) tall, built entirely of concrete and still standing proud in the landscape.

It's easy to get the impression that these heaths form a flat tableland, but they are burrowed with surprisingly steep valleys, or "bottoms". We dropped into Shappen Bottom past the tufted mire of Holmsley Bog, and crossed the long-disused track of the Southampton–Dorchester railway, savouring the spicy fragrance released by bog myrtle cones when rubbed.

Down in the hollow of Whitten Bottom, streams, pools and flooded ruts led to Whitten Pond, the wind-ruffled water steel blue, the grassy margins a brilliant green in the low afternoon sun. A broad track beyond climbed the gently domed nape of Dur Hill Down, before looping off across the heath towards the railway.

At the splendidly named Slap Bottom we steered around a group of ponies grazing the bank of a stream, and sauntered back to Burley in the cold, bright sunlight.

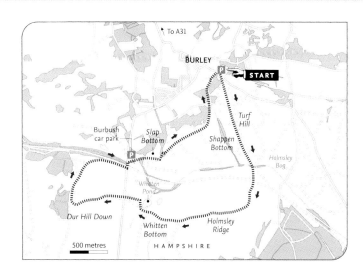

Start & finish Burley Cricket car park, Cott Lane, Burley, Ringwood BH24 4AP (OS ref SU 214029)

Walk (5¼ miles; easy; OS Explorer OL22): Cross road; down track ("Forestry Commission Burley"). In 50m left on gravel track. In nearly 1 mile cross old railway (219015); in 200m fork right (219013). In ¾ mile keep ahead (right) at fork (209010) to Whitten Bottom. Cross stream by outlet at Whitten Pond (203012); ahead to cross road at barrier (201013). On along track over Dur Hill Down. In ½ mile at post, right (194013) along line of trees, on track curving right across heath to road (201017). Left across old railway; right into Burbush car park. Aim left towards power lines; in 50m, right on path between trees, across stream into open. Ahead up slope; in 500m, left (206018) on clear track. In ½ mile at Goats Pen Cottage join gravel drive (212025); at tarred road, right to car park.

Lunch Picnic

More information Ringwood Gateway (01425 473883, thenewforest.co.uk)

FARLEY MOUNT AND BEACON HILL

You couldn't find a better place than Farley Mount Country Park for children and dogs to run about and kick up the leaves on a cold winter's day. Bright pink spindle berries lent a touch of colour to the pale grey winter woods.

In a shallow valley north of the woods we turned along a grassy farm track between rolling fields of beet and wheat stubble. In the hazel hedges, crimson stalks of dogwood sprouted green-white flowers and deeply creased leaves turning dark mauve.

A pale path of chalky mud led over the winter wheat. On the opposite slopes starlings perched on the backs of fat sheep that grazed among the vines of Chalk Vale Vineyard.

The hamlet of Ashley and its castle mound lay hidden among trees beyond a stout wall. King John stayed here often while hunting, a guest of William Briwere, described by contemporary 13th-century chronicler Roger of Wendover, as an "evil adviser" to the king.

In the fields beyond, large old beech trees, stripped of leaves, raised their graceful domed heads against the grey sky. We dropped down to the valley bottom and the Roman road from Winchester to Old Sarum, these days a narrow lane as straight as an arrow. From here a good track rose up the flank of Beacon Hill, running through groves of twisty yews.

At the crest of the down we stopped to take in a 40-mile prospect of downs and woods, ribbed ploughland and smooth grazing. By the homeward path rose a white steeple, raised in 1740 by Paulet St John to honour the horse he named Beware Chalk Pit (steed and master had miraculously survived a tumble into a deep chalk quarry).

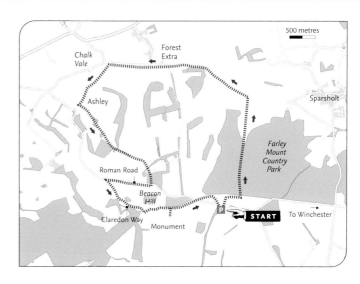

Start & finish Hawthorn car park, Pitt Down, near Sparsholt SO21 2JG approx. (OS ref SU 415292)

Walk (9 miles; easy; OS Explorer OL32): Facing away from road, from left corner of car park follow forest road north. In 250m, at barrier, follow main roadway to right. In 300m, left up forest road (417294). In ½ mile, leave trees (418303); in just under ¾ mile, left in valley bottom (418313). In 1 mile, pass Forest Extra (403319); in ¾ mile, left off road past gate (390319, arrow) on well-trodden field path. In just under ¾ mile at far side of 4th field, up steps through hedge (384311); left (yellow arrow) along field path. In 1 mile, descend to valley track (397301); right to road (399296); right. In ½ mile, hairpin back left across field (390297; blue arrow, then green arrow; "Clarendon Way"/CW). Follow CW for 1½ miles across Beacon Hill (detouring right to horse monument at 403290) to road (408293). Cross onto path; in 50m, through gate; fork left on CW at edge of trees to car park.

Lunch Plough Inn, Sparsholt SO21 2NW (01962 776353, the. littlepubgroup.co.uk)

More information Winchester Tourist Information Centre (01962 840500)

HAWKLEY AND THE HANGERS

A sunny morning, still and warm, among the great hangers of east Hampshire. Those hangers – steep-sided slopes of chalk and greensand covered in thick woodland – have enchanted poets and artists, writers and walkers since people began to look on the landscape as something wonderful and uplifting, rather than as an adversary to be wrestled with and overcome.

The sun cast long black shadows from the woods clinging to the scarp of Hawkley Hanger. Raspberries and blackberries hung in the margins of the field paths we walked. Hollow old Standfast Lane snaked deeply sunk in the greensand, overhung with coppiced hazel sprays. Fallen nuts lay scattered along the road through Empshott Green, where we picked up the long-distance Hangers Way.

The Way wound southward through the skirts of Hawkley Hanger. We walked in and out of shadows and sunsplashes, a translucent green window of beech leaves giving a glimpse of the tower of Hawkley church with its cap rising from trees. We turned through the outskirts of the village into a tangle of greenery around the multiple threads of the Oakshott Stream, then a stony lane that climbed steeply up from Middle Oakshott. A cherry plum tree overhung the path; we scooped up a few of the plump, wine-coloured fruit as we went on up the Shoulder of Mutton hill.

Edward Thomas, 20th-century poet and mighty walker, lived in Steep village at the foot of the Shoulder of Mutton. These were the views he loved – south over Steep to the rising country beyond, north to Hawkley's church and houses in a slanting patchwork of corn and pasture, woods and hanger slopes. We stared our fill, then went slipping and sliding down an ancient flinty holloway on the homeward stretch to Hawkley.

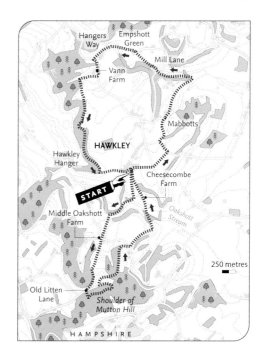

Start & finish Hawkley Inn, near Petersfield, Hants GU33 6NE (OS ref SU747291)

Walk (8½ miles; moderate; OS Explorer 133; detailed directions are highly recommended): From Hawkley Inn east to T-junction; ahead on footpath (yellow arrow/YA) to road (752294); left past Uplands. At left bend (750295, bridleway fingerpost/FP), north up field edge to lane (751299). Right to Mabbotts house (752300); follow Standfast Lane (byway). In 700m, left (755305, kissing gate) along wood edge. In 450m, approaching house, right (750306, YA on telegraph pole) across stream to Mill Lane (750307). Right; in 100m, left up woodland track to road at Quarry House (746310). Left for 300m to right bend (743310); left here over stile onto Hangers Way. Follow Hangers Way (waymark arrows, FPs) for 3½ miles via Vann Farm (740306), Hawkley Hanger (741290), Hawkley village (746291), Oakshott Stream footbridges (742283), Middle Oakshott (741279) to Old Litten Lane on Shoulder of Mutton Hill (739271). Right to waymarked viewpoint (738270). Return to Hawkley by sunken lanes – 741272 to 745278, then via Cheesecombe Farm (748286).

Lunch Hawkley Inn (01730 827205; hawkleyinn.co.uk) – a lovely welcoming country pub; great beer choice!

More information Petersfield Tourist Information Centre (01730 268829); visit-hampshire.co.uk; satmap.com; ramblers.org.uk

OWSLEBURY AND UPHAM

Apples were ripening in the gardens of Owlesbury and the old houses looked trim under their thatched roofs. It was here in Tudor times that Sir Henry Seymour of Marwell Hall, a Protestant, discovered that the priest of St Andrew's Church had been saying Latin Mass. He had the man arrested. The priest escaped, returned to the church, and was shot at the altar. It didn't pay to cross Sir Henry – he counted Henry VIII and Thomas Cromwell as his brothers-in-law.

The peaceful atmosphere today painted a different picture of Owlesbury. Beyond the churchyard we picked up the Monarch's Way path and followed it along green lanes through steeply rolling countryside.

A young roe deer was feeding on the stubble near Austin's Copse, raising its head every few seconds to flap the flies out of its ears. At Woodlock's Down Farm a beautiful young horse, black and glossy, galloped across his paddock. The paths around pretty brick and flint Upham were bounded with old hedges coming into fruit for autumn – scarlet haws, shiny purple elderberries, green-black clusters of guelder rose berries, and quadripartite spindle berries beginning to pink up.

In a furrow of earth we found a Mesolithic tool, a flint scraper with scalloped edges, perhaps 10,000 years old. A decaying beech nearby sported a great thick ruff of edible fungus, the evocatively named chicken-of-the-woods.

We crossed a Roman road, present on the map, but smoothed out of existence by the ploughing of millennia. The homeward path skirted Marwell House, then headed north across the roll and dip of harvest fields and horse paddocks towards Owlesbury, where the rooks were beginning to gather for their evening rituals.

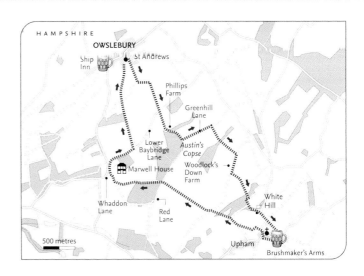

Start & finish Ship Inn, Owslebury, Hampshire SO21 1LT (OS ref SU 511233)

Walk (7 miles; easy; OS Explorer 132): From Ship Inn: left; right through churchyard; right on Monarch's Way/MW (515234) for 1 mile, crossing Lower Baybridge Lane (521226) to reach deer gate beyond Phillips Farm House (521222). Left beside Austin's Copse; left (524221) up Greenhill Lane. In 500m, right (524223, yellow arrow/YA), following YAs and fingerposts/FP); 100m past Woodlock's Down Farm, left (532216, 3-finger post); follow FPs and YAs to road at White Hill (538209). Right; in 200m, left at grass triangle to pass Brushmakers Arms pub (540206). Right at phone box. Past church, right (538206, "Owslebury"); in 100m, left ("MW", FP). Follow MW for 1¼ miles to cross Red Lane (521214). Ahead (trees, then field edge); in 400m, left through hedge (517214, YA). Follow hedge/fence on right (stiles) for 400m, then right up fenced path (513214, YA) to Whaddon Lane (512216). Right; in 200m, right (512217) up Lower Baybridge Lane. In 550m, left (517220, wicket gate, FP); two field edges, then cross valley to stile (514228); fenced path to Owslebury.

Lunch Ship Inn, Owslebury (01962 777756, owslebury.org.uk); Brushmakers Arms, Upham (01489 860231, thebrushmakersarms.com). Booking advisable at both

More information Winchester Tourist Information Centre (01962 840500)

DUNGENESS, ROMNEY MARSH

Dungeness is one of the great uncommon landscapes of Britain; a vast sheet of pebbles, the most extensive in all Europe, studded with tough fleshy and prickly plants, thronged with wild birds. Dungeness is a great wilderness, but not unaffected by man – there are fishing boats and tarry fishermen's huts, scattered bungalows, and the giant, pale grey boxes of a nuclear power station.

We followed a grassy path through the RSPB's enormous 2,000-acre reserve where pools, pastures and reedbeds lie at the heart of a great shingle wasteland. Swans sailed with nonchalant grace on the meres. "Look," exclaimed Jane. "Marsh harrier!" The big bird of prey got up quite slowly from its stance in a field of stubble and flapped off low over the reeds, the sun glinting among its wing feathers. There was great complaining among the shelducks and coots, and a party of teal sprang into the air and moved away from the vicinity of the dark destroyer as fast as they could. We saw the harrier several times after that, quartering its territory like a king and causing commotion wherever it went.

Among the birds, the yellow-horned poppies, the wide stony wastes and the gentle whisper of the wind, it was easy to forget the strangeness that the nuclear power station and its marching columns of pylons brought to the scene. We turned for home with a two-mile trudge across the pebble sheet in prospect, and there were the ghostly grey boxes and the skeleton pylon army ahead, dwarfed under the blue bowl of the sky.

We walked on, leaving behind us the plants, the birds, the pebbles and the blue sea horizon, with a blood-red sunset spreading in the west.

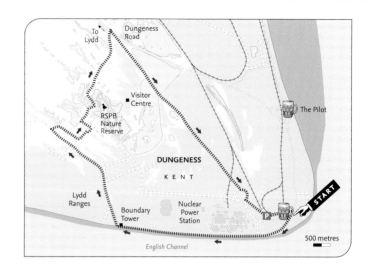

Start & finish Britannia Inn, Dungeness, TN29 9ND (OS ref TR092169)

Walk (7½ miles; easy; OS Explorer 125): Follow boardwalk near black and white lighthouse to shore. Right past power station – the hard-surfaced track by fence makes easier walking! In 1¾ miles, turn right inland by Lydd Ranges boundary tower (065167) on gravel road. In ½ mile, road bends left – in 600m, pass roadway on left (057179). In 400m, right (054181, blue topped post, Footpath No. HL33). Follow grassy path through RSPB reserve. In ⅔ mile, keep ahead at 3-finger post (059184, "Hooker's Pits"); follow bridleway blue arrows to road (063196). Right ("footpath" fingerpost), across shingle (occasional wooden posts) for 2 miles, aiming for black lighthouse. Cross road (083175); beyond old coastguard cottages, road to Britannia Inn.

Lunch Britannia Inn (01797 321959; britanniadungeness.co.uk); Pilot Inn, Dungeness TN29 9NJ (01797 320314; thepilotdungeness.co.uk)

More information Dungeness RSPB Reserve (01797 320588; rspb.org.uk/Dungeness); visitengland.com; satmap.com; ramblers.org.uk

A cold day over the North Downs of Kent at the close of winter. Along the lane on Holly Hill snowdrops still hung their heads, grubby at the end stage of their flowering. But dog's mercury had spread its tiny blooms over the floor of Greatpark Wood, and we heard a familiar introit to spring, the "tsip-tsap, tsip-tsap" of a newly arrived chiffchaff.

Sweet chestnut coppice forms a large part of these woods on the chalk and greensand escarpment. The leaves of last autumn, crisp and grey, shuffled underfoot as we dropped down to the valley road and hop fields at Great Buckland.

From the Weald Way path in Tranquil Wood we looked down on the thousand-year-old Church of Our Lady of the Meadows. The village of Dode was abandoned during the Black Death plague of 1349, but its humble church still stands.

The Weald Way forged south through hazel and chestnut coppices. Fat green buds burst from hawthorn twigs, and sheaves of green shoots showed where bluebells would soon be carpeting these woods.

At the southern edge of White Horse Wood we crossed the wet ditch of an ancient ridgeway and dipped sharply down the escarpment. At the foot of the slope ran another ancient route, the Pilgrims' Way path that brought penitents and not-so-penitents to the shrine of St Thomas Becket at Canterbury.

A pilgrim shrine that predates Becket's by perhaps 4,000 years stood on a knoll in the field beyond. The great uprights of Coldrum Long Barrow form the centrepiece of a circle of recumbent standing stones. A pagan celebrant stood singing to the stones, a stick in either upraised hand.

We left her to her devotions and went quietly away to join the Pilgrims' Way and the homeward path.

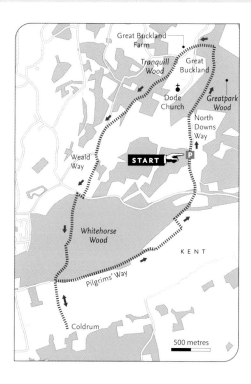

Start & finish Holly Hill car park, Meopham, Gravesend DA13 oUB (TQ 670629). NB Closes at 5pm

Walk (7 miles; easy; OS Explorer 148): From Holly Hill car park, left along road. Beyond Holly Hill House, fork right (670634) past metal barrier. In just under ¾ mile, left (673643, blue arrow/BA). At road, right (670642); in 150m, left (670644, "Vigo, Harvel"). 150m past Great Buckland Farm, left (668641, "Tranquil Wood", "Weald Way"/WW). In just over ½ mile, at gate on right (662634) don't go right (WW) but keep ahead (WW, "BA NS 246"). At road, left (659632). In 350m, on right bend, left (658629, WW) along field edge, then follow YA 235. At road (656623) dogleg right/left (WW) into Whitehorse Wood. In ½ mile (654616), descend escarpment. At Pilgrims' Way/North Down Way/NDW, right (653613); in 50m left ("Coldrum Long Barrow"). Follow path to Coldrum Long Barrow (654607). Return to NDW; right for 1½ miles to road (671624); ahead to car park.

Lunch The Villager Inn, Vigo Village DA13 oTD (01732 822305, villagervigo.com)

More information Sevenoaks Tourist information Centre (01732 450305)

KINGSDOWN AND ST MARGARET'S AT CLIFFE

At Kingsdown the white chalk cliffs shone in clear light polished and sharpened by sea and sunshine. Along the pebbly shore stood old iron winches, rusted into immobility by salt laden water and winds. Decades have passed since the village fishermen used them to haul their boats up the steeply shelving beach.

We climbed the steps at the end of Oldstairs Bay and set out on the cliff path with a stiff north breeze pushing us along.

The green sea heaved gently below, reflecting a light clear enough for us to pick out the coast of France some 20 miles off; field shapes, woods, radio masts and a long pale line of sandy beaches. Air balloons, stringbag aeroplanes, greasy swimmers and long-range shells from coastal guns – all have crossed that narrow stretch of sea.

The dastardly Sir Hugo Drax launched a deadly strike from these cliffs. Lucky for all of us that James Bond was on hand to frustrate Sir Hugo's knavish tricks and redirect the London-bound Moonraker rocket to plunge into the sea.

Ian Fleming, Bond's creator, had a holiday home at St Margaret's at Cliffe, just along the coast. We came by the spot where Fleming had Drax's men collapse the cliff onto 007, near a tall obelisk commemorating the brave Great War deeds of the Dover Patrol. Just beyond we found a magnificent view over the tight, cliff-encircled bay that cradles St Margaret's, and a zigzag of steps running down to the pebbly shore.

The homeward path led across inland fields sown with winter cereals, a landscape of long, parallel valleys and tufts of woodland, with the sea diminished to a green backdrop caught in a "V" between one slope and the next.

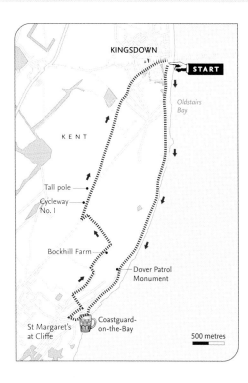

Start & finish Cliffe Road, Kingsdown CT14 8AH (OS ref TR 380482).

Walk (6¾ miles; easy; OS Explorer 138): Coast Path south for 2¾ miles to St Margaret's at Cliffe. 800m past Dover Patrol monument, left down steps to shore (369446; yellow arrow). Right to seafront. Up road beside Coastguard pub (368445). On right bend, ahead up steps (367444, fingerpost/FP). Fork right at top to road (366444); right, in 150m, fork left on Hotel Road. In 100m, left (368445, FP) up steps; on up Cavenagh Road; on up grass path (FP) to The Droveway (366448). Right; follow road for 1,000m to Bockhill Farm. 150m beyond farm, left at path junction (372455). Keep ahead up field margin path; in 600m it bends sharp left, through kissing gate; in 100m, right down tarmac track (367459, cycleway No. 1). In 400m pass tall pole on left (368464); in 100m, left through hedge; half right on path across field. In 1 mile keep left of houses (373478) to road (374481). Left; right down Upper Street into Kingsdown.

Lunch The Coastguard pub, St Margaret's CT15 6DY (01304 853051, thecoastguard.co.uk)

More information Dover Tourist Information Centre (01304 201066)

Penshurst's houses of mellow brick and Kentish weatherboard held enough olde-worlde charm to spark nostalgia for J.R.R. Tolkien's mythical Shire.

An embanked lane led west between bracken slopes, sloe bushes heavy with shiny dark fruit and hedges a-twitter with flocks of pink-breasted linnets. This is beautifully maintained countryside, giving off a whiff of money well spent. Field ditches have been dug and cleaned, new plantations of cherry, hazel and hawthorn established, hedges allowed to bulk out as food and cover for wildlife.

Along the valley stretched a line of Second World War pillboxes sprouting ivy and elder. We crossed the sluggish River Eden, where silver dace flicked with a tiny splash into the sheltering shade of alder roots. There was a whisper of wind and a shiver of leaves in the poplar groves.

This part of Kent is famous for its hops; witness the cluster of former oasts, or drying kilns, that stood at Salman's Farm. Beyond on a slope, vines had been planted, the grapes hanging from wires stretched at shoulder height. We sat on a bench to eat our picnic, looking down the rows and imagining the harvest.

Twisted hornbeams and hollies reflected a sombre light in Russell's Wood. Beyond, in Yewtree Wood, children shouted and swooped, walking the plank along the recumbent trunks of old beeches that had been thrown in storms long gone and forgotten.

Back at Penshurst youngsters were jumping with much ado into and out of the river. The walk ended with a stroll across the sward in front of 14th-century Penshurst Place, an extravagant mishmash of brick, stone, chimneys, gables and arches all picked out in the late afternoon sun.

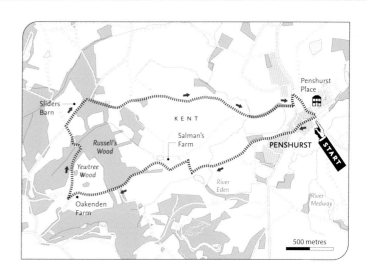

Start & finish Penshurst Place car park, Penshurst TN11 8DG (OS ref TQ 530440)

Walk (5½ miles; easy; OS Explorer 147): Down Penshurst Place drive; right along street. Past Forge Stores, right along the Warren (525436). In 1 mile at Salman's Farm, through kissing gate/KG (512432); right up track; left, and keep ahead (yellow arrow/YA). At T-junction in Russell's Wood, right (507430, YA, "441"). Opposite Oakenden house, right (501428, YA, stile), then right through KG, across fields; through Yewtree Wood. On west edge of wood cross stile (502435, YA); on to road (501436). Right; pass Sliders Barn; in 150m, right along drive (503439); follow Eden Valley walk for 1½ miles to Penshurst. Left at B2176 (525439); in 200m, right (525440, KG) through the grounds of Penshurst Place to car park.

Lunch Leicester Arms, Penshurst TN11 8BT (01892 871617, theleicesterarms.com)

More information Penshurst Place, 01892 870307, penshurstplace.com

STODMARSH NATIONAL NATURE RESERVE AND GROVE FERRY

"Keep an eye out for the beavers," advised a man festooned with wildlife cameras as we passed him in the car park at Stodmarsh National Nature Reserve.

We didn't see any of the recently reintroduced rodents on our walk around the East Kent reserve but evidence of their presence was widespread in the shape of young trees felled with a curious hinged effect, the severed parts gnawed white and smooth with fine patterns of chiselling by beaver incisors.

In the still grey afternoon, perched in the Reedbed Hide, we looked out on a bay between enormous stretches of creamy white reeds. Shoveler drakes with snowy breasts and chestnut wings went dabbling beside their drab brown mates. Among them swam teal, with yellow flashes on their afterparts, and breasts very delicately patterned in ash-grey and black.

We followed a broad and muddy path north between reed pool, ditches and sodden green acres of freshwater marsh. Stodmarsh's watery landscape was formed partly through the subsidence of old mine workings below ground, a reminder of the now-vanished Kentish coalfield.

Seductive smells of Sunday roasts emanated from the Grove Ferry Inn, where we turned back along the wide and muddy Great Stour River. An angler on the far bank hooked a roach and lifted it out, a wriggling strip of silver. We watched another hunter of the waterways, a big marsh harrier, cruising low above the reedbeds, looking for frogs and water voles.

The light began to seep out of the afternoon as we followed the homeward path, serenaded by the harsh, pig-like screech and snuffle of a water rail creeping through the reeds; another winter sound of this magical place.

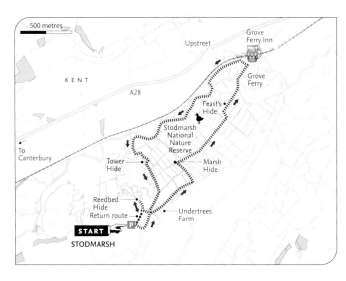

Start & finish Stodmarsh NNR car park, near Canterbury CT3 4BB (OS ref TR 222609)

Walk (4¾ miles; easy; OS Explorer 150): From bottom right corner of car park pass info board; follow track for ¼ mile to cross bridge to T-junction (223610). Left; follow "Reedbed Hide" signs to hide (222612). Return to pass bridge (don't cross); follow path ("Footpath", yellow arrows) past Undertrees Farm. In ¾ mile pass Marsh Hide (226618); in ½ mile dogleg right/left across track (233623, red arrow); follow "Grove Ferry car park" signs for ¾ mile to road (236630). Left (Grove Ferry Inn is opposite); in 40m, left ("Stour Valley Walk"). Follow riverbank path. In 1½ miles path veers inland (221620); follow it past Tower Hide (222617), then follow signs to car park.

Lunch Grove Ferry Inn, Upstreet, Canterbury CT3 4BP (01227 860302; groveferryinn.co.uk)

More information Stodmarsh NNR (0845 600 3078); explorekent.org

BUDDINGTON BOTTOM AND CHANCTONBURY RING

The blackcap that belted out its song from an ash tree by the South Downs Way was singing for a perfect summer's day. I couldn't believe the profusion of flowers and blue butterflies that bordered the ancient ridgeway as it climbed towards the roof of the downs.

The South Downs Way rose as the view opened northwards across a patchwork of dark summer woods and pale gold cornfields as yet unharvested. Far to the south the bird's beak of the Isle of Wight dipped to the sea. Soon another flinty track swung off south-west. Out of the crop fields ahead rose the multiple ramparts of Cissbury Ring, one of the Iron Age hillforts that command this countryside.

Down in Buddington Bottom I passed the Pest House, a modest cottage of brick and flint with an ominous name. In this lonely place in medieval times stood an isolation house where those suffering from the plague, cholera, smallpox and other deadly communicable diseases were banged up to recover or die – one or the other.

A grassy track led up the wooded valley of Buddington Bottom to reach the South Downs Way. Just west the early Iron Age hillfort of Chanctonbury Ring topped the hill, the circular rampart reinforced with a fine double circle of beech trees. This is a spot with an enormous atmosphere, the world spread out at your feet from the sea to the Sussex Weald.

The Ring was made by the Devil, local stories say, and he will appear to you if you run thrice widdershins around the rampart. There's a fiendish bargain on offer, of course: a bowl of demonic soup in exchange for your soul. Don't run around the Ring when you're feeling hungry is my advice.

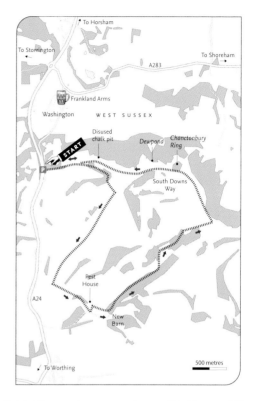

Start & finish Chanctonbury car park, near Washington BN44 3DR (OS ref TQ 125121)

Walk (5½ miles; easy; OS Explorer 121): Uphill on South Downs Way/ SDW. In ¾ mile at large grass triangle, right (130117, "Restricted Byway") downhill. In 1 mile at cross-tracks, left (121104, 4-finger post, "Wiston Estate Winery" notice). In just under ¾ mile, opposite barns at New Barn, fork left, then immediately right (130100). In 150m, where track meets lane, fork left through gate (fingerpost, blue arrow/BA); immediately left (BA). In 400m at far corner of vineyard, through gate (133104); on up path through Buddington Bottom valley for 1 mile. At top of climb, left on SDW (145113) past Chanctonbury Ring (139120). In 500m at cattle grid, fork right (134119, gate, BA) on path past dew pond. In 500m descend to gate (129121); down through old chalk pit (slippery!) to rejoin SDW (125121); right to car park.

Lunch Frankland Arms, Washington RH20 4AL (01903 891405; thefranklandarms.com)

More information westsussex.info

A perfect summer's morning over West Sussex – a blue heaven with huge white cumulonimbus clouds reaching up from the South Downs skyline, warm sunshine spreading across the countryside like butter and wood pigeons sleepily cooing in the beech trees around Burpham.

The old valley track of Coombe Lane brought us up from the village to the downs, its elder bushes and guelder rose and spindle all beginning to come into fruit. Two marsh harriers had come up from the wetlands by the River Arun, and we watched them making slow passes through the valley on their long dark wings.

The downland slopes were a maze of pale gold stubble fields where big straw bales lay doubled over. The view widened back south from Wepham Down to a flat gleam of the distant sea, the Isle of Wight lying long in a grey haze on the south-west horizon. Up on the roof of the downs the ramparts of Rackham Banks – a Bronze Age crossdyke and a hill settlement in a hollow – were spattered with scabious, knapweed and poppies. We sat idling there, the chalk-white South Downs Way ribboning east and west, the ground plunging away north to the Arun snaking through the Sussex lowlands among woods and pastures.

The ancient ridge track dipped to Downs Farm, a pretty old farmhouse marooned in a muddle of harsh modern barns and silos. Here we turned off south, dropping into a steep, silent and nameless valley. Then a last stretch beside the Arun, past an old tree-grown moated site that might well be part of the burh or fortified village established here by Alfred the Great 1100 years ago. A timeless walk, where now and then join hands seamlessly.

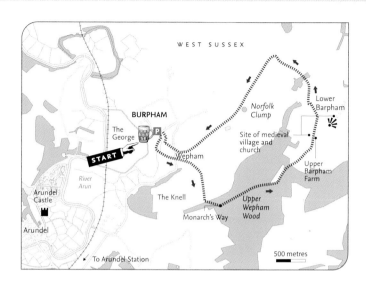

Start & finish Burpham village car park, BN18 9RR (OS ref TQ039089)

Walk (7 miles; moderate; OS Explorer 121): Right along village street; in ⅓ mile, left up Coombe Lane (044090; fingerpost/FP, blue arrow/BA). In 1½ miles at T-junction of tracks (061106), left (north) for 1½ miles to South Downs Way (051125). Left for ¾ mile. Just before Downs Farm, left (038125, "Restricted Byway"). In 100m fork right ("bridleway" FP, BA). South into valley bottom (041116); up and across tracks (044114, yellow arrow/YA) to corner of wood (044110, YA). South for ½ mile; at gateway with BAs (040102), take footpath beside it (YA) down to bottom of steps (039103). Left (BA). In ⅓ mile, right over stile (035099, YA); left across fields (stiles, YAs); keep right of moat (033094, YA); along river, back to Burpham.

Lunch The George at Burpham, Main Street, Burpham BN18 9RR (01903 883131; georgeatburpham.co.uk)

More information Arundel tourist information point in Arundel Museum (01903 882456); visitsussex.org; visitengland.com; ramblers.org.uk; satmap.com

CHICHESTER HARBOUR AND DELL QUAY

Chichester Marina lies a few miles south of the cathedral city, tucked into the eastern flank of Chichester Harbour. This muddy, meandering inland sea has many snaking creeks and widely separated peninsulas, with vast bird-haunted mudflats exposed by every falling tide. Its shore paths are perfect for an autumn morning's ramble.

The bus dropped us on the roadside, and we followed the driveway down to Chichester Marina. In the yards boats with aspirational names lay snugged down for winter: *Glowing Jade, One Life, Day Dreamer, Flight of Fancy.* Between the white walls of the yachts a pair of young Swallows (or Amazons) scudded round in a rubber dinghy.

We turned inland, walking the muddy shore path through Salterns Copse. The name stands as a memorial to the salt-making industry that flourished here in the 18th century. The shallow salterns – manmade pools with clay bottoms – held seawater, reduced to brine by the sun, then boiled and dredged for the precious salt crystals. The high cost of coal, taxes and transport put an end to the salterns just before the opening of the Chichester Canal, which might have saved them.

Halyards chinked in the morning breeze, and black-backed gulls screeched like fishwives over their tideline pickings. A flight of wigeon scooted over the water, turning and skimming down to settle beside one of the twisty rithes or creeks that furrow the harbour muds.

A quick sandwich in the dappled river light of the dark-panelled bar in the Crown & Anchor at Dell Quay, and we followed the winding path back through the fields to the marina.

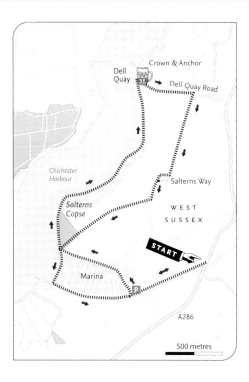

Start & finish Chichester Marina bus stop on A286, Chichester–Witterings (SU 842013), or Marina car park, PO20 7EJ

Walk (4¾ miles; easy; OS Explorer 120): Path along north side of marina into Salterns Copse (829014); fork left along shore for a little over a mile to Dell Quay Road (837028 – left to Crown & Anchor pub). Right along Dell Quay Road; in 350m, right (841027) along Salterns Way cycle path to south end of Salterns Wood. Anticlockwise round west/south edge of marina; return to car park/bus stop.

Lunch The Boat House Café, Chichester Marina, Chichester PO20 7EJ (01243 513203; idealcollection.co.uk) – booking advised

More information Chichester Harbour Conservancy (conservancy.co.uk)

EARTHAM AND GREAT DOWN

A cockerel crowed from a farmyard and pigeons cooed in the woodland known as the Rookery as we walked out of Eartham.

This corner of West Sussex countryside dips and rolls from cornfields to woods. We followed the outer row of stubbles of the recently harvested fields for the pleasure of hearing the dry stems swish and crackle against our boots.

A path in the cool shade of Nore Wood led north in a subaqueous green light to Stane Street. Out across the open landscape of the downs we followed this 2,000-year-old Roman way. The raised ridge of the agger, or road embankment, metalled with flints and mounded between ditches, still stood man-height, a seam of rabbit-burrowed earth and stones running north-east in a ruler-straight line.

From Gumber Corner, another meeting place of ancient tracks, we went south over Great Down on a ridged, grassy path between fields of dark Zwartbles lambs sporting white tail tufts. The Sussex coast spread out ahead, from the snout of the Isle of Wight on a blue-grey sea to the white miniature alps of the sunshades at Bognor's Butlins resort.

Shady green Butt Lane was floating with thistledown parachutes. We passed Courthill Farm, where the writer Hilaire Belloc found escape from his high-pressure London life in the early 1900s. A large triumphal arch stood perched on Nore Hill, a folly conceived as a picnic shelter by Anne, Countess of Newburgh, to give employment to local men out of work after the Peninsula Wars.

We came down to Eartham towards evening, the declining sun polishing the harvest patterns in the stubble fields and turning the empty flower cups of knapweed into a sprinkle of reciprocal suns among the grasses.

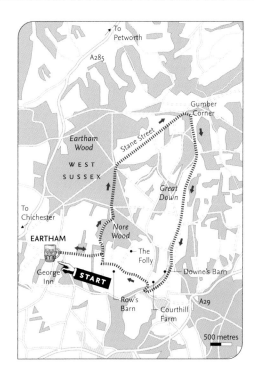

Start & finish The George, Eartham, West Sussex PO18 0LT (OS ref SU 939094); please ask permission to park and give The George your custom

Walk (8 miles; easy; OS Explorer 121): From inn, right along road; follow "Slindon"; in 100m on right bend, ahead down track (fingerpost/FP; yellow arrow/YA; pink arrow/PA). In 700m across field into wood; left (949095, "bridleway"/BW), north through Nore Wood. In ¾ mile, sharp left (952102, blue arrow/BA post). Downhill; cross track (951105, The Plain); north for ½ mile to 6-track crossing (952114, bench). Follow Stane Street ("Bignor", Monarch's Way/MW) NE for 1¼ miles. Go through gate (967126, 4-finger FP, bench). Right (MW); in 150m, right/south for 2¾ miles via Great Down, Downe's Barn (965091) and Butt Lane to road at Slindon (960086). Right; in 100m, right ("Bignor Hill"); just before Courthill Farm, left up stony lane (960088). In ½ mile pass Row's Barn (953091); round right bend; left (951092) along edge of trees. In 200m, right (949092, BA) through trees; in 200m left (FP), retracing route to Eartham.

Lunch The George pub, Eartham (01243 814340, thegeorgeeartham.com)

More information Chichester Tourist Information Centre (01243 775888); visitchichester.org; ramblers.org.uk

STOUGHTON AND KINGLEY VALE

A still, sunny day lay over West Sussex. The rumble of harrow and roller sounded faint and far off from the stubble fields around Old Bartons farmhouse. A Hereford bull stood dazed with sleepiness against the fence and permitted me to stroke his warm, dusty coat.

Up on the crest of Stoughton Down the woods hung dense and silent. I threaded the pine plantations and oak groves on Bow Hill, with sensational views opening to the south over the tidal channels of Chichester Harbour. Tree-lined tracks led on to the brow of Kingley Vale National Nature Reserve (NNR) and the rounded green Bronze Age burial mounds of the Devil's Humps. Here, I was lucky enough to bump into Richard Williamson, for 30 years the manager of Kingley Vale, now its dedicated archivist and guardian angel. "The chalkhill blues are out," he confided. Following his directions, I found the brilliant silver-blue butterflies on the tiny patch they favoured at the edge of the reserve, and spent half an hour watching them – heaven for butterflies, and pretty close to it for human beings, too. At last I got up from the sward of marjoram and harebells and went off to see the venerable yews of Kingley Vale. Visiting these bulbous trees with their arthritic limbs, all but naked of bark and extremely aged – some were old when the Romans arrived in Sussex – is like paying a call on a roomful of dignified, rather aloof Chelsea Pensioners in their birthday suits. When eventually I tore myself away from their spell, it was to follow the path dreamily up through the flower-rich meadows of Kingley Vale, before resuming the downland ridge and the flinty trackway back to Stoughton in its sun-soaked hollow.

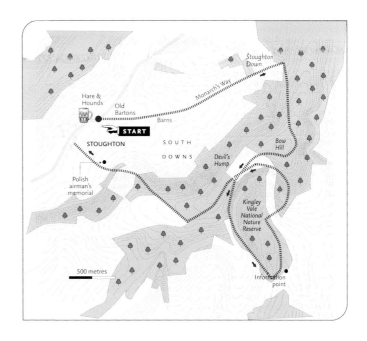

Start & finish Hare & Hounds, Stoughton PO18 9JQ (OS ref SU803115)

Walk (6 miles; moderate; OS Explorer 120): Leaving Hare & Hounds, left up road. In 200m, right at Old Bartons (fingerpost/FP, yellow arrow/YA); then fork left on gravelled track ("Monarch's Way" arrow). Pass barns (809115); on for 1 mile to 3-way bridleway FP (824121). Right; in 200m, fork left (blue arrow/BA) on narrower path through fir grove. In 600m pass BA on right; in 350m, reach track crossing by Kingley Vale NNR notice (825113; 4-way FP). Right along track for ½ mile. Just past Devil's Humps barrows, left by "Nature Trail" post (819109), through gate. Follow numbered posts anticlockwise round Nature Trail, passing information shelter at 824100, for 2 miles to return to Devil's Humps. Resume walk along track. In 300m, keep ahead by Kingley Vale NNR notice (817107; bridleway FP, BA). In ¼ mile, reach edge of wood (813105); right on track for 1 mile to road in Stoughton; right to Hare & Hounds.

Lunch Hare & Hounds, Stoughton (02392 631433; hareandhoundspub.co.uk) – a pub that knows it's a pub with excellent food, too

More information Tourist Information Point in Novium Museum, Tower Street, Chichester PO19 1QH (01243 775888; visitchichester.org); ramblers.org.uk

St Barnabas Church by Ranmore Common, Dorking

At first acquaintance Bedfordshire seems a rather nondescript county to walk in. It's hard to get a grasp on the character of this low-rolling region, with its large arable fields. Yet you soon develop a taste for the many old copses and hedgerows, the slow-flowing brooks and sudden, unexpected viewpoints from ridges you hadn't thought were there.

A glorious afternoon helps, of course. The sun blazed down out of a clear blue sky on the cottages and dark ironstone church at Church End, the southerly node of the village of Eversholt, on the eastern doorstep of Woburn Park.

We set out across a wide field of ploughland, where we picked up shards of ancient pottery and a nacreous fragment of Roman glass. One of those unforeseen Bedfordshire views opened across a rolling plain to the north-east as we stumbled across crusty ploughlands down to the trees and half-glimpsed house of Toddington Park.

Here handsome James Scott, Duke of Monmouth and by-blow of King Charles II, lived with his young lover Henrietta Wentworth, heiress to the Toddington estate. Stories say they sold her property and jewels to fund the rebellion in 1685 that attempted to put Monmouth on the throne after the death of his father. It ended badly, with Charles's brother James installed as King and Monmouth sent ignominiously to the block.

Our homeward path lay across a succession of enormous fields, mostly of thick, dark plough. There were old hedges of hips and haws, and a thread of a brook winding under elder bushes. The lichens that scabbed the elders glowed so yellow in the evening sun that it looked as though the young artists of Eversholt Lower School had been that way with their paintboxes.

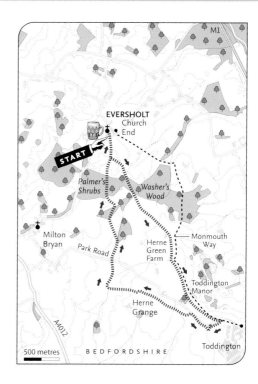

Start & finish Green Man pub, Church End, Eversholt, Bedfordshire MK17 9DU (OS ref SP 983325)

Walk (5½ miles; easy; OS Explorers 192, 193): From Green Man, left to crossroads; ahead through kissing gate/KG; cross field to KG (984320, black arrow/BLA). Bear left on path (KGs, BLAs) SE for 2¼ miles via Washer's Wood (988314), Herne Green Farm drive (995302) and Toddington Park (998297) to road on NW outskirts of Toddington (003293). Right for 200m; left along track (fingerpost); in 70m, right (BLA) on footpath WNW for 1¼ miles via Herne Grange drive (994295) to footbridge in valley bottom (984298, yellow-topped post/YTP). From here, footpath north (BLAs, YTPs) to cross Park Road (984303) and on. In 300m, fork left (985306) NW across field; then footpaths north for 1¼ miles via Palmer's Shrubs wood (983313) to Church End.

Lunch Green Man, Church End (01525 288111, greenmaneversholt.com).

More information Dunstable Tourist Information Centre (01582 891420); visitengland.com; satmap.com; ramblers.org.uk

A rainy morning over the Bedfordshire lowlands. A flock of blue tits led us south from Houghton Conquest, flitting from one hedge to the next. It was hard enough work plodding through the ploughlands, but once up on the green breast of the Delectable Hills we scooted forward with the wind in our sails and House Beautiful in our sights.

It was the local tinker's son, John Bunyan, who dreamt up the name of House Beautiful as he gazed from his native plain to Houghton House, the grand hunting lodge crowning the greensand ridge that filled his southern view. The ridge, the 'Delectable Hills' to Bunyan, may only be a couple of hundred feet high, but in this low-lying countryside it rears up to dominate the landscape. In between spells of ecstatic non-conformist preaching and dark periods in Bedford Jail for spreading sedition, Bunyan worked both house and hills into the backdrops of his Christian polemic masterpiece, *The Pilgrim's Progress*, published in 1678.

We came to House Beautiful and found it a haunting, hollow shell. We lingered in the porch, looking out on the prospect, watching slaty rainclouds and white cumulus chasing from the Midlands towards East Anglia. The heart-aching pull of a grand house in ruin is hard to explain, but today it exerted strong magic.

Siskins with canary-yellow throats and cross little eyebrows bounced in and out of the bushes as we followed the ridge lane into Kings Wood. Bluebells carpeted the floor of the ancient woodland. Down the slippery track, out across fields of medieval ridge and furrow, and back towards Houghton Conquest in gleams of weak sunshine.

In the fields as we approached the village an elderly black labrador greeted us with a hoarse bark. "Silly old fool, aren't you?" murmured his owner. I think she meant the dog.

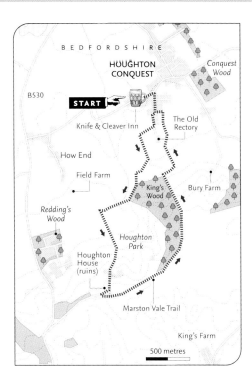

Start & finish Royal Oak pub, Houghton Conquest MK45 3LL (OS ref TL 047416)

Walk (4½ miles; easy; OS Explorers 208 and 193): From Royal Oak pub, left along High Street; left along Rectory Lane. Just before Old Rectory, right (045412, Houghton Conquest Meadows, Kings Wood). Through kissing gate, turn left. Beside 7-barred metal gate, right (045411); follow fenced path, then yellow-topped posts and Marston Vale Timberland Trail signs for 1½ miles across fields and up past Houghton Park House to entrance to Houghton House ruin (040392). Visit House; return to drive entrance. Right for 50m, then left (yellow-topped post, Greensand Ridge Walk). Follow farm track into Kings Wood (045394); permissive path down to bottom of wood (045405). Through gate; right (arrows); through kissing gate; ahead along bottom edge of coppice. In 200m, left through gate (047406, arrow); follow arrows to right of Old Rectory, back to Houghton Conquest.

Lunch Royal Oak, Houghton Conquest (01234 740459, 4-11pm Mon-Fri; from noon Sat, Sun); or picnic at Houghton House.

More information Bedford Tourist Information Centre (01234 221712); visitbedford.co.uk; ramblers.org.uk; satmap.co.uk

Aldworth slumbered along its sunny lanes. A tiny cream and green car stood outside the bike shop, an original 1937 Fiat 500.

The long lane to the Berkshire Downs ran between hedges thick with the summer's growth – angelica, cow parsley, pale pink blackberry flowers, docks brown and crisped by July heat. At Starveall cottage a patch of wild ground was bright with flowers: purple mallows and knapweeds, blue powder-puff heads of scabious, a bubbly yellow froth of lady's bedstraw.

Here the motor road expired as if it couldn't be bothered to crawl any farther. A stony lane took over, the dusty flints crunching underfoot. We crossed the ancient Ridgeway track and took the road less travelled, a grassy way between cornfields where the fat ripe ears of wheat and barley drooped earthwards on their short stalks.

A marbled white butterfly went fluttering over a bank of thistles in a blur of wings. We passed Lowbury Hill, a slightly swelling dome amid the oilseed rape. Was it here that the future King Alfred dealt the Danes a terrible beating on a winter's day in AD871 at the Battle of Ashdown? Or was it on Kingstanding Hill, at the far end of the splendid old grass track called the Fair Mile that runs straight and true, west to east along the spine of the Berkshire Downs? There's no telling the battle's exact location now, but the views from Kingstanding across Berkshire into Oxfordshire are something to savour.

We dropped down above Starveall Farm. After the heat and dust of the downland cornfields, the cool green light under the beeches of Unhill Wood was delightful. When we emerged to follow the flinty trackways back to Aldworth a whitethroat in an elder bush sang us by as though in private raptures.

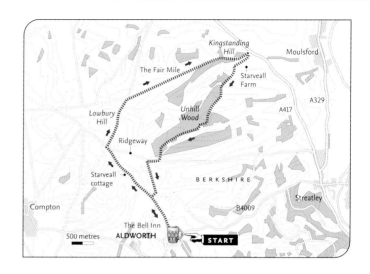

Start & finish Bell Inn, Aldworth, Streatley, Berkshire RG8 9SE (OS ref SU556796)

Walk (8 miles; easy; OS Explorers 158, 170): From Bell Inn, right to junction; right on Ambury Road. In one mile pass Starveall cottage (546809); in another ½ mile Ridgeway track crosses and forks left (540815), but take right fork (grassy central strip). In ¾ mile, just past the "Ridgeway closed to motor vehicles" notice, right (544826) along the Fair Mile for 2 miles. Just before A417, turn right through right-hand of 2 gates (573837). Half right down field slope to bottom right corner (571835). Right along drive; in 75m, left up roadway. In ¾ mile, at sharp left bend (564823), ahead on grass track (fingerpost), forking left into woods. Uphill; at start of next descent, right at pheasant feeder (564821) on grass path. In 150m, at pheasant pen (562821), left down to tarmac lane. Right; in ½ mile, at fork, ahead between waymark posts (555817). Path to stile on to driveway (553814); right to gate; right along trackway. In 200m, left (550812, "Byway"); in ½ mile, bend right (552805, "Byway") to road (551804); left to Aldworth.

Lunch Bell Inn, Aldworth (01635 578272), a rural delight (closed on Mondays)

More information visitthames.co.uk; satmap.com; ramblers.org.uk

ETON AND BOVENEY

Only just upriver from London, Eton and its famous college occupy the nub end of a flat, sprawling island between the Jubilee River and the River Thames.

Disembarking at Windsor and Eton Riverside station, we saw the great Round Tower of Windsor Castle looming large on the southern skyline. Once across the Thames and out into The Brocas we looked back to see the castle in all its magnificence, one of the classic tourist views of England.

The honk and gabble of Canada geese and the quacking laughter of mallard drakes came from the river as we walked the Thames Path west. Soon these fell behind, and we went on through a level landscape as evocative of agriculture as of leisure.

A poignant memorial stone by the river recorded Hiatt C. Baker's gift of this stretch of the bank to Eton College in memory of his son John, a member of the college killed in a flying accident in 1917. "A brilliant swimmer," recorded the proud father, "who spent here many of the happiest hours of his boyhood."

At Boveney Lock the lock keeper was on duty outside his charming cottage. Beyond we found the Church of St Mary Magdalene, now in the care of the nicely named Friends of Friendless Churches. This modest chapel, built of clunch and flint, was founded for the use of Thames bargemen.

We turned back past The Old Place, a house of mellow red brick and twisty chimneys, and followed paths over Dorney Common and North Field towards Eton. Along the neat and tidy high street were handsome ornate gateways, lovely old houses, boys and masters in white ties and tails, and a wonderful chapel and college library fit – literally – for a prince.

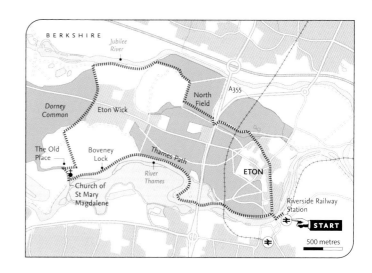

Start & finish Windsor & Eton Riverside station car park, Datchet Road, Windsor SL4 1QG (OS ref SU 969774)

Walk (6½ miles; easy; OS Explorer 160): Cross Thames on footbridge. Follow Thames Path west. In 2 miles pass Boveney Lock (945778); in 500m, at chapel, right inland (940777). At road (939778), right past Old Place; in 100m, left (fingerpost). At top left corner of field bear right (939783); in 100m, left across Cress Brook footbridge (940783). Half right across Dorney Common. Cross road at cattle grid (943786); on with stream on right to gate and cycleway (943791). Right; in 400m, pass end of footbridge (947791); in another 400m, right (951792, fingerpost, kissing gate) across field, aiming left of phone mast to cross road (954791). On across paddocks (stiles) to North Field (956789). Right; anticlockwise round field to road embankment (959785). Dogleg right/left under road; right along field edge; under railway (962783). Ahead on tarmac road, following Eton Walkway to Eton High Street (966780). Right to Thames footbridge and station.

Lunch The Boatman, Thames Side, Windsor SL4 1QN (01753 620010, boatmanwindsor.com). All customers are asked to book ahead

More information Windsor Tourist Information Centre (01753 743900)

THATCHAM REEDBEDS AND GREENHAM COMMON

A harsh scolding call sounded from dense foliage as we followed a path through the watery jungle of Thatcham Reedbeds. The crisscross of reed stems, leaves and the shadows of leaves made it impossible to spot the little sedge warbler with its subtle camouflage of brown and grey.

They have been digging gravel out of the Kennet Valley for a long time now. What's left is a string of "lakes" (flooded gravel pits) and extensive reedbeds where reed buntings and warblers nest each year.

We crossed a bridge over untroubled water, then the turbid olive channel of the Kennet and Avon Canal at Bull's Lock. Beyond the canal a crunchy lane ran south past a meadow of contented cattleland came to Burys Bank Road, on the boundary of Greenham Common.

Greenham Common used to be an RAF and US air force base, and cruise missiles with nuclear warheads were housed here from 1983 onwards. The women's peace movement established camps around the perimeter in protest, scaled the fences, danced on the missile silos and otherwise kept their cause in the headlines until long after the weapons were shipped out in 1991.

Walking the gravelly paths and climbing the former control tower for a high-level view across the common today, the contrast between then and now is astonishing. The runways for the bombers lie beneath heathland full of flowers – lady's bedstraw, centaury, viper's bugloss in vivid shades of yellow, pink and blue.

We turned off the common into a tree-hung lane that ran north to cross the dimpling River Kennet. Back on the canal, we strolled homeward among sickly smelling meadowsweet and tall spikes of purple loosestrife.

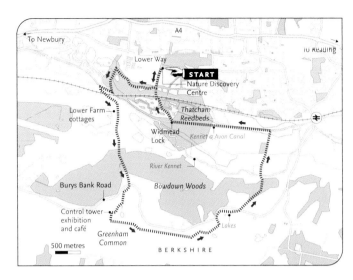

Start & finish Nature Discovery Centre, Lower Way, Thatcham RG19 3FU (OS ref SU 506670)

Walk (6 miles; easy; OS Explorer 158): Follow path on right of lake. At foot of lake, right (506667, "Reedbed Trail/RT"). In 250m, where track bends left, keep ahead on path (503667, RT), following RT signs. In ½ mile at canal, right across long bridge (500666) past Bull's Lock; in 150m, left across canal. Left on road; under railway (499666); follow "footpath" fingerposts. In 400m through gate by Lower Farm Cottages (500663), on for ½ mile to cross Burys Bank Road (502654). Up path opposite to gate on to Greenham Common. Right; in 300m pass large grey shed, then gate (501651); fork right on path to control tower (500650). Take main path south, through gate; left along wide gravel track for ¾ mile. 100m past banded waymark post, fork left (511647). Through trees, past lakes. At waymark post with double band, left (518650, gate) across road. Gravel track opposite; at T-junction, left (521654) to cross River Kennet (521655), then canal (522661). Left on towpath to Widmead Lock (509662); 50m beyond, right (banded post, gate, RT). In 500m cross railway (506666); ahead to car park.

Lunch Cafés at Discovery Centre and control tower

More information bbowt.org.uk; greenhamcommon.org.uk

Chaffinches spurting out their stuttering song, a wren squeaking and trilling, blackbirds fluting, the throaty cooing of pigeons – Combe was a valley full of birdsong.

The broad field beyond Combe village was more flint than soil. Our boots clinked with every step, disturbing a sleek and handsome brown hare. Steeply up the face of Sugglestone Down and we were up on the heights under a wide and blowy Berkshire sky. From the crest we looked back over the Combe valley, a patchwork of milky chalk soil and green wheat.

A long, flinty holloway dropped through hazel copses where sheaves of wild garlic leaves rustled and long-tailed tits swung twittering on the topmost twigs. At the bottom under Cleve Hill Down we found the Test Way footpath, a guide through the quiet hollows and inlands of these downs.

Two kites were flapping and playing over a conifer plantation, swooping together, springing apart at the last moment, while much higher overhead a pair of buzzards performed the same springtime dance.

The Test Way tilted and steepened as it climbed to the roof of the downs once more. An ancient ridgeway on Inkpen Hill ran east past the tall stark T-shape of Combe Gibbet, at whose yard ends in 1676 the murderers George Broomham and Dorothy Newman had swung. They had drowned Broomham's wife, Margaret, in a pond after she caught them in flagrante delicto on the downs nearby.

On the great Iron Age rampart of Walbury Camp hillfort we paused for a final stare out over a prospect of farmlands, villages, woods and hills, stretching away west, north and east for dozens of miles – one of the great high vistas of southern Britain.

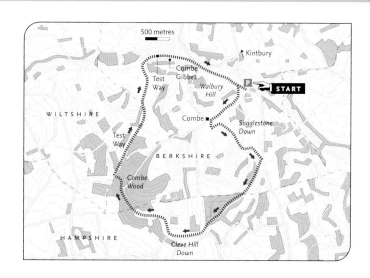

Start & finish Walbury Hill easterly car park, near Inkpen, Berkshire RG17 9EH approx. (OS ref SU 380616).

Walk (8 miles; moderate; OS Explorers 158, 131): West up trackway. In 200m, left (378616, fingerpost/FP) down path to Combe. At memorial bench, left (373609, FP) past cottages; in 200m, left (373607), then across wide field. From old fencepost (378606) path goes half right, steeply up Sugglestone Down to stile (379604). Aim for mast; path curves right to road (384601). Right (red arrow) on byway. In 1¼ miles, cross road (372587, "Linkenholt"). In 100m, right on track. In ½ mile pass adventure centre (364586; Test Way/TW joins from left). In 250m, TW forks left past barn (364588). In 1 mile, at west edge of Combe Wood (353598), TW turns right, steeply uphill. In 1 mile, right through gate (358613, TW, Buttermere Estate notice). In ¼ mile, at hedge break (359617, 3-finger post), ahead (not right) to ridge track (358621); TW right to Combe Gibbet and Walbury Hill.

Lunch Crown & Garter, Great Common Road, Inkpen RG17 9QR (01488 668325, crownandgarter.co.uk)

More information West Berks Museum, Newbury (01635 519562); satmap.com; ramblers.org.uk

ALDBURY NOWERS AND COLLEGE LAKE

As we walked out of Tring station the Chilterns beckoned us on and upward, with the green, humpbacked downland of Aldbury Nowers looking down on the railway.

It's not until you're up there in the crumbly, white clay of the 5,000-year-old Ridgeway that you properly appreciate the wildlife treasures of these chalk grassland slopes. The wild marjoram and thyme, the harebells and rockroses that carpet the steep, grassy banks are carefully nurtured by the Berks, Bucks and Oxon Wildlife Trust (BBOWT).

We followed the Ridgeway as it undulated north along the hillsides in company with the old Saxon earthwork of Grim's Ditch. Gaps between the trees gave a far prospect north and west over the green wooded plains of outer Buckinghamshire. Deep in the trees, wrens chattered in full flow, and a black and white great spotted woodpecker cocked his red-capped head as he prepared to give a beech crown a good hammering.

High on Pitstone Hill we left the Ridgeway for a bridleway that tipped back down into the valley. Here the navvies dug deep to carve out great cuttings for the railway and the Grand Union Canal. Well-tended paths led us through horse pastures to the flooded chalk quarry of College Lake.

We walked a circuit of the lake, looking for redshank and lapwing, while birdwatchers passed tantalising news of a visiting osprey that might be in the vicinity. We saw neither hide nor hair of the osprey. That didn't matter, not with the sun deciding to put in an afternoon appearance. We walked slowly back to Tring in the depths of the cutting beside the motionless, olive-green waters of the Grand Union Canal.

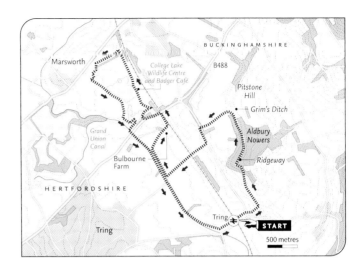

Start & finish Tring station, Hertfordshire HP23 5QR (OS ref SP 951122)

Walk (7½ miles; easy; OS Explorer 181): Cross road; right; 100m beyond right bend, left (953124, "Ridgeway"/RW) up driveway. In 50m, ahead, to turn left along RW. In 600m fork right (951129, "RW footpath", yellow arrows/YA, acorn waymarks). In ¾ mile, left at kissing gate (950139, "Bridleway") down to road (945137). Left for 250m; right (946134, fingerpost) past Park Hill and Marsh Croft farms to Grand Union Canal (939129). Right (YA) on path along east bank of canal, then past Bulbourne Farm (938135). At railway, left to B488 (938140). Left for 250m; right into College Lake Nature Reserve (935139). Walk Reserve Trail circuit. Back at Visitor Centre, right along path parallel to B488. In 250m (934137), right along road. Cross canal bridge; left along towpath for 1¼ miles to road at 2nd bridge (948121); left to Tring station.

Lunch Badger Café, College Lake Visitor Centre

More information College Lake Visitor Centre (01442 826774, bbowt.org.uk) open 9.30am–5pm; visitengland.com; satmap.com; ramblers.org.uk

CADSDEN, CHEQUERS AND COOMBE HILL

It was hard to leave the comfort and good cheer of the Plough at Cadsden, but the sound of rooks cawing among the blossoming treetops fetched us out at last along the Ridgeway into a cool, cloudy Buckinghamshire afternoon.

If you are looking for a wildflower walk, this circuit is a slice of heaven. In the beech and oak woodswe found yellow archangel, wood sorrel, delicate white anemones and carpets of blue and white bluebells. Out in the cornfields we spotted groundsel, scarlet pimpernel and beautiful yellow and violet heartsease. As for the chalky grassland of the open downs – cowslips and primroses, jack-by-the-hedge and herb Robert, speedwell and forget-me-not, guelder rose and early purple orchids.

Rounding the corner of Whorley Wood we came suddenly on the sublime prospect of the shallow valley where Chequers sits, the handsome red brick Elizabethan manor house making a centrepiece for some subtle landscaping.

Up through Goodmerhill Wood we went, following the Ridgeway to the tall Boer War monument at the prow of Coombe Hill. A pause here for a glug of water and a stare at a view of many dozens of miles across fields, woods and hill ranges, as far as Salisbury Plain and the Malvern Hills on a good clear day. Then we quit the Ridgeway for a woodland track along the edges of Low Scrubs. Peewits were tumbling over the beanfields around Dirtywood Farm and a pair of crows swooped on a red kite like fighter boys from Biggin Hill. Bandits at Angels Five!

We dropped steeply down through Ninn Wood, brilliant in late afternoon sunshine, until the Plough Inn hove up ahead, a cosy port in a green sea of leaves.

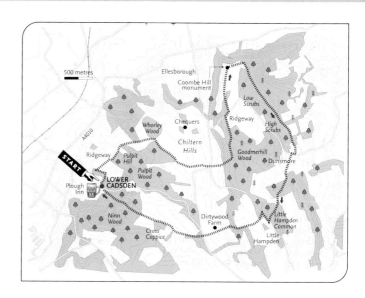

Start & finish Plough Inn, Lower Cadsden, Princes Risborough HP27 0NB (OS ref SP826045). Pub car parking only for walkers who are customers; please ring, book a table and ask about parking

Walk (7½ miles, moderate, OS Explorer 181): From Plough Inn, left along road; in 10m, right; Ridgeway (fingerposts, white acorns) for 3¼ miles to pass Coombe Hill monument (849067). In 300m, right off Ridgeway ("Bridleway") for 150m to wide crossing track. Left for 100m; right (853067) along wide track. In 200m, left on woodland track (yellow arrows/ YAs on trees) for 1 mile past Low and High Scrubs to Dunsmore (862052); Little Hampden Common (857040); Dirtywood Farm (848038); past Cross Coppice; through Ninn Wood to Plough Inn.

Lunch Plough Inn (01844 343302; theplough.pub) – it welcomes walkers

More information Princes Risborough Tourist Information Centre (01844 274795); visitbuckinghamshire.org; chilternsaonb.org; ramblers.org.uk

A cold, cloudy morning where the Chiltern Hills meet the boundaries of Bucks, Berks and Oxon. Not that the red kites were inclined to respect the county borders – they soared and wheeled indifferently over the bare woods and rain-sodden fields.

At Mill End the River Thames had forsaken its measured pace through the green meadows. The river, swollen by a whole night's rainfall, came rushing and roaring, pushing a solid skein of sinewy grey-green water through the sluices.

Heads reeling with the sound and energy of the seething water, we turned along the river bank and were instantly doused in peace and plenty. The Thames formed a broad, graceful bend, the water slow and wind-stippled as it slid smoothly past riverfront villas and their ornate wooden boathouses. Kempt lawns studded with fine cedars sloped up to Greenlands, a white wedding cake of a residence, built in 1853 for the stationery mogul WH Smith.

A great crested grebe bobbed in the midriver flow, cautiously observing a nearby tufted duck with straggly crest and brilliant golden eyes. Black-headed gulls squabbled over titbits, and a grey heron emitted a mournful shriek as it skimmed the water.

At Upper Thames Rowing Club's handsome premises we left the river and followed a snowdrop-spattered path to join up with the Chiltern Way that led across the winter wheatfields to Aston. From this elevated stance the Thames lay hidden by a fold of ground as though it had ceased to exist.

The Flower Pot Hotel at Aston exuded good smells of log fires. A venison pie (with juniper berries) and a golden pint of Boondoggle bitter here; then the final stroll beside the racing Thames towards the rumble and tumult of Hambleden Weirs.

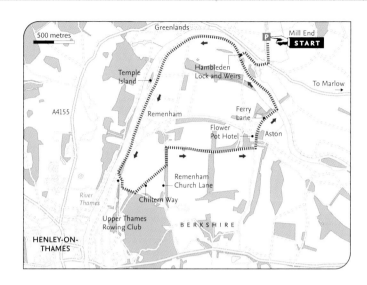

Start & finish Mill End car park, Hambleden, Buckinghamshire RG9 6TL (OS ref SU 786854)

Walk (6 miles; easy; OS Explorer 171): Right along road (pavement). Dogleg right/left across A4155 (786850); follow footpath signs ("Wokingham Way") across River Thames via Hambleden Weirs. Cross Hambleden Lock (783851); right on riverbank Thames Path for 1¾ miles. Beside flagpole of Upper Thames Rowing Club (767836), left through car park to Remenham Lane. Right; in 50m, fork left (768835, fingerpost). In 50m, left (fingerpost, "Permitted Path"); in 150m, left on Chiltern Way, Berkshire Loop (770834, fingerpost). In 400m, left on Remenham Church Lane (774837); in 200m, right (773839, kissing gate, fingerpost) on Chiltern Way. In ½ mile, just before wooden gate across path, left (782840, "Permitted Path") down to road (783842). Right into Aston. At Flower Pot Hotel (785842), left down Ferry Lane. At river, left (787845, "Thames Path") to recross Hambleden Weirs and return to car park.

Lunch The Flower Pot Hotel, Aston RG9 3DG (01491 574721, flowerpothotel.com)

More information Henley-on-Thames Tourist Information Centre (01491 576982)

HAWRIDGE AND BELLINGDON

None of the Chiltern counties north-west of London is richer in beechwoods, chalky hollows and flinty ridges than Buckinghamshire. We set out before the clock struck midday from the Black Horse Inn, just outside Chesham, where the Metropolitan Tube line runs out of track.

This is horse country, a land of paddocks and hay mangers. At Bower Farm the wind-vane figure was a polo player in mid-chukka. Up on the ridge above White Hawridge Bottom we trod heavy clay fields seeded with millions of flints. The rough nuggety soil had been the ruin of many Victorian ploughshares, whose snapped-off fragments lay rusting in the furrows.

The fine 18th-century farmhouse of Hawridge Court stands on the site of an early medieval manor, itself built inside an oval earthen bank that might date back a thousand years or more. The hedges in the valley bottom are thick and venerable, the beech woods ancient.

There's a sense of long continuity in these Chiltern hills and hollows. The local clay has gone to make good bricks for hundreds of years, and the craft still flourishes at the brickworks of HG Matthews above the woods. There were stacks of red bricks in the yard, and a good sour smell of baking brick from the wood-fired kiln beyond the sheds.

We passed the cottages at Bellingdon Farm, where DH Lawrence briefly lived in 1914 while writing *The Rainbow*.

The homeward path lay along a beautiful hillside and up between the blackly twisted beech roots of Captain's Wood, where goldfinches flirted from tree to tree and a ghostly silver sun slipped briefly out between one drifting cloud and the next.

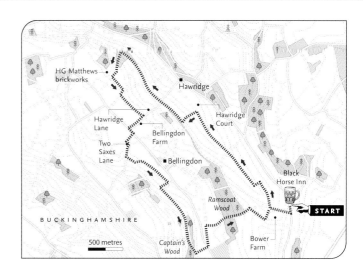

Start & finish Black Horse Inn, The Vale, Chesham, Buckinghamshire HP5 3NS (OS ref SP 963045)

Walk (6½ miles; easy; OS Explorer 181): Right along road; in 150m, right (stile) up path. At top of slope, right (961045, stile, arrow), NW along ridge for 1 mile. Beside Hawridge Court (950058), through kissing gate; left to valley bottom (948056). Right across Hawridge Lane (945059); on through 2 fields, into woodland (941064). In 300m, left (939066, yellow arrow/YA) up hill past brickworks. Left (937062, YA), SE for ½ mile; right down Hawridge Lane to road (940055). Left for 100m; right down Two Gates Lane. In ¼ mile, left (940051, YA) SE for ½ mile to lane (9460048). Right; at left bend, ahead on fenced path; at field, left for ½ mile into Captain's Wood (949040). In 200m, left over stile past Mount Nugent Farm to cross road (952039). Left on track; in 300m it bends right, then left/right (954043) through Ramscourt Wood. Into valley; right (958045) on track; in 250m, left (960043, YA) up slope; right at top (stile) to return to Black Horse Inn.

Lunch Black Horse Inn (01494 784656; theblackhorsechesham.co.uk)

More information High Wycombe Tourist Information Centre (01494 421892); visitengland.com; satmap.com; ramblers.org.uk

Mr William Liberty of Chorleywood, nonconformist brickmaker, died in 1777. In his will he stipulated that he was not to be buried anywhere within the bounds of a church. His wife, Alice, was of the same mind. And so for well over 200 years the freethinking and aptly named Liberties have lain in their brick-built tomb by the field path to Chenies Bottom.

Passing the tomb, I wondered whether Mr Liberty would have sucked his teeth at last night's Midsummer Music festival – celestially beautiful music, sublimely played, within the bounds of Latimer's Victorian church. There were wings to my heels and tunes at the back of my head as I followed the Chess Valley Walk past Mill Farm and on to Tyler's farm at the ford on Holloway Lane. The dimpling Chess, a gin-clear stream over a gravel bed, used to raise wonderful crops of cress. What a tragedy that pollution has recently put paid to the production of the crunchy and eye-wateringly peppery cress one used to buy here to chew on the way over the fields to Holy Cross church at Church End.

Back down the field slope, and on west across the Chess on a lush wet path, then up under the shade of hornbeam and bird cherry into Chenies village. History lies thick on the great Tudor mansion of Chenies Manor where King Henry VIII still walks at night, a limping ghost.

In the adjacent church, generations of Russells, dukes and duchesses of Bedford, lie entombed. I found something a little oppressive about the pomp and grandeur of the monuments looming in the Bedford chapel. It was a relief to be out under the cool grey sky again, walking the ridge path back to Latimer and looking across the river valley to where the Liberties lay free and easy among the nettles and dog roses.

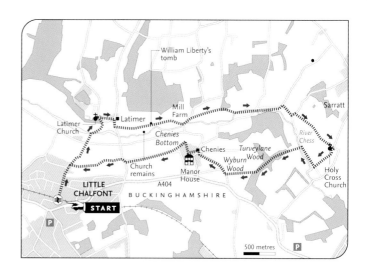

Start & finish Chalfont & Latimer Tube station, Buckinghamshire HP7 9PR (OS ref SU997975)

Walk (7 miles; easy; OS Explorer 172): Chalfont & Latimer station; left along Bedford Avenue; right along Chenies Avenue (996976). Where it bends left into Beechwood Avenue (996981), ahead into woods. At junction (997981, blue arrows/BA, yellow arrows/YA), ahead downhill to bottom of wood and kissing gate (998983). Cross road (999985) and river (000986); right to cross road (004987; "Chess Valley Walk"/ CVW, fish waymark). Follow CVW for 1¾ miles to road (031990); right; round left bend, right (033989) on path to Sarratt church and Cock Inn (039984). South gate of churchyard – valley bottom (035981); right for 400m, left across River Chess (034984; NB Wet and muddy). Chiltern Way to road (021980); right to Chenies church (016983); right at Manor, into woods. At tree with three arrows, left along upper edge of wood; ridge track to cross Stony Lane (005982); track for ½ mile to junction in woods (997981, BA, YA); left to station.

Lunch Cock Inn, Sarratt, Herts WD3 6HH (01923 282908; cockinn. net)

More information Midsummer Music festival, Latimer, every June (01494 783643, midsummermusic.org.uk); Chalfont St Giles Tourist Information Centre (01494 874732); visitbuckinghamshire.org; satmap.com; ramblers.org.uk

At Quainton in the Buckinghamshire lowlands the sails and white cap of a windmill overlook the sloping village green.

Leaving the village on the North Bucks Way, we climbed the nape of Simber Hill and Quainton Hill beyond. The views were remarkable, south to the long dark barrier of the Chiltern Hills, west and north over lower ground where whaleback hills rose from pasture striped with hedges.

Down at the foot of Conduit Hill we passed between the shallow hummocks of Fulbrook, one of several deserted medieval villages hereabouts. A path led across tussocky pasture and fields of dark grey plough to reach the road to North Marston. In a lane below the church we found a covered well with an old-fashioned pump, its stone trough bearing the sculpture of a boot.

Towards the end of the 13th century the rector of North Marston was Sir John Schorne, a renowned healer and miracle worker famed for capturing the Devil and imprisoning him in a boot. Schorne discovered the holy well during a deadly drought, and its water was said to cure gout and toothache.

The homeward path followed Matthew's Way, a rural route dedicated to the memory of "a very special little boy". His round infant face looked out of a photo placed beside the way, and we carried that image in our heads across the sheep pastures.

Under the grey cloud cap the western sky showed a crack of silver. As we approached Quainton a brown hare sprang up and darted away over the corrugations of medieval ridge and furrow, a lithe wild shape in this well-ordered landscape.

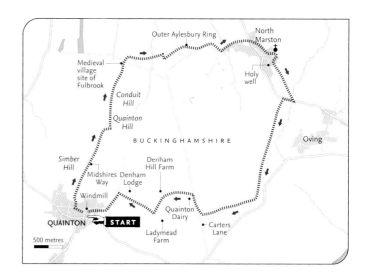

Start & finish Village green, Quainton, Buckinghamshire HP22 4AR (OS ref SP 747201)

Walk (7½ miles; easy; OS Explorer 192): At top of green, left. By playground, right (745202); follow North Bucks Way north towards Quainton Hill. In ¾ mile, at top of rise with gate and blue arrow on right (750215), left to skyline gate; fork right down Conduit Hill. Cross road (752225); half right, following Outer Aylesbury Ring/OAR) across fields. In ½ mile, under power lines, right (761228, kissing gate/KG); aim for shed and stile to road (764228, OAR). Left into North Marston. In ¾ mile, right at T-junction (774228); fork left in front of Pilgrim pub; follow lane to church (777227). From south gate, right; left along Schorne Lane; fork left by well (777225). In 30m, right (KG); follow well-marked Matthew's Way for 2¼ miles across fields to Carters Lane (765202). Right; in 400m, at Quainton Dairy, left (764205) on farm drive, passing Denham Hill Farm (759204), gates of Ladymead Farm (758202) and Denham Lodge (753204). Cross cattle grid; in 100m, left to road (751202); right into Quainton.

Lunch George & Dragon, Quainton HP22 4AR (01296 655436, georgeanddragonquainton.co.uk)

More information visitbuckinghamshire.org

BENINGTON AND BURN'S GREEN

Two renovators were busy lime-washing the chancel of Benington's Church of St Peter. They courteously moved their buckets and pulled back their plastic sheeting to let us have a peek at the extraordinary stone carvings in the church in the church – Green Men, howling faces and a king in his death throes. Out in the churchyard — either overgrown or rewilded depending on your point of view — the gravestones were half drowned in cow parsley, buttercups and miniature cranesbill.

The whole village of timber-framed houses seemed awash with greenery this spring morning. Lucky for us that the famed gardens of Benington Lordship hadn't opened yet or we might never have got away from this delightful spot.

A scribble of blackcap song, loud and melodic, followed us along the nettly verge of a barley field. Skylarks sang over the fields each side of the broad flinty track of Cotton Lane as it curled up and over the back of Great Brookfield Common.

A short stretch of High Elms Lane, a ridge road lined with pale pink campion and Jack-by-the-hedge, and we were following a shady green lane.

After a reviving sandwich and pint at the Lordship Arms on the crossroads in Burn's Green, we went on east past a dimple of ponds, walking through hay meadows waist-high with grass awaiting its first cut of the year.

The bridleway through Benington Park made a pale parting through the wheat fields. Here I picked up a big solid flint, shaped and scalloped, perhaps a palaeolithic hand axe. We crossed the fields to find Duck Lane, and turned homewards between banks of periwinkles spreading their royal blue petals like windmill sails.

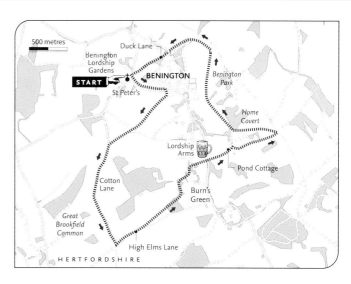

Start & finish St Peter's Church, Benington, Hertfordshire SG2 7LH (OS ref TL 297236)

Walk (6 miles; easy; OS Explorer 193): Up lane to junction; right ("Ware, Hertford"). Just past the bus shelter, right (303235, kissing gate) on permissive path. In ½ mile at arrow post, ahead (299229); in 100m, join sunken lane on left. In 300m, by brick hut (296228), fork left uphill on Cotton Lane. In ¾ mile, left up road (298215). In 500m, fork left (301217, "Benington") up track. In ¾ mile cross road at Lordship Arms public house (309226). In 300m at Pond Cottage, fork right along track (312228). In 100m fork left (blue arrow). Follow blue arrows, descending into valley. In 500m, left (318230, blue arrow post). In 500m at far corner of Home Covert, bear right (312230, blue arrow) through trees and across field. Cross Benington Park house drive; right (blue arrow) onto hill top by 4-finger post (308234). Left up hedge for 30m; right on path across field, then on left of hedges. At bottom of slope, left (309240, blue arrow); in 250m, left (306241) along green lane, then Duck Lane to Benington.

Lunch Lordship Arms, Burn's Green (01438 869665; lordshiparms.com)

More information Benington Lordship Gardens (beningtonlordship.co.uk)

St Andrew's Church stood alone in its green "God's Acre", well away from the traffic in Much Hadham's high street. The stone heads of king and queen that guarded the south door were blurred and disfigured by centuries of weathering. But they provided the inspiration for the modernistic pouting faces under regal crowns on either side of the west doorway, carved by the world-acclaimed monumental sculptor Henry Moore, a local resident.

Our way rose smoothly from the valley of the River Ash, up through meadows still sweating off the morning dew. The distinct rumble of a Stansted-bound jet formed a backdrop to the trilling of a robin from a blackthorn bush. On the path lay lime-green fruit casings like little paper chestnut trees, fallen from a wych elm in the hedge. Near Green Tye a big green dome stood in the fields like a Hollywood spacecraft – an anaerobic digester producing eco-electricity for Guy and Wright's tomato farm. Beyond the hamlet we walked the curvilinear margins of huge fields ploughed a foot deep, the furrows speckled with pebbles rounded by an ancient river long vanished.

At Perry Green stood the old white-faced farmhouse of Hoglands, Moore's home from 1940 for nearly 50 years, now the centre of the Henry Moore Foundation.

In a sheep pasture beyond the house stood a bronze sculpture, a hollow cloaked figure embracing a child, tall and calm in its stance beside a lily pond. A mound like a Bronze Age burial barrow in the neighbouring field held a recumbent female form, all curves and arches, its polished bronze mirroring the afternoon sun. Echoes of these shapes in nature were reflected in the sinewy limbs of hornbeams in the woods along the homeward path beside the river.

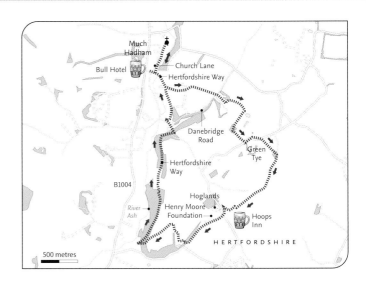

Start & finish High Street, Much Hadham SG10 6BU (OS ref TL 428193)

Walk (6¼ miles; easy; OS Explorer 194): Opposite Bull Hotel, down Oudle Lane to church (430197). Back along Oudle Lane; at corner by Two Bridges, through gate (429193, "Hertfordshire Way"/HW, "Stansted Hill"); fork left. In 200m left uphill (430191, kissing gates/KG, yellow arrow/YA). Dogleg left/right across Hill Farm drive (433191, YAs) and on. In 600m cross Danebridge Road (437190) and on ("Green Tye"). In 100m, left ("footpath"); follow HW black arrows. Before domes, fork right (441188) across footbridge. In 300m at arrow post, left (440185) to road in Green Tye (441184). Left; at Prince of Wales pub, right (444184) down lane. At thatched house, ahead. Follow HW to Perry Green opposite Hoglands (439175). Left along road; in 50m, right ("footpath 32"); ahead to road (434170). Right (fingerpost) past sculpture; cross field; through hedge (433171). In rough pasture, half right at YA post to fence (432172); then half left across pasture to KG/YA (429170). Down to valley; right on HW to Much Hadham.

Lunch Hoops Inn, Perry Green SG10 6EF (01279 843568, hoops-inn.co.uk)

More information henry-moore.org

CHOBHAM COMMON

The 1,600 acres of Chobham Common form a scrubby stretch of heathland across north Surrey. The track we were following south across the common was floored with sandy yellow soil.

Two women clopped past on ponies, one of the animals sporting DayGlo pink ear warmers. It was hard to imagine the fear which travellers in olden times felt as they ventured to cross the common, an expanse of wilderness notorious for its footpads and highwaymen.

Goldcrests went flitting through the bare treetops. We watched a treecreeper dropping down to the base of a silver birch to start another upward scuttle, looking and listening for insects hiding in interstices of the papery bark.

From Burrow Hill Green we headed north along a skein of tracks, the murmur of the M3 growing louder. On through the motorway underpass, and then a straight climb among gorse and birch to the summit of Ship Hill.

A stubby granite cross marks the spot where in 1853 Queen Victoria reviewed her troops on a summer's day. 8,000 men and 1,500 horses took part in a mock battle. Among the gallant participants were the men of the Light Brigade, destined to be decimated in Crimea the following year during their famous charge at the Battle of Balaclava.

Also present were barrels of molasses, brought to sweeten the soldiers' tea. Long after the Great Camp, a rumour persisted that the barrels had been buried to await the soldiers' return; and locals who prospected for them rejoiced in the nickname of "treacle miners".

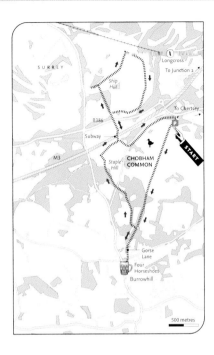

Start & finish Longcross car park, Chobham, Surrey KT16 0ED (OS ref SU 979651)

Walk (6½ miles; easy; OS Explorer 160): Path south. In 50m fork right. In ¾ mile pass post (blue arrow/BA); in 100m, dogleg right/left (975638) across track. On under power lines. In nearly ¾ mile (973632, house on left) dogleg right/left (BA) to Gorse Lane (972631). Right to Four Horseshoes pub (972628). Return up Gorse Lane. At right bend, ahead into wood (972631). Just past electricity substation, dogleg right/left (973632, BAs). In 200m, left (974633, BA). In 100m, right (BA on tree) with field on right. In 300m cross trackway (973637). At road, left; cross Staple Hill Road (970639, BA, fingerpost). Ahead for nearly ¾ mile via Chickabiddy Hill (968644), to cross M3 through subway (970647), then B386 (970650 – take care!). Ahead for ½ mile to memorial cross on Ship Hill (965655). Return to cross track (967656); ahead on track. In ½ mile round right bend; in nearly ¾ mile ahead at junction (974658, bench on left). At next junction, right (974655) for ½ mile to T-junction (969651). Left through underpass; left to cross Staple Hill road (973646); left for 800m to car park.

Lunch Four Horseshoes, Burrow Hill Green GU24 8QP (01276 856257, fourhorseshoeschobham.co.uk)

More information surreywildlifetrust.org

COLDHARBOUR AND LEITH HILL

The Surrey Weald, a great thickly wooded lens of land, lies on a band of ironstone in the shadow of the North Downs. Once it was a smoky, noisy, clangorous industrial hub, part of the medieval iron-making centre of England. You would never know it now, though, so snug and quiet lie the villages tucked into valley bottoms.

Coldharbour is no more than a scatter of cottages. We started off north along Wolvens Lane, a sun-dappled holloway under pollarded beeches. Flickers of grey and tan betrayed the movement of horse riders down parallel tracks, moving quietly and all but unseen through the woods.

A path dark with hollies and yews led west, down to the fast water race of the River Tillingbourne in its valley-bottom bed, and to the beautiful millpond at Friday Street.

From the slopes of Leith Hill, the highest point in Surrey, the view stretched many miles across the wooded Vale of Surrey and north Sussex, a smoky grey and blue prospect over the wealden landscape. From the viewing platform at the top of Leith Hill Tower, the panorama sprang further outwards, south to the South Downs around Goodwood and the trees on Chanctonbury Ring 25 miles away, north as far as a pale grey smear that might have been the Dunstable Downs 50 miles away, and the spectral towers of the London skyline.

In 1765 Richard Hull of Leith Hill Place built the 60ft (18m) brick and ironstone tower to claim a 1,000ft (300m) summit for Surrey. He lies buried here, not arrogantly at the apex of his creation, but humbly beneath its foundations, with the world climbing on his back to enjoy the sensational view he laid out for us all.

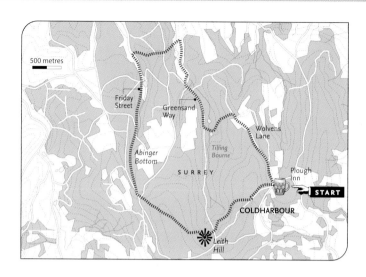

Start & finish Plough Inn, Coldharbour, near Dorking, Surrey RH5 6HD (OS ref TQ 151441)

Walk (6½ miles; easy; OS Explorer 146): From Plough Inn cross road; track to right of bench. In ¾ mile, pass Wolven Cottage Stables (145452); in 100m, left past barrier on footpath for 600m to bridleway at Tilling Springs (139449). Right (north) on Greensand Way for 1 mile; 100m past Mandrake House (nameplate), left (135465, stile) across field and Tillingbourne. Follow footpath across road (131462), west through Bushy Wood for 700m to reach track (126462; NB don't cross bridge beyond). Left to Friday Street; cross road (128458); pass Stephan Langton Inn (128456). Pass barrier at road end; bridleway south for 700m to road (127449) at Abinger Bottom. Left; fork right; on for ½ mile to crossroads (127440). At next road, left to bend; left (128438, "Broadmoor"), immediately right on track to Leith Hill Tower (139432). Follow Coldharbour Common walk and byway NE for 1 mile (141433, 142434, 144437, 146438) to Plough Inn.

Lunch Plough Inn, Coldharbour (01306 711793, ploughinn.com); Stephan Langton Inn, Friday Street (01306 730775, stephanlangton. pub); Leith Hill Tower kiosk (10am–3pm) serves tea and refreshments

More information Leith Hill Tower is open daily, 10am–3pm; satmap.com; ramblers.org.uk

A still winter's day under a sky of white and blue as we set out from the Withies Inn at Compton.

Along the road the Watts Cemetery Chapel stood tall on its mound. Mary Watts, the artist wife of the Victorian painter and sculptor George Frederic Watts, designed it as a brilliant Art Nouveau expression of grief. The exterior is packed with calm-eyed angels in flaring orange terracotta, the interior full of sombrely coloured, transcendentally beautiful cherubim and seraphim.

Mary and George Watts moved to Compton in 1891 and founded a remarkable gallery dedicated to George's symbolist work. We were tempted to spend the whole afternoon there, but the ancient holloway of the North Downs Way beckoned us away east to the banks of the River Wey on the southern borders of Guildford.

On a sandy river cliff high over the Wey we found the roofless old chapel of St Catherine, round which a notorious fair used to be held. Neither Watts painted that, but J.M.W. Turner did – a vigorous scene of fighting, drinking and sideshow action, with the throng depicted in swirling attitudes and splashing colours.

The River Wey was one of the first in England to be canalised, part of an ambitious 17th-century scheme to link London to the Channel. We walked south past neat brick lock-keepers' cottages on the edge of its quiet waters, as still and calm as a linear lake, curving with man-made artistry through meadows where last year's purple loosestrife stood brown and crackly dry.

Our homeward path lay westward through the arable parkland of Loseley Park. Rooks patrolled the furrows in fields of winter wheat, and squirrels scuttered among hazels from which they had stripped every last nut.

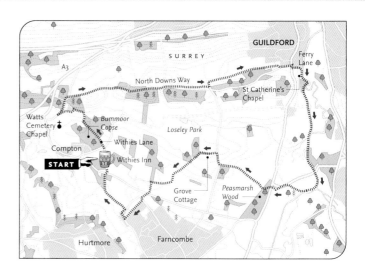

Start & finish Withies Inn, Compton, Guildford, Surrey GU3 1JA (OS ref SU 963468)

Walk (8½ miles; easy; OS Explorer 145): Right along Withies Lane; cross road; path through Bummoor Copse to junction; left, then left past Coneycroft Farm (959475, yellow arrows/YA) to road (957475). Left to Watts Cemetery Chapel, return up road for 300m; right past Watts Gallery (957477) on North Downs Way for 2¼ miles to cross A3100 (991483). Right on Wey South Path for 1 mile to Broadford Bridge (997467); right bank of river to railway bridge (995464); right on railway path to A248 (993465). Left on cycle path to cross A3100 (990465). Through Peasmarsh Wood; cross railway; field edge paths to Stakescorner Road (982468). Right; left on path via Grove Cottage (979469) and carriage drive (975466) to cross B3000 (971463) and road beyond. Path beside Copse Side for 400m to road (967459); right round right bend; first left on road to cross B3000 (964466); Withies Lane to Withies Inn.

Lunch Withies Inn (01483 421158, thewithiesinn.com)

More information Guildford Tourist Information Centre (01483 444333); visitengland.com; Watts Gallery and Cemetery Chapel, 01483 810235, wattsgallery.org.uk

EWHURST AND HOLMBURY HILL

It was a chilly February morning in Ewhurst, in the lee of the Surrey hills. Snowdrop clumps were still full and white down in the sheltered hollow of Coneyhurst Gill where the sharp, sweet song of a robin laid the archetypal soundtrack for a wintry walk in the woods.

We followed a muddy path up towards the tree-hung escarpment of the great Greensand Ridge that cradles the lowlands of the Surrey Weald. Signs of spring were already infiltrating the closed doors of winter – lamb's-tail catkins and tiny scarlet flowers on hazel twigs, rushy spears of bluebell leaves under the oaks, and an insistent bubbling of birdsong up in the high woods along the ridge. A stream stained orange by iron leachings had cut deeply into the greensand.

The Greensand Way trail strings together the promontories and heights of the escarpment, and we followed its knobbly yellow track to Holmbury Hill. In the century before the Romans invaded Kent, a Belgic tribe built a mighty fort here with ramparts and ditches as tall as three men. From its southern lip a wonderful view opens out across the Weald and away towards the South Downs about 20 miles off. On clear days walkers on Holmbury Hill can spot the semaphore flashes of the sea at Shoreham on the Sussex coast. Yet today, all was muted and misty down there.

Using gorse branches as banisters, we groped our way down a precipitous slope below the hillfort. At the foot of the escarpment the mud-squelching track of Sherborne Lane led us back through the fields towards Ewhurst, between hedges where primroses were already beginning to cluster among the hawthorn roots.

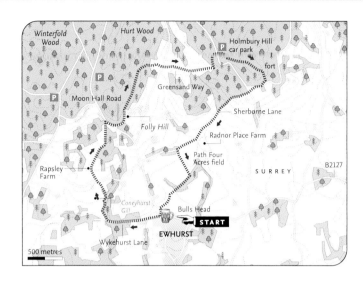

Start & finish The Bulls Head, Ewhurst, Surrey GU6 7QD (OS ref TQ090408)

Walk (6 miles; moderate; OS Explorer 145, 146): Cross B2127; follow Wykehurst Lane. In ½ mile cross Coneyhurst Gill (082407); in 50m, right (FP, stile) through trees. In 600m, left along road (081413); in 50m, right ("Rapsley") on bridleway north for ½ mile to road (081422). Right; in 100m, left up Moon Hall Road. In 200m, left opposite Folly Hill (084422, FP) on bridleway to turn right along Greensand Way/GW (085425). Follow waymarked GW for 1½ miles via Duke of Kent School (089430) and Holmbury Hill car park (098431) to Holmbury Hill fort (104429). At 150m beyond trig pillar, right (105429; warning notice) very steeply down slope to road (105428). Right; in 200m, left off road; fork right on path to left of "Wayfarers" gate (FP). Cross road (103426); down drive with staddle stones (FP). By pond, fork left (FP) along Sherborne Lane bridleway. In ¾ mile, left (093418) across driveway; footpath (FP) across Path Four Acres field, into wood (094414). Right (FP) to Ewhurst.

Lunch The Bulls Head, Ewhurst (01483 277447; bullsheadewhurst.co.uk)

More information Guildford Tourist Information Centre (01483 444333; visitsurrey.com); visitengland.com; satmap.com

FRENSHAM COMMON

It's rather amazing that Frensham Common has not sunk under the weight of its conservation titles. This 1,000-acre sandy heath in south-west Surrey is a Special Protection Area, a Special Area of Conservation, a Site of Special Scientific Interest and an Area of Outstanding Natural Beauty. It's full to the brim with butterflies, birds, insects and lizards – and it's a beautiful place for a walk on a hot summer day.

Our boots kicked up little puffs of sand as we followed a track over humps and through hollows. The sun brought rich, resinous smells from the pine trees and scented the purple heather that ran in waves to the wooded horizon in all directions.

The sandstone that underlies Frensham Common is a dark rock shot through with iron, rusted to burnt orange, warm to the touch that day. The aptly named Sandy Lane led west past a trickle of stream in the ford at Gray Walls, then out into open heath in a glassy shimmer of heat haze. A solitary lizard ran across the path in a little flurry of sand.

At Frensham Great Pond the scene changed. This big pool, created in early medieval times to provide carp for the Bishop of Winchester's table, is a great place to splash around.

The homeward path lay south of the Flashes ponds and heathland. A steep, stony path led up to the summit of the Devil's Jumps. Legend says that these three ironstone hummocks were kicked up by the Devil as he ran off with the local witches' children under his arm.

On the top we found the giant boulder that the great god Thor pitched at the Devil. Two young lovers were sitting on it, admiring the sunlit view and each other. We left them to it.

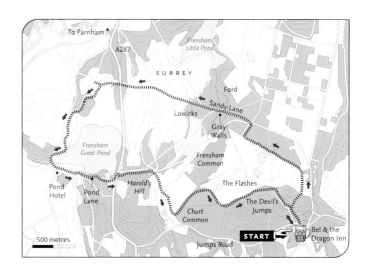

Start & finish Bel & the Dragon Inn, Jumps Road, Churt, Farnham, Surrey GU10 2LD (OS ref SU 871393)

Walk (6½ miles; easy; OS Explorer 133, 145): Left up Jumps Road; in 100m, right (fenced track) for 250m to waymark post below Devil's Jumps (870395, yellow arrow/YA). Right; in 500m, left (871400, YA) past gate; on along track. In 900m, right (864404, YA) to Sandy Lane (865405). Left past Gray Walls ford (862406) and Lowicks turning area (858407); across Frensham Common to cross A287 (849410). In 250m, left at post (847410, "Surrey Hills Cycle"/SHC); follow SHC/bridleway to Frensham Great Pond (843402). Right to road (841401, SHC); left to Frensham Pond Hotel. Left on Pond Lane to cross A287 (849399). Bridleway (SHC) to Harold's Hill; right off SHC (853399) down track/road. In 600m, left (855394, "Permissive Track") beside Churt Common, then east beside the Flashes. In ¾ mile cross track (868397); half right, steeply up to Devil's Jumps (869395); from waymark post below, right to inn.

Lunch Bel & The Dragon Inn (01428 605799, belandthedragon-churt.co.uk)

More information Frensham Common (waverley.gov.uk); Guildford Tourist Information Centre (01483 444333; visitsurrey.com); satmap.com; ramblers.org.uk

RANMORE COMMON

A lovely, crisp sunny day over the North Downs. The crocuses were out under the big oak on Ranmore Common, green lambs' tails swung from hazel twigs and, deep in the woods, a great tit rang his two-tone territorial bell. A bridleway dropped northwards through the trees towards the Polesden valley, winding among holly, yew and butcher's broom.

Down in the valley Bagden Farm stood splashed by the late winter sun. A great spotted woodpecker drummed out a rattling claim to its patch of Freehold Wood as we followed a permissive path through the valley, one of many provided by the Polesden Lacey estate. The country house lay hidden beyond flint walls and thick belts of shrubbery, but the influence of a well-maintained estate on its surroundings was plain to read in beautiful parkland treesand the excellent waymarking of paths.

Walking the tracks I recalled a visit to the house, hearing tales of Polesden Lacey's early 20th-century chatelaine Mrs Ronald Greville and her forthright manners.

Actually, Maggie Greville, despite her acid tongue, was a generous person. Born the illegitimate daughter of a Scottish brewer, she was unashamed of her origins, proclaiming: "I'd rather be a beeress than an heiress." And it's Maggie Greville we have to thank for leaving Polesden Lacey to the National Trust.

From the house, the deeply sunk old holloway of Hogden Lane rolled us down into the valley and up a long rise to the ridge beyond. Here we crossed the ancient route of the Pilgrims' Way, and turned for home along the North Downs Way.

A short detour through a grassy upland and we were clear of the trees and looking south to where Leith Hill, the highest point in Surrey, raised the impudent finger of its crowning tower.

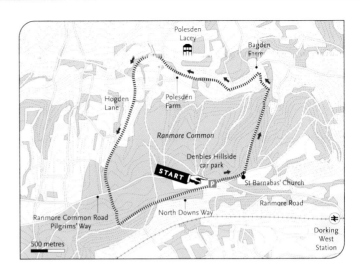

Start & finish Denbies Hillside car park, Ranmore Common Road, Dorking, Surrey RH5 6SR (OS ref TQ142504), National Trust members free

Walk (5¾ miles; easy; OS Explorer 146): Cross road; bear right on path to St Barnabas Church (145505). Left; in 100m, left on bridleway (fingerpost) north for 1 mile. Just before Bagden Farm, left by shed (148520), through gate; on with fence on right. In ¼ mile, through gate (144517, BA); left; in 30m, right (gate 33, "Run England" red arrow). Follow red arrows and Polesden Valley Walk/PVW. Just beyond Polesden Farm, right (135519, PVW); at top of slope, cross track (gates); ahead on permissive path. In 300m, through gate 20 (132522, yellow arrow); ahead on Hogden Lane, south for 1¼ miles to cross Ranmore Common Road/Pilgrims' Way (126502). Keep ahead (south) for about ½ mile; left on North Downs Way (127497, fingerpost) to car park (NB In 700m, path across open ground on right gives wide views).

Lunch Picnic or Duke of Wellington (2–3 miles away), East Horsley KT24 6AA (dukeofwellingtoneasthorsley.co.uk, 01483 282312)

More information nationaltrust.org.uk

THE SOUTH MIDLANDS

Chadlington, Oxfordshire

MISERDEN, THROUGHAM AND HIGH WOOD

The south Cotswold village of Miserden seems to have it all – shop, school, craftspeople, (occasional) buses and a cosy and welcoming pub.

Do rural Edens like this harbour serpents? Impossible to believe it as we passed a posse of happily babbling village toddlers on their morning constitutional and set out along an old country lane.

Two worlds intersected along the route from Miserden to Througham. The lane led purposefully between the two settlements, while claw-scraped mudslides in the banks marked the passage of animal highways crossing the man-made track.

A grey squirrel scampered across the lane in front of me, so intent on its course that it darted right over the toe of my boot. The sunken track, more stream than lane, rose to Througham under hazels festooned with catkins and minuscule female flowers.

We passed the handsome old country house of Througham Court, its gables pierced with dove holes. A high wall concealed a garden of cosmic design; while less abstruse but just as wonderful, a prunus on a grass triangle by the road stood covered with pink blossom, loudly humming with a smother of bees hard at work.

Another stony lane led to a pasture where seven roe deer ran in line across our path, each creature rising in turn to spring over a fence, easy grace personified.

In High Wood off-roaders had trenched the byway with ruts too deep and flooded to walk in. We teetered along the muddy margins before plunging down a hillside path to the hidden valley of the Dillay Brook. An upward slog, and a last stretch through sheep pastures under a sky milky with late winter sunlight and jingling with the early spring twittering of skylarks.

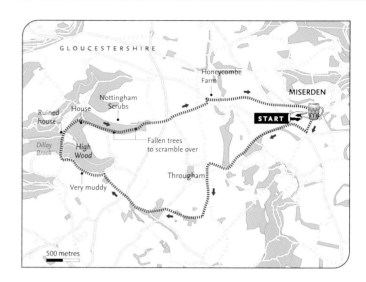

Start & finish Carpenters Arms, Miserden GL6 7JA (OS ref SO 937088)

Walk (7 miles; moderate; OS Explorer 179): Leaving pub, right; at T-junction, right; in 200m, left (933086, "Restricted Byway"). In 400m, fork left (930085); follow lane to Througham. In ¾ mile where tarmac begins, left (921081). 50m past Througham Court, ahead off right bend (921078) along lane. In 300m fork right at sheds (921075). Green lane, then field paths to road (914074). Left; fork right; at T-junction, right (912073). In 450m cross road (908076), then 3 fields to lane (905079). Left (very muddy!). In ½ mile lane bends sharp right (899081); descend on side path with wall on right. In 150m fork downhill. At bottom, cross track (899085); up path opposite. In 350m at top of rise fork right past house (901087). In 200m, ahead (blue arrow) for ⅔ mile (some fallen trees to negotiate) to gate into field (912086). Path to cross 2 roads (914087, 916087); on down to Honeycombe Farm. Path (left side of silage clamp) to road; right (ignore "Private" sign). At gate, left-hand of 2 stiles (923090); path uphill (gate, yellow arrow) across 3 fields to road (931090). On across field to road (933089); right into Miserden.

Lunch Carpenters Arms, Miserden (01285 821283, thecarps-miserden.co.uk)

More information Nailsworth Tourist Information Centre (01453 839222)

PURTON AND SHARPNESS

When the Gloucester and Sharpness Canal opened in the 1820s, the village of Purton on the River Severn became a busy little place. Nowadays it's a sleepy canal-side hamlet, full of charm and possessed of a true classic: a never-changing pub. Just down the river path we found an extraordinary elephant's graveyard of redundant boats rammed into the mud to stabilise the tide-burrowed bank between river and canal. Lovingly labelled by the Friends of Purton, *Orby, Abbey, Huntley* and *Harriett* cluster the margins of Severn in death as in life – a poignant gathering.

On down the canal, and through the abutments of a mighty railway bridge that once spanned the Severn. On the night of 25 October 1960, in a thick autumn fog and pitch darkness, two tankers collided with the bridge piers and exploded, killing five of the eight crewmen and wrecking the bridge. Plenty of people around Sharpness retain vivid memories of that awful night.

Sharpness is a rare survival, a river port still handling fertiliser, building materials and scrap metal far up the tidal Severn. We idled on the quay, watching a salt-rusted old freighter unloading bags of cement, before crossing the canal and making for the field path to Brookend.

There's definitely something other-worldly about the river country along the Severn Estuary. Following the path north from Brookend, it came as a shock to top the rise near Purton and find spread before us a 20-mile view of the long South Cotswold ridge, May Hill and the heavy tree cover of the Forest of Dean, and between them the Severn hurrying seaward. Jane and I halted, gazing our fill, before walking down the fields to Purton.

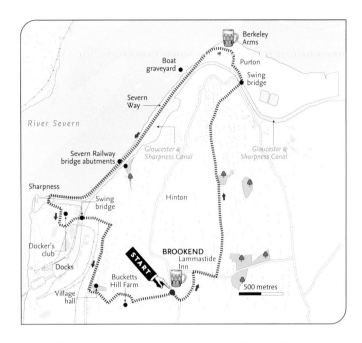

Start & finish Purton, near Sharpness GL13 9HX (OS ref SO 682042)

Walk (6½ miles; easy; OS Explorer OL14): Cross canal; left along riverside path, soon joining canal towpath (687044). NB For beached boats, detour right here. Towpath into Sharpness; cross canal (670030). "Severn Way" up steps; ahead past Dockers' Club (671029) to road. Left across left-hand of 2 swing bridges (673029). Ahead to road (677026); right ("Sharpness"). Left beside Village Hall (674021, fingerpost); paths via Buckett's Hill Farm to road at Brookend. Right; left on right bend ("bridleway") to green lane T-junction; right (686023, blue arrow) along Lip Lane. In 300m, left (689022, "footpath" stone) across fields for 1 mile to Purton (682042).

Lunch Picnic

More information Stroud Tourist Information Centre (01453 760960); exploregloucestershire.co.uk; ramblers.org.uk

ULEY BURY AND CAM LONG DOWN

Walking a circuit of the ramparts of Uley Bury hillfort on a cold, clear day, there was a regal view. We looked down to Uley and Dursley tucked under their wooded slopes, and out west across a patchwork of fields 700ft (200m) below to the River Severn sweeping round a mighty bend, with the Forest of Dean, the pointed cone of the Sugar Loaf and the lumpy backs of the Welsh hills rising beyond.

The yellow track of the Cotswold Way carried us down through leafless beechwoods, before sweeping us up the grassy nape of Cam Long Down. From the crest of the hill we saw Gloucester 20 miles to the north in a pool of sunlight, the cathedral floating high over the city, a view John Constable would have caught majestically in a blur of blues and greens.

We rollercoasted on over the hummock of Peaked Down, then descended southwards with a superb backdrop of Downham Hill, Cam Long Down and the squared-off ramparts of Uley Bury coming into view.

At Wresden Farm a horse grazed a lush meadow from which he lifted a muzzle to watch us go by. A swirl of starlings rushed overhead, tight-packed into a gang for security against marauding birds of prey, 300 pairs of wings whirring loudly enough to make the horse stare after them too.

The lane that brought us back to Uley ran between thick old hedges, its surface floored with lumps of metal scattered among the stones, the leavings of some long-gone forge. Polished by the scouring of hooves and boot soles, they made the old track shine like a pathway to an enchanted tower in some untold Cotswold fairytale.

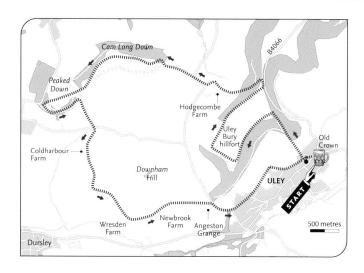

Start & finish Old Crown pub, Uley, near Dursley GU11 5SN (OS ref ST 792986)

Walk (5½ miles; moderate; OS Explorer 167): Cross B4066; path beside church; in 100m, right ("Cotswold Way Circular Walk"/CWCW) to kissing gate. Up slope, then left along wood edge to gate (789988, CWCW). Up through trees to gate; climb rampart of Uley Bury (788990), left/clockwise round hillfort for 1 mile. At north corner (788992), left to B4066; left on to Cotswold Way/CW. Descend and follow CW for 1¼ miles via Hodgecombe Farm (783992), then over Cam Long Down. On over Peaked Down; back along southern edge to rejoin CW (770992). South on CW for 300m to cross road (771988). On for ¾ mile past Coldharbour Farm (770986) to lane near Wresden Farm (774980). Left (east) via Newbrook Farm for ½ mile. At road by Angeston Grange (782982), ahead; on right bend, ahead on path (785982) to Uley.

Lunch The Dilraj, 37 Long Street, Dursley GL11 4HR (01453 543472, dilrajdursley.co.uk); open for takeaway only

More information Nailsworth Tourist Information Centre (01453 839222)

WAINLODE HILL AND COOMBE HILL MEADOWS

Perspective is a strange thing. When I was a child and free to run about and play in the fields near my home in Gloucestershire, the Red Lion inn on the River Severn at Wainlode Hill seemed a skyscraping palace, the river a mighty tideway.

Looking down from Wainlode's heights today, I see a modest red-brick pub on a bend of the Severn. Beyond lies yellow and green patchwork of hay meadows, with the Malvern Hills, like miniature mountains, 10 miles off.

Walking north up the riverbank, I remember winters when the Severn would advance across the meadows to flood our village. On this windy summer day the grasses ripple in different varieties. Tree trunks, plucked out of the Severn's banks by last winter's floods, wallow in the wind-roughened eddies of the river.

At Apperley's pink-faced Coalhouse Inn I leave the river and make east up a green valley to a viewpoint that suddenly reveals itself, forward across wet meadows to the distant Cotswold Hills.

Coombe Hill Meadows is a nature reserve these days, treasured for its rare plants, wading birds, ducks and geese, and for the marsh harriers and peregrines that hunt for frogs, water voles and small birds. As a child I just tore about ecstatically in the great open spaces. I plunged recklessly in the canal, ran as far and fast as I could, and was chased by cattle into ditches and up the pollarded willows. It was bliss.

Today I walk more soberly but just as delightedly through the squelchy meadows and along the canal where purple loosestrife grows tall and the willow leaves flick white and green in the wind. A wild and lonely place to wander, now as then.

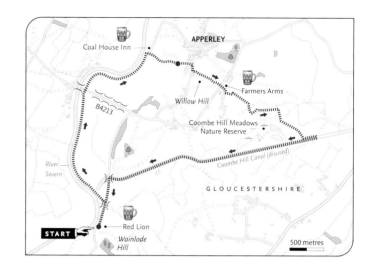

Start & finish Red Lion, Wainlode Hill, Norton, Gloucester GL2 9LW (OS ref SO 848259)

Walk (7 miles; easy; OS Explorer 179): Right (north) along river bank for 2¼ miles to Coal House Inn (855284). Right along road; in 100m, right through gateway (855283, yellow arrow/YA). Through right-hand gate ahead (YA); up through fields (stiles) to road (862282). Right; take left fork past war memorial; in 100m, left (fingerpost) over stiles, past Willow Hill and down to B4213 (866278) by Farmers Arms. Across into Wick Lane; in 100m, left through gate (867278) into orchard; on over stile; downhill across field to track (870276). Left; through gate; half right to go through hedge gap. Left, and on through hedge gap (waymark post); ahead through next gate (875275); right to waymark post (874275, YA). Left, following YAs to canal bank (878271; YA, gate, info board). Right for 2 miles to road (850265); left to Wainlode Hill.

Lunch Red Lion, Wainlode Hill (01452 730935, redlionwainlode.co.uk), open every day; booking advisable for weekend meals

More information gloucestershirewildlifetrust.co.uk

AYMESTREY

Looking back from the slopes under Beechenbank Wood, we saw the early morning mist lying as thick as bonfire smoke along the Lugg Valley. Overhead, the milky blue sky gave promise of warm weather. The pigeons on the ploughed field near Mantal Cottage seemed as lazy as the day, until we came closer and saw that they were decoys.

We dipped down to Covenhope Farm by its reservoir lake to pick up the Mortimer Trail long-distance path. It lifted us up and over the long spine of Shobdon Hill among conifers and oak glades. Holly blue butterflies flashed their brilliant underwings as they hunted moisture in the boot ruts of the path. A flash of movement drew our attention to a clearing, where a lesser spotted woodpecker swooped from tree to tree.

The view was enormous and hazy, out over the hills of the Welsh borders. We skirted the precipitous bank of Byton Common and came down to St Mary's church at Byton. Built in the south wall we found a semi-circular stone, carved almost 1,000 years ago, depicting the Lamb of God holding a cross.

From here we took the road to Lower Kinsham. A muddy bridleway shadowed the Lugg in its sinuous windings among damp meadows awash with cuckooflowers. At Lower Yeld a small boy was riding his tricycle in the ford, absorbed by the splash and sparkle of the water. If it hadn't been for the 4 miles or so we still had to go, we'd have sat for hours and watched the ford ourselves.

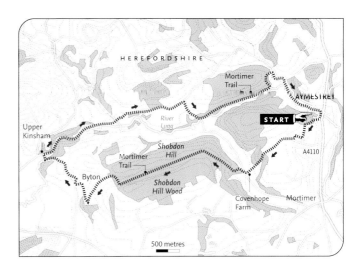

Start & finish Riverside Inn, Aymestrey, Herefordshire HR6 9ST (OS ref SO 425654)

Walk (12¼ miles; easy; OS Explorers 203, 201): Up south side of Riverside Inn (wood gates, fingerpost); up slope to gate (yellow arrow/YA); on up field by hedge to gate (423654, YA); left up path (YAs) to top of slope (422653); left along field edge to cross drive (421650, YA). Right up field edge to stile (419650, YA); cross field to top left corner. Left of farm shed (417650); through gate; to top left corner of field (415649, stile, YA). Field edges into Church Wood (412647); left to descend to forest track; left to road (413638). Right to Covenhope Farm; opposite farm, left by barn; fork right up track to Mortimer Trail/MT (406643). Left and follow MT for 3 miles via Shobdon Hill, Byton Common and Park Wood to Byton church (371642). Road to Lower Kinsham bridge (363646); bridleway east to Lower Yeld (378654); road to Lye Corner (395658) and Lye Pole bridge (398654). MT from here for 2½ miles via Sned Wood to Aymestry.

Lunch Picnic

More information Leominster tourist information centre (01568 616460); visitengland.com; satmap.com; ramblers.org.uk

Two tiny terriers came barking to their fence in Craswall, a tiny hamlet in a remote cleft of the hilly border country where Powys frowns down on Herefordshire. A pale sun was trying its best to draw aside the blankets of mist that the Black Mountains had pulled across their shoulders overnight.

Craswall's modest Church of St Mary crouched in its ring of trees. Inside, everything was plain and simple – a tiny gallery, beams shaped and bevelled by some nameless medieval village carpenter, hard upright pews. We followed a bridleway through sheep pastures, heading north to cross the infant River Monnow in a dell under alders and low-growing oaks.

Down in the cleft beyond, sunk deep into grassy turf banks, lay the silent and time-shattered ruins of Craswall Priory. The Order of Grandmont monks ran it in medieval times with a severe rule and harsh discipline. They could not have chosen a bleaker or more remote spot to build their refuge, or a more beautiful one to a modern walker's eyes. The curved apse still holds its rough altar, sandstone sedilia and triple piscina complete with stone bowls and drain holes. Over all is a profound sense of peace, and an echo of melancholy.

Up on the ridge we strode out. Suddenly the mist curtain shredded away and a stunning view lay ahead – the great steep prow of Hay Bluff and its long south-going ridge towering 700ft (200m) above us, but completely hidden until now. We stood and stared, entranced, before turning back to follow old green lanes that led down to Craswall over a succession of rushing mountain fords.

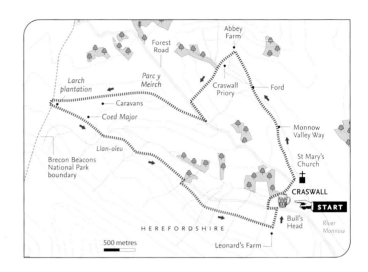

Start & finish St Mary's Church, Craswall, near Hay-on-Wye, Herefordshire HR2 0PX (OS ref SO 281363)

Walk (6 miles; moderate; Explorer OL 13): From Craswall Church (281363), right along road; immediately right, then left (blue arrow/ BA; "Monnow Valley Walk"/MVW). Follow BAs along hillside for nearly 1 mile; ford River Monnow (276375); aim across field to far top corner (275378); on through gates to Abbey Farm (274379). Left down drive to Craswall Abbey ruins (273377); on up drive to road (268373). Left; in 300 m, right (271370; "bridleway" fingerpost/BFP). Follow BA and MVW through fields for nearly 1 mile. Through gates, over stile at caravans (257374; BA); on through gate on skyline (255373). On for ¼ mile through 2 gates; at 2nd one (251373, at Brecon Beacons National Park boundary) turn left up end of larch plantation. At top of wood, left along its south side. Pass Coed Major on left (256371), down to cross stream (257369), and follow green lane/path through gates. In ⅔ mile it becomes metalled lane. At gate (268363), right (BFP) for 50m; left (BFP) on bridleway through gates. In ¾ mile, at post with 2 BAs (278357), left to road; left, and in 100m right to church.

Lunch Picnic

More information Hay-on-Wye Tourist Information Centre (01497 820144; visitherefordshire.co.uk); satmap.com; ramblers.org.uk

KENTCHURCH AND GARWAY HILL

The white tips of snowdrops were peeking in the graveyard of St Mary's Church at the gates of Kentchurch Court – a fine old dwelling, half-stronghold and half-house.

We got a glimpse of a castellated turret as we followed the lane south beside the Monnow, the river hurrying its grey waters through the valley and away towards Monmouth. Garway Hill lay squarely ahead, a bald crown above a collar of leafless trees.

We found a path that skirted the southern slopes of the hill, ascending gradually through green fields with a fine view opening across the valley, slopes and skyline softened in the haze the sun had drawn up from fields and woods lying cold and damp with winter.

At Little Adawent the proper climb began, a steep grassy path rising through bracken past mossy seeps of water and wind-twisted thorn trees. A solitary skylark sang its little crested head off.

Garway Hill has a witchy reputation. A local man once suffered the misfortune of having his wife stolen by the fairies, so stories say.

You couldn't get a less fantastical structure than the prosaic brick shelter at the top of Garway Hill. But the views today were magical anyway, west to the conical Sugarloaf, the whaleback Skirrid and the long spine of the Black Mountains; east to the Malverns and the Cotswold Hills, all dreamy and insubstantial in the cloudy air.

A green lane took us back down to lower ground, where newborn lambs would soon be calling in their feeble, treble voices, to the counterpoint of phlegmy contralto from their anxious mothers – a whisper in the inner ear from faraway spring.

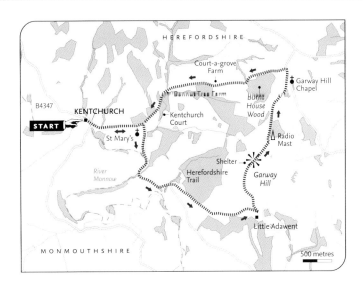

Start & finish Bridge Inn, Kentchurch HR2 0BY (OS ref SO 410258)

Walk (7½ miles; moderate; OS Explorer 189): From Bridge Inn, right; ahead ("Garway") at junction; in 800m, right past St Mary's Church (420257, "Garway"). In ¾ mile, left off road (424248) following waymarked Herefordshire Trail (gates, stiles, yellow arrows/YAs) across fields. In 1 mile, by gate on right (438243, "Little Adawent"), bear left away from wall, up broad grass track to summit shelter of Garway Hill (437251). Aim for gate on left of radio mast (440255); green lane downhill; in ¼ mile, at phone pole (441261, "Herefordshire Trail"), right to road. Left; at junction, ahead (443264, "Bagwyllydiart"). In 100m, left (443266, YA) across fields, skirting right-hand edge of Burnt House Wood and on for 1½ miles (YAs) to road at Bannut Tree Farm (423263). Left to Kentchurch.

Lunch Bridge Inn, Kentchurch (01981 241158; thebridgeinnkentchurch.com)

More information visitherefordshire.co.uk

LONGTOWN AND HATTERRALL RIDGE

The village of Longtown straggles out a mile along its back-country road in a quiet corner of western Herefordshire. On this murky morning, the Norman castle on its modest mound seemed the most upstanding feature of the Olchon Valley. We walked the round of the circular keep, under the projecting chute of Lord Gilbert de Lacy's private garderobe, and on down through the stubby curtain wall.

Strolling out of Longtown and down the pastures towards the winding Olchon Brook, the mountainous scene came gradually into focus ahead. From the riverbank, the green fields sloped up past Cayo Farm to where they abruptly steepened into the bracken-brown mountainside.

A grassy trod, one of a whole skein of paths criss-crossing these Welsh border hills, slanted up the slope and deposited us at the top on to the broad saddle of Hatterrall Ridge. Suddenly the view opened for miles westward, down into the long cleft of the Vale of Ewyas, over and across into the wild central massif of the Black Mountains. The great arches and monastery ruins of Llanthony Priory lay screened by trees and the slope of the lane, but we could see the old packhorse track to the abbey falling away into Ewyas as a hillside thread.

Here along the high lookout of Hatterrall Ridge run the remnants of Offa's Dyke. We followed it north with tremendous views on all sides, present-day lords of all we surveyed.

All too soon our homeward path appeared, a steep track sloping down the mountainside into the Olchon Valley and its sheep pastures once more. A familiar landmark beckoned us back across the fields to Longtown – the stumpy castle keep, still standing sentinel over valley, road and river.

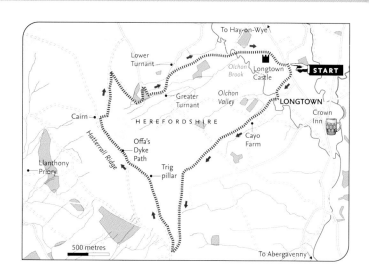

Start & finish Longtown Castle, Longtown, near Abergavenny HR2 0LE (OS ref SO 321292)

Walk (5¾ miles; moderate; OS Explorer OL13): From castle, right along road. Opposite Outdoor Learning Centre, right (322290, fingerpost). In 150m, cross stile; down field to road (320288). Through gate, left of ford; in 50m, right across brook. Left uphill via Cayo Farm (317285) through pastures for ¾ mile to foot of mountain (309279). Slant left up track for ½ mile to ridge (308270). Right on Offa's Dyke Path. In 900m, pass trig pillar (305279); in another 600m, cairn (300283); in 250m, right at cross-paths (299285, cairn). Path descends left; in 200m, pass hairpin track on right (300288); in another 350m, at path crossing, sharp right (300291) down to cross stream at fence corner (303287). Right to farm track; left to road (304289); right. In 500m, right along Lower Turnant gravel drive (308291, fingerpost). Follow white arrows (permissive path). At field with pond, through gate by pond (312293); across next field, right-hand of 2 gates (314293). Follow arrows to cross Olchon Brook (315293); cross fields, aiming for Longtown Castle.

Lunch Crown Inn, Longtown HR2 0LT (01873 860217, crowninnlongtown.co.uk)

More information Hay-on-Wye Tourist Information Centre (01497 820144); visitengland.com/herefordshire; satmap.com; ramblers.org.uk

CHADLINGTON

A hot day, and the north-eastern corner of the Cotswolds lay in glorious sunshine. Chadlington is a sprawling village, a place of rills and springs. In one of the brook meadows an old man went blithely singing through the docks and thistles, and we followed him down towards the fishing lake at Greenend.

The fields beyond the shallow dip of the River Evenlode's valley shone dull gold under the sun, mown and harvested, but not yet gathered. The woods on the ridge lay black and impenetrable in the dark dress of late summer.

We followed a broad stony lane, thick with the scent of newly mown hay, west to Pudlicote and the banks of the Evenlode.

The river wriggled like an agitated centipede between pale meadows and rustling fields of elephant grass destined for immolation in some green power station.

Swallows were fuelling up for their imminent southward flights. They flicked and zoomed like miniature fighter planes low over the stubbles, picking off insects by the thousand, snatching and swallowing as many as possible before the long, improbable journey to their African wintering grounds.

We couldn't help but admire their panache, while feeling a shiver of anxiety for their vulnerability and a pang of sadness at these last rites of summer.

We chose a crumbly seat of earth under an enormous old oak and sat for a gulp of water, looking out over the green and gold valley of the Evenlode and up overhead at a jigsaw tessellation of oak leaves against the blue and white sky.

Then we took the homeward path across Dean Common, where the Wychwood Project is turning old gravel pits and worked-out ground into flowery wetland and butterfly-friendly grassland.

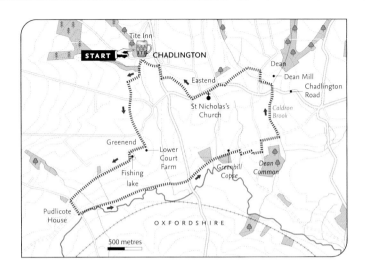

Start & finish Tite Inn, Chadlington, Oxfordshire OX7 3NY (OS ref SP 324225)

Walk (6¼ miles; easy; OS Explorer 191): From Tite Inn car park, left up road; in 50m, right ("Brook End") on path. In 200m, through gate (324222); up slope of field; cross stile; left/south (yellow arrow) to cross two roads in succession (322219, 324214). Just before Lower Court Farm, right/west on bridleway track for 1 mile to Pudlicote House. At road, left (314205); in 200m, left/east on Oxfordshire Way for 1½ miles. From NE corner of Greenhill Copse (337212), ahead to cross Grove Lane (341213). In 200m, north (344214) beside Coldron Brook to Chadlington Road (343220). Right to Dean Mill; left up drive; in 30m, left over footbridge on path to road (341222). Right; follow Wychwood Way NE to Dean (342225), then SW as bridleway to road at Eastend (336221). Right past church; right up Church Road to return to Tite Inn.

Lunch Tite Inn, Chadlington OX7 3NY (01608 676910, thetiteinn.co.uk)

More information Banbury Tourist Information Centre (01295-753752); visitengland.com; satmap.com; ramblers.org.uk

DORCHESTER-ON-THAMES AND WITTENHAM CLUMPS

A cold day under a billowing sky. St Birinus looked pinched and chilly in his niche in the chapel wall at Dorchester-on-Thames, the folds of his carved stone face seeming full of disapproval as we passed him on our way to the river.

Beyond the neat houses and gardens of Dorchester we crossed the Dyke Hills, a curious Iron Age earthwork that raises a double seam across the fields. It was built to defend a settlement established here long before the Romans came to Britain.

From Little Wittenham we climbed the short, steep path up the face of the Sinodun Hills, a double bulge of tree-topped chalk known locally as Wittenham Clumps. They draw the eye for many miles in the flat Thames-side country. On Round Hill a handy topograph picked out landmarks far and near, from the long ridge of the Chiltern Hills to the Abbey Church of St Peter and St Paul in Dorchester, the chimneys of Didcot power station, a glimpse of dreaming spires in far-off Oxford and, nearer at hand, the tower and red brick frontage of Little Wittenham's manor house below.

We followed a network of paths established by the Earth Trust across the hillfort ramparts on Castle Hill, then down towards Long Wittenham and the Thames through meadows and woodland.

The walk wheeled slowly round the fixed hub of Wittenham Clumps, away to our right across the fields. Paul Nash painted these hills again and again between the wars, trying to catch the moods and changing colours of the chalk and turf. "A beautiful legendary country haunted by old gods long forgotten" was the artist's perception of this captivating corner of the Thames, and that's as good an encapsulation as any.

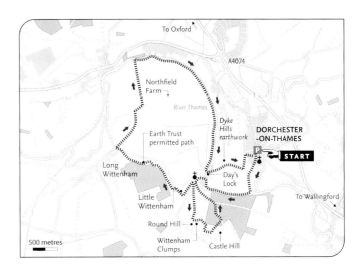

Start & finish Bridge End car park, Dorchester-on-Thames OX10 7JT (OS ref 579940)

Walk (9 miles; easy; OS Explorer 170): Ahead past chapel; south down Wittenham Lane to Thames (578932). Right; in ¾ mile, left across 3 bridges (568935); opposite Little Wittenham church, left (566934, gate). Uphill path ahead to summit of Round Hill (566928). Around clump; on to summit of Castle Hill (569926). From poem stone on far side, descend grass path through ditch. In 150m, left (572926, gate) across valley. In 250m fork right (570928) through trees. In 250m at T-junction, left (570930); downhill to Little Wittenham. Left along road; in ¼ mile, right (564931, "Long Wittenham"). In 250m, left through gate; follow permitted path parallel to road for 1 mile to road in Long Wittenham (551940). Right by thatched house ("No Through Road"). In a little more than ½ mile at Northfield Farm entrance (555949), left along green lane to Thames (553958). Right. In 2 miles, left across weir/Day's Lock (568936). Half left on fenced path; cross Dyke Hills (572937); on to Dorchester.

Lunch White Hart, High St, Dorchester OX10 7HN (01865 340074, white-hart-hotel-dorchester.co.uk)

More information Wallingford Tourist Information Centre (01491 826972); earthtrust.org.uk; satmap.com; ramblers.org.uk

William and Jane Morris spent their summers at Kelmscott Manor from 1871 onwards. William, the father of the Arts and Crafts movement, found the obscure Oxfordshire backwater a balm for the soul.

We found the manor confined in a winter jacket of scaffolding. Sulphur-yellow quinces had dropped over the garden wall. They rolled along the lane that we followed down to the rain-charged River Thames.

On the graceful curve of Eaton footbridge we stopped to admire the strength and surging power of the water, then turned east through wide green meadows whose medieval furrows each held a miniature lakelet of rainwater.

The little church of St Michael & All Angels at Eaton Hastings benefited from the proximity of Kelmscott Manor. Here we found a William Morris west window showing three ultra-romantic archangels while in the window of the north chancel Edward Burne-Jones had created a stormy St Michael, a striking characterisation.

The Thames lay distant as we walked on through the fields. The brimming ditches were lined with crack willows and ash trees distorted, bowed and twisted out of shape.

A pair of old stone bridges spanned the bifurcated Thames at Radcot. A skirmish here in 1387 between the forces of King Richard II and Henry Bolingbroke resulted in 800 men drowning in the marshes, but there were just three deaths caused by fighting – Sir Thomas Molyneux, a varlet and a boy. History records that the knight was treacherously stabbed, but one would like to know more of the misfortunate varlet, not to mention that wretched child.

Such strife in this place seemed hard to imagine as we strolled the peaceful Thames Path back towards Kelmscott.

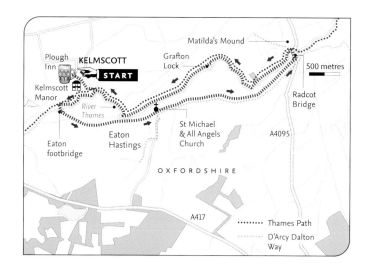

Start & finish Plough Inn, Kelmscott, Lechlade GL7 3HG (OS ref SU 249991)

Walk (7 miles; easy; OS Explorer 170): Passing stump of cross and Plough Inn on your right, fork left along road. In 150m, right (250990, "Kelmscott Manor"). Ahead beside manor ("Radcot Bridge"). In 150m, right on Thames Path (253988). In ½ mile, left across footbridge (247985). Through left-hand gate beyond cottage; left along field edges (National Trust green arrows) for 1 mile to road (263985). Ahead past Eaton Hastings church; follow D'Arcy Dalton Way east for 1¾ miles through fields (kissing gates, stiles) to A4095 at Radcot (286994). Left across 2 bridges; right (285995) on Thames Path for 3 miles to Kelmscott.

Lunch Plough Inn, Kelmscott (01367 253543, theploughinnkelmscott.com)

More information sal.org.uk/kelmscott-manor

A clear morning after a night of steady rain, with the sun diffusing a pearly light over the Vale of White Horse. Crossing the sodden paddocks on the outskirts of Woolstone, we caught a glimpse of the chalk-cut White Horse herself, cavorting with dismembered limbs across a hilltop above the vale at full and gleeful tilt as she has done for 3,000 years or more.

From Odstone Farm – a handsome house of brick and chalk clunch – an old road took us south up the steep face of the downs to join the Ridgeway. The ancient track ran broad and pale along the crest between hedges of pink spindle berries where bryony fruit hung tangled in long necklaces.

The great Neolithic tomb of Wayland's Smithy lay beside the Ridgeway in a ring of tall beeches, its southern portal guarded by four immense, roughly shaped boulders. The gold and silver trees, the weighty stones and the sigh of the wind made this a solemn place. Here the blacksmith Wayland would shoe the horses of travellers if they left a silver coin with their steeds.

The Ridgeway forged on east, hollowed and slick with trodden chalk as it rose to the crest of Whitehorse Hill and the ramparts of the Iron Age camp built up here to command a 50-mile view north over the vale. We stopped to stare at the enormous prospect, with the chalky squiggles that compose the white horse entrenched in the turf at our feet. Once every hundred years, old tales say, the horse leaps up and gallops across the sky to Wayland's Smithy to be shod by the legendary blacksmith. Now that would be something to see.

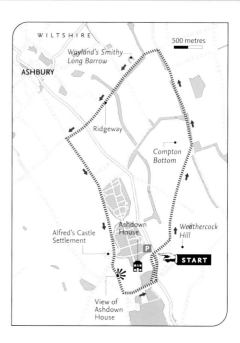

Start & finish White Horse pub, Woolstone, Oxfordshire SN7 7QL (OS ref SU293878)

Walk (6 miles; moderate; OS Explorer 170): Leaving White Horse pub, left for 150m; at right bend, ahead ("Knighton") across two fields. Dogleg left/right across Hardwell Lane (289875); on across fields (yellow arrows/YA) to cross road at Knighton (283873). On (D'arcy Dalton Way) to road at Compton Beauchamp (281871). Follow "To the Church" past barns and church; across two paddocks (YA, red discs), then field edges (276876) towards Odstone Farm. Just short of farm, left (270863) up track; across B4507 (273860); up for ⅔ mile to the Ridgeway (280851). Left, following Ridgeway east past Wayland's Smithy (281854) for 1½ miles to Whitehorse Hill. At summit, left through gate (301862, "Bridleway") past NT sign to trig pillar. Fork right beyond on grass path to White Horse (301866). Left above Horse on path, down to cross Dragonhill Road at map board (298865, gate). Half left down to gate; over left-hand of two stiles; downhill with fence on right. At bottom, left to gate into road (294871); right across B4507, down to Woolstone.

Lunch White Horse, Woolstone (01367 820726; whitehorsewoolstone.co.uk)

More information Abingdon Tourist Information Centre (01235 522711); visitengland.com; satmap.com; ramblers.org.uk

BRINKLOW, KING'S NEWNHAM AND THE OXFORD CANAL

A fine afternoon of big, blowy skies over Warwickshire. The cobbled lane of Town Yard led up from Brinklow's aptly named Broad Street to the green mound of a Norman motte and bailey castle, with far views over a countryside of corn and cattle grazing.

A good clear path led across fields of wheat. A shiver among the stalks, and a brace of partridges burst from cover almost under our feet and rattled away low across the crop.

Beside the road at King's Newnham stood a derelict tower, its parent building of St Laurence's Church long demolished. Black slit windows gave back a hard, blank stare. It was easy to see how the lone tower by the lane got its reputation as a haunted place. That reputation was enhanced when, during excavations in 1852, the corpse of a decapitated man was unearthed from the abandoned graveyard. Meticulously embroidered in black silk on his funerary chemise were the letters "TB". Nothing else was known, or has yet been discovered, about this felon and his story.

Through the fields beyond snaked the tight bends of the Oxford Canal, so winding in its course that boatmen inching their slow way through the many curves were said to be able to hear Brinklow bells ringing for matins and evensong on the same day.

As we headed homeward along the towpath a narrow boat went by, its stag party crew saluting us with beer bottles in hand. At the same moment a steam locomotive streaked by on the railway just beyond – "Mayflower", in beautiful green paintwork – passing with a hoarse triumphant cheer from her fan club perched on the bridge overhead.

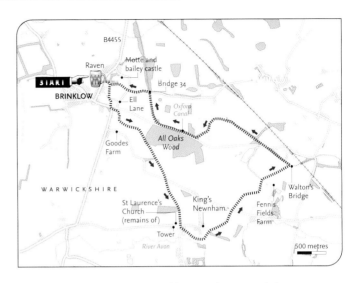

Start & finish Broad Street, Brinklow, Rugby, Warwickshire CV23 0LN (OS ref SP 436795)

Walk (6¼ miles; easy; OS Explorer 222): Up Town Yard beside Raven pub to kissing gate/KG. Right ("Coventry Way"); in 40m, right (KG) down hedge to B4455 road (437791). Left across Easenhall Road; field path south-west for 1½ miles (KGs, yellow-topped posts/YTPs) via All Oaks Wood (443786) and road crossing (446780) to road at Newnham tower (449772). Turn left then right down King's Newnham Road. In 50m, left (YTPs) between ponds; ahead along slope (not right across bridge), aiming left for KG/YTP to right of sheds. North-east across fields for 1 mile (YTPs) via road crossing (457774), skirting left of Fennis Fields Farm, to Oxford Canal at Walton's Bridge (467782). Left on towpath for 2 miles to Bridge 34 (443794). Left along road (grass verges – take care); in 350m, cross Ell Lane (440794); ahead (YTP/KG), half right across field to fence (YTP); left to Brinklow.

Lunch Bull's Head, Coventry Road, Brinklow CV23 0NE (01788 221561, bullsheadbrinklow.co.uk), open from noon every day (closed Mondays); book in advance for meals on Fridays, Saturdays and Sundays

More information Rugby Tourist Information Centre (01788 533217)

We set out along Shakespeare's Way accompanied by a tender blue sky, a cool breeze and a hazy spring sun to bring out the mellow silver and gold of the local building stone.

Parkland stretched away beside the road that led north out of Honington. Sparrows, chaffinches, rooks and wrens all loudly proclaimed the spring from greening hedges and treetops. A great spotted woodpecker drummed a hollow proclamation of ownership from its patch of woodland beyond Wagtail Spinney.

In a boggy dell we parted company with Shakespeare's Way. We got across the fast-running stream and stopped in the damp hollow beyond to clear a tangle of sticks that had dammed a spring. Watching the water bursting away from its confines in a wet sparkle took Jane and me straight back to our muddy-booted childhoods.

Walking up the field boundaries to Idlicote on its ridge, we paused to admire the superb old trees that formed the margin of the path – giant crack willows burst apart and fallen, ancient coppice stools of field maples and an ash tree split open to expose a heart of writhing tendrils more like those of an animal than a tree.

Up at Idlicote a scarecrow sat on a bench – a smooth customer in a grey homburg hat, with a pink silk kerchief in his breast pocket. Sticky paths led us up from Idlicote to a high ridge where the long views melted into mist. Before dropping down the slope into Honington there was time for a sit and stare across the plain, where the slender spire of Tredington's church rose skywards from the heart of Shakespeare's countryside.

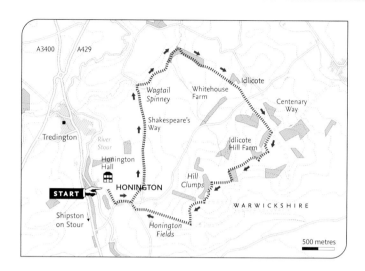

Start & finish All Saints Church, Honington, Warwickshire CV36 4NH (OS ref SP 261427)

Walk (6¼miles; easy; OS Explorer 221): Back to village street; left; opposite Barcheston turning, left ("Old Post Office"). In 40m, through metal mesh gate; through trees (yellow arrow); across field to kissing gate and road (268417). Left for 1 mile. Cross bridge in Wagtail Copse (267443), right through next gate ("Shakespeare's Way"/SW). Follow SW beside stream for 800m, right (273448, blue arrow/BA) over stream. Up through trees on right of tributary stream (BAs), then field edges. At barns (277446) ahead up field edges (BA) to Idlicote. At top of rise, ahead through gate (281443) to road. Ahead, pass tower, round left bend, immediately right between white gateposts (283442, BA). Ahead to cross road (284440), on up field edge for 600m. At top of ridge, right at waymark post (288435, "Centenary Way"/CW). Follow well-waymarked CW via Idlicote Hill Farm (288433), south end of Hill Clumps (278425) and Honington Fields (271423) to Honington.

Lunch Picnic

More information Stratford-upon-Avon Tourist Information Centre (01789 264293); visitengland.com; satmap.com; ramblers.org.uk

It was a crisp winter's day over Warwickshire, the sun picking out the gold in the Cotswold stone houses of Ilmington. A whiff of applewood smoke came down on the breeze as we followed Middle Street past medieval fishponds to the cruciform Church of St Mary.

Among the oak pews of this beautiful Norman building scurry Arts and Crafts mice, the signature speciality of the Yorkshire master carver Robert Thomson. The carpenter set these humorous little rodents in the pews and pulpit of St Mary's in the 1930s, and they still raise a smile today.

A green lane took us up the hill from Ilmington between orchards, our boots wobbling among cookers and eaters long fallen to ground.

From the crest of the hill a glorious view opened, down slopes deeply indented with the ridge and furrow of Middle Ages strip farming, away over a low-lying vale of lush green meadows to the prominent hump of Meon Hill.

After a stretch of road between hedges hung with scarlet necklaces of bryony, we swung off south-west along the well-marked Monarch's Way. Fat white sheep cropped the pastures around Hidcote Combe, the low winter sun backlighting their fleeces into spun gold.

At the foot of the lane to Hidcote Bartrim we turned east for home, leaving the wonders of Hidcote Manor gardens – "outdoor rooms" of rare beauty – for a spring visit some other day.

An ancient trackway climbs the slopes to the crest of the hills and a view west as far as the Malverns, Bredon, the Caradoc hills and into Wales. We followed this ridgeway, then descended through ribbed pastures to Ilmington, sunlit in its cradle of trees.

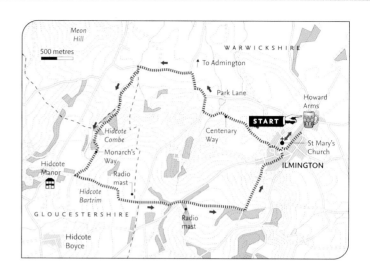

Start & finish Howard Arms, Ilmington, Warwickshire CV36 4LT (OS ref SP 213437)

Walk (7 miles; easy; OS Explorer 205): From Howard Arms, right along Middle Street; at T-junction, right, passing church to road (209435). Right, in 30m, left; follow yellow arrows (YAs). Near top of rise (207436, stile on left), bear right, follow Centenary Way for ¾ mile (YAs, yellow-topped posts) past Newfoundland Well (205437) to road (197440). Right to road (198442, "Park Lane" on map); left along road (walkable verge). In 500m pass lane to Admington (195446); in another ½ mile, left off road (187447, fingerpost) and follow Monarch's Way (MW) south-west for 1¼ miles to reach road near Hidcote (177430). Left here up restricted byway, heading east for 1¾ miles, passing two installations of radio masts (187426 and 195426). ½ mile beyond second mast, left at gate (204425), downhill beside hedge to road at Ilmington.

Lunch Ilmington community shop, Grump Street (café closed Mondays)

More information Hidcote gardens (01386 438333; nationaltrust.org.uk/hidcote); shakespeares-england.co.uk; satmap.com; ramblers.org.uk

UPPER BODDINGTON

It's an ironstone landscape here on the borders of Northamptonshire and Warwickshire, and the many handsome villages are the beneficiaries in the beauty of their building stone.

On the outskirts of the village we crossed a brook among milky-blue bells of comfrey and a froth of cow parsley newly opened. The path led us north across fields of young wheat, the pale crumbly soil free of stones and already cracked and drying under the sun.

Ahead the land heaved up into the long wooded billow of a ridge. From the top we had a wonderful view west over a great green disc of Warwickshire lowlands. Lumps and hollows in the slope at our feet betrayed the site of the medieval village of Stoneton, abandoned in early Tudor times when its arable land was converted to more profitable sheep grazing.

We made our way down past the rushy moat of Stoneton Manor, across the sheep pastures to the grassy towpath of the Oxford Canal. Walking north along its sharp curves, it was hard to believe that this clay-coloured waterway meandering inconsequentially across the plain could once have been the main communications link between London and the Midlands.

From Priors Hardwick, a picture of perfection in sun-kissed ironstone and immaculate gardens, the homeward path ran above sheep pastures whose medieval ridge and furrow showed the patterns of vanished agriculture.

As I leant on a gate to stare, a fine red fox came across the path 20ft ahead, low-slung and intent. It stopped dead still, held me at gaze for a few seconds, then turned tail and raced away to safety in the hedge.

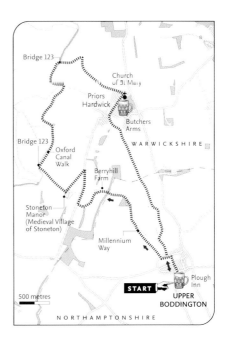

Start & finish Plough Inn, Upper Boddington, Daventry, Northamptonshire NN11 6DH (OS ref SP 483534).

Walk (8 miles; easy; OS Explorer 206): From Plough Inn, left along road; right up Frog Lane. Fork right by Hillside View; follow Millennium Way/MW waymarks north-west for 1 mile. From woodland strip (470547), dogleg right/left to Berryhill Farm; left along drive to road (464545). Right; in 600m, sharp left (466550) across field to drive (463547); in 100m, right to cross canal (458551). Right on towpath; in 1½ miles, at Bridge 123 (461568), right (SE) across fields for ¾ mile to road in Priors Hardwick (472563). Right past church and Butchers Arms; right at road; in 150m, left off bend (470559, "Hill House"). Immediately left (yellow arrow/YA) across fields (occasional YAs and black arrows), heading SSE for 1¾ miles back to Upper Boddington.

Lunch Plough Inn, Upper Boddington (01327 260364, ploughinnboddington.co.uk) – a very friendly village inn

More information Banbury Tourist Information Centre (01295 236165); satmap.com; ramblers.org.uk

A cold, still day of early spring, with the clouds layered in motionless lines over the Worcestershire hills. The low whine of an organ from the red sandstone St Kenelm's Church heralded the end of matins as we left Clifton upon Teme and headed out over ploughland. Down in the steep wooded cleft of Witchery Hole, dog's mercury had taken over the world, a brief flush of tiny green flowers at the crack of spring.

The Teme is a beautiful river. A.E. Housman called its landscape "The country for easy livers/the quietest under the sun", and there's something leisurely and seductive about the slow green flow of the river, the miniature red cliffs of its steep banks, and the winding valley it has smoothed out under hard limestone. We walked upstream along the river to Brockhill Court, with its stumpy old oasts (this was hop-growing country once upon a time) and red brick barns.

A series of shallow billowing valleys led up to a little wood, where we sat eating our cheese buns and watching treecreepers scuttling up an ash trunk.

On up past Hillside Farm, with its architecture from three eras all jammed improbably together; a steep little burst up to the ridge, and then three glorious south-going miles along the Worcestershire Way, hurdling the dips and striding along the crests with a broad plain stretching out eastwards, and the Teme to the west running unseen in its lumpy green valley far below.

Down in the valley we recrossed the dully glinting river again, and went up a long bridleway towards Clifton upon Teme, with the pocket mountain range of the Malvern Hills rising in the south in the last sunlight of the March evening.

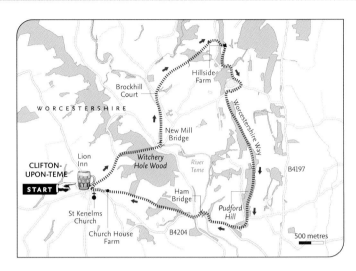

Start & finish Lion Inn, Clifton upon Teme, Worcestershire WR6 6DH (OS ref SO714616)

Walk (9 miles; strenuous; OS Explorer 204): Take signed footpath between Lion Inn and church. Follow yellow arrows (YA) into field. On far side, over left-hand of 2 stiles (716617). Ahead with hedge on left. At field end, left over stile (718619); follow hedge on right. In 50m, right over stile (YA); on to cross lower stile (YA). Aim across field to right-hand corner of Harrisfield House (719621); bear left around house, and on down to cross stile into woodland (720623). Right along waymarked track, steeply down Witchery Hole for ½ mile to road (728624). Right, then left across New Mill Bridge. Left (729625) along east bank of River Teme for ¾ mile to road at Brockhill Court (728635). Right at foot of drive (YA) through gate. Up and through next gate; right (YA) into shallow valley. Bear half right to gate (731639, faded YA). Follow valley bottom NE to stile into wood (735642). Follow path clockwise to cross stream (736642); 50m up the far bank, bear right to leave wood over stile (737643). Aim for far top corner of field (738644); over stile, and follow fence on left. Just past Hillside Farm house, left through gate (739645) onto drive; right to road (741646). Cross road onto waymarked Worcestershire Way/WW; follow it south for 3 miles to B4204 (743608). Right (take care!) for ½ mile to cross River Teme by Ham Bridge (737611). First right after bridge ("Shelsleys"); pass 2 houses, then left (736611) up bridleway. Climb through wood; in 400m, at top of first rise, dogleg left/right through gate (732612, blue arrow, "Sabrina Way"). Continue uphill with fence on right for 1 mile to Church House Farm. Left to road (717615); right to Lion Inn.

Lunch Lion Inn, Clifton upon Teme (01886 812975; thelioninnclifton. co.uk) – friendly village inn

More information temetriangle.net visitengland.com; ramblers.org.uk

Cheerful narrowboaters were drinking and chattering in the sunshine outside the Eagle and Sun at Hanbury Wharf. They lounged under the trees on the banks of the Worcester and Birmingham Canal, their neat blue and red craft moored alongside. The towpath led away north in a froth of cow parsley, and there was a soft clop-clop of bronze-brown water round the bows of *Golden Eagle* as she negotiated the narrow chamber of Astwood Lock.

From this *Wind in the Willows* dream of Olde England we moved east into fields of barley, wheat and blue-green oats. This is good growing country, the dark red earth full of pebbles smoothed by some antediluvian river.

The sun struck into the glades of Piper's Hill Wood as we followed a track among enormous old ash and oak trees. Piper's Hill was once a carefully managed woodland where local commoners enjoyed the rights of pannage (feeding their pigs on acorns) and estover (collecting fallen boughs for firewood). Such uses fell away long ago, leaving a woodland full of mighty trees, ancient and splendidly distorted.

Emerging from the wood, we climbed a grassy path to a church perched at the summit. "St Mary The Virgin, Hanbury" said the noticeboard, but we knew better. Generations of Archers from Ambridge have been married in front of BBC microphones within these crookedly sloping walls, and the bells of "St Stephen's" have rung out over the Radio 4 airwaves more times than even Joe Grundy can recall.

From the church on its knoll a path led across the broad acres of Hanbury Park. We passed the ornate oriental gates of Hanbury Hall ("Lower Loxsley Hall" to Ambridge cognoscenti) and walked homeward across hay fields.

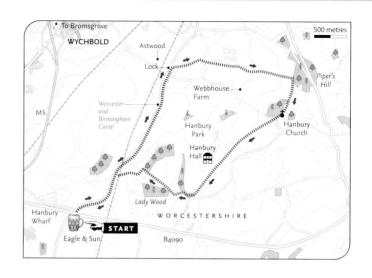

Start & finish The Eagle & Sun pub, Hanbury Wharf, Worcestershire WR9 7DX (OS ref SO 922629)

Walk (6 miles; easy; OS Explorer 204): Follow canal north; 150m beyond Astwood Lock, right through kissing gate/KG (937651). Follow waymarked Hanbury Circular Walk/HCW clockwise via Piper's Hill Wood nature reserve (956649), Hanbury church (954644) and Hanbury Hall (945637). Pass hall gates; through KG; in next field, keep same direction (trending away from hall grounds) to road (941632). Right through KG (HCW) past pond, through KG; right to waymark post at hedge corner; left along hedge; in 150m, right through hedge to corner of Lady Wood (937633, HCW). Aim slightly right up field, past pond at top (935634); down to KG; stony lane to farm drive (933636). Left; in 100m, right through gate (932635, HCW); down hedge to cross railway (929635); left along canal to Hanbury Wharf.

Lunch The Eagle & Sun (01905 799266, eagleandsundroitwich.com)

More information Droitwich Tourist Information Centre (01905 774312); download walk guide at worcestershire.gov.uk; visitengland.com; satmap.com; ramblers.org.uk

WORCESTERSHIRE BEACON AND THE MALVERN HILLS

"Some term them the English Alps," wrote the traveller Celia Fiennes in her 1696 journal after viewing the Malvern Hills for the first time. "They are at least 2 or 3 miles up and are a Pirramiddy fashion on the top." The dust of enchantment may have been in Celia's eyes when it came to estimating the height of the Malverns – the summit, Worcestershire Beacon, is only 1,395ft (425m). But there's no doubt that this dragon-backed, 7-mile chain of miniature mountains dominates both the South Worcestershire plain to the east and out towards the Welsh Borders in the west.

Less demanding to climb than they seem, the Malverns have a skein of good paths. It's hard to get lost here because the hills stand up above everything far and near.

We set out from the northern end of the range on a cold, breezy winter's day. A stony track led steadily uphill. As we climbed, the view opened out east over the red roofs of Great Malvern towards the Cotswolds, a long dark bar in the south. At the top of the track Lady Howard de Walden Drive curled away south towards the craggy peak of Worcestershire Beacon.

Up on the summit the wind blew like blue blazes. We clung to quartzite crags that have been in existence for a thousand – million years. What a prospect from here Black Mountains on the Welsh Borders to the west, Edge Hill nearly 40 miles off in the east, the Clee Hills a jagged lump in the north, the Severn estuary a salmon-pink gleam in the south.

Below Worcestershire Beacon we found the homeward way, a knobbly path along precipitous slopes stained rusty red with last summer's bracken.

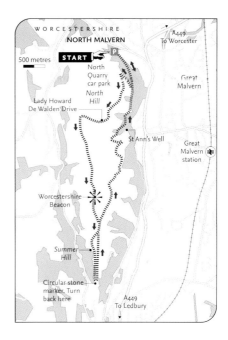

Start & finish North Quarry car park, North Malvern Road, Malvern WR14 4LT (OS ref SO 771469), £4.60

Walk (4¾ miles; moderate/strenuous; OS Explorer 190): Follow uphill track to left of ticket machine. In 600m at post with green, red and blue arrows pointing forwards, sharp right (774463) up embanked path. At top, left along Lady Howard de Walden Drive (772464). In 1 mile bear right (769453) up path to summit of Worcestershire Beacon (769452). Continue south round west side of Summer Hill. In ⅔ mile at track crossroads with circular stone marker (769442), sharp left back up stony track. In 750m, at saddle before Worcestershire Beacon by covered bin, fork right (769448) on rutted track. In 300m fork right downhill (771451). In 200m, in low saddle, fork right (771453) across rocky outcrop and on. In 300m by bench fork right (772455). Follow track downhill. Just past St Ann's Well, roadway bends sharp right downhill (771459); cross it here ("North Quarry"); right along upper track. In 300m, fork left uphill; continue to car park.

Lunch Picnic, or St Ann's Well café (01684 560285, stannswell.co.uk, open Fri–Sun 11.30am–3.30pm)

More information malvernhills.org.uk

Wallasea Island, Essex

ELY

Before monks and adventurers drained the fenland of East Anglia for agriculture, Ely was an island in a miasmic fen swamp. The town clings to a gentle swell of raised ground. Planted square across the summit of the hill above the surrounding flatlands, the graceful yet lopsided bulk of Ely Cathedral, the Ship of the Fens, draws the eye from 10 miles off.

Hops hung in the hedges, their jointed flowers not yet bloomed into that sticky, heady savour that the Victorian rural writer Richard Jefferies described as "like the half-fabled haschish ... intoxication without wine, without injurious after-effect, dream intoxication". The towpath alongside the slow-flowing Great Ouse had been cracked by the intense heatwave, and in the fields the barley ears hung low and full, awaiting the harvester.

We crossed the side arm of Braham Dock where the narrowboat *Sun* lay moored up under a limply flapping red flag. At Little Thetford, half a dozen tyro rowers were roasting in their singlets, splashing and scooping the glittering water of the river under the barked instructions of their trainer. It looked a lot of effort on such a breathless afternoon, and we were glad to flop down in the shade of a willow for a drink and a nice long stare over the baking fields.

In the distance a red and silver train bellowed like some fantastic beast. Swallows chased each other, and the tiny black silhouette of a hobby skimmed the trees on the lookout for dragonflies.

We followed the grassy track of Holt Fen Drive up to Little Thetford, and then the riverbank north again towards Ely and the high-perched Ship of the Fens as she rode the heatwave and the barley seas.

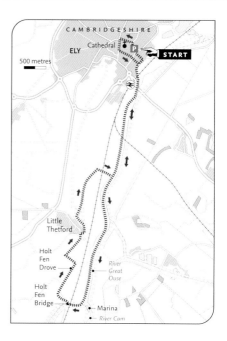

Start & finish Forehill car park, Ely CB7 4AF (OS ref TL 543801)

Walk (9½ miles; easy; OS Explorer 226): From top right corner of car park, alley to Fore Hill. Left; ahead along High Street. At end, left along Minster Place past Ely Cathedral west end (540803). On along the Gallery. In 200m, left through monastic archway (540800). Ahead through the park; cross Broad Street (543799); through Jubilee Gardens to river (544798). Right (south) on west bank of River Great Ouse for 3¾ miles. Pass marina at confluence with River Cam (534746); just beyond railway bridge, right across river path and follow Holt Fen Drove to road in Little Thetford (534760). Left; in 100m, right ("Cawdle Fen Way"). Follow path beside Thetford and Grunty Fen Catchwater drains back to river at Braham Dock (540774). Left for 2¼ miles to Ely.

Short walk (4¼ miles): Little Thetford–Braham Dock–River Great Ouse–Holt Fen Bridge.

Lunch The Cutter Inn (01353 662713, thecutterinn.co.uk). Book ahead

More information Ely Tourist Information Centre (01353 662062); elycathedral.org

GREAT FEN AND HOLME FEN

"I just love this place", said Carry Akroyd, leading the way through the trees of Holme Fen. The East Anglian fens have a passionate champion in Carry Akroyd, an artist with sharp eyes who works in vivid colours and bold, decisive shapes. I'd long admired the observant realism of her paintings, so it was a huge pleasure to be walking with her through the landscape that inspired such striking images.

Holme Fen National Nature Reserve is a lush place, as damp as a sponge. Yet the land that the trees and plants stand on has been shrinking, its level dropping, ever since drainage for agriculture began to suck the black peat dry. Beside a drove road we came to the cast-iron columns of the Holme Posts that mark Britain's lowest point, 9ft (2.7m) below sea level. In 1851 the older of the two posts was rammed into the peat until its top was flush with the ground. Today it stands 13ft (4m) tall, a measure of how far the dried-out land has shrunk around it.

At the corner of Trundle Mere we climbed into a bird hide and looked out from on high across the broad empty fens to a skyline of wind turbines and silos – a Carry Akroyd scene stretched out before us. "I try to make a portrait of a place," she said, "that's more than the sum of what you can see. But it has to be honest."

There's an ongoing scheme, the Great Fen project, to return all this countryside, nearly 15 square miles of intensively farmed land, to native fenland, managed for wildlife. What a superb vision.

We turned back through the silver birches of Stilton Roughs, the willows of Caldecote Fen and the great oaks of Home Lode Covert, to reach open flatlands once more. "It's happening, the Great Fen," said Carry, looking over the new meadows, "and it's so exciting to see it coming alive."

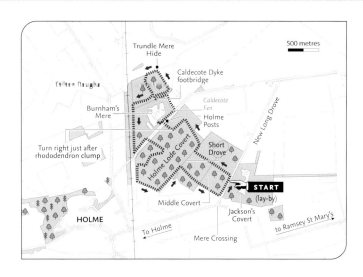

Start & finish Lay-by on New Long Drive (OS ref TL214885)

Walk (6 miles; easy; OS Explorer 227): Continue on road for 100m; left over footbridge, right on path, first left through wood for ½ mile. At T-junction on Short Drove, right (208890); in 150m, left across footbridge (209891); path bends right to T-junction; left on grass path. In 450m by "Discovery Trail" post (206895), bear left. In 250m, at rhododendrons, bear right; in 50m, right on unmarked path between trees (204893) for 200m to reach Holme Posts (203894). Cross road; left along fenced path to bird hide on Burnham's Mere (202895). Return to road; left for 250m. Where trees end just before Holme Lode Farm (204896), left past NNR sign along path. In 300m, just before T-junction, left (203898). In 250m, right over footbridge across Caldicote Dyke (201898). Right for 20m; left into trees; fork immediately right, and in 30m right again, to continue parallel with Caldicote Dyke for 300m to SE corner of wood (203899). Left on grass ride to Trundle Mere Hide (201903), turn left along wood edge. In 250m (199902), left into wood. At T-junction, right; in 100m, left; at 200899 fork right to T-junction with Caldicote Dyke (201898 – hidden by bank ahead). Right for 350m to T-junction with railway just ahead (197896). Left across Caldicote Dyke (footbridge) for ½ mile to gate onto road (198889). Left along road; in 300m, right across Holme Lode (200891), past NNR sign and on, SE along grass path. In 300m path widens into clearing; pass crooked oak on right, then in 70m turn right by pine tree with "withered arm" branch (203889). Follow grass track which winds for over ½ mile to SW corner of wood near railway (199884). Turn left along grass track; follow wood edge. In 700m, pass footbridge across drain on right (204886); keep ahead along Short Drove into wood. In 250m, right (206887) on track SE for ½ mile to ditch with cottage on your right (212883). Left for 10m; right across ditch onto New Long Drove; left to car.

WICKEN FEN AND REACH LODE

A cuckoo was calling, faint and far, across Wicken Fen National Nature Reserve. Unlike the rest of these Cambridgeshire flatlands, Wicken Fen has never been drained for agriculture. Under the National Trust's expert care for the past 100 years, it remains a flourishing, sodden, teeming green jungle, supporting wildlife that has died out or greatly diminished everywhere else.

We set out to follow a cycleway across Adventurers' Fen. What a contrast! On the east of the path, intensive agriculture in drilled green rows to the flat horizon; to the west, the lush pastures of the reserve where highland cattle and springy muntjac deer grazed, and sedgy pools stood full of geese and egrets.

We crossed the long silver finger of Burwell Lode, a man-made drainage channel, and followed Reach Lode west to Upware on a high green embankment with grandstand views across both wild fen and intensively farmed fields. The National Trust's 100-year plan, named Wicken Fen Vision, would see the nature reserve stretch all the way from Wicken to Cambridge – a restoration of the landscape that was so beloved of Richard Fielder, self-proclaimed 'King of Upware', who ruled this fenland realm with his fists and foul (but classically trained) tongue in the 1860s.

Fielder, a Cambridge undergraduate and black sheep of a well-heeled family, would smoke, drink and fight with anyone who came to his "court" at Upware's riverside pub, the charmingly titled Five Miles From Anywhere – No Hurry! When the railways brought the outside world to Fenland, Fielder and his wild courtiers melted away into oblivion. But at Wicken Fen you can still find a corner of the ancient fenland environment in which the King of Upware once reigned as Lord of Misrule.

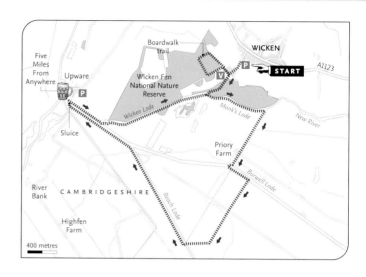

Start & finish Wicken Fen NNR, Wicken, Cambridgeshire CB7 5XP (OS ref TL565706)

Walk (8 miles, 7 miles excluding NT Wicken Fen; easy; OS Explorer 226): Walk circuit of Wicken Fen NNR boardwalk trail (optional). From visitor centre, right along left bank of Wicken Lode. In 500m bear left, then right across footbridge (560701, Adventurers' Fen); left along right bank of Monk's Lode. In ½ mile, right (539700, Cycleway post 11). Pass Priory Farm (565693) and cross Burwell Lode (564690); left along south bank of lode. Track bends south to cross Cycleway 51 (564684); on to cross Reach Lode (557678). Right along its left bank for 1¾ miles to turn right across lode at Upware sluice (537699). Back along north bank of lode. In 600m cross mouth of Wicken Lode (542696); left (yellow arrow, "Wicken Fen") up its south bank for more than a mile. Left across Monk's Lode footbridge (560701), and then return to car park.

Lunch Wicken Fen NNR café; Maid's Head, Wicken (01353 720727; maidsheadwicken.com), Five Miles From Anywhere pub, Upware (01353 721654; fivemilesinn.com)

More information Wicken Fen NNR (NT) (01353 720274; nationaltrust.org.uk/wickenfen-nature-reserve) £6.80 adult, NT members free; visitengland.com; satmap.com; ramblers.org.uk

COALHOUSE FORT AND MUCKING MARSHES

There is a haunting beauty about the landscape of the lower Thames, where the tidal water slides between banks bright with wild flowers.

Today Coalhouse Fort lay low and ominous under a grey, rain-speckled sky. We passed the old stronghold and set out north along the sea wall path where large lilac-coloured flowers of salsify bloomed among the grasses. Here, the river begins to broaden into its estuary, a forgotten corner of Essex where oystercatchers pipe on the tideline and the wind brings a smack of salt from the distant sea.

Across the river lay the ghostly outline of Cliffe Fort, where Charles Dickens sent poor little Pip in *Great Expectations* on a foggy Christmas morning with stolen "wittles" and a file for the escaped convict Magwitch. This is all moody country hereabouts, looking downriver over bird-haunted marshes and mudflats.

All the marshes hereabouts have for centuries been the dumping ground for London's rubbish. Now they have finished land-filling the giant tip on the appropriately named Mucking Marshes, and a phoenix from the ashes is arising there: Thurrock Thameside Nature Park, a big reserve of reedbeds and grasslands, woods and lakes, already up and running even as it expands and consolidates.

The senior warden gave up some precious time to show us around. Reed buntings chattered, invisible among thousands of stems, a cuckoo called, shelduck hoovered the mudflats, a brown hare scampered off. We mounted the spiral ramp to the roof of the visitors' centre and had a wonderful 360-degree view over the sullen grey river, the greened-over hills of the landfill, and floating on the western skyline the towers and spires of London, as strange and distant as a dream.

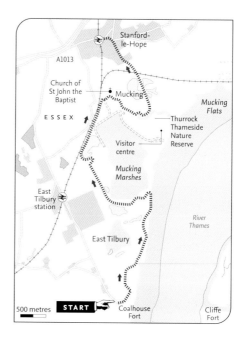

Start & finish Coalhouse Fort, Princess Margaret Road, East Tilbury, Essex RM18 8PB (OS ref TQ 690769)

Walk (5½ miles Coalhouse Fort to Stanford-le-Hope station; 5 miles, car to car; easy, OS Explorer 163): Follow seawall path north from Coalhouse Fort for 1½ miles till fence blocks path (695792). Left along fence for 1 mile. Through metal gate (684793); right through kissing gate ("Essex Wildlife Trust/TTNP") into Thurrock Thameside Nature Park. Left along path for ½ mile to lakes; right (679799) along path beside railway. In ¾ mile, path bends right just before Mucking road (683810); in 400m, bear right by warden's house (687810, "Visitor Centre" fingerpost). If doing two-car walk, follow roadway to visitor centre. If station-to-station, left at roadway in 100m (arrow) along path; in 350m, left through gate; cross sluice (691808). In 200m, fork left past metal gate (694809) to road (693812); left for 1 mile to Stanford-le-Hope station (682823).

Lunch Inn on the Green, Stanford-le-Hope SS17 0ER (01375 400010, www.innonthegreen-stanfordlehope.co.uk); TTNP visitor centre café

More information Thames Thurrock Nature Park (01375 643342, essexwt.org.uk/reserves/thurrock-thameside); Coalhouse Fort: (01375 844203, coalhousefort.co.uk); satmap.com; ramblers.org.uk

The Swan Inn at Great Easton made a perfect base for our leg-stretch through the rolling landscape of rural north-west Essex. Great Easton is full of lovely old houses, half-timbered and whitewashed, with some fine pargeting plasterwork on the walls of the former Bell Inn. Broad fields of oilseed rape surrounded the village, and crossing them felt like walking in a *Sgt Pepper*-style dream of intense, opiate yellow, all the more sense-scrambling for lying under a sky full of sharply defined grey clouds.

Apple blossom frothed in pink and white along the path to Tilty Mill, a witchy ruin caught with its curly spoked flywheels in a thicket of ivy. In the adjacent field lay the crumbling walls of Tilty Abbey. Just beyond, the magnificent rose window and chequerboard flint flushwork of today's parish church are the only reminders of the glories of the 12th-century Cistercian foundation. "Allelu-alleluia," sang the congregation, their harmony floating past us and away over the billowing cornfields. Sleek horses were grazing the paddocks at Brook End Stables. "There are wartime American air force runways hidden under these crops," said a man over his garden gate. "You'll find a window to those brave young men down in Little Easton church."

That wasn't the only memorial in the church. Beautiful medieval frescoes adorned the nave walls, and the south chapel was packed with monuments to local gentry: the Bourchiers and Maynards – ruffs and beards, armour and silks, faces lean or podgy, all lent authority and in some cases arrogance by their whiteness and immobility. Yet it was those young Americans, far from home, daily facing death, who filled my mind as we walked the fields under the growling airliners of the modern age.

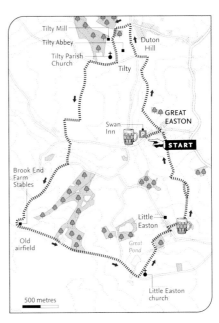

Start & finish The Swan, Great Easton, Essex CM6 2HG (OS ref TL606255)

Walk (7 miles; easy; OS Explorer 195): From Swan Inn, left; left by The Bell; field path NW to footbridge (604258), don't cross, but turn right (north) for ½ mile; left (604265) to road. Right for ¼ mile; opposite side road, left (602269) to Tilty Mill (600267); left to Tilty Abbey (600265) and road. Right for 400m; left (597264, black fingerpost) along Harcamlow Way for ½ mile; dogleg right and left (595256) to cross road (594253). On through paddocks (yellow arrows, white arrows), up field edge to road (594250). Right for ½ mile; at right bend (589245), ahead along green lane. In 100m, fork left along paddock edges to Brook End Stables (587242); left along driveway for over a mile to Little Easton church (604235). Left through Little Easton Manor gates, on past manor, through far gates, down field between ponds (606239). Up past garden fence, right to road in Little Easton (608241). Left; right down Butchers Pasture, through gate, across footbridge; half left to cross next footbridge (610245). Ahead; in 50m, right across footbridge; left to cross stile (610247). Left for 300m; right (608248) up ditch; left (yellow arrow) across ditch and field to Great Easton.

Lunch The Swan, Great Easton CM6 2HG (01371 870359; swangreateaston.co.uk); Stag Inn, Little Easton CM6 2JE (01371 870214, thestaglittleeaston.co.uk)

More information Saffron Walden Tourist Information Centre (01799 524002; visitsaffronwalden.gov.uk); visitessex.com; ramblers.org.uk; satmap.com

WALLASEA ISLAND AND THE ESSEX ARCHIPELAGO

Off the outermost tip of south Essex lies the Essex archipelago, six flat and sparsely populated islands, their coastlines closely tessellating – Potton, Rushley, Havengore, New England, Foulness and Wallasea.

All but the last two are intensively farmed, and Foulness is a Ministry of Defence establishment, off limits to the outside world. It is Wallasea where a truly remarkable project has been taking place over 20 years, a transformation from a vast blank prairie of corn and peas four miles long and nearly 2 miles wide to an RSPB nature reserve of saltmarsh and grazing, mud flats, islets and lagoons.

My last visit had been in 2007, just after the northern sea wall had been deliberately breached to let the sea in, an experiment in "managed realignment" in the face of rising sea levels and crumbling flood defences along the east coast of England.

On this cold January day it was a revelation to walk the new northern wall. Across the River Crouch lay the white and red waterfront of Burnham-on-Crouch. Between the river and the sea wall path the tide was rising where monoculture corn had once grown.

Out at the eastern end of Wallasea some three million tons of London clay have been dumped to form the islands, banks, and lagoons of Jubilee Marsh. I followed an embanked trail south across the island, passing a wooden post where a magnificent peregrine sat unafraid and stared me down as I went by.

Hereabouts a house of ill omen once stood. Known as Tylebarn, Duval's or the Devil's House, it was a well-known resort of Mother Redcap, a witch. The old lady would scarcely recognise her domain, were she to fly over it today.

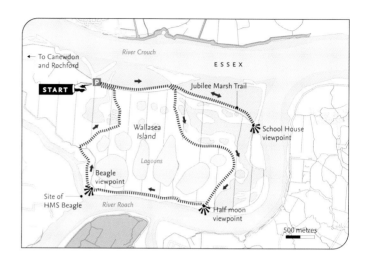

Start & finish Wallasea Island car park, Creeksea Ferry Rd, Rochford SS4 2HD (OS ref TQ955946)

Walk (6 miles; easy; OS Explorer 176): From car park, right along sea wall (Allfleets Marsh Trail). In ½ mile, right (969945, "Jubilee Marsh Trail"). In 2 miles, at Half Moon viewpoint (975925, shelter), turn west on South Trail. In 2 miles, fork right by Kim Milnes bench (953934, "car park 1.9 km"). In 100m fork right (not left past arrow) along gravel track. In ½ mile pass "Lagoons" noticeboard and hide; in another 200m left (959938, arrow post) back to car park.

Lunch Shepherd & Dog, Ballards Gore, Rochford SS4 2DA (01702 258658, theshepherdanddogstambridge.co.uk)

More information rspb.org.uk/wallasea

GEDNEY DROVE END

Gedney Drove End lies at the end of 5 miles of lonely road, out on the shores of the Wash estuary under the enormous skies of the south Lincolnshire flatlands.

From the sea bank beyond Gedney Drove End you can see what must be 40 miles of land and sea and the black distant shores of Norfolk and Lincolnshire shimmering like a mirage.

We walked the sea bank south, with the great estuary spread out on our left and massed fields of peas, kale, wheat and potatoes on our right – the soil here, reclaimed from the sea by the building of the earthen banks, is the richest and most productive in Britain. Down at the wide mouth of the River Nene we stopped to admire the twin white lighthouses that mark the channel.

Sir Peter Scott, the founder of the Wildfowl and Wetlands Trust, lived in the lighthouse on the east bank in the 1930s. It was on these marshes that he shot and wounded a goose, and saw it fall on inaccessible ground where it took three days to die. The experience haunted him and was the catalyst for his conversion from wildfowler to conservationist.

Before turning back along the Old Sea Bank through the arable fields to Gedney Drove End, we dropped down the outer slope of the sea wall and followed a muddy path through boot-high thickets of samphire to the edge of the marsh. Redshank cried, the wind hummed and brought smells of salt and mud, and up on the sea bank a flock of starlings squabbled for insects brushed out of the grass by a herd of slowly lumbering bullocks. I could cheerfully have stayed all day.

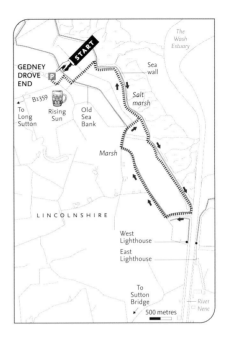

Start & finish Village Hall car park, Gedney Drove End, Lincolnshire PE12 9NW (OS ref TF 461295)

Walk (7½ miles there and back; easy; OS Explorer 249): Back towards T-junction; in 200m, left (fingerpost) to Old Sea Bank (464296). Right for 250m; left up road to cross T-junction (469296). Ahead up path to sea wall (472298). Right for 2¾ miles to gate at River Nene mouth (492264). NB: Old Sea Bank can be overgrown approaching marsh. To avoid this stretch, return along sea wall from Nene mouth to Gedney Drove End. To continue round, walk from gate, turn right along bank to road (486263); right for 600m; at left bend, keep ahead (482268, fingerpost) along Old Sea Bank for ¾ mile to road at Marsh (477279). Right; at left bend (478283), right to sea wall (481285). Left to Gedney Drove End.

Lunch Rising Sun, Gedney Drove End PE12 9PG (01406 550734)

More information Spalding Tourist Information Centre (01775 725468); visitlincolnshire.com; satmap.com; ramblers.org.uk

FOLKINGHAM AND SEMPRINGHAM PRIORY

Folkingham lies squarely across the A15 from Lincoln towards London. In the great days of coaching it was a major stopover, but the coaching trade dwindled and the railways never arrived. Nowadays the village has the air of a pleasant backwater, its mellow old houses of brick and stone marshalled around a wide and gently sloping market place, with the tower of St Andrew's church peeping between their shoulders.

We found a path that left the square and passed beside the green earthworks where Folkingham Castle once stood. Now the castle mound is occupied by a lofty stone gateway, its pediment grimly inscribed "House of Correction AD1825".

Good, clear paths led us through the enormous cornfields. The slightly rolling landscape looked at first to be an unbroken, intensive blanket of wheat, but we found the ditches and surviving hedges brimming with wild flowers.

Beside the path, feathery wild grasses made a silky border to draw the fingers through, one of those perennial pleasures of summer walking. A cuckoo called from the sunlit trees of Little Gorse; a yellowhammer chittered in the hedges. A tractor tyre seat at the crest of Beacon Hill offered a perching place and an admonition in stick-on letters: "Rest awhile, look around, be thankful."

The buildings of Sempringham Priory, founded in 1131, lay under mounds of grass but the old, restored church stood high and lonely beyond, its pinnacled tower beckoning across an immense cornfield.

In a far corner of the churchyard a circular wooden cover lay in a sunken dell. I lifted it off, to find the Holy Well of St Gilbert, founder of the priory, bubbling quietly beneath, brimful and as clear as glass.

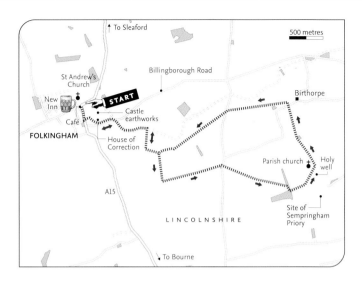

Start & finish Folkingham market place, near Sleaford NG34 0TG (OS ref TF 072337)

Walk (6½ miles; easy; OS Explorer 248): Down hill; in 150m left on fenced path between Orchard Cottage and Bradley House. Cross path (stile); ahead to stile on to Billingborough Rd (075334). Left; in 50m, right (fingerpost/FP); left on field edge path (occasional yellow arrows) for ¾ mile to path junction (082331, 3-finger post). Left ("Restricted Byway"); in 150m right (3-finger post). In 400m left by reservoir (085326) along Beacon Lane. In ½ mile cross road (093329); on across big fields; in trees at far side, right (103326). In 100m left (FP); in 200m fork left on fenced path to church (107329). NB: Holy Well in SE corner of churchyard. From NE corner, north along field edge path (3-finger post) to cross road (103337). Down right side of field; in 100m, left on path (unsigned) west across fields. In ⅔ mile cross road (094336); on (FP) to rejoin outward route.

Lunch Folkingham Shop café, open 9am–2pm weekdays; New Inn, West St, Folkingham NG34 0SW (01529 497211), open daily

More information visitlincolnshire.com; landmarktrust.org.uk

A blustery cold day at the start of spring, with bursts of snow racing across the Lincolnshire Wolds. Seen from afar, these low-rolling hills are a modest green bar on the horizon. But as you get closer, they loom up as a considerable wall, a long whaleback of limestone and ironstone rising some 300ft (90m) above the Lincolnshire plains.

Outside Tealby, the Viking Way long-distance path handed me over to a footpath running through Walesby and on through the wind-whistle fields. From Claxby I went steeply up the grassy escarpment, picturing the village's founder, one Klakkr – rather a fierce fighter, I guessed. Up in the wind, on the wold top at Normanby, I rejoined the Viking Way and followed its horned helmet symbols down to lonely Otby on its ridge, then back to Walesby, tucked into the valley below.

Walesby folk have not always dwelt in the vale. In the Middle Ages the village lay high on the Wolds, but when the Black Death arrived in 1348 the inhabitants fled their plague-ridden settlement and its church. I found snowdrops and daffodils growing on the ancient foundations of houses and fields around St Andrew's – known to generations as The Ramblers' Church. It became the focus of local walkers' expeditions in the 1930s, when it stood in romantic ruins.

I followed the Viking Way along the ridge. Near Walesby Top a herd of 40 red deer watched me pass. A flock of pedigree Lincoln Longwool sheep at Risby stared through their floppy fringes as if mesmerised. And I stared back beyond them, west, where an apocalyptic sunburst sent Blakean shafts from blackening clouds to pick out the two towers of Lincoln Cathedral on their ridge some 20 miles away in the west.

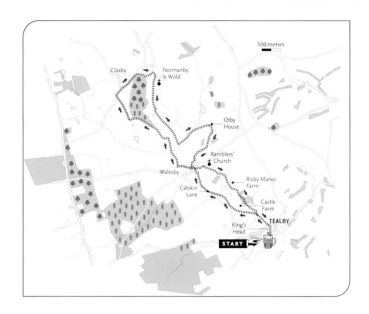

Start & finish King's Head, Tealby, Lincolnshire LN8 3YA (OS ref TF156905)

Walk (10 miles; moderate; OS Explorer 282): From the B1203 in Tealby, NW on Viking Way (VW) (157905). In the second field, left (152911); footpath to Catskin Lane (142917); ahead, then footpath (136919) to Walesby. VW along Moor Road; right (130924; "Mill House Farm"). Left at fork (129926; "Byway"); in 1/3 mile, left (127931, "Byway") to road (113942) into Claxby. Up Normanby Rise; right by reservoir (118948) up fields (yellow arrows/YA) to Normanby le Wold church (123947). VW south for 3 fields; footpath (125936, YA) to valley bottom. Left (130930; fingerpost) to end of paddock (133933); uphill to Otby House drive (139935). Right to road and Walesby. VW for 1¾ miles to Tealby.

Lunch King's Head, Tealby (01673 838347; thekingsheadtealby.co.uk)

More information Lincoln Tourist Information Centre (01522 873256; visitlincoln.com); visitlincolnshire.com; satmap.com; ramblers.org.uk

BLAKENEY TO SALTHOUSE

A mile-long creek connects Blakeney Quay with the North Sea. Looking back from the shingly shore at the distant red roofs and flint and brick walls of Blakeney, it seemed incredible that the town was once abutted by the sea. The enormous apron of salt and freshwater marshes that has grown through silt deposition along the north Norfolk coast has cut Blakeney off from the sea, but it has also made the former port a wonderful place for birdwatchers and walkers.

We turned the corner by the sea and made for the white cap and sails of the great coastal windmill at Cley next the Sea. Like its neighbour, Cley is now separated from the sea by a long mile of marshes. It too is entirely charming, with its flint walls, red roofs and narrow and curving streets. You can get spinach and ricotta filo parcels and homemade lavender bread in Cley's picnic shop – not exactly traditional Norfolk fare, but a good indicator of the change that has come to these pretty villages.

We passed under the sails of the windmill and went seaward along the floodwall towards journey's end at Salthouse. Along the marsh edge, samphire was changing colour to scarlet and yellow. A black brant goose, a rarity in from America, bobbed its white shirt-tail. Pink-footed geese in long skeins passed across the cloudy sky, and a grey seal swam off the shingle beach while he checked us over. Beach pebbles laid a carpet of many colours along the strand. Goldfinches jockeyed among yellow-horned poppies whose long seedpods quivered in the wind off the sea. Hundreds of golden plover stood huddled by a pool, close-packed like one wind-ruffled organism.

All nature seemed intent on its own business in the marshes, indifferent as to whether we were walking there or not.

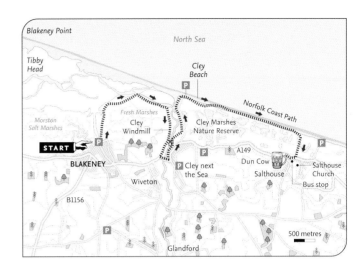

Start & finish Blakeney Quay car park NR25 7ND (OS ref TG028441)

Walk (6½ miles; easy; OS Explorer 251): From car park, climb steps and walk seaward along floodbank ("Norfolk Coast Path"/NCP), following path for 2¾ miles to Cley next the Sea. Follow road through village (take care; narrow, sharp, blind corners). In 500m, left (045439, signed) to Cley Windmill. Follow NCP seaward along floodwall to Cley Beach for 1 mile, then right (east) along shingle bank for nearly 2 miles. Opposite Salthouse Church, inland (078444, yellow arrow) to A149 (076437). Left to bus stop/ right to Dun Cow pub. Return to Blakeney by Coasthopper bus.

Lunch Dun Cow pub, Salthouse NR25 7XA (01263 740467; salthouseduncow.com)

More information Wells-next-the-Sea Tourist Information Centre (01328 710885; visitnorfolk.co.uk); visitengland.com; satmap.com; ramblers.org.uk

Just behind the houses and the big, flint-built Bailey Gate in Castle Acre's main street, a great castle stands in ruins on its 100ft (30m) mound. Fortified in the 12th century by the de Warenne family, it still looms strikingly severe and dramatic.

We followed the ancient thoroughfare that brought friend and foe to the walls of Castle Acre, a route known nowadays as Peddars Way, to where the River Nar dimpled over shallows of flint and sand across a wide ford.

At South Acre, St George's Church stood by the roadside. Inside we admired the ornate, 20ft (6m) tall medieval font cover and the intricately carved foliage of the old rood screen.

Beyond South Acre the sandy lane of Petticoat Drove climbed out of the shallow Nar Valley through corn and beet fields. A rising wind whistled in the tops of ash and sycamore as we passed Three-Cocked-Hat Plantation. Dropping down a long grassy lane towards the River Nar again, we caught glimpses through the hedges of tall blocks of flint masonry, the remnants of West Acre's Augustinian priory.

The Nar Valley Way led homewards along duckboard trails, over squelchy ground and on past the juicy reedbeds and marsh ground of Castle Acre Common. This valley was nicknamed the Holy Land for its many religious houses, and on the outskirts of Castle Acre we found the Cluniac priory established by William de Warenne at the same time as the castle.

Guarding the monastic buildings stood the tall west front of the abbey church, superbly built and engineered, sculpted with a row of stone heads more pagan than Christian.

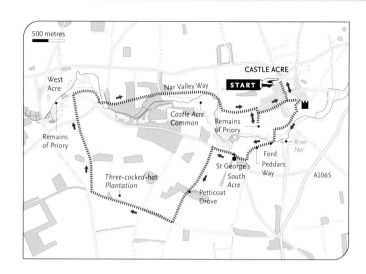

Start & finish Castle Acre, near King's Lynn, Norfolk PE32 2AE (OS ref TF 816152)

Walk (7½ miles; easy; OS Explorer 236): Follow signs to castle (819152); walk ramparts. From SE corner of precinct (820150), right along Nar Valley Way/NVW. At Bailey Street, left (819150, "Peddars Way"/PW). In 100m, right (PW) up Blind Lane. In 100m, fork left (white acorn); at T-junction (816148), left past ford (816146). Just beyond Church Farm, right along road (812143). Pass South Acre church (810143); in 350m, left (807144, "Restricted Byway") up Petticoat Drove. In ¾ mile, right at grain silos (801133, "Circular Walks"/CW); in ¾ mile, right (788137, CW), north for ¾ mile to cross road (785148). In ¼ mile, cross NVW (785151); bear left ("public footpath") across common. At ford, right along road (789151); in 50m, left (NVW) for 2 miles back to Castle Acre.

Lunch Picnic by River Nar ford

More information Castle Acre castle and priory, english-heritage.org.uk; Kings Lynn Tourist Information Centre (01553 763044)

It feels strange that Hunstanton, a Norfolk coastal resort, faces west rather than north or east. The town sits on the eastern flank of the Wash, a mighty tidal basin into which four great rivers drain – the Nene, Welland, Great Ouse and Witham.

The cliffs to the north of Hunstanton are remarkable to behold. They form a striped sandwich of rock, the white chalk on top separated from the rusty orange carrstone by a band of red chalky limestone.

We walked the sands and clambered among the rounded and thickly barnacled boulders on the beach. At the feet of the cliffs a litter of big chalk slabs showed how unstable and prone to falls the structure is. Stretched out among the rocks we found the cast-iron skeleton of the steam trawler *Sheraton*, wrecked in 1947, now slowly rusting into dissolution.

At Old Hunstanton the cliffs dipped. The orange carrstone disappeared beneath the shoreline, the white chalk followed suit and a line of sandhills took over the northeastern march of the coastline.

The coast path ran between dunes and grassy hinterland. Everything that can withstand salty winds and retain rainwater flourishes here.

Beyond Holme Dunes we emerged from the sandhills to find the sea suddenly close inshore, a fan of sand spreading beyond an apron of creek-cut saltmarsh to the east.

We turned inland along a zigzag of flood banks guarding grazing marshes reclaimed from the sea and made for the red roofs of Thornham across the fields as evening began to close in.

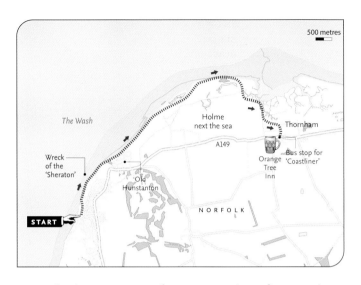

Start & finish Hunstanton seafront PE36 5BQ (OS ref TF 672409)

Walk (6½ miles; easy; OS Explorer 250): From Hunstanton seafront, turn right along beach (low tide) or Norfolk Coast Path along cliffs to Old Hunstanton. Continue along Coast Path (waymarked) to Thornham. Opposite Orange Tree inn (733432) take Coastliner bus back to Hunstanton.

Lunch The Orange Tree, Thornham PE36 6LY (01485 512213; theorangetreethornham.co.uk) – excellent village inn, perfectly placed at walk's end

More information Holme Dunes, norfolkwildlifetrust.org.uk; Coastliner bus timetable lovenorfolk.co.uk

DUNWICH AND DINGLE MARSHES

A tangle of trees has almost smothered Dunwich's famous "last grave". The solitary curly-topped headstone of Jacob Forster, however, still clings to the cliff edge above the hamlet on the Suffolk coast, the last relic of the church of All Saints that toppled to the beach in 1922. Just inland, the grand flint walls and gateways of Greyfriars Priory enclose an empty square of grass.

These remains are all that speak to us today of medieval Dunwich, the great trading port whose churches, hospitals, squares and houses were consumed by the sea. It made a sobering thought to take with us as we set out across the green hinterland of Dingle Marshes. A brisk wind pushed us along the flinty tracks through copses of old oak and pine trees.

Beyond Dingle Stone House stretched the great reedbeds of Westwood Marshes, burnt orange and green, whispering in a million scratchy sibilants. Over all floated the kingly black silhouette of a marsh harrier, circling with deliberate flaps of its wings as it scanned the reeds for mice and frogs.

We crossed the Dunwich river and came up on to the shingle bank. An instant switch of view and perspective, out over a slate-grey sea and round the curve of the bay to Dunwich under its sloping cliff and the distant white sphere of Sizewell nuclear power station.

Among the shore pebbles, a flat black stone caught my eye. It was a worked flint tool, dark and ribbed, snugly fitting in my palm, its edges scalloped by some ancient maker. Dunwich Museum has it now – one more stage on its journey from hand to hand through the millennia.

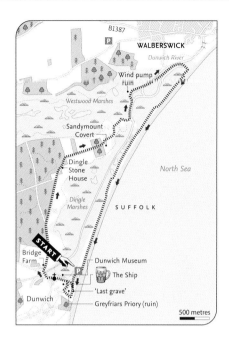

Start & finish Dunwich car park, Suffolk IP17 3EN (OS ref TM478706)

Walk (6¾ miles; easy, OS Explorer 231): At car park entrance, left up footpath (fingerpost, "Suffolk Coast Path"/SCP arrow). Just past "last grave" on left (479704), turn right through Greyfriars wall, across monastery site, through archway. Right along road; in 100m, left down footpath (fingerpost) to road with Dunwich Museum on right (477706). Left; fork right at church ("Blythburgh"). In 150m, right past Bridge Farm (474707) along SCP. In 1½ miles, leaving Sandymount Covert (483728), fork right along marsh path. In ¾ mile, just past the wind pump ruin (487737), right down steps, over footbridge, along boardwalk. In ⅔ mile, right across footbridge (495742, SCP) to shingle bank; right to Dunwich.

Lunch The Ship at Dunwich IP17 3DT (01728 648219; shipatdunwich. co.uk) – a cosy, friendly village inn

More information Southwold Tourist Information Centre (01502 724729; southwoldtouristinformation.co.uk); thesuffolkcoast.co.uk; satmap.com; ramblers.org.uk; Dunwich Museum open March– October, varying times (01728 648796, dunwichmuseum.org.uk)

Lavenham is ridiculously pretty, its high street an unbroken run of wonderful medieval buildings, each one more cranky, crooked and colour-washed than the last.

A cold west wind blew out of a wintry sky as we followed the trackbed of the old Long Melford branch railway out of the town. Arable land lay on either side, the heavy dark soil sliced by recent ploughing into long gleaming furrows. We watched a trail of seagulls following a distant tractor, each new furrow no sooner opened than lined with screeching, squabbling birds.

Spring was beginning to knock on winter's door. Hazel catkins trembled in the wind, daffodil spears were pushing up along the hedge roots, and over the open fields the first skylarks of the year poured out their continuous, ecstatic song. But winter was not done yet. Grey-headed fieldfares, overwintering from Scandinavia, flocked round a stark concrete wartime pillbox, crowds of goldfinches twittered in the treetops, and the mud of the winter rains lay black and stodgy underfoot.

Beyond the bare skeletons of beech and oak in ancient Lineage Wood we traversed fields of river-rolled pebbles to cross a tangle of old moats at Balsdon Hall farm. The yellow-faced 17th-century farmhouse lay tucked away behind trees, a remote setting among the fields. A characteristic rural Suffolk landscape, agricultural and unsmartened. Sugar beets lay heaped in roadside ramparts 10ft tall, and the great flint tower of Lavenham Church rose across the waves of ploughed earth like a landlocked lighthouse.

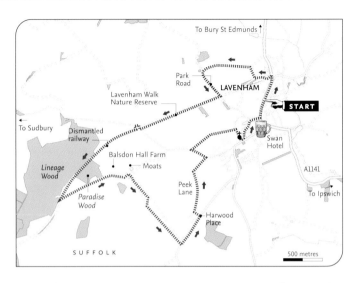

Start & finish High Street, Lavenham CO10 9QA (OS ref TL 915491)

Walk (5¾ miles; easy; OS Explorer 196): Up High Street, over ridge and down. In ⅓ mile fork left (017496, "Lavenham Walk"). In 100m, left along old railway. In 100m, right ("Dyehouse Field Wood"). In 200m right by bench (914497, "St Edmund Way") across field. Left along hedge. At Park Road, left (908497); in 300m, right along old railway (911494). In 1⅓ miles, Paradise Wood ends on left (893484); in another 300m, left (891481, arrow post) on field track. At Balsdon Hall Farm, follow farm drive between buildings (898484) to 3-arrow post at fork, with Balsdon Hall on right (900484). Ahead across fields to road (906476). Left; in 400m, left up Harwood Place (808480). In 50m, right ("Byway") along Peek Lane for ½ mile to road (909487). Left; in 200m, right (907487, fingerpost) on field path to road (913490). Right to Lavenham Church. Leaving south door, left along south side of church, then north side of graveyard to kissing gate. Follow tree avenue and walled path to Hall Road (914492); right to High Street.

Lunch Swan Hotel, High Street, Lavenham CO10 9QA (01787 247477, theswanatlavenham.co.uk)

More information Lavenham Information Point (01787 247983)

ORFORD AND BUTLEY FERRY

A pure blue-sky morning, a dreich, drizzly afternoon, and in between one of the classic walks of coastal Suffolk.

Orford is a pure delight, a self-sufficient coastal settlement at the end of a long road. Not that the village faces the bracing tides of the North Sea directly – the monstrous shingle spit of Orford Ness, 10 miles long and still growing, cut Orford off from the open sea hundreds of years ago.

The strange pagoda shapes of long-abandoned Ministry of Defence nuclear laboratories straddled the pebbly spine of Orford Ness. We turned downstream along the flood banks of the River Ore, looking back to see the red roofs of Orford bookended by the village church and the octagonal tower of Orford Castle.

We made inland for the dusty road to Gedgrave Hall, where the breeze carried a beautiful tarry whiff from Pinney's fish smokery near Butley Ferry.

A local ferryman skilfully balanced the forces of wind and tide as he rowed us across Butley River in his muddy little dinghy.

We crossed the back of Burrow Hill, at 50ft (15m) a mountain hereabouts, and followed broad, flowery lanes inland for miles to Chillesford. It was slow, heavenly walking in calm, clear air through a seductively beautiful coastal landscape.

In Sudbourne Park on the homeward stretch, cricketers in their whites were preparing for their Sunday match. Bowlers pounded the nets, batsmen practised immaculate strokes they would never execute and as the umpires emerged from the pavilion the first spits of rain were felt on the wind, in true traditional style.

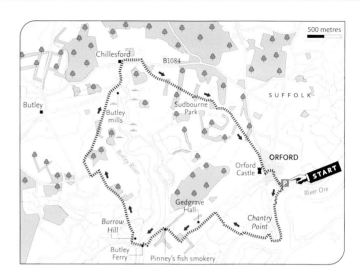

Start & finish Orford Quay car park, Orford, Suffolk IP12 2NU (OS ref TM 425496)

Walk (10 miles; easy; OS Explorer 212): From quay, right along seawall for 1½ miles, passing Chantry Point. At tide, gauge where River Ore bends SW, bear right off seawall path through gate (416485, "Suffolk Coast Path, Orford Loop", SCP/OL). Up grassy lane for ½ mile to road (409490). Left; 500m past Gedgrave Hall, right (401483, "Butley Ferry") past Pinney's fish smokery (397485), following SCP to Butley Ferry (393482). Cross Butley River; ahead through gate; in 150m, right through gate (390482, SCP); follow well-marked SCP for 2½ miles via Burrow Hill (389485), Coulton Farm (382498) and South Chapel (380496) to road at Butley Mills (383515). Right to B1084 in Chillesford (386522); right past Froize restaurant. In another 100m, right (391522, SCP/OL, "Orford 2¼"); follow marked SCP back to Orford.

Lunch Picnic

More information Butley Ferry runs 11am–4pm Saturdays, Sundays and bank holidays; £2 (07913 672499, butleyferry.org); Ipswich Tourist Information Centre (01473 258070); visitsuffolk.com; satmap.com; ramblers.org.uk

Snowdonia National Park, Wales

Arenig Fawr ("Great High Ground"), the summit of a curving ridge at 2,802ft (854m), stands at the eastern edge of the Snowdonia/Eryri National Park, some way apart from the region's more celebrated peaks.

At least three times over the years we'd had Arenig Fawr in our sights, and three times we'd been rained off. Now here we were at the foot of the track on a beautiful morning. The well-found track led us across thistly hillsides to our first sighting of Llyn Arenig Fawr, a sheet of wind-stippled water, steel-blue in the shadow of a tall corrie of dark crags with pink screes chuting down towards the lake.

By the dam a little one-room bothy, immaculately clean, offered basic shelter. From there the track steepened beside the corrie, a good old puff upwards on a path whose rocks sparkled in the sunshine. A couple of fences to hop and we were out into a wild upland, the path undulating through boggy patches before turning up loose screes and rocky steps towards the ridge.

The slope of the climb hid the conical summit of Arenig Fawr till we were nearly there. Up at the trig pillar we found a stone-walled shelter and a poignant memorial to the eight-man crew of a USAF Flying Fortress bomber, killed when their plane crashed here on a night training flight in 1943.

The promised mountains stood clear and dramatic all round – the dinosaur spine of the Clwydian Hills and the four billows of the Berwyns to the east, Cadair Idris looming like a hunchbacked beast in the south-west, and away to the north-west the shoulders and pointed head of Snowdon/Yr Wyddfa itself, just brushing the gathering cloud.

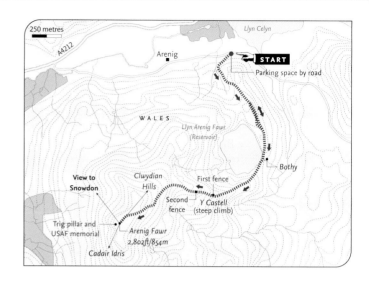

Start & finish Car parking space just east of Arenig, near Bala, LL23 7PA approx. (OS ref SH 846395)

Walk (7¼ miles, strenuous; OS Explorer OL18): Through gate, follow track for 1½ miles to Llyn Arenig Fawr. Cross ladder stile by bothy (850379); follow path, gentle gradient at first, then a rocky and steep climb from 400m at bothy to 600m at fence ("Y Castell" on map). Cross fence (842373); up to cross second fence 40m beyond corner where you join it (839374). From here on, path rocky and stumbly – watch your step! Path bears right round rocky outcrops, then makes a long leftward curve across the slope. In ½ mile path bends right and climbs (832372), a few cairns mark it from here. Near the summit, aim for a prominent post above, then trig pillar at 2,802ft/854m (827369). Return same way.

Lunch Picnic

More information walkingbritain.co.uk; snowdonia.gov.wales

THE BEGWNS

There are parts of the Welsh Borders that are neither rugged mountains nor agricultural lowlands, but rather semi-wild uplands where sheep and cattle roam freely and a walker can step out along grassy pathways in every direction. The Begwns are a fine example, a rolling ridge of common land north-west of Hay-on-Wye that separates the Brecon Beacons/Bannau Brycheiniog from the hills of southern Radnorshire.

We set out west from the hill road south of Painscastle on a midday of brisk wind and hazy blue sky. Our inland track became a potholed lane where foxgloves grew among the stone slabs of the walls. We passed the tumbledown farm of Bailey-bedw, the house roof in holes, an elder bush rising from the chimney pot like a puff of green smoke.

Beyond Bailey-bedw, sheep were gobbling turnips in a field beside the track.

The track swung up and over a shoulder of hill, then bent back on itself to climb to the Roundabout. This conifer plantation perches at the brow of the Begwns inside a circular wall, commanding a really spectacular view. We gazed our fill, south to the tumbled heights of the Brecon Beacons and the ship's prow of Hay Bluff as pale as a lead cutout in the haze, north across the Painscastle Valley to where the green patchwork of pastures rose into dun-brown moorland.

A grass track took us down from the Roundabout to Monks' Pond, flat on its saddle of ground in a golden collar of flowering gorse. The margins of the water were spattered with white blooms of water crowfoot. We walked a circuit of the wind-ruffled lakelet, and headed back home over the grassy shoulders of the Begwns.

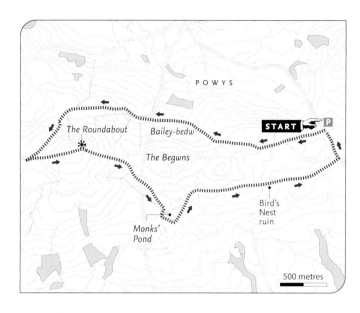

Start & finish Parking bay at cattle grid, Croesfeilliog near Painscastle, Powys HR3 5JH (OS ref SO 182445)

Walk (5½ miles; easy; OS Explorer 188): Cross road; follow track west along lower, right-hand edge of Access Land with fence on right. In ¼ mile cross stony track (177444). Two green tracks diverge here; take left one to ridge (175444). Right here (west) along rutted track, soon becoming tarmac lane. In ¾ mile cross road (163447); in ½ mile, pass track to "Top of Lane" (156448). In 100m, fork left on to grassy path, which bends left over shoulder west of Roundabout. In 600m, at large pond on right, turn left (149443) uphill to Roundabout (155444). From gate, head along spine of Begwns, bearing right across road (161440) to Monks' Pond. From NE corner (166438), head for angle of wall; north, then east on track with fence, then wall on right. In ½ mile join farm track at Bird's Nest ruin (176440); ahead to road (183442); left to car.

Lunch Picnic; there's a nice spot at the Roundabout

More information visitwales.co.uk

CAERFANELL HORSESHOE

The Nant Bwrefwr waterfall came sparkling down from the heights of Craig y Fan Ddu, chuckling over its gleaming black and red rocks as though at the folly of walkers who'd bust a sweat climbing the Brecon Beacons/Bannau Brycheiniog on a glorious summer morning as hot and sunny as this. Wild thyme and tiny white flowers of heath bedstraw jewelled the sedgy grass as we went slowly up towards the ridge. Up there a welcome breeze was blowing from the precipitous valley of the Afon Caerfanell. We circled the rim to where the infant river tipped over the edge and cascaded down through a clutter of boulders. Bog cotton trembled like trapped swansdown over the surface of a pool framed in sphagnum moss as green and cool as a freshly cut lime.

The flat high heads of Fan y Big and Cribyn looked over the moorland to the north-west. We went on along the cliffs, past shaggy hill ponies and newly shorn sheep, to the far side of the valley. Here two jumbles of weather-pitted aluminium and a memorial cairn marked the site of a wartime air crash. Today it couldn't be a more peaceful place, looking south through the jaws of the cleft to the blue ridges of the South Wales valleys, one behind another till they merge into the sky.

From the cairn at the end of the ridge we dropped steeply off the promontory, making across a grassy upland to descend beside the Afon Caerfanell. Following it down the valley and back to the car we found orchids in the bogs, blue butterwort under the rocks, and a whole rake of families splashing and swimming and making the most of the waterfalls of the hastening, beautiful Caerfanell.

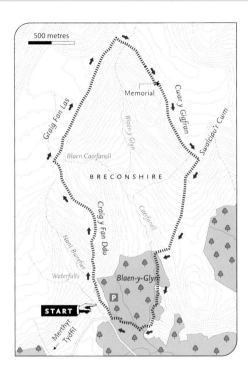

Start & finish Upper Blaen-y-glyn car park, near Pontsticill, Powys CF48 2UT approx. (OS ref SO056176)

Walk (5½ miles; moderate/hard; OS Explorer OL12): Return across cattle grid, immediately right on stepped path, steeply up to ridge (054183). Where path flattens, bear right; follow rim of valley clockwise for 1½ miles to saddle at head of valley where Blaen-y-Glyn cleft descends (057206). Right on path to aircraft crash memorial (062200). Steep path ascends on left of stream gully; right along top of Cwar y Gigfran crags to cairn (067192). Bear half right, steeply down; on across upland plateau to wall; right down to Afon Caerfanell (062183). Left over stile; follow riverside path. In ½ mile, just before valley bends left (east), turn right by footpath fingerpost across footbridge (061174). On through kissing gate; in 50m, left at junction; in another 50m, before concrete footbridge, right up steep path between two streams. At top, where trees open to left, turn left on wider track, which bends right to car park.

Lunch Red Cow, Pontsticill (01685 384828); Pubs/tearoom in Talybont-on-Usk; nearest tearoom (March–Oct), Old Barn, Ystradgynwyn, Merthyr Tydfil CF48 2UT (01685 373175)

More information Brecon Beacons National Park (01874 623366; breconbeacons.org); visitwales.com; satmap.com; ramblers.org.uk; theaa.com/walk-and-bike-ride

GREAT ORME AND PARC FARM

The high Victorian hotels of Llandudno stand in a long line around the curve of the bay, buttressed by the two bulbous headlands of Great and Little Orme and backed by the distant mountains of Snowdonia. It all makes a fine setting for a walk to explore the rugged charms of Great Orme, where the National Trust owns 145 acres of land, Parc Farm.

The peace of a cold, cloudy morning lay over Happy Valley Gardens as we climbed their pathways, then on up steps to the crest of a natural limestone amphitheatre.

Great Orme is a giant lump of limestone, in profile like a barking dog with muzzle raised to the north-west. We passed the farmhouse of Penmynydd Isa and then Powell's Well, before dropping down to St Tudno's church perched above the sea. Inside we found intricate medieval Celtic stonework, and a fine dragon snarling in the shadows above the chancel window.

We headed west towards the Orme's seaward snout over a moor patched with limestone pavement and scattered with big erratic boulders left by the retreating glaciers 10,000 years ago.

On over the brow of Bishop's Quarry where hundreds of lovers, rogues and wanderers have spelt out their names in white limestone fragments. A sensational view over the Conwy estuary to the mountains of Snowdonia, stamped on a stormy sky in flat grey-blue silhouettes as though cut in profile from the lead and slate they are founded on. And then the skeltering path of the Zig Zag Trail, steeply down through windblown heather, rocks and cliffs to the gentle pathways of Haulfre Gardens and Llandudno's promenade once more.

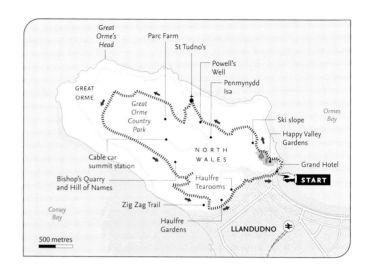

Start & finish Happy Valley Road, Llandudno LL30 2LR (OS ref SH 782828)

Walk (6 miles; moderate; OS Explorer OL17): From Grand Hotel, Alex Munro Way up to Happy Valley Gardens; follow Happy Valley Summit Trail ("To Summit"/TS arrows, blue-ringed posts) up past ski slope to St Tudno's (770838). Up road for 200m; path forks right (TS) uphill; in 150m turn right on track, keeping wall on left, anticlockwise for 1½ miles to SE corner below summit station (765831). Ahead past yellow-ringed post over hill; aim half left for black-ringed post near boulder (769828); follow "To Town" signs back.

Lunch Haulfre Tearooms, Haulfre Gardens LL30 2HT (01492 876731)

More information visitllandudno.org.uk; Parc Farm: nationaltrust.org.uk/projects/wildlife-and-farming-on-the-great-orme; Great Orme: greatorme.org.uk; conwy.gov.uk/thegreatorme

The River Severn's estuary was at a fantastically low ebb as we crossed the "new" bridge on a day of no cloud.

Downriver the little hump of Denny Island off Portishead stood marooned in a huge desert of sand.

Llanvihangel Crucorney lies in the River Monnow valley that forms the eastern boundary of the Black Mountains and Brecon Beacons/Bannau Brycheiniog. It's a great jumping-off point for walks westwards into those mountains, but today we were aiming east to climb the Skirrid (Ysgyryd Fawr, the "big split one").

The Skirrid is made of tough old red sandstone lying in a heavy lump on top of thin layers of weaker mudstone – hence its history of slippage. We came up to it in cold wind and brilliant sunshine across fields of sheep, skirting its western flank through scrub woods, gorse bushes blooming yellow and holly trees in a blaze of scarlet berries.

The ascent is short, steep and stepped, but it's the sort of "starter mountain" that families with six-year-olds can manage. Once at the peak in this unbelievably clear weather we gasped to see the landscape laid out in pin-sharp detail a thousand feet below and 50 miles off – Malverns, Black Mountains; farmlands rising and falling towards the Midlands and Gloucestershire; the slanting tabletops of Pen y Fan and Cribyn over in the Brecon Beacons; Cotswolds, Mendip, Exmoor; the South Wales coast trending round into Pembrokeshire.

Nearer at hand a grey streak of softly glimmering sea showed the tide rising in the Severn Estuary past Brean Down's promontory, the slight disc of Flat Holm and the hump of her sister island Steep Holm, their lower edges lost in mist so that they looked like floating islands in some fabulous sea.

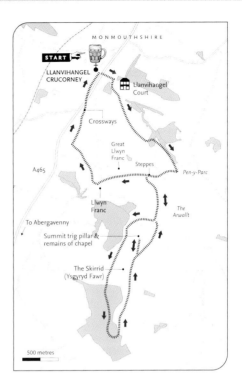

Start & finish Skirrid Mountain Inn, Llanvihangel Crucorney, Abergavenny NP7 8DH (OS ref SO 326206)

Walk (6½ miles; strenuous; OS Explorer OL13): Opposite church, lane (gateposts) to cross A465. Down drive; right at wall (325204); follow Beacons Way/BW arrow waymarks. Pass wood-framed barn; in 100m, right (328202, BW, gate). Follow BW across fields to lane at Pen-y-Parc (336192). Right; beyond "Steppes" house, left (332191, stile); follow BW to foot of Skirrid (333186). Right on path along west side of Skirrid to rejoin BW at southern foot of mountain (327169). Follow BW up to Skirrid summit (331183). Return; in 200m, sharp left beside hollow (331181); path descends to north foot (333185). Retrace BW back to lane at Steppes (332191). Left; in ½ mile, opposite Llwyn Franc, right (325190, gate, fingerpost "Crossways"). Follow hedge on right to gate/stile (325192). Half left across field, crossing Great Llwyn Franc drive (324193); on down to Crossways House (323200) and Llanvihangel Crucorney.

Lunch Skirrid Mountain Inn, Llanvihangel Crucorney (01873 890258, skirridmountaininn.co.uk)

More information Abergavenny Tourist Information Centre (01873 853254, visitwales.com)

Cwm Idwal is a very popular place, and here was the proof in a procession of sturdy, bare calves, red rolled-down socks, big boots and sticks clattering up the stone-pitched path towards Llyn Idwal, lying hidden in its dark, dramatic bowl of cliffs.

Soon we struck off the main path and followed a stony trod across bog feathery with cotton grass, then up the steep mountain cleft where Nant Bochlwyd came jumping down from rock to rock in a rush of foam. Up over the rim of the cleft we found Llyn Bochlwyd lying flat under the sombre cliffs of Glyder Fach, a wind-rippled mountain lake in a hollow of green bilberry, as quiet and lonely as could be.

The outline of Llyn Bochlwyd mirrors almost exactly that of Australia. We took great delight in walking the Gold Coast from Sydney to Cairns – so to speak – before making for the saddle of ground that looks down on Llyn Idwal lying as dark as tarnished copper 600ft (180m) below.

A very steep rocky chute of a path landed us on the shore of Llyn Idwal, and from there we took the high road south, a slanting path rising under the tremendous crags of Glyder Fawr to reach a tumbled boulder field. Delicate starry saxifrages grew here, their white flowers powdered with bright scarlet dots of anthers. Along with royal blue butterwort and tiny green stars of alpine lady's mantle, they made a delightful mountain meadow to walk through before we descended the rough path to Llyn Idwal.

We walked its gritty beach and looked our last on the Glyder cliffs, now wreathed in curls of mist, before turning down the homeward path in a whirl of flitting meadow pipits.

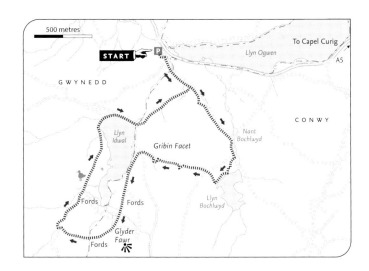

Start & finish Ogwen Warden Centre, Nant Ffrancon, Cwm Idwal car park LL57 3LZ (OS ref SH649603)

Walk (4½ miles; hard; OS Explorer OL17): Up stone-pitched path at left side of warden centre. In 350m path bends right (652601); ahead here on stony track across bog; steeply up right side of Nant Bochlwyd to Llyn Bochlwyd (655594). Right (west) on path for 400m to saddle (652594); pitched path to Gribin climbs to left, but you keep ahead, then very steeply down to Llyn Idwal (647596). Left along lake. At south end take higher path (646593) slanting up to boulder field; take care fording torrent at 642589. Arriving face to face with a very big boulder (640589), go right down the side of it, then left across rocky grass to find downward path (640590), steep in places, to Llyn Idwal and visitor centre.

Lunch Picnic

More information Ogwen Warden Centre (01248 602080) or Betws-y-Coed Tourist Information Centre (01690 710426; visitbetwsycoed.co.uk); eryri-npa.gov.uk

A cold autumn morning, with the Snowdonia/Eryri mountains steaming with cloud. We were looking for a high and handsome walk, something tastily mountain-flavoured but without actually ascending too far.

You can't see either from the upland car park at Llyn Eigiau, high above the Conwy Valley and bang in the middle of the Carneddau range. In fact, they lay well-hidden until we had climbed the old quarry track round the shoulder of the tongue-tinglingly named Clogwynyreryr and were deep in the hidden valley behind.

Dulyn was the first to slide into view across the cleft, a dark sliver of water in a bowl of rock-scabbed cliffs 500ft (150m) high. But it was Melynllyn we came to first, skirting an old quarry building where a great cast-iron flywheel stood buried up to its axle in rubble. The slate around Melynllyn is studded with tiny particles of abrasive quartz, and first-class hones or whetstones were quarried here to sharpen the scythes and sickles of Victorian Britain.

The clear water of Melynllyn lay hidden until the last moment. As we gazed, a fish jumped and disappeared. A steep track led down to Dulyn, black and still under its cliffs. The twisted fingers of an aircraft propeller reached out of the water like a demon hand in a Tolkien setting. As many as 20 planes have crashed into the cliffs above Dulyn over the years, and their engines and wing parts still litter the rocks. It was a hauntingly beautiful place to sit before taking the long homeward path.

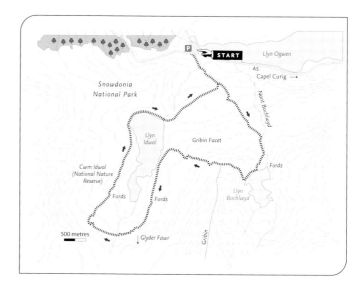

Start & finish Llyn Eigiau car park (OS ref SH 731662)

Walk (6 miles; moderate/difficult; OS Explorer OL17): Cross stile at east end of parking place (732663); follow paved path. Cross stile (727666); follow track past sheepfold and up shoulder of Clogwynyreryr for 1¾ of a mile to ruin near Melynllyn Reservoir (706656). Ignore footpath on map; continue along track to SE corner of reservoir (703658). Follow track skirting to right of crags, down to reach Dulyn Reservoir. Follow path above bothy (707664), along hillside above Afon Dulyn. Pass Scots pine clump; cross first stream (709669), then fence by ladder stile. Cross Ffrwd Cerriguniawn (713671), and another ladder stile (715673). Cross Afon Garreg-wen (718675); then head right, aiming downhill for white dam ⅓ mile away. Ford Afon Dulyn below dam (725675); follow track to Maeneira farm ruin (728673) and on to re-cross stile below sheepfold (727666) and return to car park.

Lunch Picnic

More information Betws-y-Coed Tourist Information Centre (01690 710426; visitwales.co.uk); ramblers.org.uk

NEW QUAY TO ABERAERON

We had plotted the tides as best as we could, so it was a relief to descend New Quay's steep streets to the harbour and find the beach section of the Wales Coast Path still passable. We skirted the slippery rock promontory that makes a barrier to walkers at high tide, and went on round the classic curve of sand that rims New Quay Bay.

Pale grey cliffs banded with extravagantly squeezed and distorted strata formed a backdrop to the beach. Tiny fingernails of fractured shells paved the sand. Beyond the headland a stream trickled out of the woods, and we sat by the stepping stones to watch pied wagtails flitting and hovering above the water to snatch their insect feast from mid-air.

Halfway along the stony beach of Little Quay Bay we found steps leading up from the shore. After a glance back at the kayak paddlers in the shallows we climbed a shady lane through the woods. In a garden at the top lay a venerable railway carriage, now with a second lease of life as a summerhouse.

The Wales Coast Path ran through steep pastures with the sea sighing low on our left.

Ahead, the great curve of Cardigan Bay was clouded and hazy, the distant finger of the Lleyn Peninsula lying on the sea like a bar of mist. Down in the cleft of Oernant a stream came sparkling down through falls and spillways it had carved in the rocks.

Down to cross stream clefts on wooden bridges; up again to breast the next brackeny hill. Finally we were given a view from a summit gate over Aberaeron, the shipbuilding and trading port, laid out in Georgian elegance around its harbour on a grey stone shore.

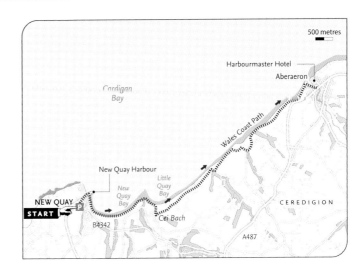

Start & finish Church Road car park, New Quay, Ceredigion SA45 9PB (OS ref SN 387599)

Walk (6½ miles; moderate; OS Explorer 198): Down Church Street to the harbour. If high tide means beach impassable, continue up Glanmor Terrace to B4342 (388597). Left; in ¼ mile, left down Brongwyn Lane (390596) to shore. If beach passable, walk round curve of New Quay Bay to the far point (405599). Continue along beach for 400m to Cei Bach Road end (409597). Up steps; right up road; just past caravan park, left up drive (409595, "Coast Path"/CP). In 100m, left before farm building; through gate (CP); follow well-marked CP along coast to Aberaeron. Return by bus T5.

Lunch Harbourmaster Hotel, Pen Cei, Aberaeron SA46 0BT (01545 570755, harbour-master.com), stylish, friendly, bustling place

More information Aberaeron Tourist Information Centre (01545 570602, www.discoverceredigion.co.uk); visitwales.com; walescoastpath.gov.uk

The Afon Disgynfa rushed towards the 200ft (60m) cliff, gathered into a bulge of glass-clear water at the very rim, then hurled itself into space. Prone on a spur of beaten earth beside the cliff, I watched the cascade drop away. Up here at the top of Pistyll Rhaeadr, the tallest waterfall in Wales, everything – mossy rocks, slippery stones, lichen-encrusted larch and hazel – spoke of the damp, clean air of the surrounding Berwyn Hills.

Down on the footbridge at the base of the cliff, the waterfall itself is all the view one needs. I watched spellbound as the fall came hissing lazily out of the mist-whitened sky in lacy skeins, toppling gracefully into a halfway basin before bounding out through a natural bridge of polished black rock and crashing on down towards the spray-shrouded pool at the bottom.

I lingered a long time on the bridge. Then I turned and followed a path between mossy trees scarred with ancient penknife carvings of lovers' names. Out on the hillside the path dropped between house-high boulders fallen from the sharp ramparts of Craig y Mwn, the Mine Rock, far above.

The path threaded the hillsides where lambs tottered after their mothers. I stopped for a word with the farmer at Tyn-y-wern – the cost of feed, the price of lambs, the hard winter of 1982 when Pistyll Rhaeadr froze solid and daring souls went ice-climbing up its face. Fondling the head of Nell the ancient sheepdog of Tyn-y-wern, I leant on the farmyard gate and sniffed woodsmoke, silage and wet grass, the essence of spring in the Berwyns, all underpinned by the distant murmur of the great fall.

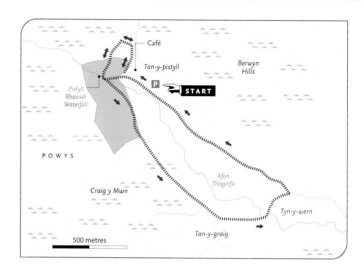

Start & finish Pistyll Rhaeadr car park, SY10 0BZ approx.; near Llanrhaeadr-ym-Mochnant (OS ref 075294)

Walk (3 miles; moderate; OS Explorer 255): From car park, down road to end; right behind public lavatories, up signed path (yellow arrows) that zigzags steeply uphill. At top, track continues to arrow pointing through gate (fingerpost) to top of waterfall. Please take great care: slippery rocks, unfenced 60m (200ft) drop! Return same way to foot of fall; cross by footbridge; follow path through trees, over fields, across mining spoil to Tan-y-graig and road at Tyn-y-wern. Left to car park.

Lunch Tan-y-Pistyll Café (01691 780392; pistyllrhaeadr.co.uk/cafe)

More information Llangollen Tourist Information Centre (01978 860828); www.visitwales.co.uk

PRECIPICE WALK AND FOEL OFFRWM SUMMIT

The Cynwch made a dull mirror of its steep, glacier-scoured valley. I was setting out on this brisk day to explore the Precipice Walk high above.

A rocky path, clear on the ground but tricky to find footing on, led round the northern nose of a tall ridge before edging back along the brink of the precipice. The slope down to the river 700ft (213m) below was steep and tree-hung, vertiginous in a couple of spots. But the views were quite sensational, out to the mouth of the Afon Mawddach's estuary below its headland, south to where Cadair Idris sprawled in full majesty of ridges, cliffs, corries and peaks against the clouds.

The Precipice Walk rounded the southern end of the ridge and fell away to the lake shore and a level stroll back to the car park. But I wasn't quite satisfied. On the other side of the road rose Foel Offrwm, the "Hill of Sacrifice", a tall knobbly eminence crowned with an Iron Age hillfort. The views from up there ought to be sensational too.

And so they were, once I had slogged up the zigzag path, past a tempting resting bench and on up to the tumble of stones that once formed a sturdy defensive wall for the ancient stronghold at the summit. By the curious square cairn I revolved slowly, taking in one of Snowdonia's finest prospects – the lumpy Rhinogs and the serpentine Mawddach to the west, the Arans and Are to the east where I had climbed last year, the long, tented back of Cadair Idris capturing the whole of the southern skyline, and away to the north a hint of the tall mountains that form the roof of Snowdonia.

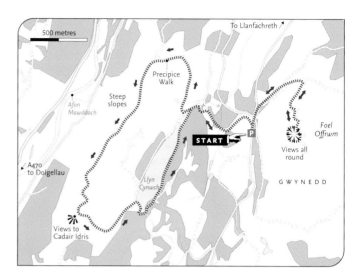

Start & finish Precipice Walk car park, near Dolgellau, LL40 2NG (OS ref SH 745211)

Walk (5½ miles in total, Precipice Walk 3½ miles, Foel Offrwm 2 miles up and down; moderate/strenuous; OS Explorer OL23): Turn right along marked path at top of car park. In ½ mile through gate marked "Danger; Deep Drops" (741212); in 100m uphill along wall. Follow it to right then follow the obvious "Precipice Walk" circuit. Watch your feet on this rocky path! Back at car park cross road and follow lower track parallel with road. In 250m, before gate, fork right (748212, "Foel Offrwm" on marker stone) up side path, through gate and on. In 250m fork right up path ("Copa Foel Offrwm"). In 100m bend right with the path, and keep climbing in same direction. At bench, fork back left (750213 approx.) on path to summit cairn (750209). Return same way.

Lunch Picnic

More information snowdonia.gov.wales/walk/precipicewalk; visitwales.com

THE PRESELI HILLS

The Preseli Hills march east to west across the heart of west Pembrokeshire and the Golden Road marches with them, an ancient drove road and highway that hurdles their peaks. We followed the Golden Road as it climbed gently up the flanks of Foel Eryr, the Eagle's Peak.

A topograph by the summit cairn specified places in view and their distances, but it could never catch the splendours of the extraordinary view. Lundy lay like a sleeping sea dog, 50 miles off in the south, the shadowy shapes of the Cambrian mountains far to the north, west to Skomer and Ramsey islands, and in the east the dragon humps of Worm's Head.

Then it was down over sedgy ground to the lonely farm of Pen-lan-wynt, where thorn trees bent by the wind lined the hedges. This is a land of small farms and smallholdings: the stone cottage of Gernos Fawr in a watery dell full of runner ducks, the hillside farm of Gernos Fach, where a young sheepdog leapt gymnastically between the high bars of a gate to welcome us.

Beyond the farm a moorland track led away, the cold cloudy sky reflected in its peaty pools. Standing stones stood in the heather a little way off the track, a hip-high pair sloping close together and a fine solo stone of man-height, crusted with lichens and upright in a little circular moat of water.

We crossed the road and climbed a boggy old path that snaked up the wet hillside of Rhwngyddwyffordd. Ponies with tangled manes moved reluctantly off the track as we followed it to the saddle. Here we turned for a final stare over bog and hillside, coasts, islands and distant mountains, before a last homeward stretch along the miry ridgeway of the Golden Road.

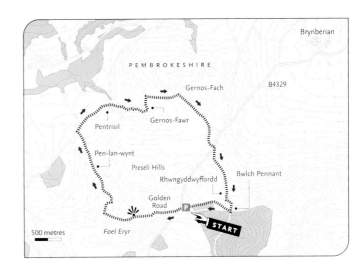

Start & finish Bwlch Gwynt car park, near Tafarn-y-bwlch, Pembrokeshire SA66 7RB (OS ref SN 075322)

Walk (6½ miles; moderate; OS Explorer OL35): Cross B4329; path to Foel Eryr summit (066321). Keep same line descending. At fingerpost with arrow (061321), right on path. In 300m, at another fingerpost with arrow (061324), fork left, soon bearing downhill to wall. Right to 4-finger post (060327); follow wall to Pen-lan-wynt farm (058330). Follow blue arrows/BA to track (057333), then road (055337). Right; 250m beyond Pentrisil, right (062342, "Tafarn-y-bwlch, Pembrokeshire Trail"). Follow track past Gernos Fawr (069341, BAs); up green lane to gate (069344); right (bridleway fingerpost) to Gernos Fach (075343). Right (fingerpost) on track to B4329 (084337). Right; in 350m, fork left (082333, BA) up hill track for ¾ mile to fence at Bwlch Pennant (085321). Don't go through gate; turn right along fence to car park.

Lunch Tafarn Sinc, Rosebush SA66 7QU (01437 532214, tafarnsinc.co.uk)

More information Fishguard Tourist Information Centre (01437 776636); visitwales.com

Only the upperworks of St Davids Cathedral tower are visible as you enter the smallest city in Britain. The first sight of the cathedral is so unexpected that it takes your breath away. You step through the arch of Porth-y-Twr gatehouse, and there, filling a hollow far below, lies this magnificent and enormous church, with the ruin of the most spectacular 14th-century Bishop's Palace just behind.

Green lanes and country roads took us down to the southern corner of Whitesands Bay. On the far side of the tan-coloured strand, the rocky promontory of St David's Head ran a long finger westward into the sea.

The Pembrokeshire Coast Path leads along the coast at the very edge of green and purple cliffs whose dense sandstone has fractured into slanted faces as smooth as slate.

Ramsey Island, long and low-slung with two humps of hill, lay square-on across a mile or so of very turbulent water in Ramsey Sound.

Ramsey is an RSPB reserve these days, but the old farmhouse where the Griffiths family once stuck out the tough island life still stands. From a tiny fingernail of beach at the southern end came a thin hooting. With binoculars we made out a little gathering of seal pups in white fur, nerving themselves for the short journey to the waves and their new lives as creatures of the sea.

Soon, Ramsey Island was behind us. The path led in and out of tiny coves and beaches. We skirted the slit-like inlet of Porthclais, and headed inland past the ancient Chapel of St Non, mother of St David, with the last of the daylight transferring a silver sheen from the sea to the darkening sky.

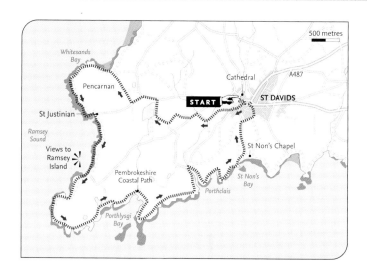

Start & finish St Davids Cathedral, Pembrokeshire SA62 6RD (OS ref SM 752254)

Walk (10 miles; easy; OS Explorer OL35): From town centre follow Goat Street ("St Justinian's"). Bear left at "Merrivale"; on down Catherine Street. Opposite Ramsey Gardens, right (749252, blue arrow) down lane. In ½ mile at road, left (743252). In 200m, right ("Ty Newydd Farm"). In 400m, right at road (737250). In 500m, left at T-junction (736254, "St Justinian"). In 500m right (731254, "Pencarnan"). At Pencarnan entrance, fork right (728258, "Public Path to Coast Path"). At coast, left on Pembrokeshire Coast Path/PCP for 6½ miles via St Justinian's (724252). Porthlysgi Bay (731238) and Porthclais (741242) to St Non's Bay (750243). Inland off PCP at kissing gate (fingerpost) past Chapel of St Non to road (752244); left for ¾ mile to St Davids.

Lunch Picnic; The Bishop's Inn, Cross Square, St Davids SA62 6SL (01437 720422, thebish.co.uk)

More information St Davids Visitor Centre (01437 720392)

SUGAR LOAF

On a still afternoon in the Brecon Beacons/Bannau Brycheiniog the Grwyne Fawr River ran dark and noisy under the single arch of Llangenny bridge. It was a stiff pull up the hill out of Llangenny, following a wet green lane full of cress and pennywort. Lost lambs scampered in front of us, calling "Ma-a-aaa!" as their mothers answered gruffly from beyond the hedges. Soon the Sugar Loaf stood ahead, a green hill rising to a broad domed top, the kind of mountain that beckons rather than threatens.

What the hell is a sugar loaf? Well, children, if you're sitting comfortably … that's how granny used to buy her sugar, in tall conical blocks with rounded tops. They came out of the moulds in the sugar factory that way; it was easier to slide the crystallized lump out of a cone than a cylinder or cube. Bingo! That simple!

Up above Cwm-cegyr – "hemlock valley" – a wide green cart track left the shelter of the larch groves and headed for the craggy summit of the Sugar Loaf. What a fabulous view from the top: the upturned longboat shapes of the Black Mountains along the northern skyline, the whaleback of Ysgyryd Fawr rising on the east, the rippling spines of the Valleys' hills in the south-west, and farther in the west the ground climbing towards the Brecon Beacons proper.

A bunch of beautiful semi-wild horses with wind-tossed manes and tails followed us off the Sugar Loaf, one cheeky fellow nibbling at Jane's hat and hair. Soon they rollicked off to a water hole, plunging their muzzles in with loud sighs of satisfaction, while we went on down through fields honeyed by the declining sun.

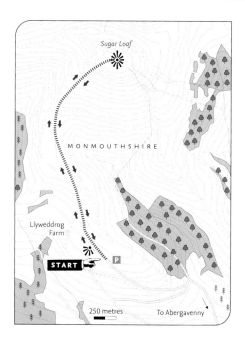

Start & finish Dragon's Head Inn, Llangenny, near Crickhowell, Powys NP8 1HD (OS ref SO240180)

Walk (6½ miles; moderate/hard; OS Explorer OL13): Cross bridge; left uphill past Pendarren gatehouse. In 150m, right ('Castell Corryn'). Ahead for 100m, over stile, left uphill to cross stile. Right (yellow arrow/YA) to stile into road (244179). Cross road; follow green lane (fingerpost, then YAs) for ¾ mile, first along lane, then with fence on left. By Cwm-cegyr, track comes in on right (254175); follow it, rising for 200m, then bearing right along fence and on uphill for ½ mile to corner of larch grove (260183). Bear right into dip; steeply uphill for 500m to where main track to Sugar Loaf crosses path (265182). Left to summit (272188). Left along ridge to end; follow broad path off ridge. In ¾ mile keep ahead (right) at fork (260190). In another 300m, fork right again. At foot of slope, follow wall to right. At bottom right corner, through gate above Gob-pwllau (blue arrow); follow stony lane through wood and on to Pengilfach (246190). Right along lane; in 50m, ahead (right) down to road (242191). Right for 350m to Tycanol (244194). Left here (fingerpost); cross 2 stiles; follow path downhill through orchard and on (YAs), taking right forks downhill to Grwyne Fawr river (238190). Left for ¾ mile to Llangenny.

Lunch Dragon's Head Inn (01873 810350) – welcoming country pub

More information Crickhowell Tourist Information Centre (01873 811970; www.visitcrickhowell.co.uk); ramblers.org.uk; satmap.com

A sunny spring afternoon over South Wales, with a blustery wind gusting along the coast of the Gower Peninsula. The view opening westward over Three Cliffs Bay had me stopped and stunned on the brink – cliffs black in shadow, mirror-grey in sunlight, with the big, squared foot of Great Tor planted solidly at the water's edge, dividing a 3-mile curve of creamy, pristine sand. The strata of the cliffs stood tilted almost vertically, as rough as the coarsest sandpaper with their coating of uncountable millions of barnacles.

Down in Pobbles Bay I crept through a wave-cut arch in the promontory, and followed the sinuous Pennard Pill stream to teeter across its precarious stepping stones. Sandy paths led round the plateau of the promontory, almost an island, of Penmaen Burrows, where the chambered cairn of Pen-y-Crug has crouched for 5,500 years, under a monstrous capstone of dully shining quartzite.

Back on the mainland I followed lanes winding inland and back towards the coast among wildflowers including the last celandines and first wild strawberry flowers. I climbed the steep sandy face of Penmaen Burrows and came to enchanted Pennard Castle looking over Three Cliffs Bay.

History says that this badly sited stronghold was smothered by blown sand in AD1300, but legend tells of a princess who came there to be married and found herself at the mercy of its drunken garrison. They also attacked fairy guests, who buried the lot in a sandstorm.

I walked the homeward path along the cliffs, looking across the Severn Sea at the blue spine of Exmoor and picturing the princess and the bullies entombed in the dunes. Or did she escape, as some tales tell, to live happily ever after with the fairies?

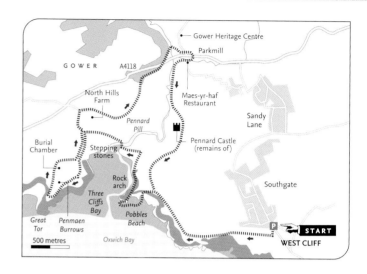

Start & finish West Cliff car park, Southgate, Gower (OS ref SS 554874)

Walk (7 miles; moderate with steep parts; OS Explorer 164): This is a low-tide walk. Set off shortly after low water. If Pobbles Beach is covered by sea, follow cliffs to Pennard Castle and return. West along cliffs for 1 mile, descend to Pobbles Beach (540878). Through rock arch; follow Pennard Pill to cross stepping stones (538883). Left up path. Near top, left (534884, "Penmaen Burrows" fingerpost) downhill, then uphill; clockwise round Penmaen Burrows; back to fingerpost. Left to T-junction (534887); right past North Hills Farm, along path to cross A4118 (542891). Up lane opposite, in 200 yards, right to re-cross A4118. Go left of Maes-yr-hâf Restaurant (545892, "Three Cliff Bay"); cross stream, right (blue arrow) through woods for ½ mile. Climb steeply to Pennard Castle (544885). Right along cliffs to car park.

Lunch Refreshments North Hills Farm shop, Gower Heritage Centre tearoom, Maes-yr-hâf Restaurant

More information www.mumblestic.co.uk; www.visitwales.co.uk; www.gowerlive.co.uk/swansea-tide-times/

YSTRADFELLTE AND NEDD FECHAN

It takes a good positive community such as tiny Ystradfellte to keep a pub, post office, church and village hall going these days in such a small and out-of-the-way place.

Down at Porth yr Ogof, unearthly groans and roars issued from a cave in which the Afon Mellte went churning and twisting invisibly through subterranean narrows. A file of youngsters in hard hats and caving overalls came up the path, grinning with excitement at what they had seen.

A narrow, stony lane, all mud and moss, led us over a green hillside and down into a parallel valley, where the Nedd Fechan River rushed beneath Pont Rhyd-y-Cnau, the "bridge at the ford of the nuts". Hazels overhung the water, but squirrels had gathered all the nuts for winter.

We walked upriver beside the Nedd Fechan, feeling its cold breath on our cheeks. The rain-swollen water hurried over rapids, fed by tributaries that tumbled down through the woods in stepped waterfalls. Pwll Du, the black pool, lay quiet, a dark silver disc in a cave mouth at the foot of a crag. We scrambled up a steep little path and teetered along at the rim of the gorge, ducking under silver birch boughs crusty with white and green lichens.

A farm track across the river led up to Cefn-ucheldref, the "back homestead", a lonely clutch of mossy ruins on the hillside. A final crossing of the Nedd Fechan and we followed an old bridleway eastwards over a sedgy upland, until the neat white houses of Ystradfellte appeared below in a twinkle of lights through the dusk.

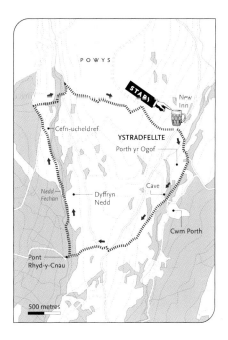

Start & finish Ystradfellte car park, Brecon Beacons CF44 9JE (OS ref: SN 930134)

Walk (6 miles; strenuous in parts; OS Explorer OL12): Right by New Inn, past church; cross river; in 200m, right (932130, stile, yellow arrow/YA). Path SSW to car park for Porth yr Ogof cave (928124; detour down to right to see cave). At road, right; just past "Cwmporth" sign, left (blue arrow) on bridleway SSW for ¾ mile to cross road into lane (919117, "Nedd Valley"). In 200m, left through gate, down steep lane to Pont Rhyd-y-Cnau bridge (912116). Don't cross; go right (north) up riverbank path. In 500m, at Pwll Du (912121), climb above pool; follow narrow upper path with fence on right (steep slope to river – take care) for 500m to cross river (912126). Track (occasional YAs) for 900m to Cefn-ucheldref ruin (909135). Right along track above; in another 350m, right (908139, unmarked track); cross river (911140); left at road above. In 200m, right (913141, gate, "Ystradfellte" fingerpost) on bridleway east across rough upland for ¾ mile to gate in angle of walls (924138); green lane to Ystradfellte.

Lunch New Inn, Ystradfellte (01639 720211, waterfallways.co.uk)

More information breconbeacons.org; visitwales.com

Sherwood Forest, Nottingham

CASTLETON AND LOSE HILL, PEAK DISTRICT

Castleton lies cradled in a natural amphitheatre of hills whose rocks are seamed with rich deposits of lead. This early in the year there were few visitors in the show caves and Blue John shops. Most folk moving in the hills around Castleton were walkers such as ourselves, only too delighted to be stretching the winter slackness away.

Below the rocky gorge of Winnats we looked back to see the black ruin of Peveril Castle perched like a raven on its crag above the huddled houses of Castleton. In the chill dark mouth of Peak Cavern, below the stronghold, once squatted a whole tribe of rope-spinners, their lungs and joints sacrificed to the dampness they needed to tease the fibres together. Lead miners lived and died in even worse case. What desperate conditions our ancestors put up with, just because they had to.

A bunch of schoolchildren were munching sandwiches at tables outside Treak Cliff Cavern. "We've done our big walk already!" they squeaked proudly. Tired? "Naah! We're going to play football when we get back to the hostel!" Outside the Treak Cliff Cavern, we crossed the bumpy old mine-spoil ground with its velvety nap below the striated cliff of Mam Tor, and went crabwise up the long slope to Hollins Cross on the ridge. Up there the wind blew at double strength, smacking and shoving us along the flagged pathway towards the big dark cliff of Back Tor. Here with a KitKat apiece we snuggled down and took in the view north up the long valley of the River Noe.

Edale village was a scatter of toy houses far below and the old start of the Pennine Way up Grindsbrook Clough cut a deep dark scar into the fellside. A step more along the ridge to the summit point of Lose Hill, and we were looking down on the glorious length of the Castleton valley – our forward view for the homeward path.

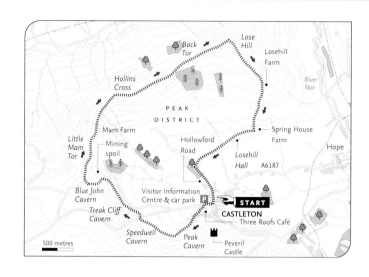

Start & finish Castleton Visitor Information Centre, Castleton S33 8WN (OS ref SK149830)

Walk (5½ miles; moderate; OS Explorer OL1): Cross road; up lane by 3 Roofs Café. At road, right (148828); uphill ("Speedwell Cavern"), then field path to cross road at Speedwell Cavern (140827). Left-hand path (yellow arrows) above Treak Cliff Cavern (136831) to Blue John Cavern (132832). Right to road; right to car park; across waste ground under Mam Tor Cliff to Mam Farm (133840); up hillside to Hollins Cross (136845); ridge to Back Tor and Lose Hill (153854). Paved path down to cross stile (155851); bear right for 100m to cross another stile; left along fence, then downhill through trees (157848). In 30m, just before fingerpost, right downhill to bypass Losehill Farm. Lane downhill to Spring House Farm. Just past house, right along lane (156840, "Castleton" fingerpost) past Losehill Hall. Where drive swings left, keep ahead through wicket gate (152838). Ahead across fields, then along lane to road (148835). Ahead into Castleton.

Lunch Picnic on Back Tor

More information Castleton Visitor Information Centre (01629 816572; peakdistrict.gov.uk); peak-experience.org.uk; ramblers.org. uk; Peak District walking festivals: www.visitpeakdistrict.com/ walkingfestivals

DERWENT EDGE AND LADYBOWER RESERVOIR

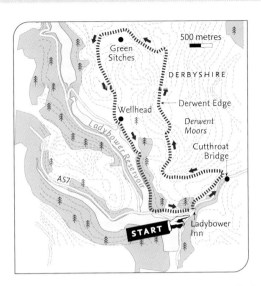

It was one of those Peak District days you can only dream of: a gauzy blur of sunlight over moors and pastures, enough bite in the wind to fill the blood with oxygen. "I've been absolutely longing for this," Jane said, looking up at the Derwent Moors, "a day up somewhere high and wild."

The broad moor paths glittered with mica, their sandy gritstone pebbles rumbling quietly under our boots as we climbed to Whinstone Lee gap and a most stupendous view up Ladybower Reservoir. The wind blew like a mad thing, making the tears fly from our eyes as we followed a dark stone wall north towards the tors of Derwent Edge. Wheel Stones and White Tor, they stood out in drama on the skyline, piled towers of rocks shaped and slit by wind and frost. Climbing across Access Land up to the Edge tested our leg muscles and lungs, but once up there in the wind and sun we grinned like fools at a 30-mile view streaming away in all directions.

A paved path led north up the length of Derwent Edge and we followed it past the outcrop of Dovestone Tor. Beyond stood the Cakes of Bread, flat folds of stone like giant piles of pancakes. It was quite a wrench to leave these outlandish stones, but a great wide moor was beckoning to the northwest.

The moors are the antithesis of virgin country. The hand of Man lies emphatically on them. Through deforestation, sheep grazing, mining and abandonment they have been stripped to the barest of elements – heather, moor grass, rock, water. By rights they should be dismal, frightening places. But for a walker in search of absolutely nothing between him and his maker, they are sublime. Descending the lane to Ladybower Reservoir and the long walk home, I felt like a man in the company of friends.

Start & finish Ladybower Inn, Ladybower Reservoir, Bamford S33 0AX (OS ref SK205865). NB Please ask permission to park, and give the inn your custom

Walk (9 miles; hard; OS Explorer OL1): From Ladybower Inn climb steep path to north-east. At top of incline, don't fork left; keep ahead, to descend almost to A57 at Cutthroat Bridge (213875). Turn left uphill, then left (west) along bridleway for 1 mile to Whinstone Lee gap (198874). Path splits in 5 here; take marked bridleway to right of National Trust "Whinstone Lee Fields" sign, following wall north along fell side. In 3/4 mile pass "Derwent, Moscar" sign (198884); aim half right uphill across trackless Access Land to White Tor on ridge (198888). Left along ridge track for 1 1/3 miles by Dovestone Tor to Bradfield Gate Head. 200m before trig pillar on Back Tor, left at stone marker pillar (198907) on stony path going NW over moor. In 1 mile (185912) join wide grassy track on Green Sitches. Go through ruined wall; in 100m fork left (182911); almost immediately left again, aiming for fingerpost (180905). Follow "Ladybower" and "Footpath" fingerposts, with tumbled wall as guide, past plantation (182903) and on for 3/4 mile to Lanehead Farm (184892). Descend (yellow arrow) to road at Wellhead (184887). Left on lakeside track for 1 2/3 miles to bridge (195865). Left fork uphill between houses becomes hillside track, descending to Ladybower Inn.

Lunch Ladybower Inn (01433 651241, ladybower-inn.co.uk) or picnic on Derwent Edge

More information www.visitpeakdistrict.com/walkingfestivals; ramblers.org.uk

GOYT VALLEY, ERRWOOD HALL AND SHINING TOR

The Goyt Valley lies just west of Buxton, a north–south cleft in the moors, tree-shaded and floored with two long and gracefully shaped reservoirs. A skein of paths leads along the River Goyt and up to the moors that stretch away on either hand.

The humpback packhorse bridge that spans the river below Goyt's Clough Quarry stands witness to the importance of the valley as a crossing point for goods in times gone by.

We climbed a stony track that steepened beside a tumbledown wall, its stones sparkling with mica in the sunshine. Up at the crest a thoroughly trodden path led to the summit of Shining Tor and a tremendous view – west over a hazy Manchester to vague mountain outlines towards the Clwydian Range in Wales, east over waves of Peak District heights, further south to the sharp shark's tooth of Shutlingsloe.

Now came a couple of miles of heavenly ridge walking, going north along an airy saddleback by way of Cats Tor where the brilliantly coloured bow shapes of paraglider sails appeared suddenly from below as though magically conjured out of the hill.

At Pym Chair (named after a highwayman said to have lain in wait hereabouts for unwary wayfarers), we turned down the road and back into the Goyt Valley along the slopes of the Errwood estate.

We descended the slopes, plucking and eating ripe bilberries till our hands were red. The ruin of Errwood Hall stood forlorn above a stream, a run of Italianate arches hinting at its former glories.

Here we picked a handful of wild strawberries and savoured their sweet bursts of flavour one by one as we followed the riverside path back down the Goyt Valley.

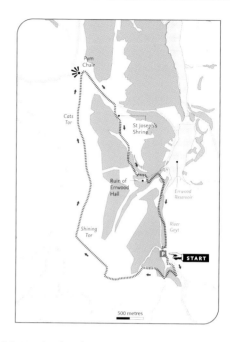

Start & finish Goyt's Clough Quarry car park, near Buxton, Derbyshire SK17 6TT approx. (OS ref SK 011734)

Walk (7½ miles; moderate; OS Explorer OL24): From Goyt's Clough Quarry/GCQ, right along road. In 150m, right past wooden barrier; bear left through old quarry on track above road. At 3-finger post, right (014730, "Stakeside") through wood. Follow "Shining Tor" signs up to stile at crest (000730). Right; in 250m, left (001731, fingerpost) to Shining Tor (995738). Right along ridge for nearly 2 miles to Pym Chair (996767). Right on path beside road. In ½ mile, right (002761, "Errwood" fingerpost); follow "Errwood" past chapel (002759) and on. In ¾ mile, right in valley (006749, "Errwood"), then left before bridge ("Errwood Hall"). At Hall, follow path passing below ruin; in 50m, left down steps (008747); left along lower drive with river on right. In 400m pass metal barrier and "Errwood Hall" sign (010748); right on cobbled path, following "GCQ". In 650m cross road (011741); follow "Riverside Path". In 750m path climbs to road (011735); right to GCQ.

Lunch Picnic

More information Buxton Tourist Information Centre (01298 25106); visitpeakdistrict.com

In 1932 working-class youngsters from depression-hit Manchester and Sheffield, frustrated at being barred from the privately owned countryside around the cities, staged a Mass Trespass up to the great moorland plateau and gritstone crags of Kinder. On a lovely crisp morning we went up the narrow road from Bowden Bridge with Kinder Edge in our sights and these young heroes on our minds.

The long path up to the moor led us above Kinder Reservoir, through the heather and bilberries of White Brow, then steeply up the rocky cleft of William Clough, whose beck sluiced in cataracts over the boulders. The full sweep of Kinder Edge stood out to the east, a sharply cut skyline of dark rock outcrops traversed by diminutive figures of walkers.

From Ashop Head we climbed to the long escarpment of Kinder Edge and followed it for mile after mile, the wind nudging us, the gritstone crunching under our boots, looking out over a magnificent view to Manchester and the far hills of Wales. The rock outcrops had been cut and smoothed by wind and weather into multiple shapes: shark fins, dog heads, ogre noses.

We picnicked on a rock beside the trickling river at the head of the cleft of Kinder Downfall and went on to where the Pennine Way fell away east towards its starting point at Edale. A good long stare down the delectable green Vale of Edale and we were trudging westward down an endless lane home, thankful to those hearty lads and lasses from long ago whose bold law-breaking laid the foundations for today's Right to Roam over these moorlands and mountains.

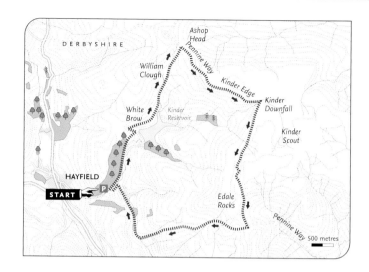

Start & finish Bowden Bridge car park, Hayfield, Derbyshire SK22 2LH (approx. OS ref SK 049870)

Walk (9 miles; strenuous; OS Explorer OL1): Continue up road. At Booth Sheepwash, cross river (051876); in 100m, take path (yellow arrow). In 250m, left to reservoir gates; up cobbled bridleway on left. In 300m, left (054882, "bridleway" sign) up to gate. Right ("Snake Inn") for 1½ miles (White Brow, William Clough) up to Ashop Head (065900). Right on Pennine Way (PW) along Kinder Edge for 3½ miles. Beyond Edale Rocks, where PW turns left for Edale, right (081861) through gate; lane for 2¾ miles down to Kinder Road and car park.

Lunch Sportsman Inn, Kinder Road SK22 2LE (01663 741565)

More information Kinder Scout mass trespass walk, nationaltrust.org.uk; visitengland.com; satmap.com; ramblers.org.uk

MILLER'S DALE AND HIGH DALE

I don't walk with my geologist godson as often as I'd like, but when I do he opens a window onto the hidden but wonderful world of what lies underground. On this hot summer's day on the White Peak it was all about limestone.

A lung-busting flight of steps lifted us through the trees and out of Miller's Dale into an upland of cattle grazing and stone walls. "Ah, a productid," said Andy, pointing to the wall of Lydgate farmhouse where the edge of a fossil shell stood slightly proud of the stone. "A creature with a hinged shell that lived buried in the seabed mud and let its feeding tendrils trail out to grab any food that passed." I ran my fingers across the shell and tried to imagine the immensities of time and circumstance between that form of life and my own.

We crossed the walled fields to walk between the grassy jaws of High Dale, a little narrow valley between high folds of ground. I asked my godson what formed this deep cleft. "A stream underground excavated a cave in the porous limestone, digging away till the roof collapsed into the bottom."

A steep path led down to the old cycle path in the shadows of Miller's Dale. On a cutting wall I put my hand on an enormous dark stain splashing the red and white limestone. "That's what happens when giant land masses collide and the seabed gets ripped apart," my godson told me. "Superheated magma came gushing out into the cold water and cooled instantly into this tongue of volcanic rock. It happened maybe 350 million years ago, and it's still here."

What a remarkable thought to carry away from this really magical walk.

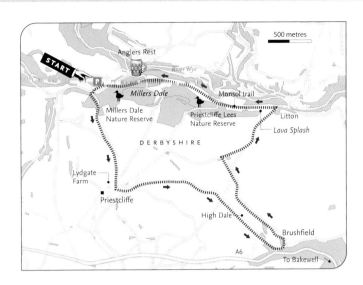

Start & finish Miller's Dale car park, Wormhill, Buxton SK17 8SN (OS ref SK 138732)

Walk (5 miles; moderate; OS Explorer 149): From car park entrance, right under railway bridge. Right on B6049; in 50m, left up path (137731, fingerpost); in 100m, right up steep steps to gate at top (138728). Across fields; walled lane (139726) to Lydgate Farm (140721). Left ("Brushfield"); in 40m, fork right by cottage (gate). At T-junction left (142721); in 100m, right (wall stile, yellow arrow/YA) across fields and through High Dale. In 1 mile at SE end of dale, through gate (156715); fork left uphill on road. At Brushfield follow "Priestcliffe" and "Miller's Dale". Follow stony lane for ¾ mile to T-junction (152724); right ("Priestcliffe Lees Nature Reserve", YA). Across field; bear left down steep path into Miller's Dale. Left along Monsal Trail (158729). In 1 mile, just before viaduct, fingerpost (142732, "Lime kilns"). Return to Monsal Trail; left across viaduct to car park.

Lunch Anglers Rest, Miller's Dale SK17 8SN (01298 871323, anglersrestmillersdale.co.uk)

More information visitpeakdistrict.com

BURROUGH HILL, LITTLE DALBY ESTATE AND SOMERBY

The track to Burrough Hill ran through pastures corrugated by medieval ridge and furrow and nibbled to billiard-table smoothness by sheep.

The ramparts of Burrough Hill's splendid Iron Age hillfort stood ahead, an undulating line of turf-covered stone whose hollows spoke of millennia of weathering, trampling and quarrying. We walked the circuit, pausing at the topograph to spy out the hazy towers of Leicester, the red-brick smear of Melton Mowbray and the charmingly named Robin-a-Tiptoe Hill.

The path led steeply down the north face of the fort, and on through the cool avenue of ash and beech in Rise Hill Spinney. A seat placed for the northward view was presented by two foresters, Jack Atton and Terry Darby, who spent nearly 20 years in the 1980s and 1990s planting the trees that now cover these hillsides.

Turning south, we followed the Leicestershire Round long-distance path through the parkland of the Little Dalby Estate, looking back to where Little Dalby Hall peeped from a collar of trees. A short, sharp climb led to uplands characteristic of these Leicestershire wolds, broad cornfields and plough, the hedges dotted with pink spindle berries, where the dip and roll of the land hid the nearby fort on Burrough Hill.

Beyond Somerby we skirted the rim of a dry valley where ridge-and-furrow corrugations plunged down the flanks, testament to the exploitation of every bit of land by our hungry medieval ancestors. Under a pearly evening sky we made for the ramparts of Burrough Hill, now in full view ahead once more. The homeward path skirted the hillfort, a green track through thickets of gorse above which rooks flocked on their homeward flight.

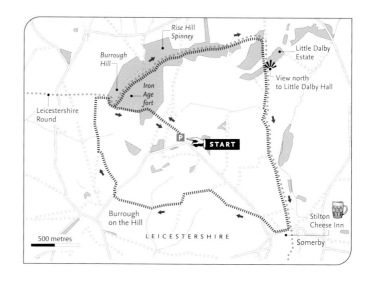

Start & finish Burrough Hill car park, Burrough Road, Somerby, Leicestershire LE14 2QZ (OS ref SK 766115)

Walk (6 miles; easy; OS Explorer 246): Up signed track to Burrough Hill. Clockwise round ramparts via topograph. At north side near cut tree trunks (761121), descend past yellow-topped post/YTP to gate (763122, YTP, yellow arrow/YA) and on. In 450m, ahead through wood (767124, "Leicestershire Round"/LR). In just under ¾ mile, at T-junction, right (775126, "Dalby Hill Path") and follow YTPs. In 300m, up steps (775123); diagonally across field; follow LR/YTPs for 1 mile to road in Somerby (778106). Right; in 200m, right (776105, "The Field") to cross road (775107). On across fields ("Public footpath to Borough on the Hill"). In 400m, at kissing gate, right (771108); follow fence on your right (YAs) round the top of the dry valley. Descend to cross the stream (763107); aim for the pole on the knoll, then to the left of the house with the prominent window. Right at road (758109); in 50m, left (YTPs) across fields. In ¾ mile at YTP with LR arrows (756119), right past Burrough Hill to car park.

Lunch The Stilton Cheese Inn, Somerby (01664 454394, stiltoncheeseinn.co.uk)

More information leicscountryparks.org.uk

HOBY, GADDESBY AND FRISBY-ON-THE-WREAKE

A cool morning above the Leicestershire Wolds, and neighbourly conversations developing over the garden fences of Hoby. The village, perched on a ridge overlooking the valley of the River Wreake, trails its mellow red-brick buildings along a street as bendy as the snaking meanders of the river through the meadows below.

I followed a path beside the Wreake, passing the handsome square tower of All Saints Church at Rotherby, and then the crocketed spire of Brooksby's Church of St Michael – just two of the dozens of churches on the Leicestershire Wolds built and embellished by medieval wool wealth.

This is long rolling country, with shallow descents to gravelly rivers and gradual climb to the next ridge where we had long views over mile upon mile of cornfields. The stony track of the Midshires Way ran south past a sand and gravel quarry, the conveyors and elevators dribbling their loads onto ever-growing cones of pinkish diggings. On the opposite side of the track an old quarry flooded for nature conservation showed the other side of the extraction coin with its sailing mallards and reedbeds a-chatter with warblers.

At Gaddesby we detoured to St Luke's Church, where a line of gurning little faces looked down from the wall, some medieval stone-carver's humour that spanned the ages. Then we were heading north over the undulating corn fields on the Leicestershire Round footpath.

In Frisby-on-the-Wreake we passed the stump of the old preaching cross and found the homeward path across the ridge and furrow pasture. In the willows by the river cattle sheltered from the hot afternoon sun, and a cream-coloured bull exchanged loving nose-licks with his dappled grey bride-of-the-moment.

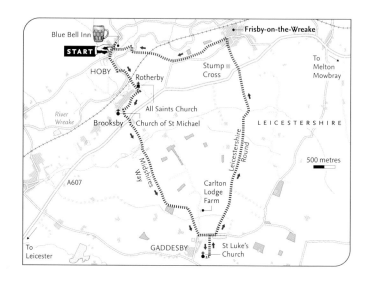

Start & finish Blue Bell Inn, Hoby, Melton Mowbray LE14 3DT (OS ref SK 670175)

Walk (8½ miles; easy; OS Explorer 246): From Blue Bell Inn, left along village street. In 200m, right ("Brooksby"); in 50m, left (kissing gate, "Rotherby"). Path between cottages and river; cross river (671169); cross railway to road at Rotherby church (675165). Right to Brooksby; left at road (672161). Cross A607 (671359) and on, following Midshires Way (yellow arrows/YAs and yellow topped posts/YTPs). In 1½ miles, approaching Carlton Lodge Farm, right (686141, stile, YTP) across fields to road (689135). Cross into Pasture Lane. In 300m, just beyond Rose Cottage driveway, left through hedge (692135, "Frisby on the Wreake", YTP). Follow Leicestershire Round/LR for 2¾ miles to road in Frisby-on-the-Wreake (694175). Right; fork left to corner of Main Street and Water Lane (694177). Right; follow LR for nearly 1 mile to corner of Rotherby Lane (682171). Fork right off LR, on path aiming for Hoby Church. Cross railway (677133), then river; follow LR into Hoby.

Lunch Blue Bell Inn, Hoby (01664 434247, sites.google.com/site/bluebellhoby)

More information Melton Mowbray Tourist Information Centre (01664 480992)

HUNGARTON

Early morning in the Leicestershire Wolds, I slipped out of Hungarton past grazing horses and over a kale field, my boots already clotted with dark clay soil. Sheep came running up to lick my fingers with their stiff tongues and butt my knees gently with their woolly foreheads.

The 15th-century moated manor of Ingarsby Old Hall, presides in isolation over a field of hummocks and hollows, seamed across with deep old trackways – all that's left of the deserted village of Ingarsby, the property of the canons of Leicester Abbey in medieval times.

Ingarsby is one of half a dozen abandoned medieval villages in this rolling corner of Leicestershire. From Ingarsby I followed a slowly plodding horse across fields trenched with the ridge and furrow of strip farming, up to Quenby Hall. This magnificent red-brick Jacobean pile, a palace in the wolds, is a more showy order of architecture than the domestic enclave of Old Ingarsby. The village of Quenby lay reduced to a patch of ridge and furrow in the smooth, lawn-like parkland. Beyond, the abandoned settlement of Cold Newton echoed the Ingarsby model, all slopes, humps and slanting house platforms.

I followed the gentle green valley of the Queniborough Brook. A bedlam of cawing from the rookery in Carr Bridge Spinney; the handsome pale stone Baggrave Hall on a knoll above its still lake. The park still carried faint ridges of the vanished fields of Baggrave village. There is deep poignancy in such landscapes. But the well-laid hedges around Waterloo Lodge Farm, and the beautifully looked-after sheep in the homeward fields, were proof that not all the old agricultural traditions are gone from this countryside.

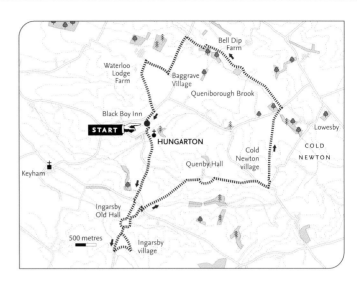

Start & finish Black Boy Inn, Hungarton, LE7 9JR (OS ref SK690075)

Walk (8½ miles; moderate; OS Explorer 233): From Inn, follow main street south. Left along Church Lane; follow path to road (691066). Ahead to T-junction (688059). Ahead over fields (fingerposts, stiles, yellow posts/YP). Cross brook (686055); bear right for 50m (yellow arrow/YA), then left (YP, YA) over stile. Follow YA through farmyard to road (686054). Right past Ingarsby Old Hall. Just before bridge, left (684050, fingerpost, YP) through Ingarsby deserted village. Aim for tree on skyline; left here to road by Old Hall (685053). Forward for ½ mile to cross road (689058, YP); follow bridleway for 1½ miles, up field slopes (YPs), passing right of Quenby Hall and following drive to road (713064). Right; first left ("Lowesby"); fork left past cottage, through gate (YA), through Cold Newton deserted village. Through gate at bottom of slope (716067); follow YPs north beside stream. In 300m, look for YP and YA on right. Cross stream; in 150m don't recross brook where blue arrow indicates (716072), but keep ahead (YA). In 200m, left across stream (YA); right to road (717077). Right; in 150m, left (YA) up right bank of Queniborough Brook for ¾ mile (YAs, YPs). At corner of Carr Bridge Spinney (708086), YA points left downhill to cross brook; don't take this! Instead, keep on right side of brook and go ahead through hedge opposite (YP) and on. In ⅓ mile, cross track to Bell Dip Farm (704089). In corner of next field, left over stile (YA) to cross brook. Right along far bank (YA) to road (698091). Left past Baggrave Hall. At top of rise, right (695085; "bridleway") up Waterloo Lodge Farm drive. Just before farm, left over stile (690087; YP). Aim for far left corner of field; over stile in hedge (YA, YP); aim left of buildings; follow YPs to cross drive (691079). Diagonally left across field to road (692077); right to Black Boy Inn.

A late winter sky of chilly blue lay over Northamptonshire, lending a glow to the deep orange ironstone of Badby's houses. Mention of the River Nene usually brings to mind an image of the broad, mud-choked tideway that empties into the Wash, but here, a hundred miles away, the Nene crawls below overshot willows, an infant stream narrow enough to jump across.

Trees shaded the golden houses of Newnham along the village green. The path ran through the churchyard where the arcaded memorial to Eric Newzam Nicholson of the 12th Lancers stood wrapped in creepers and ivy tendrils, looking out of its thicket over classic English countryside of sheep pastures corrugated by medieval ploughing, wooded ridges and well-laid hedges. Rooks cawed in the oaks around the farming enclave of Little Everdon with its handsome buttery gold houses.

There were big views all round from the summit of Everdon Hill. Storm-battered cedars and wide gleams of water heralded Fawsley Park, the two slender arms of its man-made lake cradling the estate church on a knoll – another dream of settled tranquillity in the heart of England.

The peaceful woods of the Fawsley Estate provided a refuge and haven for Joseph Merrick, the Elephant Man, during the late 1880s, in the last stages of the mysterious affliction that grotesquely distorted his face and body. Travelling from London in a private railway carriage to avoid the public consternation caused by his physical appearance, Merrick stayed in the gamekeeper's cottage as the guest of Lady Louisa Knightley. Walking back to Badby we pictured the outcast man in these bluebell woods, free to stroll among the trees, pick flowers and feel at ease for the only time in his life.

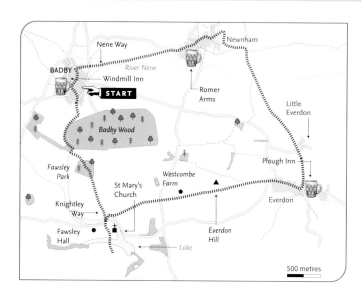

Start & finish Windmill Inn, Badby, Northamptonshire NN11 3AN (OS ref SP559589)

Walk (7½ miles; easy; OS Explorer 207): From Windmill Inn, left through Badby. Opposite Maltsters Inn, right down Court Yard Lane (560592). Follow well waymarked Nene Way for 3 miles via Newnham to road at Little Everdon (594580). Forward; in 150m Nene Way goes left (595579), but keep ahead on road to Everdon, past church and on. At top of village, left ("Fawsley"). In 100m, right (590576; fingerpost, black arrow/BLA); follow BLAs for 1 mile to cross road near Westcombe Farm (573573). Through gate, up field to gate (570572); follow BLAs to road (566570). Right, round bend to Fawsley Church (565568); return to bend; left on Knightley Way (KW). Follow KW for 1 mile through Fawsley Park and inside west edge of Badby Wood (559580). Leaving wood (559584), aim diagonally right across field; follow KW to Badby Church (560587). Right to Windmill Inn.

Lunch Romer Arms, Newnham NN11 3HB (01327 705416); Plough Inn, Everdon NN11 3BL (01327 361606, theploughinneverdon.com); Windmill Inn, Badby NN11 3AN (01327 311070)

More information Daventry Tourist Information Centre (01327 300277); satmap.com; ramblers.org.uk

When the National Trust took over Canons Ashby in 1981, the Tudor country house in gently rolling Northamptonshire countryside was a wreck, its gardens run wild. Such decay was hard to imagine on this brisk spring day with volunteers tending the tulip beds and topiary in the immaculate gardens, and others ready to fill in the story of the ironstone house and its dark panelled rooms gathered tightly round a tall courtyard.

At South West Farm a couple of guinea fowl went scuttling across the road with their characteristically furtive air, hunched down in spotted cloaks of feathers as though guilty of some misdoing.

The trees around the priory fishponds were loud with birdsong – chaffinches, blackbirds, great tits, blackcaps and song thrushes giving it their best springtime chorus. The path led round the margins of enormous fields of wheat. In their hedges white blossom of sloe and pink of crab apple gave promise of a fruitful autumn six months hence.

Up on the crest of the land we turned along a ridge road with long views over the plough-striped undulations of the countryside. The verges of the road were lined with trees, wide grassy strips that told of past animal droving.

Oxford Lane, our return route to Canons Ashby, was another broad green highway. The old green road has lost its easterly hedge to modern farming. The soil of the wheatfields that bordered it was thick with flint, chert, fossil shells and pebbles rolled smooth and round by some great prehistoric river.

Bluebells hazed the ground under the larches, pink bonnets of milkmaids spattered the damp ditches, and a few early bees went buzzing among the white blackthorn blossom.

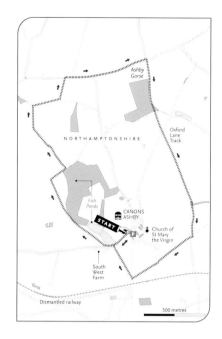

Start & finish Canons Ashby house, near Daventry, Northamptonshire NN11 3SD (OS ref SP 577505); National Trust pay car park; limited parking also available at the church

Walk (5 miles; easy; OS Explorer 206): From car park, right down road. Just past South West Farm, right (573503, fingerpost) on field path, following arrows. In ¾ mile, at "Private" notice (568512), left along farm track, then hedgeside track. In ½ mile at oak tree with arrows (564519), right with hedge on right. In 400m left up hedge (568520) to road (568521). Right; in just under ¾ mile, opposite road on left, right down Oxford Lane hedged track (578525, "Byway, Macmillan Way"/MW). In ½ mile MW bears right (580516), but keep ahead. In ½ mile cross road (584508) and on. In 400m right (584504, gate, arrow); half left across pastures till right-hand hedge meets fence (579501). Through 3 kissing gates, across footbridge; on across field to cross road (577499, fingerpost). Field path to road at South West Farm (574503); right to car park.

Lunch Crown Inn, Weston NN12 8PX (01295 760310, thecrownweston.co.uk); NT tea room at Canons Ashby

More information nationaltrust.org.uk

WADENHOE

We left the pale limestone walls and thatched roofs of Wadenhoe, climbing gently from the valley of the River Nene into pastures of medieval ridge and furrow cropped by fat ginger-coated bullocks. A pair of red kites circled overhead. Along an old trackway we fingered the pink leaves of blackthorn bushes whose sloes hung in thick dark clusters, ripe for the gin bottle.

Through Lilford Wood on a speckled carpet of brown and yellow elm leaves to a view at the far end across a ploughed field to the stone shell of Lyveden New Bield, Sir Thomas Tresham's never-completed dream of a country lodge. Tresham, a staunch and devout Catholic, died in 1605, shortly before his son Francis became embroiled in the Gunpowder Plot. Disgrace and financial ruin followed for the family, and the unfinished lodge (a mansion in all but name) and its adjacent pleasure gardens were left to fall into decay.

Lyveden New Bield has been preserved and its grounds restored by the National Trust. We explored the eerie hollow skeleton of the lodge, with its fine carvings of discreetly placed Catholic symbols, and climbed the moated mound behind for a view over the whole fantasy landscape. Then we took the homeward path through Lady Wood, where the wonderfully distorted limbs of ancient oak trees held up a canopy of quince-coloured leaves.

Long-tailed tits and siskins thronged the trees down by the River Nene, feasting among the seed cones of alders. We spotted a marsh tit, a rare sighting and a delight. And in the recesses of Wadenhoe's box-backed church I found an old friend of ours – the Green Man, carved by some anonymous medieval mason seven centuries ago, hiding in the shadows with a secret smile.

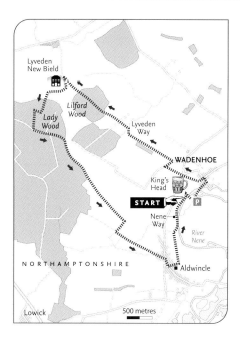

Start & finish Village hall car park, Wadenhoe, Northamptonshire PE8 5ST (OS ref TL 011833)

Walk (8½ miles; easy; OS Explorer 224): From car park back up village street to the top; turn left and follow waymarked Lyveden Way/LW for 2½ miles to Lyveden New Bield (984853). Continue following LW for ½ mile to edge of Lady Wood (980850). Right; in 100m, left off LW into wood. Pass picnic tables; path south through wood for 300m to junction. Right to observation tower (978848); left to meet LW at wood bottom (978844). Left along LW for 1½ miles to pass brambly, iron-fenced pond on left in a field (993830). In another 400m, LW goes left at green lane (996827), but you turn right along lane. In 300m, left (994825) on field path to Aldwincle. At main village road, right (004820); in 200m, left ("Nene Way" fingerpost) across paddock. In 200m, left at field edge (007820) on Nene Way to Wadenhoe.

Lunch National Trust café at Lyveden New Bield; King's Head pub, Wadenhoe (01832 720024, wadenhoekingshead.co.uk)

More information Lyveden New Bield, 01832 205158; nationaltrust.org.uk; visitengland.com; satmap.com; ramblers.org.uk

CLUMBER PARK

Henry Douglas, 7th Duke of Newcastle-under-Lyme, founded the Chapel of St Mary the Virgin by the lake at his family seat of Clumber in 1889. The church of deep pink sandstone stands as tall and elegant as many a cathedral, full of glorious stained glass by Charles Kempe, delicate wood carving and stone demons.

It was the 2nd Duke, handsome Henry Pelham-Clinton, who poured his money into landscaping Clumber Park and creating its great serpentine lake in the mid-18th century. We walked the lake as far as the dock where the 4th Duke once kept a miniature frigate, with a sailor employed full-time to tend it. The path looped inland and back to the water, where tufted ducks sailed with brilliant white flanks and intense golden eyes. A mother coot scooped seeds from the lake surface to feed her tiny, scarlet-faced chick, beak tip to beak tip.

Beyond the lake we turned off across a belt of heather, broom and silver birch – a wild contrast to the neatly contrived artificiality of the landscaped park. A bridleway led through the birch and pine of Hardwick Wood to the outskirts of Hardwick, built as an estate village for the park, its cottages with steep ornamental gables and giant chimney stacks. In the E-shaped yard of the model farm a peep through a chink in a barn door disclosed a collection of beautiful old agricultural wagons in the gloom.

A long stretch by the southern shore of the lake, looking across to the chapel spire, and we were crossing the Palladian arches of Clumber Bridge. Coots sat tight on their domed nests in the shallows, and a duck of mixed parentage submerged its head ecstatically in the lake, sending showers of diamond droplets flying in all directions.

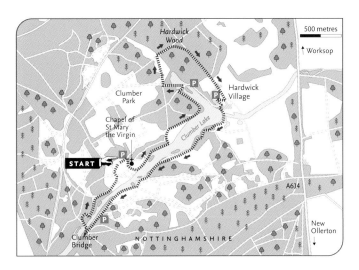

Start & finish Clumber Park main car park, near Worksop, Nottinghamshire S80 3AZ (OS ref SK625746)

Walk (6 miles; easy; OS Explorer 270): From car park follow "chapel". From chapel (627746), left along lakeside path. At Boat House dock, left (632748), heading north close to fence. In 150m, right through stone gateway; pass gate on right; at pair of stone gateposts, right on gravel path. At "In The Wood" info board (633755), right across neck of lake, then left along causeway road. In 300m beyond lake, right off road (631756, "16" marker on left side of turning) on gravel path. In 400m, right along road (630759); in 200m, right ("Bridleway") on bridleway. At road (634760), right into and through Hardwick. At T-junction, right (639754); opposite farmyard, left past log barrier and National Trust "no parking" sign ("Route 5"). In 50m, left across water (639752); follow path along south side of Clumber Lake. In 1¼ miles, meet road at a car park (623740); continue along road. In 300m, right across Clumber Bridge (621738). Fork right along road. In 150m, right past log barrier on woodland path. At road with barrier, right to car park.

Lunch Clumber Park tearooms

More information Clumber Park (01909 544917, nationaltrust.org.uk/clumber-park); experiencenottinghamshire.com; satmap.com; ramblers.org.uk

SHERWOOD AND BUDBY FORESTS

Dozens of young Robin Hoods in Lincoln green hats were dashing about with bows and arrows, shooting the tree trunks in the outskirts of Sherwood Forest. A fair number of them made it as far as the Major Oak, but once past this colossal thousand-year-old veteran, the clamour of young voices fell behind.

The wide woodland track of Robin Hood Way took us west through the heart of Sherwood Forest, where immensely distorted and swollen old oaks raised arthritic limbs in the shadows. These tremendously characterful trees owe their survival to their imperfections. Had they stood straighter and taller, they would have been cut down for timber long ago.

When medieval fugitives from justice such as Robyn Hode hid out in Sherwood, the Forest was 100 times its current size and covered 150 square miles of country. Nowadays it all fits comfortably into two square miles. Somewhere toward the middle we found the Centre Tree and turned north along a grassy bridleway into Sherwood's northerly neighbour, Budby Forest. Here the trees opened out into a broad heathland of golden bracken and purple heather.

The track swung south again through a stretch of wood pasture grazed by long-horned cattle with chocolate-brown coats and white streaks up their backs, a stylish combination. We stopped to admire their sleepy stolidity, and reckoned that the Merry Men would have been exceptionally pleased to encounter such slow-moving lunches on the hoof. Hollywood has dandified the doings of such as Robyn Hode, but the life of a Sherwood Forest outlaw must have been pretty tough. You had to grab your opportunities when every man's hand was against you.

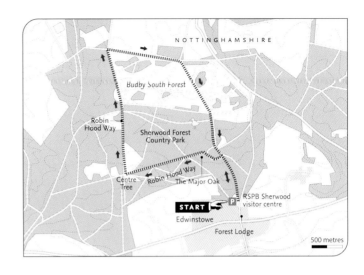

Start & finish Sherwood Forest Visitor Centre, Edwinstowe, Nottinghamshire NG21 9HN (OS ref SK627677)

Walk (5 miles; good forest tracks; OS Explorer 149): From Visitor Centre, follow signposted Major Oak walk. Just beyond Major Oak, fork left (not through gate) and follow Robin Hood Way/RHW green arrows. In ¾ mile at Centre Tree, right (607676, "public bridleway") on RHW for 1¼ miles. At crossing with 7-finger post, right (604695, "Budby"). In ¾ mile at crossing (616694), right through kissing gate; fork left on grassy bridleway for 1 mile. At bird table on left (622680), left to Visitor Centre.

Lunch Forest Lodge, Edwinstowe NG21 9QA (01623 824443; forestlodgehotel.co.uk)

More information Sherwood Forest Visitor Centre (01623 823202; nottinghamshire.gov.uk); experiencenottinghamshire.com; satmap.com; ramblers.org.uk

SILVERHILL WOOD AND PLEASLEY PIT

At the summit of the hill in Silverhill Wood Country Park, we came to a seated figure in bronze, a miner in helmet and pit boots, holding up his Davy lamp and scanning it for signs of gas. It was the only clue that beneath the woodland and the hill itself lay the pit heap of Silverwood Colliery, one of 75 Nottinghamshire coal mines now closed but commemorated on a plaque below the statue.

Nottinghamshire county council has done wonders hereabouts, greening the area's colliery sites, turning slagheaps into woods and industrial railways into multi-user paths. The hill summit at Silverhill Wood is said to be the highest point in Nottinghamshire at 672ft (205m), a claim fiercely contested by several other "highest points" locally.

Standing beside the bronze miner we saw Lincoln Cathedral's towers 30 miles away on the eastern skyline, the crooked spire at Chesterfield and the outline of Bolsover Castle to the north, and north-east the slim chimney at Pleasley Pit, our next aiming point on this walk.

At the bottom of the hill we found the Teversal Track, an old railway in a tunnel of large oak, ash and beech, with views out into a landscape of dip and roll. A tremendously tall embankment crossed the tiny wriggling stream called Merril Sick, beyond which the old line came to Pleasley Pit, closed in 1986 and now a country park and mining museum.

A right-angle of two old railways led homeward through more gently rolling countryside. The wind stripped lemon-yellow leaves from the trackside hazels and laid them on the path. We landed back at Silverhill Wood aware as never before of the roadways, levels and shafts hidden silent and abandoned under these fields and hills.

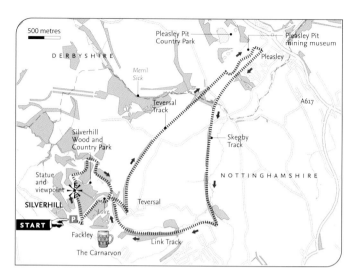

Start & finish Silverhill Wood Country Park car park, Silverhill Road, Fackley, Nottinghamshire NG17 3JL (OS ref SK 470616)

Walk (8 miles; easy; OS Explorer 269): From side of car park furthest from entrance, follow path. In 100m, left past info board, uphill to miner's statue (471621). Down steps, left along trail. In nearly 1 mile pass between lakes (477620). Left beside lake to Teversal Track (480617, "Pleasley 2 miles"). Left for 1¾ miles to T-junction at "Pleasley Country Park" sign (495640). Right to Pleasley Pit museum (499643). Through car park; left along Pit Lane; in 100m, right along Skegby Track (501643). In a little over 2 miles at "Skegby Track" sign, right (494616) onto Link Track (sign). In 1 mile at "Silverhill" sign (479615) keep ahead and fork right on narrow path to road (478616). Dogleg left/right over barrier into Silverhill Wood Country Park. In 400m left at lakes; left (477620) back to car park.

Lunch The Carnarvon, Fackley Road, NG17 3JA (01623 559676, thecarnarvon.co.uk)

More information nottinghamshire.gov.uk; pleasleypittrust.org.uk

HAMBLETON PENINSULA

Upper Hambleton stood high and handsome on its green ridge this autumn morning, its rosy stone houses glowing in clear sunshine under a china-blue sky. It was the village's hilltop position that saved it when the Gwash Valley was flooded in the 1970s to create the giant man-made lake of Rutland Water.

Ever-expanding Peterborough's thirst for fresh water saw the villages of Middle and Nether Hambleton drowned beneath the reservoir's rising waters, but their elevated neighbour escaped the tide. Now Upper Hambleton sits in solo splendour across the neck of a long peninsula extending into the great sheet of water that lies at the heart of Britain's smallest county.

We found a pathway down to the water's edge below the village and followed a gravelled track where cyclists and pedestrians share access along the northern shore of the peninsula. The far shore, a smother of trees, was splashed beautifully in scarlet, gold and green.

The track wound along the lake shore through the skirts of Armley Wood, where ash, oak and hazel leaves filtered the sunlight into translucent shards of lime and lemon. Beyond the wood the path rose among fields all a-clatter with a tractor and harvester reaping a crop of maize.

At the tip of the peninsula we turned back along the south shore, looking across to the spire at Edith Weston. Pairs of teenagers were scudding about in sailing dinghies, chivvied by instructors yelling from a rubber boat. On an isolated ness stood the Jacobean mansion of Old Hall, gabled and mullioned, sole survivor of the two drowned villages, marooned on the shore beside the water that swallowed them.

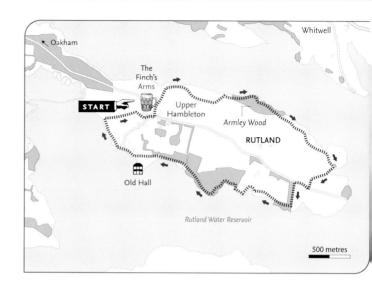

Start & finish The Finch's Arms pub, Upper Hambleton, Rutland LE15 8TL (OS ref SK 900076)

Walk (5 miles; easy; OS Explorer 234): From The Finch's Arms, left along village street. In 150m, opposite pillar box, left down drive (fingerpost) to lake shore. Right along shared-access trail, clockwise round peninsula. In 4½ miles pass driveway to Old Hall (899071); in a further 500m, right over stile (895075, yellow arrow). Up field to top corner (898076); cross successive stiles; narrow fenced path to Upper Hambleton. NB The shared-access track is very popular with cyclists at weekends, so keep your eyes and ears peeled.

Lunch The Finch's Arms, Upper Hambleton (01572 756575, finchsarms.co.uk)

More information Rutland Water Visitor Centre (01780 686800); discover-rutland.co.uk; visitengland.com; satmap.com; ramblers.org.uk; Anglian Water Birdwatching Centre, Egleton, Oakham LE15 8BT (01572 770651, rutlandwater.org.uk)

ABDON AND BROWN CLEE

A circular bank surrounds Abdon's little red Church of St Margaret's, the sign of a very old, probably pre-Christian site. People have been working and living for millennia in the valleys around the Clee Hills and in the ramparted forts that crown their basalt peaks. Looming at the back of Abdon is Brown Clee, a great whaleback of green, purple and red that blots out half the eastern sky and, at 1,770ft (540m), it's the highest peak in Shropshire.

On this bright winter morning big clouds bustled across from the sunlit uplands of Wenlock Edge out to the west. A field path led us from the straggling houses of Abdon down to Cockshutford.

Clee Liberty Common beyond lay pitted with the hillocks and holes of former coalpits and quarries. Above stood the neat oval ramparts of Nordy Bank, rare among hill enclosures hereabouts in having been left undamaged by the quarrymen.

Twisted old silver birches flanked the sunken track that meandered across the common to the radio mast at Clee Burf. From this great ringfort we had a fine view south to the stepped profile of the much-quarried Titterstone Clee.

We headed north on the Shropshire Way along the spine of Brown Clee, passing the memorial to airmen killed nearby in crashes during the Second World War.

At the topograph on Brown Clee's summit rampart we marvelled at an incomparable prospect all around the horizon from Cader Idris and the Berwyns to the west and Brecon Beacons to the south, to the Peak District hills in the north-east and Birmingham's towers in the east. The Wrekin, the Malverns, Cannock Chase and Wenlock Edge, all drenched in sun under a china-blue sky.

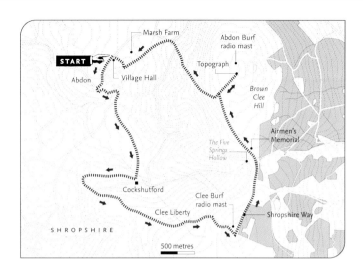

Start & finish Abdon Village Hall, Abdon, Craven Arms, Shropshire SY7 9HZ (OS 576868)

Walk (7½ miles, moderate; OS Explorer 217): Left down road; left at junction (574863); in 600m, opposite last buildings on right, left off road (577862), then fork right, following yellow arrows/YA across fields for ¾ mile to Cockshutford (579851). Cross lane, up steps; right (YA) beside hedge for ½ mile to stile (573852, YA). Left to road. Left; in 300m, at second Clee Liberty Common notice, right (573850) up gravel track for 1½ miles to Clee Burf radio mast (593843). Left on Shropshire Way/SW; in Five Springs Hollow, through right-hand gate (596854, "SW main route"); past airmen's memorial (596855). In ¾ mile, by gate on left, right (591863) to topograph by Abdon Burf radio mast. Return; go through gate (blue arrow); down track to road (586869). Right to junction; left ("Abdon Village Hall"); in 100m, left on path (fingerpost). In 400m, pass Marsh Farm; in 200m, right to stile (578867); up hedge to stile into road by car park.

Lunch Tallyho Inn, Bouldon SY7 9DP (01584 841811, thetallyho.co.uk), 3 miles

More information Ludlow tourist information centre (01584 875053); shropshiretourism.co.uk; satmap.com; ramblers.org.uk

CLUNTON AND BURY DITCHES

On this cool spring morning Clunton was as quiet as anywhere under the sun. Green slopes rose steeply on all sides, crowned with dark conifer woods, cradling the little village in a fold of the Shropshire hills. Looking back from the side of Clunton Hill, it might have been an alpine rather than an English scene.

A field path led steeply up to the tangled ways of Merryhill Plantation. A quick phone call confirmed that its forbidding forestry notices were long out of date. We swung down the track and out into lambing fields, where the northward view made us gasp, a painter's ideal of hill country with patchwork fields, snaking lanes and artfully placed spinneys. This was the Walcot Estate bought by the soldier of fortune Robert Clive ("Clive of India") in 1763, with the vast riches he acquired during colonial service with the East India Company.

Down in the valley we joined the Shropshire Way, a dusty white road running west between banks of violets, bluebells and star-like wood anemones.

On Sunnyhill we came to Bury Ditches, a great oval hillfort built 2,500 years ago with four concentric rings of ramparts and ditches. Uncountable Iron Age slaves and prisoners-of-war lived and died while mounding these prodigious earthworks. We walked a circuit of the ramparts, taking in the view – the long whaleback of the Clee Hills, Long Mynd and Wenlock Edge in the east, the quartzite upthrust of the Stiperstones on the northern skyline, and Corndon Hill looming bulkily over the huddled houses of Bishop's Castle. Then dropped down the woodland tracks and out in brilliant sunlight over the long slopes back to Clunton.

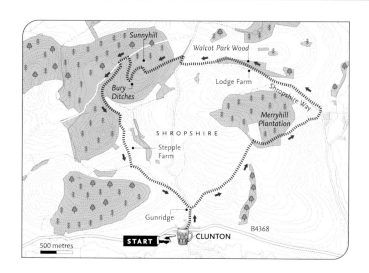

Start & finish Crown Inn, Clunton, Shropshire SY7 0HU (OS ref SO 335814)

Walk (7½ miles; moderate; OS Explorers 201, 216): Left up minor road to Bury Ditches. At No 5, Gunridge (353817), right; left through kissing gate; over stile. Footpath uphill (stiles, yellow arrows) NE for nearly a mile to cross belt of woodland (345827, YA). Right to stile into Merryhill Wood; track descends to gate (350828, YA), then down fields to meet Shropshire Way/SW in valley (356838, YA). Left along SW for 1½ miles to road beyond Stanley cottage (334839). Right/left into Bury Ditches car park; first path on right (red markers) to Bury Ditches hillfort (328838). At gate on west side (326836), right on track; follow red trail markers for ½ mile north to meet SW (325840), then SW to cross forest road in valley (322836). Grassy track descends; in 200m, red markers turn left across stream; right here (321834) on track SE to leave wood (324831, kissing gate). Right on farm track to Stepple (325826). Left of buildings; right through gate (YA); follow path SE (YAs, stiles) to Clunton.

Lunch Crown Inn, Clunton (01588 660265, crowninnclunton.co.uk)

More information Bishop's Castle Walking Festival (walkingfestival.co.uk); shropshiretourism.co.uk; visitengland.com; satmap.com; ramblers.org.uk

THE STIPERSTONES

The Stiperstones are easy enough to explain geologically: outcrops of quartzite about 500 million years old, spread along a mile or so of heathery Shropshire ridge on a westerly spur of the Long Mynd.

It's their contrary aspect – jagged upthrusts of naked rock in the midst of smoothly rolling countryside – that has cloaked them in all manner of strange and demonic myths. Walking towards Cranberry Rock at the southern end of the line, it was disconcerting to find the harsh outline of the tor suddenly appearing, as though the ground had disgorged it all in a moment.

The path among the Stones, rocky and full of angular quartzite lumps, required careful watching. We followed it through the heather past Cranberry Rock and Manstone Rock to the Devil's Chair – more like a giant and uncomfortable chaise longue of unforgiving stone.

Wild Edric the Saxon, Lady Godiva and all the witches and warlocks of Shropshire have the Devil's Chair as their trysting spot. And here the Devil reclines in stormy weather, watching between the lightning bolts for the ruination of Old England. On that day, it's said, the Stiperstones will sink back whence they sprang – into the bowels of Hell.

We descended a steep grassy path among old lead mine workings to the village of Stiperstones, 1,000ft (300m) below. Down there, with the Stones shut away from sight by steep hillsides, it was hard to bring their otherworldly atmosphere to mind. But as we headed home along a track that skirted the ridge, we saw their ragged profiles lit by the setting sun and a spectral half-moon that sailed up out of the ridge. The Stiperstones stood sentinel, a ghostly guard above our homeward path.

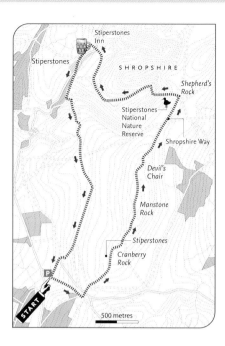

Start & finish The Bog car park, near Stiperstones, Shropshire SY5 0NG (OS ref SO 358978)

Walk (5 miles; strenuous; OS Explorer 216): Follow Shropshire Way/ SW signs to right of pond; follow path, up steps, through kissing gate (arrow). Ahead along gorsy bank to kissing gate; left to cross road (362976). Follow SW "main route" for 1 mile along ridge past Cranberry Rock (365981), Manstone Rock (367986) to Devil's Chair (369992). In another 600m, SW turns right (371996); keep ahead here. In 350m, at crossing and cairn by Shepherd's Rock (373999, yellow arrow/YA, "Cross Britain Walk"), left down grassy path to road in Stiperstones village (363004). Left past Stiperstones Inn; in 400m, hairpin left (361002, fingerpost); cross stile; right, steeply up fence for 300m. Left at post (359999, arrow); cross stile, pass NNR notice; steeply up through trees to cross stile at top (361996). Half left across field; right (361994) on stony lane for 1 mile to road (359980) and car park.

Lunch The Bog Visitor Centre, Stiperstones (01743 792484, bogcentre.co.uk)

More information The Bog Visitor Centre (see above); visitengland. com; satmap.com; ramblers.org.uk

CANNOCK CHASE AND THE TRENT CANALS

A table full of cheery Midlands pensioners were getting to work on their ice-cream sundaes as Jane and I left the Barley Mow and set off across Milford Common into the woods of Cannock Chase. An ancient no man's land of hummocks and hollows, Cannock Chase mine heaps and quarry scoops, has been greening over for centuries. This is what the neighbouring Black Country would look like if the Industrial Revolution had not ravaged it.

We followed the Heart of England Way, then the Staffordshire Way, up sandy rides flanked by venerable, deeply fissured silver birches, and by bilberry bushes whose green shoots had been nibbled down to the woody root by hungry deer.

The Chase is a place in which to get lost, a wanderer's paradise where a million West Midlanders come for recreation and are never seen again — not by Jane and me today, anyway. Dogs splashed after sticks in the pools of Sherbrook Valley, and over in Abraham's Valley a great spotted woodpecker flashed scarlet, white and black as he gave a hollow oak a battering. From the green enclosures of Cannock Chase we emerged into the open country through which the River Trent snakes round the northern edge of the Chase. The sky expanded and the ground smoothed out into broad, flat river meadows in which the mansion of Shugborough Hall lay like a giant wedding cake on a croquet lawn.

You can't have a Midland scene without canals, and so it turned out here; the Trent and Mersey to carry us north along its towpath to Haywood Junction, the Staffordshire and Worcestershire to lead us past grebehaunted reedbeds and fields of spring lambs to the Barley Mow and the borders of Cannock Chase once more.

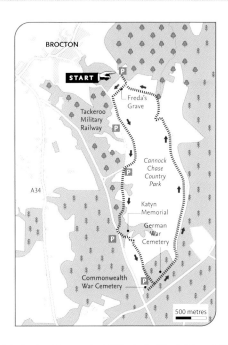

Start & finish Barley Mow pub, Milford, Stafford ST17 0UW (OS ref SJ973212)

Walk (8½ miles; easy; OS Explorer 244): Cross A513; left along Milford Common. Opposite Shugborough Park gates, 2 paths diverge (975210); take farther one (bridleway fingerpost) past one pond to another (974207). "Heart of England Way" (fingerposts) to Mere Pits (978201); left ("Trail 5, Punchbowl"); in 250m, right on Staffordshire Way (981202) for 1⅓ miles. At pools (986186) left across Sher Brook; up and over into Abraham's Valley. Left (999186) for 1⅓ miles (blue arrows) to car park. Follow road across A513 (004207) to Navigation Farm bridge (004213). Left along Trent & Mersey Canal to Great Haywood Junction (995229); left along Staffs & Worcs Canal to Tixall Bridge (975216). Left down road to Milford Common and Barley Mow pub.

Lunch Barley Mow pub (01785 665230)

More information Stafford Tourist Information Centre (01785 619619; enjoystaffordshire.com); cannockchasedc.gov.uk/visitors; ramblers.org.uk

A cool, windy Staffordshire afternoon and the Duncombe Arms in Ellastone was packed with sharp-dressed wedding guests. Out in the fields beyond St Peter's Church, ewes and lambs stared at us as though they had never before seen human beings, before quickly turning tail.

The land dipped and rolled, trending away northwest to where the Weaver Hills rose in three green hummocks against a blue sky piled high with massive whipped-cream clouds.

Wootton Hall, with its tall, domed portico, stood in parkland carefully groomed and preserved. Black lambs and sleek horses grazed under the lime trees.

Coffee and a sticky treat apiece at Daltons Dairy Shop on the edge of Wootton gave us a burst of energy to climb the slopes of the Weaver Hills beyond. Up at the trig pillar a tremendous prospect unfolded round the compass, north to the limestone heights and clefts of the White Peak, south over the great Midland plain, stretching away to a level horizon.

We followed a path east along the ridge, down towards the rough bracken-brown swell of Blake Low. Tiny calves stood staring beside their mothers and a big brown hare ran pelting away in a panic.

At Stanton we got into Field Lane, a narrow country road that brought us south by slow degrees to Ellastone. In a cottage garden at the bottom of a steep hollow lay the remnants of Ousley Cross, a medieval waymark on a pilgrim route to the shrine of St Bertram at Ilam.

The evening air was full of birdsong and lamb cries as we crossed the pastures towards St Peter's Church, its rose-coloured stone walls lit by the sun declining in the western sky behind the Weaver Hills.

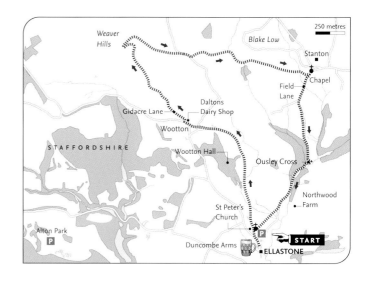

Start & finish Ellastone Parish Hall car park, Ellastone, Ashbourne DE6 2HB (OS ref SK116434)

Walk (7½ miles; moderate; OS Explorer 259): Left up Church Lane. Right by Blenheim Cottage; follow path (stiles, yellow arrows/YAs) across fields for ¾ mile. At Wootton Hall Farm, kissing gate (115446); left to lane, right to Wootton. Follow "Green Hill"; at junction, ahead (105451, "Leek"). In 150m, right (104452) past Dalton Farm along Gidacre Lane, then footpath (stiles, YAs). In just over ½ mile "Public Footpath" post (098458, "Wardlow") to gate/stile (097461). Half right up to stile at top of wall (096464). Left to ladder stile, then to trig pillar (095464). North through gate; right over stile (096465, YA), right (east) on field path (stiles, YAs) for ½ mile to road (104463). Right; 50m after right bend, left (106462, "Weaver Walk"). Down 3 fields to cross stream (112463). Right along stream; in 350m, same direction (stiles) for ¾ mile to Field Lane at Stanton Chapel (125459). Right; in 1½ miles, just past Northwood Farm, right (121438, stile, "Weaver Walk") across fields to Ellastone Church.

Lunch Duncombe Arms, Ellastone DE6 2GZ (01335 324275, duncombearms.co.uk)

More information enjoystaffordshire.com

HAMPS VALLEY, RUSHLEY DALE AND THROWLEY OLD HALL

Setting off from humpbacked Weag's Bridge, I followed the Manifold Way's cycle path past the looming cliff of Beeston Tor, its grey limestone face seamed with cracks and caves. The path snaked to and fro across the dry Hamps, the verges spattered with yellow rattle and common spotted orchids.

A side path led up through Old Soles Wood and on up Soles Hollow into open sheep country. I crossed the long ridge of Mere Hill with spectacular views east to the gorge of the River Manifold and the tent-shaped upthrust of Bunster Hill at the entrance to Dovedale. These iconic hills, dales and uplands of the Staffordshire/Derbyshire border are a walker's dream.

Below Slade House a deep and sinuous dale, seemingly nameless, runs eastward. As soon as I got into it I found slopes of unimproved grassland thick with wildflowers – intense blue milkwort and harebells, and masses of greeny-white greater butterfly orchids.

Things soon got a little more challenging as the path wriggled under sycamores and hazels in a dank, damp tangle of herbage. I walked with head bowed, watching for slippery stones, hands raised out of the way of stinging nettles, like a surrendering soldier in a jungle.

Out of the stingers at last, I came to the tumbledown farm and neat holiday cottages of Rushley, and turned up the long open-sided road to Throwley Hall farm. On a knoll rose the blackened stone ruin of Throwley Old Hall, tall and stark, its Tudor mullioned windows looking out blankly over medieval ridge and furrow fields to the deeply carved cleft of the Manifold Valley.

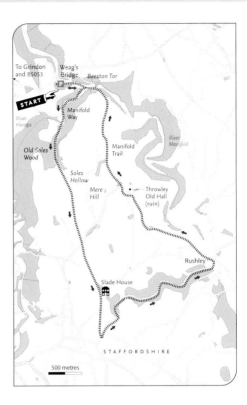

Start & finish Weag's Bridge, Grindon ST13 7TX (OS ref SK 100541)

Walk (7 miles; moderate; OS Explorer OL24): Pass bridge (don't cross); ahead on cycle path (Manifold Way/MW). In ¾ mile after third bridge, left off MW (101534, gate, "Old Soles Wood") up woodland path. In just over a ¼ mile through gate (100529); up cleft. In 500m left through gate (102525, yellow arrow/YA); right along wall for ½ mile to cross road (104517). Follow drive to Slade House (107510). Through farmyard (fingerpost "Calton"), then gate (YA). Grass path to next gate (107508); fork left (stile), down hedge to bottom. Left (107504, gate, YA) along dale bottom path for 1½ miles to road at Rushley (124514). Left; in 100m, left up road ("Manifold Trail"/MT). In 1 mile pass Throwley Old Hall (111525); on to farmyard; left ("Calton"). Immediately dogleg right/left through wicket gate (110526, YA, MT). Half right to corner of wall (108528); track to gate beside trees (108529); down slope to gate (107533, MT); follow MT back to Weag's Bridge.

Lunch Picnic

More information peakdistrict.gov.uk; enjoystaffordshire.com

Hawnby Hill, Yorkshire

BLACKSTONE EDGE AND GREEN WITHENS RESERVOIR

Around Blackstone Edge the gritstone moors roll away, breezy uplands that are a godsend to anyone bent on getting out of the former manufacturing towns of Lancashire and Yorkshire for a good day in the open air.

From the White House Inn we crossed the road and followed the broad stony track of the Pennine Way. The path surface had broken down under millions of footfalls into sand and quartz, a creamy, honeyed hue.

A short, cobbled section of Roman road led up to the Aiggin Stone, a medieval waymark pillar set up to guide benighted or mist-beguiled travellers. From here the Pennine Way rose to Blackstone Edge, a classic gritstone ridge with cliffs jutting westward like ships' prows.

The narrow, stumbly path headed south down a long slope into the rushy declivity of Redmires and Slippery Moss.

Beyond Slippery Moss, the M62 cuts the moor with a roar and rush. We turned away to follow a trickling leat of water across the peat and heather to Green Withens Reservoir, a classic of municipal sandstone architecture built in the 1880s in the middle of nowhere to supply Wakefield with water. From here the path ascended the dimpled face of Green Withens Edge before meeting Rishworth Drain and curling back towards the Aiggin Stone.

As we came level with Rishworth Drain, a big bird of prey, its pale wings tipped with black, came flapping easily along the waterway. "Hen harrier," we exclaimed on the same breath. We watched spellbound as it launched itself downwards and pounced into a grass tuffet, then resumed its flight, having missed its grab.

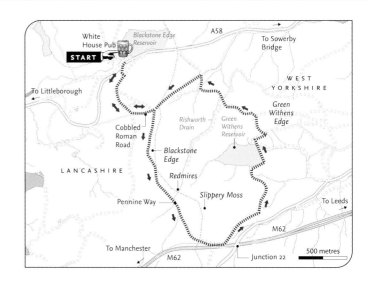

Start & finish The White House Pub, Blackstone Edge, Halifax Road, Littleborough OL15 0LG (OS ref SD 969178)

Walk (7½ miles; moderate; OS Explorer OL21): Cross road; follow Pennine Way/PW, then path beside Broad Head Drain. In 800m, left through gate (970169); up cobbled road to Aiggin Stone (974170). Right on PW (gate, National Trail acorn), southward by Blackstone Edge and Redmires. In 1¾ miles PW turns right to cross M62 (984147); don't cross, but keep ahead with motorway on your right; then follow path on right of leat (986148) to Green Withens Reservoir (991160). Right along two sides; 100m beyond far end, right beside leat (991165). In 150m, left across leat. Follow path across moor, up Green Withens Edge; near the top, left on crossing track (991169). In ½ mile at Rishworth Drain (986172), fingerpost points right ("Baitings Reservoir"); but keep ahead here. In 700m left across footbridge by pool (982176); bear back left on rutted Old Packhorse Road to Aiggin Stone; retrace steps to White House Pub.

Lunch The White House Pub, Blackstone Edge (01706 378456, thewhitehousepub.co.uk)

More information moorsforthefuture.org.uk; yorkshire.com

BUCKDEN BECK AND BUCKDEN PIKE, WHARFEDALE

This walk starts along one of the most beautiful waterside paths in the Yorkshire Dales, a cornucopia of waterfalls, clear pools, wild flowers and birds of the uplands. The banks of the beck were spattered with the bright colours of low-growing plants, well sheltered in the narrow valley.

The beck came jumping from pool to pool, sluicing down rocky cliffs hung with dense mats of sodden mosses. Its trickle and bounce, the energy in its scouring of flat stone and moulding of flanking rocks, were in tune with the dipper that bobbed and curtsied on a branch of hawthorn overhanging a pool.

In the dark little hollow where the first tall waterfall hissed down its rock face, the path made a hairpin bend and climbed precariously to a narrow cleft in the limestone outcrop, up which we scrambled. A repeat performance above the second fall and the climb eased off.

Up ahead, the vee of the valley was blocked by a great orange-yellow heap of spoil from the Buckden lead mine that once roared and hammered up in this remote spot.

Up at the 2,303ft (702m) summit of Buckden Pike we sat to catch our breath and take in the view – north over an immense lowland, south towards the Peak District and west to where the Three Peaks of Yorkshire stood clear in their characteristic shapes – Whernside's rising ridge, Ingleborough's tall double hump and the sloping leonine profile of Pen-y-ghent.

The descent across the moor and through a network of stone walls was glorified by the sunlit westerly prospect up Langstrothdale, the dale sides undulating downward in a smooth succession of limestone ribs and sloping green pasture.

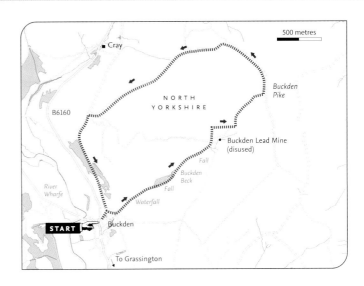

Start & finish National Park car park, Buckden BD23 5JA (OS ref SD 943773)

Walk (5 miles; strenuous; OS Explorer OL30): Leave car park through gate (Cray Gill Bridge, Buckden Pike). Right (Buckden lead mine) along wall, then left on path on left bank of Buckden Beck. Path soon becomes narrow and twisting. Just before first tall waterfall, path hairpins back to left (947776 approx.), then short scramble up rock outcrop. Same again just before second tall fall (948776 approx.). Above second fall, cross fence before changing to path on right bank. In ½ mile at mine site (954781), up left side of spoil heap, on into ruins. Just before arched entrance, left on path (wall on left). In 100m right uphill beside wall on left. Follow this clear path uphill for 800m to angle of wall (961786). Left (ladder stile) to trig pillar on Buckden Pike (961788). Ahead by wall, then follow clear path, slippery and rocky in places, for 2¼ miles back to Buckden.

Lunch The Buck Inn, Buckden BD23 5JA (01756 761933; thebuckinn.com)

More information National Park Visitor Centre, Grassington (01756 751690; yorkshiredales.org.uk)

CLAPHAM AND INGLEBOROUGH CAVE

Reginald Farrer of Ingleborough Hall travelled all over the wild lands of China, Tibet and Upper Burma to collect seeds for the plant collection he established around his family home in the North Yorkshire village of Clapham. Some thought him mad, especially when he took to firing seeds out of a shotgun to scatter them evenly along the crevices of Clapdale. It was a pleasing picture to have in the mind on our way up the cobbled lane that travels in tunnels and artificial stone-walled canyons through the grounds of Ingleborough Hall and on up to the limestone fells beyond.

Beyond the sullen grey cliffs of Robin Proctor's Scar we crossed the sloping fields and found the path up to Norber, a slanted upland where retreating glaciers dumped hundreds of sandstone boulders on the limestone pavements 10,000 years ago.

Pen-y-ghent's lion face poked out of a welter of dark grey cloud ahead as we made for the lane up Crummack Dale in a spatter of rain. A grass track brought us up to the ridge at Long Scar, where the tremendous view encompassed Pen-y-ghent, the elongated purple back of Ingleborough ahead in the north, and away to the south the bulk of what we guessed to be Pendle Hill far off in Lancashire.

On the way down to Clapham we stopped off for a tour of Ingleborough Cave. Down in the depths our young guide Sam blew out his candle and plunged us into the profoundest blackness. Candles were all those first explorers had to light their way in 1837 when they first ventured into this now famous tangle of caves and cramped passages.

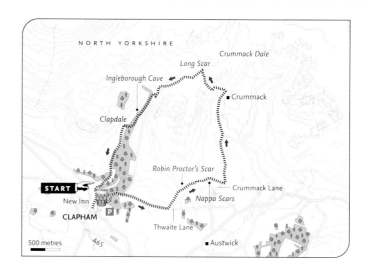

Start & finish National Park car park, Church Avenue, Clapham, North Yorkshire LA2 8EF (OS ref SD745692); pay and display

Walk (7½ miles; moderate; OS Explorer OL2): From car park, right up Church Lane; fork right by church, up cobbled lane. Follow "Austwick" for 1 mile along Thwaite Lane. Where field wall angles in on left, turn left over stile (760692, "Norber"). Half right to far wall corner (763695, stile); on to fingerpost (766697); left ("Norber") to plateau and erratic boulders (766700). Back to fingerpost; left, downhill to cross wall (768698); under Nappa Scars to Crummack Lane (772697). Left for 1¼ miles to Crummack. Pass "Bridleway" fingerpost; at next fingerpost (772715, "Sulber") left uphill. Follow grassy track; in 300m, bear right below scar; at crest (768719), left on track for 900m past cairn, downhill to gate into lane (758716). Left down lane; in 250m, right over wall; down to lane in valley; left past Ingleborough Cave Centre (754711). In 250m, right (blue arrow) through gate, up to Clapdale farm (751708); left on track to Clapham.

Lunch Reading Room Café, Clapham (01524 251144; claphambunk.com)

More information Ingleborough Cave (01524 251242; ingleboroughcave.co.uk); Ingleton Tourist Information Centre (01524 241049; ingleton.co.uk/inginfo.asp); yorkshire.com; visitengland.com; satmap.com; ramblers.org.uk

A gorgeous sunny morning in Malham laid special glory on the neat stone cottages, the bird-haunted gardens and the stone bridges across Malham Beck, and I was already entranced as I struck out through the pastures on the paved path to Janet's Foss.

In a narrow, tree-shaded cleft, the waterfall of Janet's Foss sluiced down a mossy slide in twin tails of white water. Beyond the jaws of Gordale Scar open, steep slopes rose to 500ft (150m) crags of jagged pale grey limestone, five hundred feet (150m) tall. The Scar is a vast cave, burrowed out by raging floodwaters at the end of the last Ice Age. The roof collapsed, leaving a giant chasm twisted into the body of the Dales.

"We're not sure about the climb," said a couple, returning crestfallen from the depths of the Scar. But it proved a sheep in lion's clothing, an upward scramble beside a jetting cataract and through an upper chamber choked with striated boulders where another water fall tumbled in lacy folds from a crack in the dark walls overhead. No wonder Gothic painters and poets loved Gordale Scar; in these awe-inspiring depths it's only natural to picture the Devil creating the chasm with a thunderous stamp of his cloven hoof.

At the top of the gorge, I came out into wide, windy uplands striped with stone walls and pale terraces of naked stone, where Malham Tarn lay flat and steely. Here I turned back along the Pennine Way, through the high cleft of Dry Valley to reach the crazed limestone pavement at the rim of Malham Cove. The eerie metallic squeak of a peregrine echoed from the enormous amphitheatre of the cove, a towering limestone cliff and all that remains of an ancient waterfall higher than Niagara. As a coda for this walk of natural extravagance and superlatives, it couldn't have been better.

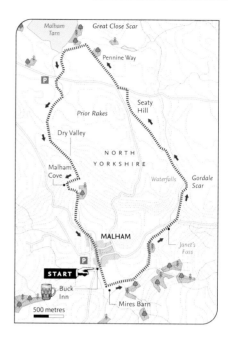

Start & finish Buck Inn, Malham, North Yorkshire BD23 4DA (OS ref SD 901627)

Walk (7½ miles; moderate/hard; OS Explorer OL2): Buck Inn, Malham – Mires Barn (902624, "Janet's Foss") – Mantley Field Laithe, Janet's Foss (911633), Gordale Bridge, Gordale Scar (915641) steep scramble: see below for details. Path NW to Street Gate (905656) – National Trust road to Pennine Way (898664). Left (south) on Pennine Way for 2¾ miles via Tarn Foot car park (894658); Comb Hill, Dry Valley (894646, marked "Watlowes" on OS Explorer) and Malham Cove. Signposted detour from road at Gordale Bridge to top of Malham Cove. NB Detailed directions recommended.

Lunch Buck Inn, Malham (01729 830317; buckinnmalham.co.uk)

More information Skipton and Craven Tourist Information Centre, Coach Street, Skipton (01756 792809); yorkshiredalesandharrogate.com; ramblers.org.uk; satmap.com; Crickhowell Walking Festival, Black Mountains (crickhowellfestival.com)

HAWNBY AND BILSDALE

In this southern corner of the North York Moors, every heathery summit seems only to lead you to another higher crest, each wooded dale bottom to precipitate you into one even lower. Within five minutes of setting out from the Inn at Hawnby I looked up to find the hamlet high above me; ten minutes later Hawnby had been swallowed by the landscape, not to be seen again till the last few steps of this beautiful walk.

The land hereabouts is hard on its farmers. At Crow Nest I found a roofless ruin in a zigzag tumble of yard walls. A boulder-strewn moor loud with the complaint of curlews and lapwings led down into the inbye fields of Bilsdale. Across the dale fat lambs cried in the fields around Carr Cote, where they were gathering the sheep for shearing. I climbed up through bracken, then away across the purpling moor where red grouse chicks scuttered off, their mothers whirring low over the heather as they shrieked: "Back! Back! Back!" Up on the crest a broad yellow sand road led south past the lonely moorland farm of Low Thwaites towards Easterside Hill and Hawnby Hill.

Up on the thyme-scented summit of Hawnby Hill I sat by the conical cairn, looking down the precipitous slopes into Ryedale and picturing the Hawnby Dreamers. Three modest local men, Chapman, Cornforth and Hugill by name, fell asleep upon these moors one day in the 1740s, and dreamed identical dreams of repentance and salvation. They sacrificed their reputations, their livelihoods and the tied cottages they lived in to set out immediately and walk 100 miles to hear John Wesley preach.

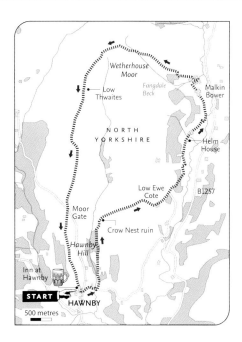

Start & finish Inn at Hawnby, North Yorkshire YO62 5QS (OS ref SE542898)

Walk (10 miles; moderate; OS Explorer OL26): Follow "Osmotherley", then "Laskill" on tarmac to cross stream. In 100m, left/north (547899) on bridleway (occasional blue arrows/BA) for 1 mile to Crow Nest ruin (547914). Track ENE for 1 mile across moor to Low Ewe Cote (561918). Green lanes NE, then north up Bilsdale for 2¼ miles via Helm House (569934) and Malkin Bower (570944) to Fangdale Beck. Left by Chapel Garth (570946) across footbridge; left through garden gate, right between buildings, into lane rising west uphill through gates (BAs) for ⅓ mile to final gate (563949). Trackless path WNW (aim slightly left of mast) for ¾ mile to line of grouse butts (552954). Left along them, then continue same direction to sandy moor road (548954). Left; 200m past Low Thwaites, fork right (543942); track south for 1½ miles to Moor Gate (540917); ahead up path to top of Hawnby Hill (540910). South, and descend to Inn at Hawnby.

Lunch Picnic

More information Thirsk Tourist Information Centre (01845 522755; visitthirsk.org.uk); visitengland.com; satmap.com; ramblers.org.uk

INGLETON WATERFALLS

People have been doing Ingleton's Waterfalls Trail since the days of stovepipe hats and crinolines, and this steep, tree-hung circuit of the two moorland rivers that rush together in Ingleton village to form the River Greta continues to be one of Yorkshire's prime outdoor attractions.

Setting off from Ingleton along the narrow path that shadows the River Twiss, we were almost at once enclosed in the dark walls of a gorge, with the river running fast among mossy stones splashed with dipper droppings. The trail climbed the wall of a canyon above swirling holes where the south-going river chased round and round before escaping, sculpting semi-circular hollows in the rock walls with a continuous swallow and gurgle.

A long view upriver showed Pecca Falls crashing down a staircase of slippery rock steps. Beyond the cascade the trail left the trees and followed a curve of the Twiss. A wonderful view opened ahead towards Thornton Force, pride of the walk, descending a series of rapids before hurling itself in a 50ft (15m) free fall into a smoking pool. Above this thunderous weight of water we followed a walled lane into the mist.

Below Twisleton Hall the River Doe echoed and hissed in its own steep-walled canyon, leaping down towards Ingleton and its confluence with the Twiss through S-shaped channels carved through the shale by the force of water alone. We crossed above potholes boiling with toffee-coloured bubbles, and skirted backwaters where the surface lay marbled with scarcely moving patterns of foam. Below the white wall of Snow Falls the path snaked past money tree and on through mossy old quarry workings, to emerge at the foot of the gorge with the church and houses of Ingleton lying beyond.

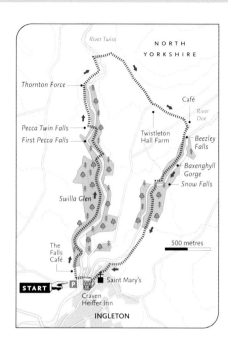

Start & finish Waterfalls Walk car park, Ingleton, North Yorkshire LA6 3ET (OS ref SD693733)

Walk (4½ miles; moderate/strenuous; Explorer OL2): From car park follow waymark arrows up River Twiss, along lane via Twisleton Hall Farm (702751) and down River Doe.

Lunch Falls Café (015242 41617; www.thefallscafe.co.uk)

More information Ingleton Tourist Information Centre (01524 241049); www.ingleton.co.uk/inginfo.asp; ingletonwaterfallstrail.co.uk; yorkshire.com

Littondale is tucked away, a secluded cleft running north-west from its parent valley of Wharfedale. If people venture to Littondale, it's usually to glimpse Arncliffe, the gorgeous stone-built village where the first few series of *Emmerdale* were filmed.

I climbed the steep hillside out of Arncliffe, where a mass of wild flowers – milkwort, bird's-foot trefoil, lady's bedstraw, hawkbit and rockrose – grew like little jewels on the slopes.

A gate in the summit wall led to the downwards track into Wharfedale, the valley spread out at my feet in patchy sunshine, with the clustered stone houses of Starbotton and Kettlewell under the long back of Cam Pasture, and miniature dots of sheep feeding in a maze of meadows boxed in by drystone walls, each field with its own handsome stone-built barn.

Down at Starbotton I followed the Dales Way beside the River Wharfe through flat pastures glinting gold with buttercups in the pale sun. The Wharfe ran slow and darkly viscous around its many meanders. This seemingly tame river can be fierce in spate. Starbotton was wrecked in one terrible flood in 1686. Thomas Cox recorded in his *Magna Britannia Antiqua & Nova*: "The rain descended with great violence for one hour and a half; at the same time the hill opening, and casting up water to a prodigious height, demolished several houses, and filled others with gravel to the chamber windows. The affrighted inhabitants fled for their lives."

At Kettlewell I turned steeply back up the daleside, scrambling on limestone crags to the top of the moor. Then it was a descent over sedgy grass, precipitously down the rocky sides of Park Scar, and over the little humpy bridge into Arncliffe.

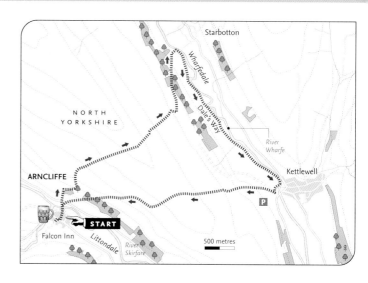

Start & finish Village green, Arncliffe, North Yorkshire BD23 5QE (OS ref SD931718)

Walk (7½ miles; strenuous; OS Explorer OL30): Take lane-way opposite water trough; cross river; at bend (932721) up steps, through gate, up fellside to cart track bridleway (932723). Turn right along it for 1 mile to go through gate at crest (941730). Down for ½ mile to circular sheep pen ruin near gate in wall (951736, 3-finger post). Left down to bridge over Wharfe (951745). Don't cross; turn right along the Dales Way for 1¾ miles to Kettlewell. At bridge (967722), hairpin back right up stony track, through gate. In 50m, turn left, steeply up fields. Rocky staircase through outcrops (964723); on up grassy path. In 600m, right over ladder stile (958723); on up to two ladder stiles in quick succession at crest (952722). Down for 1 mile to gate into Park Scar (938721). Steeply down to road (934721). Right, then left into Arncliffe.

Lunch There are plenty of places to choose in Kettlewell

More information Grassington National Park Centre (01756 751690); yorkshiredales.org.uk; satmap.com; visitengland.com; ramblers.org.uk

Railway, road and river all wriggle close together through the Ribble Valley at Long Preston. Lumpy fells flank the elongated village on the east, and we were heading up there on a peerless day of unbroken blue sky over the western fringes of the Yorkshire Dales.

We made for Scaleber Lane and a long, gentle climb northwards with the midday chimes sounding below. We crossed Long Preston Beck in its rocky bed and went upstream. Stepping stones across Bookil Gill Beck brought us to Langber Lane, an old walled lane running confidently north. In Langber Plantation a tree creeper inched up a pine trunk, snicking insects out of their hiding places behind the pink bark scales.

Pale knobbly ramparts of limestone appeared ahead, Warrendale Knotts and Attermire Scar. Below them Stockdale Beck cut through the outcropping strata, tumbling in long hissing tails of white water down tall steps of limestone in a water-delved gorge.

From the heights another walled way, Lambert Lane, ran south through sheep pastures to meet Edge Lane, the old hill road from Long Preston over to Settle. Today in warm sunshine the gritstone walls and the sandy track sparkled cheerfully. In proper old-time winter weather the bumpy and winding hill road must have been a fearsome prospect for drovers and benighted travellers.

Edge Lane rose to the heathery heights of Hunter Bark, highest point on the old road. We stood and stared round at the 50-mile view – Ingleborough flat-topped in the north-west, the long green stretch of the Craven lowlands running away west, and down in the south-west the hummocks of the Bowland Fells and the grey upturned hull of Pendle Hill.

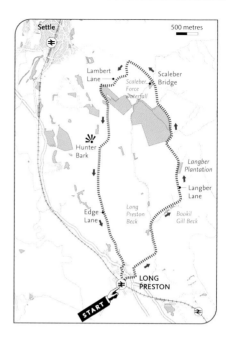

Start & finish Long Preston railway station, near Settle BD23 4RY (OS ref SD 834579)

Walk (8½ miles; easy; OS Explorer OL2): Up B6478; cross A65 into Church Street; left at church. In 200m, right (836583, "Langber Lane") up Scalehaw Lane. In 700m cross Long Preston Beck (842586); left beside beck. Pass New Pasture Plantation; cross Bookil Gill Beck (840592). Don't cross next footbridge, but fork right through gate and uphill, heading to right of skyline barn. In ¾ mile ford Bookil Gill Beck (847600); left on Langber Lane track for 1½ miles to road (841623). Left; in 200m, left at Scaleber Bridge through wicket gate (841626, "Scaleber Wood") to view Scaleber Force. Back to road; left; in ½ mile, left (835630, "Pennine Bridleway"/PB, "Lambert Lane"). In about ¾ mile, left at road (828625, "PB Long Preston"). In 150m fork left beside wood (828624); follow Edge Lane for 2¾ miles to road in Long Preston (834583). Right; at A65, left. Right down Greenbank Terrace; left on footpath (834581) to B6478; right to station.

Lunch Town End Farm Shop, Scosthrop, Airton BD23 4BE (01729 830902, townendfarmshop.co.uk) for takeaway picnic food

More information Settle Tourist Information Centre (01729 825192, yorkshire.com)

MARSDEN AND WESSENDEN MOOR

It's a long time since the buzzer at Bank Bottom Mill summoned half the working population of Marsden. It stands redundant at the bottom of the town, as big as a cathedral, acres of windows and grey-slate roofs round a central tower and an octagonal chimney.

We followed a laneway among these ruins, then on to a great grass bank, filling half the skyline. The dam of Butterley Reservoir is an impressive sight, even when floodwater is not cascading down its spillway.

Blakeley Reservoir, high above, is smaller and wilder. Here we stood and looked back along the twisting valley with its man-made lakes, insinuated at the turn of the 20th century to feed industrial Huddersfield's mills and wells.

Walking the Pennine Way across these moors used to be a purgatorial flounder among bogs and peat hags. Nowadays thousands of old mill flagstones give dry passage across the morass. This afternoon's westward walk beside Blakeley Clough was a pleasure, striding firm-footed as the sun burst from behind the clouds and turned the moor grass to a sea of wind-ruffled gold.

The moor-top reservoirs of Black Moss and Swellands lay side by side in modest beds, their water the polished indigo of a lobster's shell. On the shore of Redbrook Reservoir the Pennine Way met Standedge Trail, whose stony path we followed, chased by an icy wind. It carried us down from the hills and back to Marsden by way of a narrow-walled lane, from which we looked down over the terraced houses along the valley and the tall black chimney of the great mill complex, standing silent at the foot of the town.

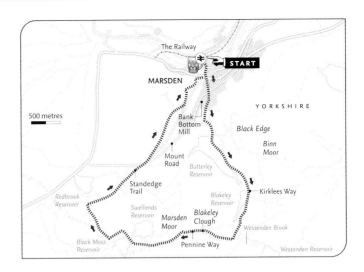

Start & finish Marsden railway station, Marsden, West Yorkshire HD7 6AX (OS ref SE 047118)

Walk (7 miles; moderate; OS Explorers OL21, OL1): Cross canal, walk downhill. At left bend, right across river, past church. Cross Towngate; along weir side. Cross Mount Road; up Binn Road. In 100m, fork right by Marsden Industrial Society between Bank Bottom Mill buildings (048111); on along lane to Butterley Reservoir dam. Up steps on left (049106); at top, right on Kirklees Way (fingerpost) for 1 mile to top of Blakeley Reservoir. Right on Pennine Way (054091, fingerpost) over Marsden Moor for 2 miles. Just before Redbrook Reservoir, right (027094) along Standedge Trail (unmarked, broad track). In ¾ mile cross Mount Road (037101). Up Old Mount Road; in 50m, fork left ("Hades Farm"). In 900m, right (042110, "Marsden Heritage Trail", Point 15) down walled lane to track (044111). Left past house; walled lane for 300m to gate on left of farmhouse (044113). Right along house wall; ahead through 2 gates (yellow arrow); down sloping field, following gully to bottom left corner (046115). Cross stile; right down lane to road; left across A62; return to station.

Lunch The Railway, Marsden (01484 841541, railwaymarsdenhuddersfield.co.uk)

More information yorkshire.com/places/west-yorkshire; satmap.com; ramblers.org.uk

MUKER AND KELD, SWALEDALE

A brisk west wind, a chink of sun in the Swaledale clouds after days of rain over North Yorkshire, and the clatter of walking sticks on the road outside Muker Teashop where Jane and I were finishing our Yorkshire rarebits.

A walled lane led up the sloping fellsides behind the village, the grazing fields dotted with the square-built farmhouses and small stone barns so characteristic of the Yorkshire Dales. Sun splashes and cloud shadows chased across the hills.

It was a joy to be alive and walking up there in the face of the wind, climbing the old stony road to the crest of Kisdon Hill and following it down to Skeb Skeugh ford and the huddle of grey stone houses at Keld, the Norsemen's well-named "place by the river". On the outskirts of Keld, Jane and I joined the glorious and notorious long-distance treadmill of the Pennine Way, but only to cross the rain-engorged Swale. East Gill Force jetted down its black rock staircase and into the river with a muted rumble and hiss, and here we swung away from the Pennine Way and made for Crackpot Hall's dolorous ruins.

"Don't miss Swinner Gill," we'd been advised by Nick and Alison Turner, the owners of Muker Teashop. "It's really something special." It was lead mining subsidence that put an end to Crackpot Hall, and the ruins and spoil heaps of the Dales' great lost industry lie all around – stone-arched mine levels, a tumbledown smelt mill deep in the cleft of Swinner Gill, and the precarious trods or tracks of the lead miners. All lay silent this afternoon, with the dale sides rising sharply to the sky, the beck sluicing below, and a breathtakingly beautiful prospect opening southward towards Muker down the sunlit floor of Swaledale.

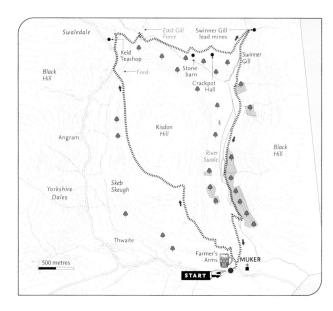

Start & finish Muker Teashop, Muker, Richmond, North Yorkshire DL11 6QG (OS ref SO910979)

Walk (6½ miles; moderate/hard; OS Explorer OL30): Leaving Muker Teashop, left; left again up lane by Literary Institute. Forward; right by Grange Farm, left up its side ("footpath to Keld"). Follow lane; then "Bridleway Keld" (909982) up walled lane for ½ mile. Pennine Way/PW forks right, but continue for 30m, then bear right uphill by wall (903986; "Keld 2 miles"). At top of slope follow wall to left; climb to open hilltop. Follow green road (fingerposts) over hill, down to ford beck, right along road. On left bend, right (893009; "Keld only") into Keld. Right down gravelled lane (893012; "footpath to Muker"). In 300m, left downhill ("PW"). To return direct to Muker, turn right and follow PW. To continue walk, cross River Swale footbridge; left to reach top of waterfall. Where PW forks left, turn right along track (896011; "bridleway" fingerpost). In ½ mile pass stone barn; in another 100m pass engine and steering wheel sunk in ground (!). In 50m fork left (904009) on stony track to Crackpot Hall. Aim for house above; then follow path (progressively narrower) into Swinner Gill. Where path forks opposite ruined lead mine buildings, take lower fork to fingerpost; turn back sharp right (911012; "Muker") down narrow path to ford beck (911008; NB If beck too swollen to ford safely, retrace steps to Crackpot Hall and follow main track south towards Muker). Continue along path for ¼ mile to join main track; continue down Swaledale on left (east) bank of river for 1 mile. Cross Swale by footbridge (910986); right (yellow arrow) for 50m, then left along meadow path for ½ mile back to Muker.

OSMOTHERLEY AND CLEVELAND WAY

Early on a cold morning I followed the Cleveland Way north out of Osmotherley. Vague shapes of Pennine ranges lay out to the west on the edge of sight, under a sky ribbed with cloud. A side path lined with simple wooden crosses inscribed with the Stations of the Cross led up to a lonely Lady Chapel, object of pilgrimage and still used for worship.

Another sidetrack led down through the trees of Mount Grace Wood among bluebells and wild garlic, to where the remarkably well-preserved Mount Grace Priory lay sheltered below the escarpment.

From the Priory, I climbed back up to the Cleveland Way and resumed the walk, up through South Wood to where larch and firs gave way to silver birch and young green bilberries. On the eastern skyline ran the hummocky dark spine of Osmotherley Moor, the sombre-coloured escarpment edge trending north to where the sharp breaking-wave profile of Roseberry Topping stood against the sky.

Out on Scarth Wood Moor a paved path wound palely over the heather. Suddenly an intent dark shape scuttled across – a handsome black grouse, his bright-scarlet crest erect, legs strutting.

Here I left the Cleveland Way, cutting back south by way of Cod Beck Reservoir, as cold and still as a sheet of tin among its trees. Above the lake I found High Lane, a track perhaps dating from Neolithic times, down which Scottish drovers in former days would drive trains of up to 300 cattle to markets in Thirsk and York. It was a great way to head towards Osmotherley, staring out over 50 miles of lowland country, picturing those hardy men and their charges slowly plodding south across these moody northern moors.

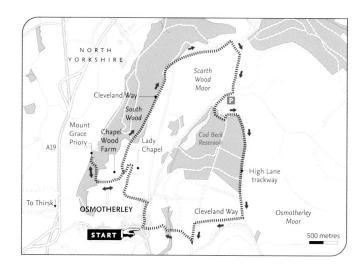

Start & finish North End, Osmotherley, North Yorkshire DL6 3AA (OS ref SE 456972). More car parking at Cod Beck Reservoir, 1½ miles north

Walk (6¾ miles, 8 miles including Mount Grace Priory detour; moderate; OS Explorer OL26): Follow Cleveland Way/CW (white acorn and fingerpost waymarks) for 2½ miles north to road on Scarth Wood Moor (473003). Right beside road for 1 mile to lower car park at Cod Beck Reservoir (468992). Left (kissing gate, footbridge) into trees. In 50m, left up left bank of stream; at edge of trees, left (470990, ladder stile); bear right to High Lane trackway (472991). Right for 1 mile; 400m beyond end of trees, right across chain (473974) on grassy track. In ½ mile cross horse gallop (465973); left down path; in 30m, right (465970, CW) on CW to Osmotherley. Detours: (a) Lady Chapel, signposted from 453977; (b) Mount Grace Priory, follow yellow arrows downhill from Chapel Wood Farm (452980) along field edges, then through wood to Priory (448985) and return.

Lunch Golden Lion, Osmotherley, Northallerton DL6 3AA (01609 883526, goldenlionosmotherley.co.uk)

More information Cleveland Way northyorkmoors.org.uk/ clevelandway; Mount Grace Priory nationaltrust.org.uk/mount-grace-priory; ramblers.org.uk; satmap.com

PATELEY BRIDGE

Business-like bunches of walkers were assembling in Pateley Bridge car park in a clatter of boots and sticks. Everyone wanted to grab hold of a day such as this, with enormous white clouds slowly drifting in a blue sky across Nidderdale. Yet this steep, rolling country has a mysterious way of swallowing its walkers, and we scarcely saw another soul all day. We followed the waymarked Nidderdale Way west along a narrow farm road between carefully maintained stone walls that sparkled with minute, intense winks of sunlight. The steep fields were striped with walls that wriggled like snakes up the undulations of the daleside and vanished over the top into sombre-coloured moorland, where heather burning operations were sending up curling towers of oily smoke.

We followed the lane down to Ashfold Side Beck through a tremendous slump of old lead-mine workings. Below the ashen tips a cluster of tumbledown buildings and a great rusty cogwheel and shaft showed where 19th-century miners had processed the precious and poisonous ore. Cornishmen, Irishmen, Scots and Welsh laboured here for the Prosperous and Providence Lead Mining Company, working the Wonderful and Perseverance Levels – names that say everything about the triumph of hope over experience.

Back along the beck and up over the fields to Stripe Head Farm, where the farmer in cap and gumboots was helping a ewe newly delivered of twins. "I'm out at 11pm to check on them this time of year," he said, "and out at 5.30am too." The newborn lambs staggered about and cried until they found what they were looking for under their mother's shaggy pelmet of wool stained dark by the winter. Then you couldn't hear a sound out of them.

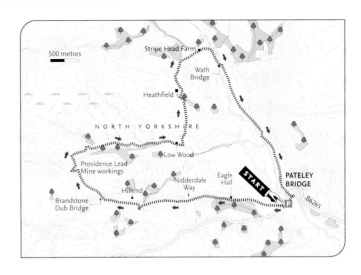

Start & finish Showground car park, Pateley Bridge, North Yorkshire HG3 5HW (OS ref SE157654); pay and display

Walk (7 miles; easy/moderate; OS Explorer 298): From car park, left along B6265. Pass turning to Ramsgill; in 50m, right (fingerpost, yellow arrow) up laneway to road (155654). Dogleg right/left ("Ladies Rigg"), and follow path through fields past Eagle Hall, following left-hand hedge/fence to meet Nidderdale Way/NiW at corner of wood (147655). Turn right along road, following NiW. In 1 mile, fork right at Hillend along lower lane (131653, "Ashfold Side, Cockhill"; NiW). In 700m cross Brandstone Dub Bridge (124655); follow stony lane to left. In ½ mile follow path down through ruin of Providence Lead Mine workings to cross Ashfold Side Beck (119611). Follow NiW downstream for 1¼ miles. Beyond Low Wood, left off lane (138664, NiW, "Heathfield"). Up field edge, through Spring House farmyard (138665); half right across next field to gate; on along track by wall. In 500m pass Highfield Farm; on down to Heathfield and Grange Lane (138673). Left along road. In 250m, 100m before Pie Gill drive, right through gate (137676, fingerpost). Follow left-hand wall; cross stile; half right between garage and wall. Keep wall on left till it bends left; aim half right for gate below (139679). Down track to Stripe Head Farm; through gate to right of buildings; down to road (141680). Right; in 500m, left ("Wath") across bridge (145677); right on NiW along River Nidd for 1¾ miles to Pateley Bridge.

Lunch The Sportsman's Arms, Wath (01423 711306; sportsmans-arms.co.uk)

ROSEBERRY TOPPING

A pale grey, windy sky streamed south over the North York Moors. Well wrapped against the foul weather, Jane and I followed a bowed but sprightly old lady up the lane to Aireyholme Farm.

James Cook spent his boyhood here in the 1730s, before the sea and the explorer's life claimed him. Roseberry Topping was a whalehead of a hill above the farm back then. Now it takes the shape of a tsunami wave in a classical Japanese painting, a convex green back rising to tip suddenly over at the summit in a great vertical cliff face of rugged broken rock. It was a giant landslip in 1912 that sent the western half of the hill crashing and sliding into ruin.

We followed a zigzag path, well patched with stones, steeply up to the crest of Roseberry Topping and one of the best views in the north of England – the long escarpment of the Cleveland Hills pushed out their ship's-prow profiles one behind the other into the great wide vale of the River Tees. A mess of chimneys lazily emitting coils of smoke showed where Teesside lay, still a heartbeat of industry in the north-east.

We followed the Cleveland Way down off the hill and up again to skirt the edge of a sombre dark moor at Great Ayton, all the way south to where the thick sandstone needle of the Captain Cook monument rose on its ridge. "A man of nautical knowledge inferior to none, in zeal, prudence and energy superior to most" eulogized the inscription. "Long will the name of Capt. Cook stand out among the most celebrated and most admired benefactors of the human race."

We drank to that with bottled water as we sheltered under the obelisk and watched the moors and hills smoking under a rolling sea of cloud.

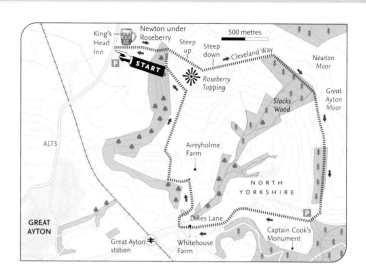

Start & finish Great Ayton station TS9 6HR (OS ref NZ574108)

Walk (5½ miles; hard; OS Explorer OL26): From station, cross bridge; on up road. Left at White House Farm down lane (577110); in ⅓ mile, nearing Aireyholme Farm, left over stile (578115; "footpath"); over next stile; ahead with wood on left. Ignore stile on left; over stile in corner of field (576115); right on path towards, then up Roseberry Topping. From summit (579126) follow Cleveland Way (CW) pitched path east, down and up to gate at edge of plantation (588127); right (blue, yellow arrows) on CW for 1¾ miles to Captain Cook monument (590101). Face back the way you came up CW, and take next path to left, aiming to go between two prominent gateposts. Follow path (yellow arrows) down through Ayton Banks wood; cross track near bottom (585104); continue down out of trees to angle of wall on right (584104). Right along sunken lane. In ½ mile, nearing Dikes Lane, left down stony track (578108; "Fir-Brook"); in 200m, right through gate; cross field to farm track (576107); left to station.

Lunch Picnic

More information Great Ayton Tourist Information Centre (01642 722835); yorkshire.com; ramblers.org.uk; satmap.com

RUNSWICK BAY

Runswick Bay, pride of the North Yorkshire coast, is an utterly charming, easel-friendly jumble of red-roofed, white-walled houses. They stand piled in one corner of a perfectly semicircular bay whose cliffs have been assiduously quarried and mined over the centuries. The steep green slopes are patched with the black scars of landslips and at their foot lie pebbles of black, red, ochre, cream and chocolate — colours that betray the presence of a treasury of minerals.

This is a dangerous coast for contrary currents and winds. Runswick Bay's lifeboat is not just there for show, and the crew were always traditionally drawn from local fishermen.

Beyond Hob Holes caves we climbed a steep flight of stairs and were away along the cliffs, looking ahead to where Whitby Abbey stood in Dracula-style ghostliness on the headland, eight miles off as the fulmar flies.

We skirted above landslip bays where dense undercliffs of heather and grass never see a human footfall, and turned back inland through fields corrugated with medieval ridges and furrows. The grassy foundations of a Roman lookout tower lay low on a hump of ground. The tower's minders evidently came to a bloody end at the hands of German barbarian pirates; archaeologists unearthed their skeletons, together with that of their dog, crushed in the ruins.

We followed the track of an old railway on a great curve through the fields, and dipped down through the trees to Runswick Bay once more. On the shining strand we stopped to collect a hoard of sea-smoothed stones, tide-rinsed and gleaming in our fingers.

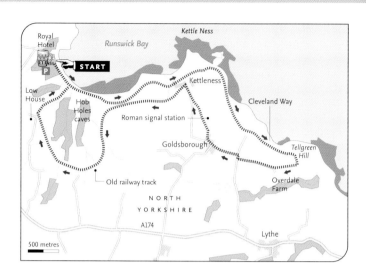

Start & finish Runswick Bay car park, North Yorkshire TS13 5HT (OS ref NZ810160); pay and display

Walk (9 miles; moderate; OS Explorer OL27): Right along beach. In ½ mile, just past Hob Holes caves, right (815154, Cleveland Way/CW acorn symbol) up rock, then wooden steps to cliff top. Follow CW for 2¾ miles. At Tellgreen Hill headland, right inland (850145; "Lythe" fingerpost). In 150m, yellow arrow/YA points ahead, but go right here to Overdale Farm drive (847143): ahead to road (840144). Right to Goldsborough (836147). Follow "Kettleness"; in 50m, right ("footpath") through farmyard; on through gate (YA) down green lane. Through gate (836148, YA); half left via Roman lookout tower mound (835151) to shed in field corner. Over stile (YA); down to chapel (833153); over 2 stiles to road; right into Kettleness. Left along old railway track (832155) for 2½ miles. Beside Low House, right off railway (807151) on track down to beach (812156); left to Runswick Bay.

Lunch Royal Hotel Runswick (01947 840215); beach café, Runswick Bay

More information yorkshire.com; visitengland.com; satmap.com; ramblers.org.uk

THIXENDALE

With the air of one who'd heard it a thousand times before, the landlord of the Cross Keys echoed: "What's a Painslackfull? Listen, if I have to tell you, I've got to kill you to keep the secret." I ordered one sight unseen, and went out into the garden of Thixendale's little pub to wait for it and to savour the cold, bright, windy day that had descended over the Yorkshire Wolds.

The village of Thixendale, near the deserted medieval village of Wharram Percy, lies down at the junction of half a dozen of the small, snaking, flat-bottomed valleys they call "dales" hereabouts.

My Painslackfull turned out to consist of … well, I couldn't possibly reveal that. But it was fantastically delicious. Wiping my mouth and burping pleasurably, I made my way up the adjoining valleys of Thixen Dale and Milham Dale.

The view west from the Roman road on the ridge above was sensational, and quite unexpected in these apparently flat lands: 40 or 50 miles across the Vale of York towards the hazy outlines of the Pennine Hills.

I walked down into the silent, sleepy and perfectly ordered village of Kirby Underdale, whose Norman church held a strange surprise: a blurred sandstone carving of Mercury, Roman god of good luck and swift action. Setting back by way of Painsthorpe Dale and Worm Dale, I pictured the sculptor at work with careful devotion, long before Christianity first blew like a breeze across these secret dales.

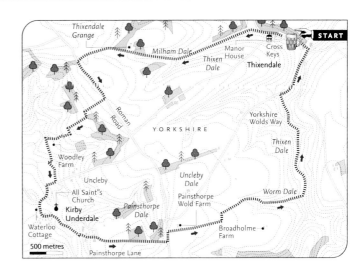

Start & finish Cross Keys Inn, Thixendale YO17 9TG (OS ref SE845610)

Walk (8½ miles; moderate; OS Explorers 300, 294): From Cross Keys Inn turn left for 50m, to road; right through village past Uncleby turning. 50m beyond village sign, left through gateway (838612, "bridleway"). In 50m, bear left (blue arrow/BA) up Thixen Dale. In ¾ mile fork right through gate (826608, "Chalkland Way") up Milham Dale. At Thixendale Grange (819609), left along drive to Roman road (811607). Left for ⅓ mile; at fingerpost on left of road, turn right (815602) down left side of hedge. At bottom of field, left to cross stile. Down hedge, through gate (812599); on down through next gate; follow left hedge down past Woodley Farm. At bottom of field, left through gate (807596; yellow arrow/YA). Follow hedge; on across field to join track (YA); follow it for ¼ mile to road (808590); right to pass Waterloo Cottage. At T-junction, left into Kirby Underdale. Left by phone box to pass church. Beyond church road bends left; right here over stile (811584; fingerpost, YA). Cross paddock; through gate (812583); left (YA) past Beech Farm; right (815583) up Painsthorpe Lane for ⅔ mile to Roman road (825582). Left ("Malton") for 150m; right ("bridleway" fingerpost) along farm track past Painsthorpe Wold Farm. In ½ mile, track bends left, then right. On this right bend (833586) keep forward (BA) for 30m, then right with hedge on right. Through gate (835588, BA), bear right for ½ mile down Wormdale. At junction with Thixen Dale (845589), left (fingerpost, YA) along Thixen Dale bottom for 1 mile to road (841603); right to Thixendale village.

Lunch Cross Keys Inn, Thixendale (01377 288272)

Buttermere, Cumbria

The cattle at Wood Farm were frisking in their pastures on this early spring morning. Walking the walled lane at the foot of the Peckforton Hills, we found crinkle-edged hart's-tongue ferns sprouting from chinks between the sandstone blocks. It's sandstone that shapes this landscape, particularly the great ridge that undulates north to the outermost crag where Beeston Castle stands. The castle occupies one of the most sensational sites in England, right at the lip of a 330ft (100m) cliff, with a superb prospect across 30 miles of country in all directions.

We looked around the exhibition down at the castle gateway (bronze axe heads and stone spinning weights, Civil War bullets and drinking flagons), then climbed through the massive sandstone gatehouse and wall towers of the outer ward, and on up through pine trees to the inner ward gatehouse and the tiny, lumpy stronghold at the peak. Pennine and Welsh hills, Liverpool Cathedral, the Wrekin and Chester – all lay there in open view, with the Victorian folly of Peckforton Castle rising on its crag a mile away southward.

It's claimed that in December 1643 eight Royalist desperadoes forced the surrender of the Roundhead garrison after they climbed the western crags. Some say the treasure of King Richard II lies at the bottom of the castle's well. It's certainly a hauntingly beautiful spot. Walking back to Burwardsley I kept turning round to gaze at the castle on the crag, an image to fix in the inner eye and carry away with me.

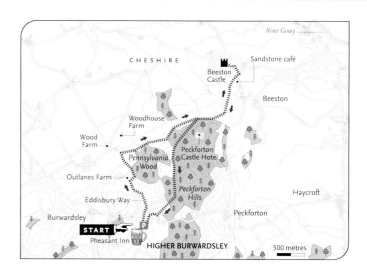

Start & finish Pheasant Inn, Higher Burwardsley, Tattenhall, Cheshire CH3 9PF (OS ref SJ523566)

Walk (6½ miles; moderate; OS Explorer 257): Right out of Pheasant car park; along lane. In 300m, left down field (524568, fingerpost, yellow arrow/YA) with hedge on left. Over stile (Eddisbury Way/EW); down to road (522571). Right; follow EW round Outlanes Farm; on across fields. Approaching Wood Farm, cross double stile (519577, EW); half left across stile by gate; right along field edge. Over stile at far end (522578); half left across field, through boggy dell (YAs). Half left across field beyond, to fingerpost at far top left corner (527580). Follow lane to join Sandstone Trail/ST (533583). Ahead on ST for 1 mile, crossing road (539588), to reach next road (540590). Ahead to Beeston Castle (537593). Return along ST for 2¼ miles to road just east of Higher Burwardsley (529567). Right to Pheasant Inn.

Lunch Pheasant Inn, Higher Burwardsley (01829 770434; thepheasantinn.co.uk); Sandstone Café near Beeston Castle gatehouse

More information Chester Tourist Information Centre (0845 6477868), visitcheshire.com, visitengland.com, Beeston Castle (01829 260464; english-heritage.org.uk/beeston), sandstonetrail.com

SHUTLINGSLOE AND WILDBOARCLOUGH

Ridgegate and Trentabank reservoirs gleamed dully between their pines and silver birch trees as. I forged ahead across the sedgy uplands on a pitched path that led to a scramble up to the gritstone peak of Shutlingsloe, the "Matterhorn of Cheshire".

At the summit of this mini mountain I was lord of a 100-mile view from the Pennines to the Trent, the Long Mynd to the Clwydian Hills of Wales. A few minutes to stand and stare, and I was scrambling down for the path to Wildboarclough, a quiet valley of easternmost Cheshire. The wild gritstone hills and moors of the Peak District rose all around. Old stories say that the last wild boar in these hills was hunted down to death in this steep little valley.

I followed a field path west along the flanks of the Clough Brook, then up the cleft below Oakenclough. Stopping to listen, I could not hear a single sound but the trickle of the brook. Over the damp shoulder of High Moor and down to the Hanging Gate Inn on its escarpment edge, with a most tremendous view out west over tumbled farmlands to the Cheshire plain stretching into misty distance.

The bare stone bluff of Tegg's Nose lifted its dark grey hump ahead as I walked the homeward stretch, north along the waymarked Gritstone Trail that knits together a fine string of these coarse sandstone hills. Hawthorns were thick with scarlet berries, or "peggles" as the great naturalist Richard Jefferies used to call them. I tested them with a squeeze of the fingers: still hard as rock, so that I wondered how the fieldfares and redwings of winter were going to gobble them down.

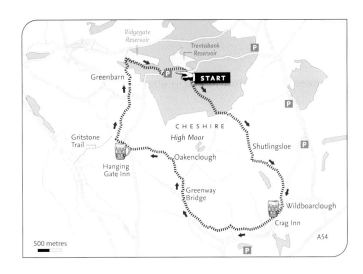

Start & finish Trentabank Visitor Centre car park, Langley, Macclesfield SK11 0NS (OS ref SJ 961711)

Walk (7½ miles; moderate; OS Explorer OL24): Pass Visitor Centre; follow "Shutlingsloe" signs for 2¼ miles SE to Shutlingsloe summit (977696). Path SE to farm road (983691); right. Just past Crag Inn (981685), right on field path west through 7 fields (yellow arrows/YA, coloured circles) to lane (970681), road (964685) and Greenway Bridge. Right (963687, YA) here beside Highmoor Brook. In 300m, left across brook (963690). Follow YAs to cross Oakenclough drive (961695); left on path west across moor to Hanging Gate Inn (952696). Cross road; down footpath beside inn; right to road (951698). Left for 150m; right/north on Gritstone Trail/GT north for ¾ mile. On house drive, right off GT at telephone pole (952712), following YAs to Ridgegate Reservoir (952713). Right on path to car park.

Lunch Leather's Smithy pub, Clarke Lane, Langley (beside Ridgegate Reservoir), SK11 0NE (01260 252313, leathersmithy.co.uk); Hanging Gate Inn, Potlords (07999 382236, thehanginggate.com)

More information Macclesfield Tourist Information Centre (01625 378123)

From the little resort town of Arnside we climbed a walled lane, then followed peaceful green paths through Red Hills Wood. From the crest of Arnside Knott beyond we got a most sensational view. Huge sprawling sands were uncovering themselves as they slid free of the sea's grey blanket. The River Kent was a sinuous coil of silver, its seaward movement seen as a writhing snake among the tan and mauve sandbanks. To the north and west, beyond a green apron of marshland fringing the estuary, stood the rugged profiles of the Furness Fells and their sister fells of South Lakeland.

We crossed the grassy top of Arnside Knott among juniper, yew, gorse and brambles. A solitary walker inched along like an ant far below, dwarfed by the sands he was striding on. A topograph gave further clues about the peaks and ridges to the north – Helvellyn and Striding Edge, Skiddaw and Bowfell, Coniston Old Man and the westward hump of Black Combe – all these in view from the Knott's modest elevation of 522ft (160m).

Down at Park Point we found a slanting ledge of rock from which to scramble down onto the shore. Jane went barefoot on the ribbed sand while I clambered over the limestone rubble in boots, looking for fossils. Rounding Blackstone Point we found the outgoing Kent's channel suddenly near at hand, with a fine view up the estuary to the centipede legs of Arnside's railway viaduct.

We reached the resort in time for an ice cream with the tide still ebbing. Arnside was a busy port till the 1850s, when the building of the viaduct caused the harbour to silt up. Then tourism took over, a new source of prosperity for the little town with the mighty views.

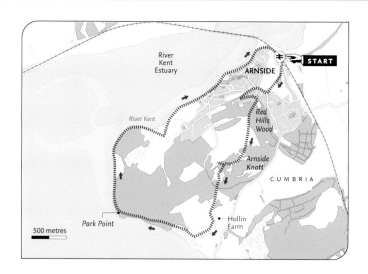

Start & finish Arnside railway station, Cumbria LA5 0HQ (OS ref SD 461788)

Walk (6½ miles; moderate; OS Explorer OL7): From station, left along road. Pass Milnthorpe turn; in 100m, right ("Silverdale Road" fingerpost). Right at Silverdale Road (459783). In 200m, left (457784, "Arnside Knott"). In 150m, left (456784, "High Knott Road"); bend left by "Windrush"; in 250m, right (457783, "The Knott") through Red Hills Wood. Through kissing gate (456780); head uphill to bench and gate (456776). Follow main path to another bench and on, soon descending. Round sharp left bend (452772); down through gate in wall (452770). Ahead on path outside trees. At Hollins Farm, right (451766, "Far Arnside"). At road, right (450764, "Park Point"); ahead through holiday park. At Shore Close fork right ("Bridleway"); at Knott Drive fork left. Follow woodland path back to Arnside. Be aware that woodland path from holiday park is stony and stumbly; shore option is for low or falling tide. Low tide option: Descend to shore just north of Park Point (437769); shore path back to Arnside.

Lunch Ye Olde Fighting Cocks, Arnside LA5 0HD (01524 761176, fightingcocksarnside.co.uk)

More information Arnside AONB Centre (01524 761034)

BUTTERMERE AND GATESGARTH

From the tiny settlement on its isthmus Coming down the road into Buttermere village, we ducked into the diminutive Church of St James to gaze out of the window dedicated to the supreme guidebook writer and illustrator Alfred Wainwright.

The beautiful lake of Buttermere shares its name with the village that stands on an isthmus separating it from Crummock Water. On this cold winter morning tough guys and gals wrapped in cocoons of winter clothing were heading for the surrounding heights. We were after something more modest today: the low-level circuit of Buttermere that's one of the peachiest short winter walks in the Lakes.

Soon we were on a stony path that threaded its way along the southern lake shore among the lemon-yellow larches and wind-tattered silver birches and sycamores of Burtness Wood. Sourmilk Ghyll came rushing down its rocky cleft with tremendous noise and presence. High overhead the crumpled peaks marched south-east along the flanks of the valley: Red Pike and High Stile beside us, Robinson and Grasmoor opposite.

At the far end of Buttermere, Fleetwith Pike rose magnificently, a sharp angle of fell running up to a peak with the knobbly spine of Haystacks alongside.

From Gatesgarth Farm and the hump-backed valley road we took the homeward path along the northern shore. A flock of Canada geese with white chinstraps and shirt fronts bobbed on the lake, discussing our passing with hen-like clucks and coos. A rock scramble and a short splashy tunnel through an outcrop, and we descended to Wilkinsyke Farm at Buttermere village, as eager for tea and stickies as though we'd truly been storming the heights.

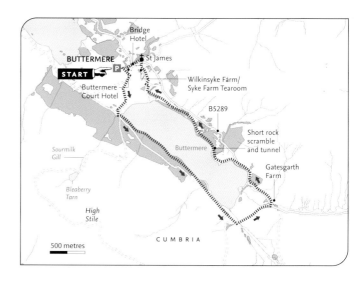

Start & finish Buttermere village car park, CA13 9UZ (OS ref NY 174169)

Walk (5 miles; easy/moderate; OS Explorer OL4): From car park, through kissing gate; right along path ("Lake", then "Buttermere"). In 600m at gate with NT contribution box (174164), right; continue on track along south side of Buttermere for 2 miles to Gatesgarth Farm at lake head (195149). Left along B5289 (take care – narrow road with bends); in 600m, left off road (192154, fingerpost "Buttermere village"). Follow north side path. In 700m, short rock scramble (approx. 187158); short tunnel follows. At foot of lake, keep ahead at fork (178164, fingerposts) to Wilkinsyke Farm and road (176169). Left to car park.

Lunch Syke Farm Tea Room, Wilkinsyke, Buttermere CA13 9XA (01768 770277; emayon.com)

More information South-side path, though rough and rocky in places, is recommended for wheelchair users in *Accessible Walks in the Lake District & Cumbria* by Mike Routledge (Pathfinder Guides; pathfinderwalks.co.uk)

CAUTLEY SPOUT, THE CALF AND BOWDERDALE

At noon under a blue sky, hens were clucking and sparrows chirping at the Cross Keys at Cautley. This old temperance inn is a pub with no beer (you're welcome to bring your own), but it's got just about everything else, including home cooking, enough books to stock an extremely erudite library, and that indefinable air of welcome and comfort that a weary walker dreams of finding.

But first we had to earn our ease. The Cross Keys has a wonderful view of Cautley Spout, a waterfall that tumbles some 650ft (200m) down a dark rock cleft in the eastern flank of the Howgill Fells. A track led through sheep pastures to the foot of the fall, and from here on it was a steep puff up a path of rocky steps. It was the first time I'd ever used a stick on a walk, and I certainly was glad of it.

At the top we crossed the fall, suddenly diminished to a trickle hardly wide enough to wet the boots. A stony track led off west beside Force Gill Beck into a silent upland, the heart of the Howgills. Green and gold carpets of opposite-leaved saxifrage grew close to the chattering beck. A lonely sheepfold had been nicely restored, and sheep had congregated there as though the shepherd might return at any moment.

Up on the skyline a tremendous westward panorama suddenly burst out, fold upon fold of east Cumbrian hills towards the Lake District. We turned along the ridge on the broad track of the Dales High Way, followed by a long descent to the secret valley of Bowderdale and the homeward path.

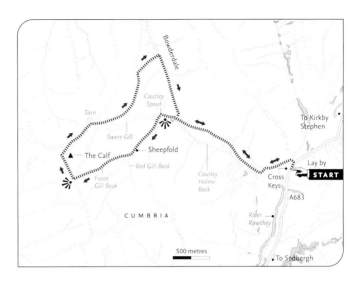

Start & finish Car parking bay on A683 at Cross Keys Inn, Cautley, near Sedbergh LA10 5NE (OS ref SD 698969)

Walk (6 miles; moderate with one steep climb; OS Explorer OL19): Down steps; cross River Rawthey; left on path to Cautley Spout. Steeply up beside waterfall. At top, left across Swere Gill (680975); follow path on right bank of Red Gill Beck. In 600m, just beyond sheepfold ruin (676971), fork right up path beside Force Gill Beck, then up to meet Dales High Way/DHW on skyline (669967). Right; follow DHW to The Calf trig pillar (667970) and on. In 600m at tarn (671964), follow path as it bends right and descends into Bowderdale. Either follow it to bottom of dale, or in ¾ mile turn right at small cairn (677980 approx.) on grassy path shortcut to dale bottom (680982 approx.). Right on path to foot of Cautley Spout (683975); return to Cross Keys.

Lunch Picnic, or Cross Keys (Fridays 9.30am–5pm, Saturdays and Sundays 9.30am–4.30pm)

More information cautleyspout.co.uk

A cold wind over Cumbria, blowing across the fells around Dufton. The last time I was here, walking the Pennine Way, I had fallen in love with the trim little farming village in its neat green dale.

Goldfinches were tentatively cheeping in the leafless sycamores of the stone-walled lane up Pus Gill's cleft, and the bubbling cry of curlews, so hauntingly evocative, came down from the moors where they would be pairing up for nesting and rearing.

Looking back above Pusgill House, we saw Dufton cradled in green, the wide vale of the River Eden beyond and, standing magnificently on the western skyline, the humpy backs of the Lakeland fells.

Once we had skirted the sharp cone of Dufton Pike and turned up the narrow side dale of Threlkeld Side towards the moors, the green road we were following became rocky and dark, and the sides of the dale sloped thick with tumbled boulders and charcoal-coloured slack. Lead miners of former days had burrowed the cleft into a warren of pitch-black levels, and their smelting kilns, spillways and spoil hummocks lay all around. Above the desolation lay the high moor, where we found a stone-built shooting box on the bank of cold and steely Great Rundale Tarn. Coming unexpectedly over the skyline, we shocked a pair of Canada geese who were sailing on the tarn, contemplating connubiality; frantic honking and splashing signalled their displeasure.

It was too damn cold to hang about. We turned along the beautiful wooded valley descended and that lies like a secret behind the nape of Dufton Pike, and were soon back on the Pennine Way and bowling down to Dufton.

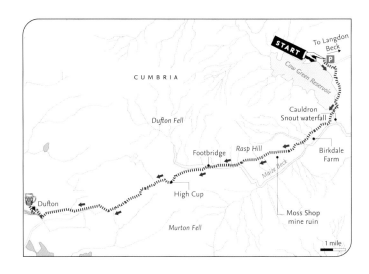

Start & finish Dufton car park, near Appleby-in-Westmorland, Cumbria CA16 6DB (OS ref NY690250)

Walk (8½ miles; moderate; OS Explorer OL19): Right along road from car park, round left bend; on following right bend by Old Dufton Hall, ahead on stony lane ("Pennine Way"/PW). In 150m, at foot of slope, PW forks left; but keep right here (692252; "bridleway") and up walled lane for 3½ miles, passing Pusgill House (696257) and mine workings of Threlkeld Side, to reach shooting box by Great Rundale Tarn (729283). Return for 2 miles past mines. Under Dufton Pike, right over wall stile at yellow-topped post (704268); down to another post; over stile, and right along track through Great Rundale Beck valley (yellow arrows). At clapper bridge (692273), left on PW to Dufton.

Lunch Stag Inn, Dufton CA16 6DB (01768 351608; thestagdufton.co.uk); Post Box Pantry, Dufton (07903 358081; postboxpantry.co.uk)

More information Appleby-in-Westmorland Tourist Information Centre (01768 351177), visitcumbria.com, ramblers.org.uk, satmap.com

ENNERDALE WATER

Ennerdale Water is the most westerly lake in the Lake District, and the quietest of all those easily accessible. The only road beside it is the crunchy forestry track that we followed along the north shore.

Big tranches of forest clothe the lower slopes of Great Borne and Starling Dodd on the north side. We moved from shadow to sun splashes under silver birch, rowan, ash and larch, looking up and beyond the trees to see the pink splotchy shoulders of Red Pike and High Stile, 2,000ft (610m) above us against the cloudy sky.

Ennerdale is a shapely valley, scoured by a glacier high on Great Gable to the east. The glacier pushed its moraine or rubbly foot down the valley towards the sea, piling up a long tongue of rocks where the River Liza runs into the lake. We turned down across this rough grassy hinterland before setting back westwards along the steeper and stonier southern shore of Ennerdale Water.

It seems incredible that a scheme should be afoot to bury nuclear waste in the granite rock below this lake. But that's the situation. The lake is deep, dark and cold, a broad trench of water full of life – salmon and trout, and the rare Arctic char, a race of fish sealed into the valley when the glacier retreated.

A scramble up and down the slippery rocks of Angler's Crag, polished to a shine of red and green by millions of boot soles. Then a last section round the west end of Ennerdale Water, looking east to Pillar and Pillar Rock, guarding the mountain approaches to Ennerdale as they have done for the past 400 million years.

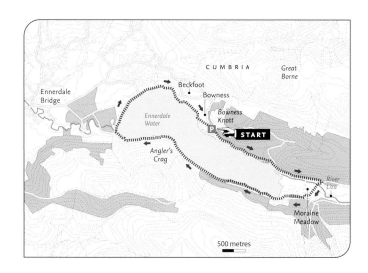

Start & finish Bowness Knott car park, Croasdale, Ennerdale Water CA23 3AU (OS ref NY 110153)

Walk (7½ miles; moderate; OS Explorer OL4): Left along track, clockwise round lake. In 1½ miles, pass modern bridge on right (131143); in another 350m, fork right (134142) down to cross 2 footbridges. Bear left through ruined wall; head across pasture for gate in plantation wall (131138). Go through; right along track; in 100m, right through gate. Left on the outside of plantation wall and on along south lake shore. In 2 miles, scramble over outcrop of Angler's Crag (103149); on clockwise round lake. In 2½ miles, path turns inland at Bowness to car park.

Lunch The Gather Café (01946 862453, thegatherennerdale.com); Fox and Hounds Inn (01946 861373, foxandhoundsinn.org); Shepherds Arms (01946 861249, shepherdsarms.com), all at Ennerdale Bridge

More information The Gather Café (see above); golakes.co.uk; nationaltrust.org.uk/ennerdale; ramblers.org.uk; satmap.com

GLENRIDDING DODD AND SHEFFIELD PIKE

Mine host Mark Hook pointed out of the dining room window at Mosscrag Guest House – "That's Glenridding Dodd. It's a shame people don't go up there from Glenridding any more. The Victorians did, and they knew a good view when they saw one."

In the Lake District it's handy to have a B&B host who knows the local fells inside out. Within five minutes Mark had pencilled out the route on my map. It didn't seem too fearsome, even though some of the contours looked a little close-packed for comfort.

Half an hour into the walk I paused to catch my breath, not for the first time. If our genteel ancestors really did "ascend" Glenridding Dodd by this 45-degree channel of rubbly stones, they must have been made of stern stuff. At the summit of the Dodd, a towering lump of rock scabbed with pale outcrops, I saw what they had perspired to see, a fabulous prospect down the southern length of Ullswater.

With a travel-stained copy of Alfred Wainwright's *Guide to the Eastern Fells* in hand, I negotiated a steep and rugged path up Heron Pike, splashed between the peaty tarns and stood by the cairn on Sheffield Pike, lord of a most superb view – north up Ullswater, east to the long line of the High Street ridge, west into the great green clefts under Glencoyne Head, and south to the blade-like profile of Helvellyn.

Wainwright hated the lead mines whose remnants scar the upper end of Glenridding. But I enjoyed the descent through those incredible banks of multicoloured spoil, hanging in the sky like the sword of Damocles over the former smelting mills dwarfed at their feet.

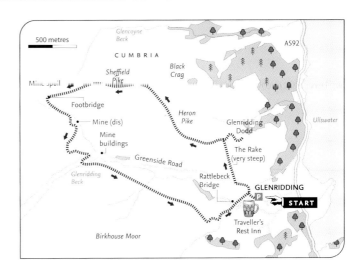

Start & finish Glenridding car park CA11 0PD (OS ref NY386170)

Walk (7 miles; hard; OS Explorer OL5): From car park follow signs to Traveller's Rest Inn (382170). 100m past pub, right ("Greenside Road"). Fork left ("Greenside Mine"); past 2 cottage terraces, through gate at cattle grid, then right up zigzag path; in 100m, right (yellow arrow) up steep stony track to wall at saddle (378175). Don't go through gate; follow wall to right; in 150m, right up track to summit of Glenridding Dodd (381175). Return to gate; don't go through, but keep ahead, with wall on right, along path (grass, then stones). Steeply up ridge of Heron Pike, then across boggy grass for ¼ mile to summit of Sheffield Pike (369182). From summit aim west for long ridge of mine spoil. Cross Swart Beck by footbridge (359179); left along mine track; steeply down to mine buildings. Just before buildings, right (364174; "Red Tarn, Helvellyn"). In 200m, left across Glenridding Beck; left along hillside path for almost a mile. At fork by big boulder with wall, left downhill; follow wall; through gate by ladder stile (376167). Down stony path; cross Glenridding Beck by Rattlebeck Bridge; Traveller's Rest Inn; car park.

Lunch Traveller's Rest Inn, Greenside Road, Glenridding CA11 0QQ (01768 482298)

More information Ullswater Tourist Information Centre, Glenridding car park (01768 482414); golakes.co.uk; ramblers.org.uk; satmap.com

MELLBREAK AND CRUMMOCK WATER

Setting out from the Kirkstile Inn, the northern face of Mellbreak looked so dark, sheer and forbidding that we wondered how on earth we were to get up there.

Yet once we'd reached the slippery screes that fan out down the mountain, it was easy enough – a bit of zigzag, a lot of hard breathing and upward effort, and we were standing proud at the northern summit cairn. The view from the 1,668ft (508m) northern peak of Mellbreak must be one of the best in the Lake District – back over Loweswater and north as far as the misty spread of the Solway Firth and the grey humps of Scotland's Galloway hills; east across Crummock Water to the pink screes of towering Grasmoor; north to the great mountain spine of Red Pike, High Stile and High Crag; west to the long green ridge of Hen Comb and Loweswater Fell rising across the deep, unpopulated valley of Mosedale. A steep, skeltering path dropped us into Mosedale. Down there a green track skirted the western flank of Mellbreak in wonderful isolation and silence. If Mosedale ever had farms, fields and folk, they are long forgotten. Here were swaths of bog grazed by Herdwick sheep, and watery dells full of orchids, sundews and flowering sedges, all caught in a cradle of shapely fells.

Down on Crummock Water we turned north along the lake shore. What were the islet of Low Ling Crag and its tiny tombolo beach of grey shaley stones created for, if not for swimming in the cool lake water on a hot summer afternoon?

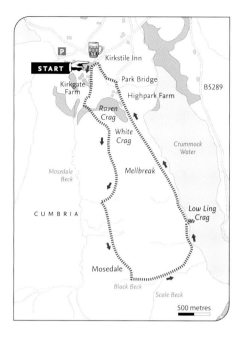

Start & finish Kirkstile Inn, Loweswater, Cumbria CA13 0RU (OS ref NY141209)

Walk (6 miles; hard; OS Explorer OL4): From Kirkstile Inn fork right off left bend; immediately right ("No Through Road"). Country lane south for ½ mile past Kirkgate Farm. At gate, lane curves right (139202); ahead uphill between trees. On open fell, keep ahead to bottom of scree (141199). Bear left; zigzag up (steep, skiddy!) to north summit of Mellbreak (143195). Ahead into dip. In 500m path bears right to a fork, 50m before rock outcrop on main path (145190). Fork right here on faint path, steeply down to track in Mosedale (141186). Turn left (south) for 900m, to pass metal gate. Shortly afterwards track curves left and follows the lower line of the bracken; keep ahead here (144178), aiming for curved peak of Red Pike. In 350m, go through gate in fence on bank (146175); descend to turn left along track by Black Beck (146174). Pass 3 footbridges (152174; 155175; 156178) but don't cross any of them. On reaching Crummock Water, bear left (north). Nearing north end of lake, in 1¼ miles, branch left (149197) up path through bracken which bisects angle with stone wall ahead. Reaching wall (148199), follow it to Highpark Farm. Turn right through gate in wall (145202); left through gate; on along stony lane. Cross Park Bridge (145205); fork left to Kirkstile Inn.

Lunch Kirkstile Inn (01900 85219; kirkstile.com)

RAVEN STONES AND GREENFIELD BROOK

From Binn Green car park a good flat path led us north beside Yeoman Hey and Greenfield reservoirs. Their waters rippled lightly, as though the valley winds were chiselling millions of scallop shapes in shiny black slate.

We passed the tall grassy wall of Greenfield dam. There was fine Victorian attention to detail in the rusticated facings of sluices channelling moorland streams down to the reservoir. High above ran the black gritstone edges or cliffs of the valley rim, where tiny figures of early bird walkers posed on tors sculpted by weather and time into crenellations and towers.

At the head of the valley we crossed a sluice and turned aside into Birchen Clough. Greenfield Brook came rushing down over boulders and rapids, a puzzle to get across. We teetered and hesitated, then hopped and flopped from rock to rock before climbing by hand and boot tip up the steep rough path on the other bank. Past a waterfall, kinder gradients took over. We recrossed the brook and followed a squelchy trail up to Raven Stones Edge. Here, looking down the valley, I pictured in awe the grinding power of the glacier that carved these cliffs tens of thousands of years ago.

The path led away across the moor, where vibrant magenta heather was in bloom, to reach a gritstone memorial cross to James Platt, MP for Oldham, who died in 1857 when his shooting companion stumbled and accidentally shot him. A dark monument in a dark rocky wilderness, from which we descended towards the valley and the man-made lakes still brushed with sunlight far below.

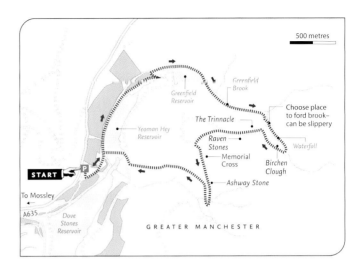

Start & finish Binn Green car park, Dove Stone Reservoir, Oldham OL3 7NN (OS ref SE 018044)

Walk (5¼ miles; strenuous; OS Explorer OL1): From lower car park, steps ("Reservoirs & Trails") descend to road. Left ("Yeoman Hey"). Follow roadways along left banks of Yeoman Hey and Greenfield reservoirs; 700m beyond Greenfield Reservoir, right across culvert (038050), up Birchen Clough, on right bank. After 100m, choose place to cross (boulder-hop – may be impassable in flood). On up left bank; 100m above waterfall, choose place to recross (040056) on to path slanting right up to Raven Stones (037048). Follow path along edge for 400m, then trending left from 033048 across moor for 400m, till Dove Stone Reservoir in view. Left (030047) on clear track up knoll; on past Memorial Cross (031044) and Ashway Stone outcrop (032042). In 150m, sharp right on lower path; in 150m, immediately below Ashway Stone, fork left (031042) on path downhill for ½ mile to cross Yeoman Hey dam (022046). Left to Binn Green.

Lunch Picnic

More information visitpeakdistrict.com

Pendle Hill is the witchiest hill in England – mostly, but not entirely, on account of the notorious trials of 1612 when ten local men and women were hanged at Lancaster for practising the dark arts.

Today it rode under a great breaking wave of cloud. As we climbed the steep, stone-pitched path to the summit, skeins of mist came drifting across, turning Pendle House farm below into a washy watercolour.

At the top we followed a grassy track to find George Fox's well, a modest, urban-looking trapdoor in the hillside. Raising it revealed a silver tankard chained to the lid, ready to be lowered into the well. I drank a scooped handful from the spring below – ice cold, glass clear and sweet. Fox, young and full of spiritual zeal, refreshed himself here in 1652 having just experienced an epiphanic revelation on Pendle's summit that drove him to go forth and preach, and to establish the Quaker movement.

We forged south through the mist along the crest of Pendle, on a cairned track that soon turned and plunged down out of the murk. Big views opened eastward as we followed a rutted bridleway at the foot of the hill, down to where the Ogden Water's shallow flow wound out of steep-sided Ogden Clough to fill the twin reservoirs that lie above Barley.

Coming back into the village we passed the site of Malkin Tower, lair of the Pendle witches – according to their persecutors. Who knows what Alizon Device, Chattox, Old Demdike and Mouldheels were really up to? Whatever it was, their shadows still lie long across this beautiful valley and the hill that overhangs it.

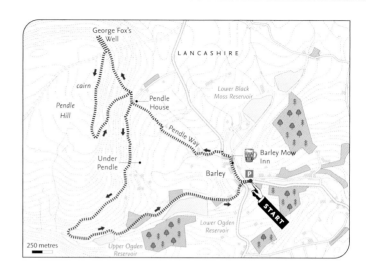

Start & finish Car park, Barley Picnic Site, nr Nelson, Lancs BB12 9JX (OS ref SD823403)

Walk (6¼ miles; moderate/hard; OS Explorer OL41): Turn right through village; left by Meadow Bank Farm; follow waymarked Pendle Way/PW across fields to Pendle House Farm (809412) and up steep slope to top of Pendle Hill. Right over stile (806418) to visit George Fox's Well (200m along path). Return over stile; right for 100m; left/south along PW for ½ mile, past trig pillar (805414). Where PW forks right (804409), keep ahead on grooved path, curving left to rim of escarpment (805408). Descend to Pendle House Farm. Right along bridleway, with wall on left for ¾ mile, past Under Pendle (808404), to where bridleway turns left (807401). Keep ahead through kissing gate, down to Ogden Water (801397). Left along PW past Upper Ogden reservoir; road past Lower Ogden reservoir to Barley.

Lunch Barley Mow, Barley, Pendle BB12 9JX (01282 690868; barleymowpendle.co.uk) – welcoming, walker-friendly pub

More information The Cabin Café and Information Centre, Barley picnic site (01282 696937); Clitheroe Tourist Information Centre (01200 425566); visitlancashire.com; visitengland.com; satmap.com; ramblers.org.uk

CLOUGHA, FOREST OF BOWLAND

Young lambs cried, ewes blared and a curlew emitted haunting cries from the slopes of Clougha as we skirted the stone stronghold of Cragg Farm. Sunlight slanted across the folded fells that climbed southward into the great upland wilderness of the Forest of Bowland. Nearer at hand, our aiming point of Clougha ran as a high line stretched against a pale blue summer sky.

Beyond the slit-windowed wall of Skelbow Barn – more fortress than hay store – we turned uphill beside the musically burbling Sweet Beck. A faint path led up beside a nameless stream trickling over mats of slippery moss, heading for higher ground through tough old heather sprigs and acid-green bilberry.

Up at the heights of Clougha, three rectangular stone monoliths stood side by side in a sea of grey stony clitter. Close up, they proved to be an installation by the landscape artist Andy Goldsworthy – Clougha Pike Chambers, a trio of sentry boxes with beautiful elliptical openings. We sat next to the sculptures to gaze out across the hillside and listen to cuckoos calling from Cragg Wood far below.

A Land Rover track proved a reliable guide on our descent from Clougha. A mother grouse clicked frantically to her three fluffball chicks to stay low and invisible as we walked by. Out in front unrolled a most stupendous 100-mile view over the low-tide immensities of Morecambe Sands, the widening arms of the Lakeland and north Wales coasts, and a blur on the western sea horizon that might have been the Isle of Man.

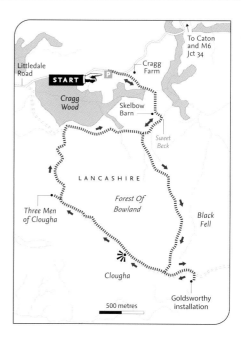

Start & finish Little Crag car park, near Caton, Lancaster LA2 9ET (OS ref SD 546618)

Walk (5½ miles; moderate; OS Explorer OL41): Leave car park, right along road. In 100m, right by cattle grid, over ladder stile, past Cragg Farm on field track. In 700m, left through gate at Skelbow Barn (551613). In 100m, right uphill with wall on right. Through gate; in 150m, left over ladder stile (551611). Right along wall; in 100m, beside gate, left up track on left of beck (not green embanked track on your right), aiming for tree. After tree continue, keeping about 100m from wall on left. In 300m, make for stony track, bearing left round hillside, parallel with wall. About 700m after leaving tree, track curves right/south (553606) for ¾ mile to meet a four-wheel-drive track (552596). Left to Goldsworthy installation (556595); return along four-wheel-drive track. After 1¾-mile descent, track turns sharp left near Cragg Wood wall for steep descent into gully (541612); right here on path along north edge of "access land" for ¾ mile to ladder stile (551611), Skelbow Barn and car park.

Lunch Picnic

More information Lancaster Tourist Information Centre (01524 582394); visitlancashire.com; satmap.com; ramblers.org.uk

COCKERHAM TO CONDER GREEN

A glorious afternoon on the west Lancashire coast under wall-to-wall blue sky. We walked the green fields of Cockerham with the Bowland moors rising in the east, Blackpool Tower tiny and familiar down in the south-west, and the Lake District fells around Helvellyn and Scafell Pike standing as if cut from pale blue card on the northern horizon.

Down at the sea wall a great flat apron of saltmarsh lay spread at the edge of Cockerham Sands, cut with wriggling channels.

The seawall path ran past Bank End and Bank Houses, remote farmsteads among flat green pastures out at the edge of the land. As the coast turned north we came to Cockersand Abbey, or what remains of it – a curious semi-rectagonal chapter house among angles of walls, its soft red sandstone rubbed into dimples and hollows by 800 years of wind and weather.

Cockersand Abbey was founded on this lonely shore as a leper hospital. When the site was excavated in the 1920s, archaeologists found fragments of lead and coloured glass from the windows that were smashed at the Dissolution of the Monasteries. The abbey ruin became a source of readyworked building stone.

From Cockersand Abbey we followed the windy coast path north to Crook Farm, with Heysham Power Station looming massively ahead like a 1950s suburban house designed by an ogre. Soon it was behind us, and we followed the grassy imprint of Marsh Lane over sheep pastures to Glasson Dock. A dip into the cornucopia of goodies in the Port of Lancaster Smokehouse here, and a last stretch on a railway path into Conder Green above the golden marshes of the Lune Estuary.

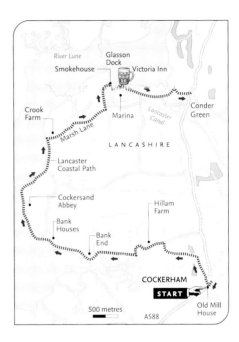

Start & finish Cockerham car park (OS ref SD 465525)

Walk (7 miles; flat and easy; OS Explorer 296): Follow A588 south and round right bend at junction with B5272. in 50m, right beside Old Mill House. Follow lane; through garden at top; through kissing gate at end of garden (464524, yellow arrow/YA). Follow fence on right downhill; follow YAs along field edges, round cottage (462529). Leave cottage garden over stile; ahead over field and footbridge (YA); follow ditch/fence on right for ½ mile to Hillam Lane (455531). Left past Hillam Farm; in ½ mile, right (449528) along sea wall. Follow Lancaster Coastal Path/LCP north for 3¾ miles via Bank End (441528), Cockersand Abbey chapter house (427537), Crook Farm (431550) and Marsh Lane to road at Glasson (443556). Left, then right to Glasson Dock. Cross swing bridge (445561); cross road by Victoria Inn; right along LCP. In ¾ mile, cross bridge (456560); right to Conder Green. Bus 89/89H or taxi (01995 607777) to Cockerham.

Lunch Picnic

More information Lancaster Tourist Information Centre (01524 582394); visitlancashire.com; visitengland.com; satmap.com; ramblers.org.uk

TRAWDEN AND WYCOLLER

Trawden lies in a narrow dale – the name signifies a trough-like valley – between the old mill towns of Nelson and Colne and the high empty moors of the Lancashire–Yorkshire border. We left this cheerful village, which was gearing up for a festival with stalls and silver bands, and climbed a cobbled lane south towards the open country.

Out in the fields well-tended gritstone walls divided the large, square pastures. The cockerels and dogs of Trawden made Sunday music far below, their cries fading under the sharp alarm calls of curlew in the sedge as we gained height towards the twin Coldwell reservoirs.

An old moor lane led east at the foot of the rough slopes of Boulsworth Hill. Rutted and walled, its slabs indented by boots, hoofs and cart wheels, it gave superb views north over the fields and farmsteads of Trawden Forest, a Saxon hunting ground gradually overtaken by farming, milling and mining. Back west rose Pendle Hill, burdened with legends of witches and spells, but now just a beautiful hill in the sun.

Deep, brackeny cloughs brought streams twisting down to the south. We crossed Turnhole Clough and followed the Brontë Way down to the shell of Wycoller Hall, Charlotte Brontë's model in *Jane Eyre* for Mr Rochester's lonely house of Ferndean.

A glass of pink lemonade in the little tearoom at Wycoller; then we found the homeward path through fields where sheep lay panting in the shade of upright gritstone slabs that served for fencing.

The pale blue shoulder of Pendle Hill rose on the far skyline as an aiming point, and from down in Trawden the thump and blare of a silver band came blasting across the sun-scorched fields.

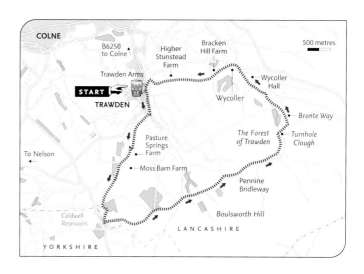

Start & finish Trawden Arms pub, Trawden, Lancashire BB8 8RU (OS ref SD 912388)

Walk (8 miles; field paths and moorland tracks; OS Explorer OL21): Fork left off B6250 up lane at Trawden Arms. In 450m, cross road (912384); follow fingerposts to right of Trawden Literary Institute and garages to field path (911383). Ahead uphill by wall past radio mast (909378), Pasture Springs Farm (908377) to Moss Barn (907374). Right along front of house; yellow arrows/ gate/stile into plantation. Left on path through trees for 400m to stile/ footbridge on to moor (905370, yellow arrow). Half right, aiming for turbine, to wall stile (903367), then gate on to road (903364). Left; in 350m, left on bridleway (903361); follow "Pennine Bridleway", "Wycoller". In 3 miles cross Turnhole Clough (941379); in 300m, left (943381, "Wycoller") down to Wycoller (933392). Follow road past tea shop, over bridge; in 200m, on right bend, through wooden gate (930394, fingerpost) on right of farm track. Path west across fields for 1¼ miles by Bracken Hill Farm (927392) and Higher Stunstead (916390) to B6250 in Trawden (912389); left to Trawden Arms.

Lunch Trawden Arms (01282 337055, trawdenarms.co.uk); Tea Wycoller Tearoom (01282 868395, wycollercraftcentre.co.uk)

More information trawdenparishcouncil.org.uk; visitlancashire.com; satmap.com; ramblers.org.uk

WINTER HILL AND RIVINGTON PIKE

Aiming for the 1,000ft (300m) needle of Winter Hill TV mast on a chilly morning, we made out a network of paths coming from every direction, climbing to converge at the summit of the hill.

At the top a cold wind whistled and groaned through the skeletal radio towers. To the west the promised view over Morecambe Bay, Blackpool Tower and out to the mountains of Snowdonia was hazed out to a milky blur under a streaky blue sky.

Winter Hill has an ominous name. Memorials are widespread, one to a Scottish traveller murdered here in 1838, another to the victims of an aircraft crash in a snowstorm in 1958.

A broad braided track dropped down from Crooked Edge Hill to the cheerful Pike Snack Shack, where a cuppa and a sticky slab fortified us for the homeward trek. A rocky road led away west below the dark castellated bulk of the tower on Rivington Pike, an 18th-century hunting lodge, to reach the wonderful folly of the Pigeon Tower, a slender rocket of a building that called out for a Rapunzel to let down her hair. It was built in 1910 by Lord Leverhulme as part of his remarkable project to lay out Italianate and Japanese terraced gardens on the slopes below.

Rich men's foibles notwithstanding, Rivington Moor and Winter Hill are democratic places. Bolton, Bury, Wigan and Blackburn lie below, the hill and its open spaces tantalisingly in sight. In a mass trespass in 1896 10,000 people broke down private gates and occupied the ground. It would take another hundred years for the moor and hill to be declared open access land for all, but today the folk from all around can walk where they will.

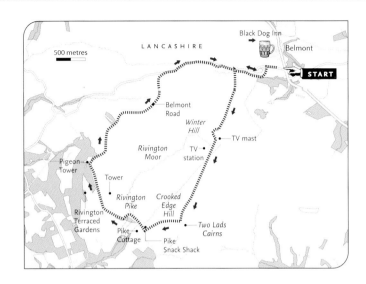

Start & finish Black Dog Inn, Church Street, Belmont BL7 8AB (OS ref SD 674158)

Walk (7½ miles; easy; OS Explorer 276): Up Church Road. In 400m, left on path round Ward's Reservoir. In 700m, just before car park up on right, left across stream (666158). Uphill beside tumbledown wall. Where it bends left (665155), ahead up path, aiming for tall TV mast. At top of Winter Hill, bear right around fence to road (661148). Left and follow road. In ¾ mile on left bend, right at fingerpost (657136). Cross footbridge; ahead to reach Two Lads cairns on Crooked Edge Hill (655133). Right on broad path (ignore yellow arrow waymark post), descending to Pike Cottage and Pike Snack Shack (649132). Right along stony roadway for 1¼ miles to Pigeon Tower (640143). Fork right here along stony Belmont Road for 1½ miles to meet Rivington Road (653158). Right to car park (665159) and reservoir path back to Belmont.

Lunch Pike Snack Shack, Pike Cottage BL6 6RU (07949 338820)

More information rivingtonterracedgardens.org.uk; visitlancashire.com

High Force, Durham

The Teesdale town of Barnard Castle on a busy weekday was bustling, friendly and packed with local shops. Some of these were not entirely traditional in produce, however; goat-curry pasties were wowing the shoppers at the Moody Baker.

We passed the gaunt, broken walls of the castle that overhangs the Tees. Down by the river we stopped beside the rushing white bar of the weir just in time to catch sight of a dipper alighting there. It bobbed its white-shirt front energetically up and down before skimming off upriver in flight as straight as an arrow. We followed it along the Teesdale Way, an undulating path now rocky, now muddy, that shadowed the river through beautiful woods of young limes and beeches.

On this woodland walk, every flowering thing popped out and was displaying ensemble, taking advantage of the short northern spring – wood anemones white and purple, bluebells and stitchwort, primroses side by side with red campion. Wild garlic and celandine, violets next to wild strawberries, forget-me-not, speedwell and water avens – it was altogether an astonishing display.

Opposite Cotherstone we found the most perfect picnic spot in Teesdale, a primrose bank from which we looked down through young ash leaves to the river snaking noisily round a bend. Pied wagtails curtsied on the rocks, swallows skimmed the water, and a fisherman stood knee-deep and cast for a trout.

We descended to cross the Tees, then climbed to the return path along the rim of the dale. A bolt of rain, a whistle of wind, a crash of thunder and a spatter of hail like buckshot on our backs. Then brilliant spring sunshine spreading like butter across the pastures at Cooper House.

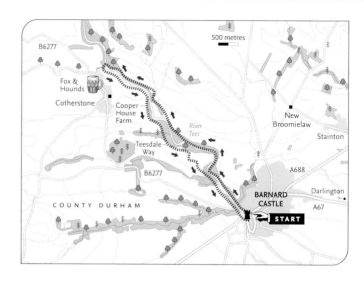

Start & finish Barnard Castle long-stay car park DL12 8GB (OS ref NZ 051163)

Walk (8½; moderate; OS Explorer OL31): Right up main street to right bend; left ("Castle"); follow "Riverside Walk and Cotherstone" down to River Tees. Follow Teesdale Way/TW upstream for 3½ miles. Opposite Cotherstone, descend to 2-finger TW post on far side of gorse meadow. Left here (014202) across River Tees and tributary (013201). To visit Cotherstone, turn right here; to continue walk, climb steep bank opposite and follow TW for 3½ miles downstream to Barnard Castle. At B6277 (045167), left across Tees ("Cycle Route 70"); right into town.

Lunch Picnic; or Fox & Hounds, Cotherstone (01833 650241, cotherstonefox.co.uk)

More information Barnard Castle Tourist Information Centre (03000 262626), thisisdurham.com; visitengland.com; satmap.com, ramblers.org.uk

CRONKLEY FELL, DURHAM DALES

There's something perfect about the blend of springtime sights and sounds in this twisting cleft in the Pennine Hills – the rumble and chatter of the young Tees in its rocky bed, the high volcanic cliffs between which it snakes, the poignant cries of curlew and lapwing nesting in the sedgy fields, and above all the brilliant colours of the exquisite little flowers that bloom for a short, unpredictable season across the craggy back of Cronkley Fell.

Setting out on a cold, wind-buffeted morning, we had no idea whether the flowers would be out. Yet in a damp bank beside the farm, sunk among masses of marsh marigolds, we spotted the pale yellow orbs of globe flowers, a signal that spring was at least attempting to elbow winter out of the way.

Behind Cronkley Farm we climbed between the juniper thickets of High Crag into the grassy uplands, where the old droving track called the Green Trod runs up the nape of Cronkley Fell.

A succession of "exclosures", wired off to make them impenetrable to the nibbling sheep and rabbits, harbours the rarest of Upper Teesdale's spring flowers, delicate survivors of a post-Ice Age flora that has vanished from the rest of upland England. We knelt on the stony ground to take in these miniature beauties at eye level – deep-pink bird's-eye primroses, tiny white stars of spring sandwort and the intensely, royally blue trumpets of spring gentians.

At last, we tore ourselves away, frozen and entranced. We descended to the Tees and returned along the brawling river.

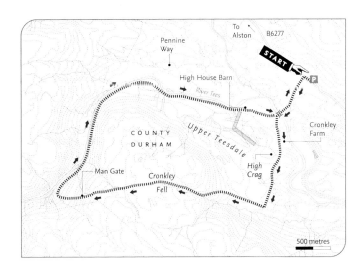

Start & finish Forest-in-Teesdale car park, near Langdon Beck, Co. Durham DL12 0HA (OS ref NY 867298)

Walk (7 miles; moderate; OS Explorer OL31): Right along B6277; in 100m, left down farm track. Skirt right of first house (864296); down to wicket gate (yellow arrow/YA); on, keeping right of Wat Garth, to track. Join Pennine Way (PW) and cross River Tees by Cronkley Bridge (862294). Follow PW and YAs past Cronkley Farm, into dip (862288), up rocky slope of High Crag and on along paved track. In 500m, left across stile (861283). PW bears left here, but continue ahead uphill by fence. Through kissing gate (861281); in 100m, turn right along wide grassy Green Trod trackway. Follow it for 2 miles west across Cronkley Fell (occasional cairns). Descend at Man Gate to River Tees (830283); right along river for 2½ miles. At High House Barn (857294), aim half left across pasture for Cronkley Bridge; return to car park.

Lunch Picnic

More information ramblers.org.uk; thisisdurham.com

FROSTERLEY AND THE OLD QUARRIES, WEARDALE

From the daleside village of Frosterley we followed the Mineral Valley Walk as it rose to run round the rim of an old quarry. Sunk below the level of the fields were big lumpy spoil heaps, delvings and trackways, their awkward angles smoothed and softened by the grass that covered them in a green velvet nap. Looking down on this from the striated limestone crags of the former quarry faces, it was hard to imagine the thunderous noise, the dust, the hard labour and raw surroundings of a hundred years ago.

Beyond the quarry we turned down the gorge of the Bollihope Burn on a former railway track. A red grouse scuttled away in a panic. The path squeezed between adjacent rock faces where streaks of dusky red hinted at the presence of iron. Across the burn some hopeful lead miner had driven a speculative adit, a tunnel leading from a crude hole into utter darkness.

A flight of steps led up to open sheep pastures, hillside farms and a glimpse of long ridges of moorland. Then we dropped back down beside the Bollihope Burn, looping back to Frosterley along the rim of Harehope Quarry, another huge subterranean moonscape repurposed as an ecological education centre. Field classrooms, wildlife ponds, summerhouses and a wind turbine have taken over from heavy machinery, rubble mountains and polluted pools.

On the way we crossed the dry bed of a stream. There below the footbridge were great slabs of Frosterley marble, dark rock smoothed by water and patterned with an intricate jumble of white fossils. It was remarkable to think of the journey this ancient seabed deposition made in medieval times, cut and shaped to rise in polished glory in Durham Cathedral, pride of the Prince Bishops, 20 miles away across the hills.

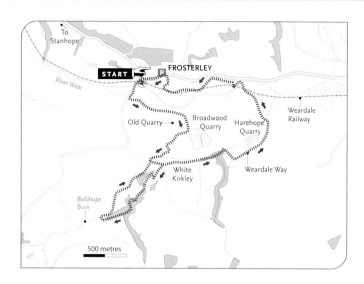

Start & finish Frosterley car park, Frosterley DL13 2QW (OS ref NZ 026370)

Walk (5½ miles; easy; OS Explorer OL31; Frosterley Walks leaflet downloadable at durham.gov.uk): Right along A689. Left ("White Kirkley") across River Wear. In 150m, left (022367) beside chapel ("Mineral Valleys Walk"/MVW). In ½ mile, right at kissing gate (029365, MVW); keep fence on right round quarry rim. Through gate (027362); down slope; right (MVW) to road (025360). Left (MVW); by bridge, right (026360, stile, MVW) along Weardale Way/WW. In ¾ mile, pass (don't cross) bridge (020354); in 40m, right up steps; right at top to gate. Left up fence; in 150m, right (020356) on field track to road (025360). Right; in 150m, left (026360, stile) on WW. In 700m, by footbridge on right, ahead (033361, stile, "Permissive Path"); in 150m, left along WW (035360). In 500m, at gate, WW turns right (039363); left down road. In ½ mile at level crossing, don't cross (036368); bear left on path. In 600m, right to cross railway (030368); ahead on lane to Frosterley churchyard (026368) and Front Street.

Lunch Frosterley Inn, Front Street DL13 2RH (01388-528493)

More information Durham Dales Centre, Stanhope (01388 527650), thisisdurham.com; northpennines.org.uk; Harehope Quarry (07807 002032), harehopequarry.org.uk

HANNAH'S MEADOW

There aren't many proper old upland hay meadows left in England, but the one at Low Birk Hatt farm in Baldersdale is an absolute beauty. That's thanks to Hannah Hauxwell, the lone woman who farmed these fields in an entirely traditional way until her retirement in 1988, and also to Durham Wildlife Trust, which took them on, renamed them Hannah's Meadow, and continued the good work.

We stepped into the sparse little exhibition in Hannah's Barn below High Birk Hatt farmhouse, and then followed the Pennine Way beside the meadow. Not yet cut, its sweet vernal grass and sedges were full of old hay meadow flowers such as yellow rattle, knapweed, moon daisies and the blue powder puffs of devil's-bit scabious.

From Low Birk Hatt the squashy, puddled track of the Pennine Way led us up and out on to Cotherstone Moor.

On a wild open upland, unfenced for miles under a gigantic sky, we found an alternative loop of the Pennine Way and followed it back north. Above the path the flat-topped gritstone granite outcrop of Goldsborough stood proud of the moor – a miniature table mountain, whose sheer southern crags are only seen by sheep and walkers. We lingered under the rocks, admiring their weather-cut striations and the brilliant purple heather lining their ledges, and then dropped back down over many stone stiles into sunlit Baldersdale and the homeward path. Lapwings creaked in the sedgy fields, oystercatchers zipped down the wind, and every blade of grass squeaked and sparkled underfoot.

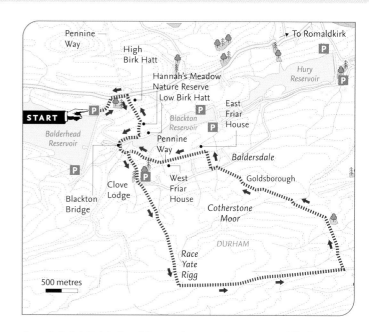

Start & finish Balderhead Reservoir car park, near Romaldkirk, Co. Durham DL12 9UX approx. (OS ref NY929187)

Walk (8 miles; moderate; OS Explorer OL31): Walk back to "Hannah's Meadow" gate; go through, and down lane ("Pennine Way"/PW). At gate (933190), right to Hannah's Barn exhibition. Return to PW; follow it past Low Birk Hatt (936184), across Blackton Bridge (932182). Fork left (no waymark) across beck. At triple PW fingerpost (934181), right up stony track to road beyond Clove Lodge Farm (935177). Ahead; in 200m, right (PW) across Cotherstone Moor. In 1 mile, at Race Yate, cross stile in fence (942161, PW). In 100m, left off PW through gate (blue arrow/BA); follow grassy track (sometimes faintly marked on ground) east for 1⅔ miles. At gate where wall and fence meet at Ladyfold Rigg, left (969164, BA) along Bowes Loop of PW. In ½ mile, at cross-wall by ruin (965171), go through left of two gates. In 20m fork left, aiming for crags of Goldsborough. Cross Yawd Sike (stream) by railed footbridge (960174); carry on below left slope of Goldsborough. At crest beyond (952178), fork left aiming for West Friar House Farm. At road (948179, PW), left for 100m; right down drive to East Friar House. Down left side of byre (acorn, yellow arrow/YA); left over stile (946182, YA); follow PW/Yas west through fields and stone stiles to Low Birk Hatt and car park.

Lunch Picnic

More information Middleton-in-Teesdale Tourist Information Centre (01833 641001); thisisdurham.com; visitengland.com; satmap.com; ramblers.org.uk

If an alien walker inquired the season and place to catch upland Britain at its very best, I'd direct him to spring in the Durham Dales, here in Upper Teesdale with the Tees blustering down the valley.

On a cool grey afternoon we gazed from the Swingy Bridge (officially Wynch Bridge, a bouncy span) upriver to where the Tees poured in creamy cascades over its jagged bed and down the rocky steps of Low Force waterfall. As we followed the Pennine Way upriver a muted roar and rumble heralded High Force, a tossing wall of peaty brown water crashing 70ft (20m) down three huge steps of the Whin Sill, the dolerite intrusion that shapes the dale. We stood at the brink, watching the fat lip of water curl downward into space and thunder off its walls into the rocky basin at the foot.

Along the path juniper bushes yielded a savour of gin when pinched. Once past the quarry at Dine Holm Scar the view lifted into an altogether wilder prospect, with long ridges of moorland ahead. On the way up the knobbled knoll of Bracken Rigg the path ran beside a fence excluding the sheep, and there on the other side, safe from the nibbling teeth, was a little clump of bird's-eye primroses, tiny and deep pink with egg-yolk yellow "eyes" – remnant flora of the postglacial tundra still thriving up here.

We descended to Cronkley Farm and recrossed the Tees where sandpipers were pattering on the pebbles. The homeward way lay just above the dale road, a path through pastures where brown hares scampered off, lapwings tilted earthward with creaking cries, and young blackface lambs ran to the admonitory bleating of ewes in ragged fleeces still stained with winter.

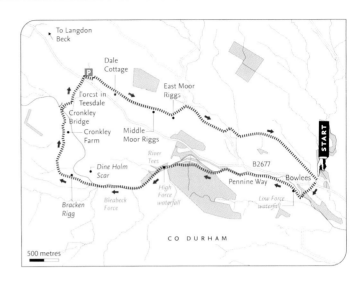

Start & finish Bowlees Visitor Centre, near Middleton-in-Teesdale DL12 OXF (OS ref NY 907282)

Walk (8 miles; moderate; OS Explorer OL31): From Visitor Centre cross B6277; path to cross Wynch Bridge (904279). Right on Pennine Way for 4 miles to cross Cronkley Bridge (862294). Pennine Way turns left, but follow track ahead. In 50m ahead up flagstone path. At top, right through gate (864294); through next gate; left past barn. Through wicket gate; past house, follow drive to road (866299). Right; in 100m left through car park; left; in 100m, right (868299) past school and cottages. Wall stile to field path; lane from Dale Cottage (872296); field path from Middle Moor Riggs (877293). Pass ruined East Moor Riggs (880292); in next field, half left to bottom right corner. Gate by corner of house; follow drive to road (884294); right. In ½ mile on right bend, ahead (890289); follow walled lane for 1½ miles to Bowlees.

Lunch Langdon Beck Hotel, Forest-in-Teesdale DL12 OXP (01833 622267)

More information Middleton-in-Teesdale Tourist Information Centre (01833 641001); thisisdurham.com; northpennines.org.uk

After the last of Durham's coastal pits closed in 1993, a remarkable operation named "Turning the Tide" led to a clean-up of the cliffs, the beaches and the steep wooded valleys known as denes. Following the clifftop path south from Seaham Harbour, we couldn't believe this was the same colliery coast that we had once known.

Blast Beach, got its name from the blast furnaces of the adjacent ironworks, which covered the beach with a thick layer of grease and sludge. Mixed with coal waste from Dawdon Colliery, this scab of industrial slag was dubbed "minestone" by locals.

We walked across Blast Beach, marvelling at the contrast between the barren layer of minestone and the rich flora that has developed under the cliffs – buttery yellow bird's-foot trefoil, intensely purple bloody cranesbill.

Up on the cliffs again, we strolled the grassy meadows where bee orchids grew in clumps. On the sheltered beach of Hawthorn Hive a man was collecting sea coal into a sack.

Easington Colliery's beach was once a wasteland where a gaunt gantry dropped a continuous stream of mine filth into a blackened sea. Now it's a beautiful sweep of pale pebbles on which the waves break in white foam.

From here we struck up the path into Castle Eden Dene and walked up into Peterlee through a green canopied cleft full of ferns and water-sculpted rocks. Goldcrests squeaked in the treetops and the underworld below the trees was hazed and smoky with bluebells.

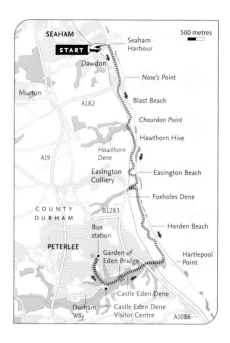

Start & finish Seaham Harbour, Co. Durham SR7 7DR (OS ref NZ 431494)

Walk (10 miles; moderate; OS Explorer 308): Follow coast path south for 7½ miles via Nose's Point and Blast Beach (437478-439469), Hawthorne Dene (440461 – steep steps down to beach or inland route crossing railway), Fox Holes Dene (440434) to Hartlepool Point (455407). Pass the foot of a track inland; take next path inland up Castle Eden Dene. Under railway (451405), across A1086 (448405); on for 1 mile to cross Garden of Eden Bridge (438399). Right up waymarked Yew Tree Trail to Visitor Centre (427393). Ahead up Stanhope Chase; across Durham Way; path ahead to edge of playing field (426397). Right for 150m; left up right side of playing field; path ahead through North Blunts woodland to Peterlee bus station (428407).

Lunch Picnic on the cliffs or beaches

More information Castle Eden Dene Visitor Centre (0191 586 0004), durhamheritagecoast.org

The old railway rose gently between bushes of gorse and young juniper. The wind carried lamb cries and the liquid territorial calls of nesting curlew – "Cur-leek! Cur-leek!"

Lumpy mounds of spoil bore witness to lead mining in the not-so-distant past. Nowadays the moors are managed patchwork-style for grouse, with coarse grey patches of old heather left for shelter and bright green young shoots for food.

We left the Waskerley Way and followed a stony track down to the long dam wall and wind-rippled water of Hisehope Reservoir. A feeder channel paved with stone led away east across the moor. Fenn traps had been placed on poles that crossed the channel to catch four-legged predators hunting the grouse.

A side path ran off north across the moor, soon descending to cross the deep-sunk Backstone and Hisehope burns in a steep little gully. From here the landscape changed to thistly meadows crossed by the faintest of cart tracks. The lonely farmhouse of Cushat Leazes drooped sadly, slate roof falling in, walls patchy where handily shaped stones had been robbed for wall-mending, a reminder of just how tough life is for the upland sheep farmers.

We followed a green path over rough pasture to climb the steps to the brink of Smiddy Shaw Reservoir. The view back across the moors we'd tramped disclosed a big dark marsh harrier sailing close to the heather, a lapwing rising to scold it away with urgent, creaking cries.

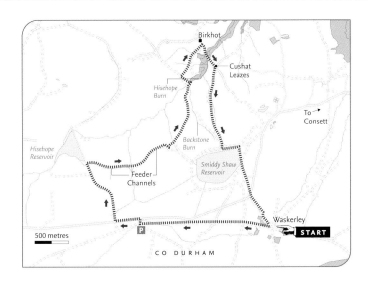

Start & finish Waskerley Farm car park, Consett DH8 9DZ approx. (OS ref NZ 051453)

Walk (6 miles; easy; OS Explorer 307): Right along Waskerley Way/ WW. In 1¼ miles at next car park (033453), right; left beside road. In 250m right on track to Hisehope Reservoir. Just beyond house, right (025462) along channel. In just under ¾ mile round right bend to footbridge (037464). Left here on moor path for just over ¼ mile to Backstone Burn. Follow right bank; cross burn at confluence with Hisehope Burn (040473). Left to cross burn. Up bank; in 150m, right over ladder stile (039474). Ahead across grass on track. In 100m edge left to raised bank; follow it to ford (039476); on to reach wall on left. Follow it to house (041479). In dip, right on grassy drive. Cross bridge (042477); in 200m pass Cushat Leazes ruin; bear right (044475) on green path. In just over ¼ mile through wall gate (043470); ahead on moor track; steps up to Smiddy Shaw Reservoir (044464). Left; at car park (047462) left to road; right to corner (048457); left to car park.

Lunch Picnic

More information thisisdurham.com

STANHOPE BURN, DURHAM DALES

When a beautiful day like this one arrives over the moors and valleys of west Durham, everyone wants to be out and about. The chatter and fuss of the other visitors were soon overlaid by the quiet chuckle of Stanhope Burn as we walked up its narrowing dale against the flow.

The hillsides north of the village wore the velvety nap and lumpy complexion that betokens a lead-mining landscape. In the throat of the valley, we found the pitch-black levels and abandoned buildings of old workings, where local miners earned their crusts through hard and health-shattering labour.

Nowadays Stanhope Burn runs clean and sparkling. Grey wagtails flirted their yellow underbellies on the stones, and a dipper bobbed its white shirtfront mid-stream under a bridge.

Above the mine buildings we left the valley track and followed a narrow path across hillsides where swallows cut low arcs across the heather. We forded and re-forded the shallow burn, and headed south across trackless moorland.

A line of wind-tattered conifers on the skyline formed a handy aiming point. When we had come up to them, we found ourselves by Park Plantation with its long encircling wall and swathes of grey and brown stumps of recently harvested trees. The sun blazed and the wind blew fiercely as we followed the wall south, leaping over boggy sikes or streams that wound through the heather to join Stanhope Burn.

We turned off along a farm track by Mount Pleasant and Pease Myers (also called Mires), and dropped down to Stanhope through woods where late bluebells and early purple orchids glowed under beech trunks striped with sunlight.

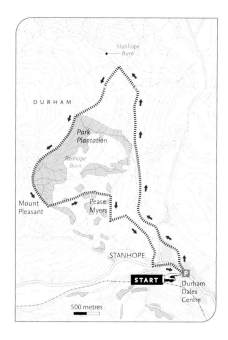

Start & finish Durham Dales Centre, Stanhope, Co. Durham DL13 2FJ (OS ref NY 996393)

Walk (8¼ miles; rugged moorland walking; OS Explorer 307): Right along A689; in 200m, right up Garden Close; dogleg right/left to Chapel Street. Left; right up footpath to kissing gate; on up with hedge on left to track (995396). Left to cross B6278 (991400). Track on right of Stanhope Burn for 1¼ miles to disused mine (987413); continue north on right of burn for about ¾ mile. Ford burn near derelict cottage (987425); ford again just west of bend; ford again to south bank in 500m by access land notice and gate (983431). SSW over trackless moor, aiming for right-hand edge of conspicuous line of conifers ahead. At corner of Park Plantation, follow wall SW, then SE for 1½ miles; then left (970404) through gate. Track past Mount Pleasant (972405) and Pease Myers to road (982406). Right; in 450m left to Widley Field (984402). Half right across field to far right corner stile (986401). Left; in 50m, left (stile) into wood; right on path for ½ mile to Stanhope.

Lunch Durham Dales Centre tearoom

More information Durham Dales Centre (01388 527650, durhamdalescentre.co.uk); thisisdurham.com; satmap.com; ramblers.org.uk

The friendly and hospitable Forest View Walkers Inn at Byrness lies in a wild corner of the Cheviot Hills. From the forestry hamlet I followed the Pennine Way up through the trees, and soon turned off on a forest byway that dipped to the valley of Cottonshope.

I walked up the road to the lonely farm of Cottonshope whence a faint path climbed through rough grass pastures, swerving in and out of the boundary of Otterburn Ranges, to meet the Pennine Way on Ravens Knowe.

What a splendid view from the cairn up here. To the north-east the rounded bulk of Cheviot lifting gently to the cloudy sky, the flanks rolling and tumbling down to where I stood. South and west, lower ground with hills and forests running to the Scottish border. To the east, the barely perceptible path up which I'd come, falling away into the Cottonshope Valley. South from Ravens Knowe it was all forest, great swathes of the coniferous cladding that has adhered to the Redesdale hills since the area was planted between the world wars of the past century.

I turned for home along the boardwalks and squelchy corners of the Pennine Way, accompanied by a flittering meadow pipit. Catcleugh Reservoir came into view, a wedge of steely water among the trees. The Pennine Way descended among tuffets of bilberry and sphagnum, before suddenly slanting precipitously down a staircase of rocks.

Down in Byrness the little Church of St Francis of Assisi holds a stained-glass window in memory of those who died constructing Catcleugh Reservoir late in the 19th century. A very poignant and touching memorial.

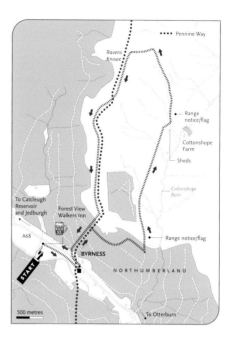

Start & finish Otterburn Green, Byrness NE19 1TS (OS ref NT 764027)

Walk (7½ miles; moderate/strenuous; OS Explorer OL16): From Forest View, right along Otterburn Green; past village hall and on. At A68, by church, left along cycleway (771023, "Pennine Way"/PW). In 50m cross A68 (take care!); left up path. In 100m, go through hedge (PW); on through gate into trees (769026); continue up PW. In ⅓ mile, at 3rd major crossing track, right off PW (773030). In ¾ mile, left along Cottonshope Road in valley bottom (773030). In 1½ miles, just past farm sheds, left up track beside range flagpole and notice (789049). Follow clearly seen route for 1¼ miles over moorland to cairn on Ravens Knowe (781061). Left along Pennine Way for 2¾ miles back to A68; retrace steps to Byrness.

Lunch Picnic

More information Between Cottonshope and Ravens Knowe, path veers in and out of Otterburn Ranges boundary. Ranges may be closed if live firing; ring Range Control (01830 520569) before setting out. You can check firing times at gov.uk/government/publications/otterburn-firing-times

Druridge Bay is designated a heritage coast and a site of special scientific interest. This 7-mile curve of beach from Amble to Cresswell is unspoilt, a simple and grand arc of dull gold sand backed by flowery dunes, with crashing steel-grey waves coming in off the North Sea under huge overarching skies.

A flight of ringed plover twinkled in black and white across the ribbed pools that had collected in the sands. On the landward side of each sandy ridge in every pool, a skin of gritty black had collected; tiny flecks of coal, sifted out of the low-lying hinterland behind the beach and filtered through the dunes by the trickling flow of tiny burns. The richness of the bird and flower life here, the windy solitude of the beach, made it easy to forget that this is coal-bearing country.

A couple of miles along the beach we cut inland through the dunes and past the wetlands and wildfowl lakes of Druridge Pools. Isolated in the fields beyond stood the lonely ruin of Low Chibburn Preceptory, a medieval chapel and hospital of the Knights of St John built on the ancient pilgrim route to Holy Island. The Hospitallers' refuge has done duty in its time as a grand dower house, a cattle shed and a Second World War pillbox.

Before setting back for the beach and the return walk, we wandered slowly round the ruin, admiring its finely carved piscina, its arched windows and handsome stonework, survivors of changing fortunes over the course of 700 years in this remote corner of the Northumbrian coast.

Start & finish Druridge Park Visitor Centre, near Amble, Northumberland NE61 5BX (OS ref NZ 272998)

Walk (6½ miles; easy; OS Explorer 325): From car park, follow "Beach". Path through trees, then dunes; down steps on to beach (273996). Turn right/south for 1½ miles. Where the dunes dip to a pool and Dunbar Burn, pass a pipe (broken in two) across the beach (277972). Continue along beach for 500m, then turn inland between tank blocks through gap in dunes (277965), past concrete blockhouse. Through fence gap (North Sea Trail "N" waymark); right along road; in 200m, left between boulders (275966) on path (yellow arrow/YA) past Druridge Pools and on across two fields (YAs) to Low Chibburn Preceptory ruin (266965). Return same way. As you near Visitor Centre, look for wooden steps up through dunes.

Lunch Picnic; Visitor Centre café (open daily in the summer, weekends in the winter)

More information visitengland.com; northumberland.gov.uk, 01670 760968; satmap.com; ramblers.org.uk

Romantics of all kinds and conditions can do as I did this blowy day on the Northumberland coast – gird their loins and follow the ancient pilgrim path to Holy Island over the wide tidal sands. Tall rough poles mark the straight way, with barnacle-encrusted wooden refuge towers for foolish virgins to clamber into if beset by a rising tide.

It was a good hour's walk. But this was a heavenly way to cross to Holy Island, or Lindisfarne, to give it an older and lovelier name. Holy Island village is still partly a fishing community, mostly for crab and lobster these days. People come to Lindisfarne for its peace, its small-scale beauty and its remarkable monastic history. St Aidan of Iona established a monastery on Lindisfarne in the 7th century. St Cuthbert became its hermit bishop and saintly icon. The "most beautiful book in the world", the illuminated Lindisfarne Gospels, was crafted here.

This little island off the Northumbrian coast kept alive the flickering light of Christianity during the Dark Ages; and when Holy Island was reoccupied after the Norman Conquest (the monks having fled Danish raids in AD875) a wonderful new monastery was built here.

Lindisfarne is full of marvels. Wind and weather have sculpted swirling shapes in the red sandstone walls of the church, whose "sky arch" springs 50ft (15m) in the air, seemingly unsupported. Inland, the humps of the Cheviot Hills began to fade under rain. The island's strollers vanished into the tea shops and I was left alone to walk the north shore dunes, savouring the wind and showers.

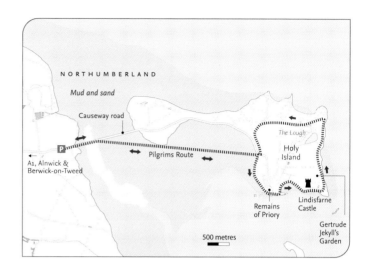

Start & finish Holy Island causeway car park, Northumberland TD15 2PB approx. (OS ref NU079427)

Walk (10 miles including sands crossing, 3½ miles island circular; easy; OS Explorer 340): From car park follow causeway, then pilgrim route posts, to Chare Ends on Holy Island (NB see below!). Follow road to Priory ruins (126418 – signposted). Return to Market Square; between Crown & Anchor and Manor House Hotel, follow path to shore. Left round harbour; on to castle (detour to Gertrude Jekyll's Garden – 136419). Continue on coast path, past The Lough and National Nature Reserve notice. Follow path to left along line of dunes for ½ mile to meet fence at NNR notice (129433). For island circular, left through gate, ahead to village. For sands crossing, keep ahead for ½ mile; bear left (122433) with causeway on right, to rejoin posts at Chare End.

Lunch Plenty of options in the village

More information Berwick-upon-Tweed Tourist Information Centre (01670 622155), www.lindisfarne.org.uk, visitnorthumberland.com, ramblers.co.uk, satmap.com

The steam trains of the South Tyne Valley railway were slow enough by all accounts, but travellers in the slowest of them could never have had the leisure to spot all the wild flowers that Jane and I saw as we started from Featherstone Rowfoot along the footpath that now runs along the old railway. Along the farm lane to Lynnshield, black and brown heifers tittuped and snorted in pastures where oystercatchers circled above their nests, crying their sharp "pik, pik" alarm calls. Beyond the farm we headed south at the rim of Park Burn's deep canyon, where the burn rushed over rocky falls.

We picnicked under a footbridge, watching sand martins popping in and out of their nest holes in the banks. Then it was on south by way of dusty spoil heaps of old coalpits, and a tangle of dubious paths around the steading of West Stonehouse. Here we paused for a superb view north over miles of moor and upland.

Down again through sheep pastures into the wide green valley of the River South Tyne. It was hard to equate the sluggish dark tideway through Newcastle upon Tyne with this young river of clear water, running fast round islets of pebbles piled up in winter floods. We followed it north to where the great grey bulk of Featherstone Castle raised its battlements and window arches.

Just upstream stood an abandoned clutch of stark red-brick buildings, black-windowed and sinister: the remnants of Camp 18. Here after the Second World War German officers were put through a process of "denazification" before being repatriated to help to rebuild their ruined country. The three senior officers who ran Camp 18 were all Jewish. It was a humane, far-sighted initiative, the first step in the process of Anglo-German reconciliation.

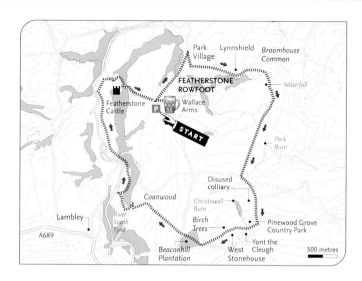

Start & finish Featherstone Park car park, Featherstone Rowfoot, near Haltwhistle NE49 0JF (OS ref NY 683607)

Walk (8 miles; easy; OS Explorer OL43). North up old railway (Haltwhistle). In ½ mile, cross railway at Park Village (687615); right along road; in 150m, left/west for ¾ mile past Lynnshield (695612, yellow arrows/YAs) to Broomhouse Common (700613). South for ½ mile to cross Park Burn footbridge (700605). Green Lane, then road south to junction (696595); left to top of hill (699587); right through Pinewood Grove Country Park to West Stonehouse. Skirt anticlockwise round barn and houses to gate (YA) and ladder stile/LS to farm track by Birch Trees house (694586). On to LS at corner of Beaconhill Plantation (689583). Through plantation (YAs) to cross road (686586, LS). Downhill (YAs) to farm at Coanwood (681590). Waymarked path SW to road (678590); sharp left down through gate (Lambley Bridge); right/north beside river for 1¾ miles. At Featherstone Castle, right (673612) up road to car park.

Lunch Wallace Arms pub; Blenkinsopp Castle Inn, Castle Home Park, Brampton CA8 7JS (01697 747757)

More information visitnorthumberland.com; satmap.com, ramblers.org.uk

WEST ALLEN VALLEY AND MOHOPE MOOR

We climbed the lane past the old lead-mining hamlet of Keirsleywell Row, its grassed-over spoil heaps as prominent as Viking burial mounds, then on up towards Mohope Moor on a broad rubbly track between stone walls. All around the land lay open under the sun, green fields striped with walls and dotted with handsome pale stone farms rising to darker moor tops that rolled out of sight.

A cold wind blew out of the southwest into our faces as we reached an old sheep dip flanked by square stone sheep passes in the lane walls (these allow flocks to move between fields while keeping out cattle). A boggy track led away south across the long upland waste of Mohope Moor, its line indicated by waymark posts among the peat and moss. The broken shell of a curlew egg, its olive surface scribbled with tarry streaks for camouflage, lay by the way. Nearby we saw two large pellets, ejected by some raptor with a mixed diet, that were a clotted mass of fur, feathers, small bones and fragments of marine shells.

At the black stream of Lower Blackish Cleugh we turned back towards the West Allen Valley, tramping through rushes and down a grassy walled lane to find the homeward path along the pebbly flood meadows of the Mohope Burn.

Beyond Malakoff Bridge, flashes of silver showed along the riverbank. Sand martins darted into and out of their nesting cavities in the overhang of the bank. Their young stood like impatient Deliveroo customers at the threshold of each hole, squeaking as they waited for the next beakful of nutritious insects to be delivered.

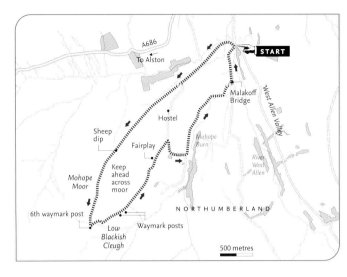

Start & finish Ninebanks Bridge, Chapel Bank, Hexham NE47 8DB (OS ref NY 782524).

Walk (OS Explorer OL 43, 31): Take road signed "Mohope". In ¾ mile at left bend, keep ahead (774518, "Isaac's Tea Trail, Long Cross"); climb stony lane for 1 mile to stile at sheep dip (763508, "Welcome to the Moor" signboard). In 100m, track bends right; keep ahead here, over stile, then follow waymarked posts (yellow arrows/YAs) across moor. Bring binoculars to spot the posts. In ¾ mile, the sixth post (2 YAs) stands on far bank of Low Blackish Cleugh stream (759497); don't cross stream but turn left, aiming a little left of farm on distant slope. In 300m you'll see line of posts ahead; follow to wall corner (765499); walled green lane to road at Fairplay (769506). Ahead; in 300m, sharp right (771510). In 450m, on right bend, keep ahead (774507, "Redheugh, Malakoff Bridge"); follow waymarked path for 1 mile to Malakoff Bridge (782518); left on road to car.

Lunch Take a picnic

More information Hexham Tourist Information Centre (01670 620450); visitnorthumberland.com

VINDOLANDA AND HADRIAN'S WALL

Hadrian's Wall retains, in greater or lesser ruin, its observation towers and guard-posts, and the roads and townships that served it. The Wall forms the most remarkable monument in Britain to those energetic, organised and lifeloving invaders, the Romans.

How incredibly angry the tile-maker of Vindolanda must have been when that stupid pig walked all over the nice new clay flooring he'd left out to dry in the sun. A surviving tile from the spoiled batch, on display in Vindolanda's museum just south of the Wall, carries the prints of the pig's incurving toes, as sharp today as the hour they were dinted 2,000 years ago.

Walking the rushy meadows a mile or so to the south, I looked up at the thin line of Hadrian's Wall as it rode the rollercoaster crags of the Whin Sill, the volcanic rampart that strides across the neck of Northumberland. Arriving at the wall, a stepped path swooped me up the crests and down into the hollows of the dolerite sill, passing the sites of the milecastles and turrets where conscripts from the Low Countries paced and shivered and looked out into the debatable lands to the north from where the wild Picts might come screaming at any moment.

The old house and barns of Hotbank Farm lay huddled on the slope of Hotbank Crags, their walls much patched with Roman stones. Here I left Hadrian's Wall and headed across the vallum and down flowery meadow slopes, with Vindolanda spread below me in the evening sunlight.

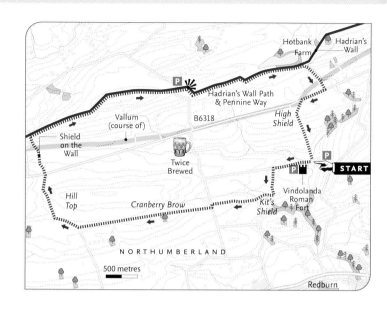

Start & finish Vindolanda car park, near Bardon Mill, Northumberland NE47 7JN (OS ref NY767664)

Walk (8 miles; moderate; OS Explorer OL53): From Vindolanda car park, left along road; in 100m, left through gate, down track; in 400m, right (766660) on path (stiles, yellow arrows/YAs). NB After passing barn at Kit's Shield (764659), negotiate tree blocking path! Skirt Layside (760659, YAs); on to road (756658). Left, then right along lane ("Cranberry Brow") for 1⅓ miles to road (735655). Right (fingerpost) on drive to Hill Top; on to road (730659). Right to cross B6318 (729663, stile, "Shield on the Wall"). Path along field wall, then diagonally left across Roman Vallum ditch to Hadrian's Wall (727669). Right along National Trail for 3 miles to Hotbank Farm (771680). Leave National Trail here; right down farm drive to B6318. Right along grass verge for 400m; left (770674, stile, "Vindolanda") across field, aiming to cross stile on left of High Shield house (769672, YA). Left to stile (YA); down fields with fence on left. In 2nd field, fence trends away left, but keep a beeline ahead to stile and road at bottom (772665). Right to Vindolanda car park.

Lunch Vindolanda Café

More information Vindolanda (01434 344277; vindolanda.com), National Park Centre; visitengland.com, satmap.com, ramblers.org.uk

YEAVERING BELL AND AKELD

In the farming hamlet of Akeld, just outside the regional capital of Wooler, stands a bastle, a reminder of a savage history. These fortified farmhouses – with their tiny windows, "upstairs" doors and walls many feet thick – date from the days when the Scottish Borders were aflame with cattle-thieving and feuds.

Above Akeld, a winding path led us away through bracken and heather across the hunched back of White Law. We dipped into a hollow, then climbed past the circular foundations of ancient beehive huts to the summit of Yeavering Bell. This high and handsome hill is the king of the north Cheviots, its knobbly brow encircled by a great wall – once 10ft (3m) thick, now scattered – and crowned with a cairn.

Up there we sat, catching our breath and savouring the view – the chequerboard plain stretched north at our feet, a steel-blue crescent of North Sea, and the rolling heights of the Cheviots as they billowed away south into the heart of the range. Then it was down from the peak and on through the bracken to find the broad green road of St Cuthbert's Way striding purposefully through the hills.

The hard rock outcrop of Tom Tallon's Crag rode its heathery hilltop like a salt-brown ship pitching in a russet sea. We passed below the crag, then followed a grassy old cart track into the cleft of Akeld Burn. Suddenly all the birds of the air seemed to be flying about us – meadow pipits in undulating flight, kestrels and sparrowhawks hanging in their hunting stances, and a raven flapping with a disdainful "cronk!" out over the northern plains before us.

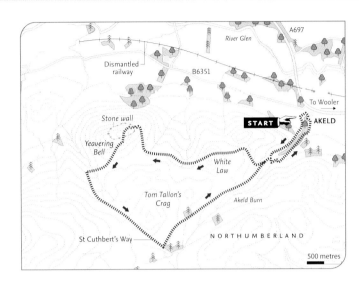

Start & finish Akeld, near Wooler, Northumberland NE71 6TA approx. (OS ref NT957297)

Walk (6 miles; moderate; OS Explorer OL16): Walk through farmyard; up track (blue arrow/BA). Pass to right of Gleadscleugh cottage (952290); through next gate; in 100m, right over stile (950288; yellow arrow/YA). Follow path, bearing right up left rim of stony Glead's Cleugh. Follow YAs on posts for 1¼ miles over White Law (943290) and down to stile and gate in fence under Yeavering Bell (932290). Path up to saddle to right of summit; at wooden pallet marker (931294), left on path to summit cairn (929293). Follow path half left off summit, through scattered stone wall (928292); here fork right (YAs, "Hill Fort Trail") to St Cuthbert's Way/SCW at stile (923287). Left, following SCW for 1 mile. Pass Tom Tallon's Crag; through gate in wall (933278); in 300m, at near corner of conifer plantation, turn left off SCW through gate (935277); follow track to Gleadscleugh house. Right (951289, BA) on track to right of house; zigzag across burn; on by wall; follow yellow arrows to Akeld, passing bastle (958294) on your left.

Lunch Picnic

More information Wooler Tourist Information Centre, The Cheviot Centre, 12 Padgepool Place (01668 282123); visitnorthumberland. com; visitengland.com; satmap.com; ramblers.org.uk

SCOTLAND

Old Man of Hoy, Scotland

COIGACH GEOTRAIL, ACHILTIBUIE

The rugged peninsula of Coigach in northwest Scotland is famous for its Peter Drake, a sea fisherman and our guide on this walk, was a prime mover in establishing the 45-mile Coigach Geotrail around the shores of the peninsula's wild beauty and its geological treasures.

In the bay of Camas a' Bhothain stood a ruined salmon bothy. Beyond ran a layer of rock in red-grey sheets pressed close together. "The oldest inhabitants of Coigach," Peter said. This very finely layered limestone is a stromatolite, a structure created by microbes that clung to rocks around the shore of a lake about a billion years ago. It represents the earliest form of life yet discovered in Europe.

On the shore beyond the bay, a smear of red rock told a dramatic story. About a billion years ago an asteroid measuring half a mile across slammed into the planet at 25,000 miles per hour, a dozen miles from where we stood. The shock of the impact liquidised the Earth's crust in the vicinity and spattered it far and wide in a splash of ejecta, or molten rock.

Stuck in the ejecta we found greenish fragments of the asteroid, and a sprinkling of tiny globules like acne on a teenage face – the spherical lapilli, or droplets of molten rock that cooled and hardened as they fell out of the sky from the massive volcanic cloud that billowed up above the site of the strike.

We rounded the corner of the peninsula and found ourselves staring at an eastern skyline clouded but magnificent – the mountains of Inverpolly, horizontally striped sandstone a billion years old, all that's left of the landscape that lay here before the giant glaciers of the Ice Ages scraped most of it away.

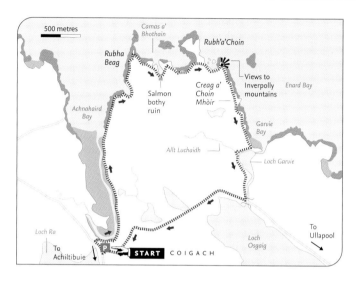

Start & finish Loch Raa car park, Achnahaird IV26 2YT approx. (OS ref NC 021123)

Walk (6½ miles; moderate; OS Explorer 439): From Loch Raa car park, head north along west side of Achnahaird Bay, either on shore or along sheep path near cliffs. In 1¼ miles cross deer fence (023142; stile). Follow coast to salmon bothy ruin in Camas a' Bothain (029145). Continue across neck of Rubha a' Choin peninsula (034146). Along rocky beach; up headland and turn right to cross deer fence (038142). Continue south down Garvie Bay, then along west bank of river to road bridge (040129). Right for 1½ miles to car park.

Lunch Picnic from Achiltibuie Stores (01854 622496); Summer Isles Hotel (01854 622282; summerisleshotel.com)

More information Downloadable trail map and notes available at visitcoigach.com; nwhgeopark.com; visitscotland.com

COIRE MHIC FHEARCHAIR, BEINN EIGHE, TORRIDON

It was a beautiful warm morning when we set off from the car park on the Torridon – Kinlochewe road. The stony path led up between the white screes of Coinneach Mhor and the blocky grey cliffs of Stuc a' Choire Dhuibh Bhig. We crossed a mountain torrent by way of stepping stones to reach an otherworldly upland. Great rugged tents of mountains stood pitched on a green plateau where a constellation of steely lochans lay glinting. This is the heart of Wester Ross, a roadless wilderness whose eagles and otters outnumber its human inhabitants.

A rush-choked lochan quivering with water boatmen and dragonflies showed where we were to turn off for the climb round the dark bulk of Sail Mhor, the most westerly "finger" or buttress of Beinn Eighe. The path rose steadily, with enormous views of sea-like waves of hills, till we came in sight of the waterfall sluicing down the rock wall that underlies the hanging corrie in the palm of Beinn Eighe.

A last upward scramble, and we were looking into a giant geological crucible. On the left, the pale shattered rock of Ruadh Stac Mhor; in the centre at the back of the horseshoe, three great grey buttresses in the face of Coinneach Mhor; and on the right, Sail Mhor's purple-black wall of pinnacles and columns. At their feet, the long dark lake of Loch Coire Mhic Fhearchair, reflecting the peaks that hung more than a thousand feet above. It's a view to give anyone a proper sense of their own insignificance in the scale of time and change, as these mountains experience such things.

We stripped off and crept into the shallows of the loch, cold and refreshing after the long hot climb, as smooth as olive oil on the skin.

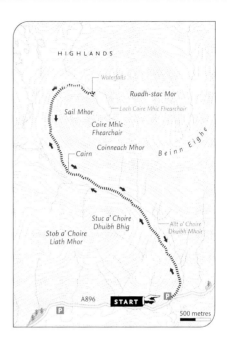

Start & finish Car park on A896, 6 miles SW of Kinlochewe (OS ref NS959568)

Walk (7 map miles, about 9 miles actually walked; strenuous; OS Explorer 433): Start of path is marked "Public Footpath to Coire Mhic Nobaill". Follow this well-maintained path. In 1¾ miles, cross stepping stones (947589). In another ¾ mile, at the far end of a rushy lochan, fork right at a cairn (935594) and follow path for 1¾ miles up to Loch Coire Mhic Fhearchair (940611). Return same way.

Lunch Picnic

More information visitscotland.com; satmap.com; ramblers.org.uk

Creag Meagaidh National Nature Reserve, lying between Spean Bridge and Kinloch Laggan, has embarked on an ambitious programme to recolonise this rugged mountain landscape with the native flora and fauna that have been destroyed by overgrazing and deforestation.

Long-horned Highland cattle put their heads up from the lush grazing in the floor of Aberarder Forest to peer through their luxuriant fringes and watch us go by. We walked a rising path through woods of young birch, oak and alder, free to grow now that the sheep have been removed and the deer controlled.

At the top of the rise the path left the trees and curved west across open moorland tufted with bog cotton. Below in the glen the Allt Coire Ardair snaked and sparkled in its rocky bed. Northwards rose the flattened pyramid head of Coire a' Chriochairein, and round in the west hung the high, rubble-filled notch called The Window that marks the northern edge of cliff-hung Coire Ardair. A lichened rock lay by the way, the parallel lines in its flat surface gouged out 10,000 years ago by the glacier that formed the precipitous glen.

The top of the glen was blocked by a low barrier of heath and grass, concealing the moraine or mass of rock and rubble that the head of the glacier had pushed before it up the valley, like dust before a broom. From its ridge we looked down to Lochan a' Choire, suddenly revealed like a conjurer's trick – a little glass-still lake under black, snow-streaked cliffs.

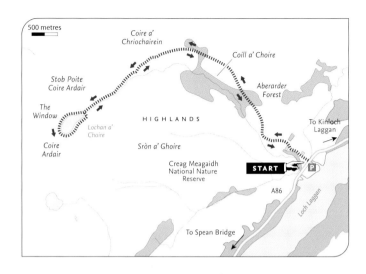

Start & finish Creag Meagaidh NNR car park PH20 1BX (OS ref NN483873)

Walk (8½ miles; moderate; OS Explorer 401): From car park follow red trail (otter symbol). In 500m pass to right of toilets/buildings (479876). Follow path on the level, then up steps; fork right at top (474879; "Coire Ardair") on clear stony path for 3 miles to Lochan a' Choire (439883). Return same way. Don't forget midge repellent!

Lunch Picnic

More information Creag Meagaidh NNR (01528 544265; www.nnr-scotland.org.uk/creag-meagaidh); visitscotland.com/natural; satmap.com; ramblers.org.uk

THE DEVIL'S BEEF TUB, MOFFAT

It was a long, steady climb through bracken and heather, then among the young trees along the Tweedhope Burn. Rowan berries glowed a deep burnt orange, and the indigo berries on recently planted juniper bushes gave a spicy tang of gin when crushed and sniffed.

At the watershed, soggy and boggy, a neat elliptical cairn stood at the turning point of the Annandale Way, a rollercoaster path along the backs of Chalk Rig Edge, Great Hill and Annanhead Hill. Here we perched on a handily placed bench, looking down into the plum-coloured shadows of the Devil's Beef Tub, source of the River Annan.

A stranger to the area 300 years ago would never have happened upon this remote, tight and formidably steep-sided hollow, some 500ft (150m) deep, nearly sheer from rim to bottom. Here the cattle-raiding Johnstone family would graze the beasts they had stolen, confident that no one would ever find them.

The secluded hideaway was also a refuge for the 17th-century religious dissenters known as Covenanters. One of them, John Hunter, was chased up the slopes by dragoons in August 1686 and shot like a dog when caught. In 1745 a Jacobite prisoner managed to break free from his captors while crossing the rim of the Devil's Beef Tub, and escaped by rolling like a barrel down the plunging braeside while wrapped in his plaid.

We descended from Annanhead Hill and crossed the rushy bump of Ericstane Hill. Following the homeward path in bright evening sunshine, we looked back towards the darkly shadowed Devil's Beef Tub, picturing the tumbling Jacobite.

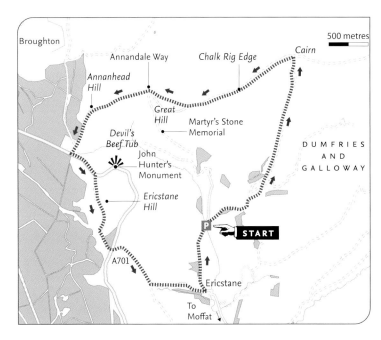

Start & finish Car parking space (OS ref NT 073117) on farm road between Ericstane (077116) and Corehead (073124)

Walk (7½ miles; strenuous; OS Explorer 330): Bear right along grassy track. Follow Annandale Way (AW waymarks) for just under 1¾ miles, gaining height beside Tweedhope Burn to reach cairn at watershed (084138). AW turns left with fence; follow it over hills for 2 miles to descend to A701 (056127). Left; in 400m, right (059124, AW) across Ericstane Hill to cross A701 (061115). Follow field track; in ½ mile on right bend, left off AW through gateway (065110). Follow track down to Ericstane (072109); left to car.

Lunch Hugo's Restaurant, 4 Bath Place, Moffat DG10 9HJ (01683 221606, hugosmoffat.uk)

More information bordersforesttrust.org

THE DEVIL'S STAIRCASE, GLENCOE

There's an air of menace, faint but definite, that clings to the Pass of Glencoe as the road from Fort William threads it between the jagged ridge of Aonach Eagach and the massive, troll like faces of the Three Sisters of Glencoe. These volcanic mountains are dark and precipitous, giving the impression of hanging threateningly over the road even on a crisp winter day with clear sky and glassy visibility. That haunted feeling may derive from the notorious 1692 Massacre of Glencoe, when dozens of members of the local MacDonald clan were murdered by soldiers billeted in their houses or died of exposure as they fled through a snowstorm to hide in the mountains.

A couple of miles down the glen, the mountains draw further back from the road and the atmosphere lightens as the glen broadens. Here, we set off from the packed car park at Altnafeadh for a morning's saunter up the Devil's Staircase.

It was one of those "Watch your step, take the next zig and zag as they come, how long to the top?" slogs up the Devil's Staircase, but at last the path smoothed out at the bealach. Here, we turned off the West Highland Way on to a narrow stony track that rose across slippery slabs and squelchy black bog to the modest cairn at the summit of Stob Mhic Mhartuin, 1,300ft (400m) above the floor of Glencoe.

From here, the southward view over the glen burst out in all its glory. Twin mountains stood opposite, their volcanic history written in their crumpled faces, Buachaille Etive Beag on the right looking east across the tightly squeezed glen of Lairig Gartain at her big sister Buachaille Etive Mòr. Snow streaked the gullies on Buachaille Etive Mòr, and a party of hikers were outlined against a grey sky as they inched their way towards the summit.

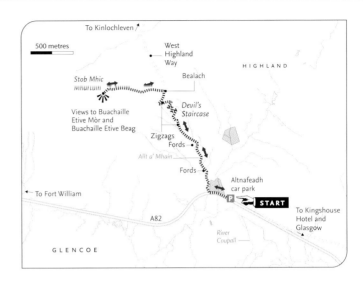

Start & finish Altnafeadh car park, Ballachulish, Glencoe PH49 4HY (OS ref NN 221563). Check the weather (mwis.org.uk) and choose a clear day for the best views. Hill-walking gear is advisable

Walk (3½ miles; moderate; OS Explorer 384): From the A82 turn north up West Highland Way (WHW), keeping left of forestry. Climb 850ft/259m up the Devil's Staircase zigzags to the bealach or pass at 1,797ft/548m. Just before the big cairn (216575) at the bealach, go left off WHW on a clear path that becomes rocky, boggy and steep in places. In ½ mile it bends left to climb to the summit of Stob Mhic Mhartuin (2,319ft/707m). Return the way you came.

Lunch Kingshouse Hotel, Glencoe, Ballachulish PH49 4HY (01855 851259; kingshousehotel.co.uk)

More information visitscotland.com

FORVIE NATIONAL NATURE RESERVE

On a brisk, windy day with a cloudy sky hurrying rain showers out to sea, the dunes of the Forvie National Nature Reserve looked dun and drab as we followed the coast path among their shaggy camel humps. But that first dull impression gave way to astonishment at the richness of their flora – spatters of white heath bedstraw, stout northern marsh orchids with richly purple flower heads, pink streamers of ragged robin, wild pansies with lower lips of cream and yellow.

At North Broad Haven a sour, fishy whiff heralded a teeming colony of kittiwakes. We lay on the cliff edge above a guano-whitened sea stack where a row of cormorants sat on a line of untidy nests. The nestlings craned their heads up to rub the throats of their parents, stimulating them to regurgitate the fish they'd brought back in their crops.

Down on the beach at Rockend we strode south on firm sand to the boundary of the ternery. Here sandwich, common and little terns have their summer breeding ground; and once we had crossed the dunes and were perched looking down on the Ythan Estuary, we could see them lined up head to wind in hundreds on the mud flats. Beside our homeward path along the river a great congregation of eider ducks lay moulting, the males with green neck flashes and black toupés with centre-partings like 1920s cabaret cads.

These handsome, bulky birds gobble the estuary's mussels whole, grinding them small in their gizzards. Forvie NNR offers the eider a place of safety, as it does the terns, the wild flowers and the dunes that have been growing and shifting along this coast since Stone Age man came hunting here.

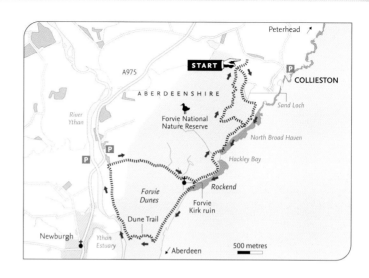

Start & finish Forvie NNR Visitor Centre, Collieston AB41 8RU (OS ref NK034289)

Walk (8½ miles; easy; OS Explorer 421): From Visitor Centre follow "To the Reserve". Through gate; turn left along gravel track towards line of cottages (Red Route or Heath Trail, with occasional waymark posts). Along right side of Sand Loch to coast (036281); right along dune path above sea. In 1½ miles, descend to beach at Rockend (023265). Continue along beach for ¾ mile to rope barrier at ternery (014253). Turn right into dunes past tern sign on pole; follow Dune Trail to Ythan Estuary (009254). Right up estuary path for 1 mile. Opposite info shelter, turn right (005269). Follow Dune Trail posts for 1 mile to Forvie Kirk ruin (021266); then follow "Hackley Bay" to coast (023265). Left up coast for 1¼ miles. At Red Route post (033276), left inland on Heath Trail. At marker post at far side of small loch, don't turn right; keep ahead. At "Shortcut" post bear left; at next post, fork left (032284) to return to Visitor Centre.

Lunch Picnic

More information Forvie NNR Visitor Centre (01358 751330; nnr-scotland.org.uk), visitscotland.com, satmap.com, visitaberdeen.com

LITTLE WYVIS

It's one hell of a climb to the pride of mid-Ross, the 3,432ft (1,046m) crown of the great whaleback mountain called Ben Wyvis – too much, really, for this scorcher of a summer's day.

But Little Wyvis, a couple of miles to the south-west, looked just the job at 2,507ft (764m), a good upward pull on a fine stony track and no one else to share the mountain with us.

The zigzag track rose up the flank of Little Wyvis, the sun striking a million diamond winks out of its mica-sheathed rocks. We plucked juicy bilberries, sweet and sharp on the tongue, beautifully refreshing to the upward climber.

At the summit of Little Wyvis we found a small rocky cairn infested with scores of bees. Ben Wyvis rose to the north, a double hump with precipitous slopes facing in our direction. Through binoculars we saw the red and yellow dots of walkers sweltering in the sun as they struggled up the leg-twanging ascent. Standing by the cairn we took in a truly stupendous view, from the lumpy mountains of Torridon way out west to the long sea lochs at Dornoch in the east, a vista of green mountains and steely waters.

On the way down two plump birds stood on a rock, staring us down. White patchy bellies, feathery feet, salt and pepper backs, and a bold red eyebrow on the male. A pair of ptarmigan, no less – my first ever sighting of these elusive birds of the high mountains. And just beyond them a mountain hare motionless under a peat bank, his ears short and neat, his pelt ridged. What a thrill.

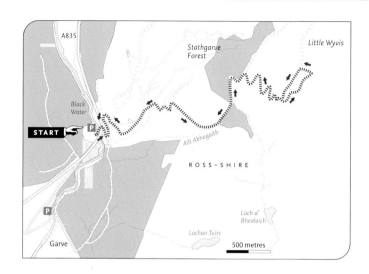

Start & finish Car park on A835 Inverness–Ullapool road (OS ref NH402639)

Walk (7 miles there and back; strenuous, OS Explorer 437): Cross A835 (take care!); left for 100m; right up roadway. In 50m, left past gateway post (ignore warning sign – it's aimed at 4x4 drivers). Follow gravel track. In ½ mile pass barn (407640); on through deer gate. In another mile, at second gate, left up track (418640). In another ½ mile, track forks (422646); continue to right here, up zigzag track. In ¾ mile, just below summit at 2,296ft/700m, rough track goes left (427643); ignore this and keep ahead upwards. Go through remains of fence, and on up to summit cairn (430645). Return same way.

Lunch Picnic

More information Inverness Tourist Information Centre (01463 252401)

A good squirt of Avon Skin-so-Soft, incomparable deterrent to the midges, and we were off along the river with the high hills of Galloway cut sharply against white cumulus and blue sky, the profile of Mulldonoch standing tall across Loch Trool, the grey-green teeth of Cambrick Hill beyond.

Up beside the roughly squared lump of Bruce's Stone we gazed across the head of the loch to the slopes where Robert Bruce's ragged guerrillas had whupped the mail-clad asses of the English in 1307. We crossed a miniature gorge of black rock walls by way of Buchan Bridge and followed a hill path through the bracken into the lonely side cleft of the Gairland Burn.

A hillside track led us up among boggy patches jumping with tiny green and yellow frogs, upstream beside the glassy oxygenated waters of the burn.

We skirted steely dark Loch Valley and climbed beside ancient animal pens of massive boulders to reach imperial-blue Loch Neldricken, its waters bright with bog bean, its white and salmon-pink beaches etched in crescents under the shoulder of The Merrick.

Down in Glen Trool once more we crossed the head of Loch Trool and turned back along a swooping path through the forest. Cuckoos made call and response across the sunny valley, and the loch waters sparkled as though a generous, invisible hand had scattered diamonds there.

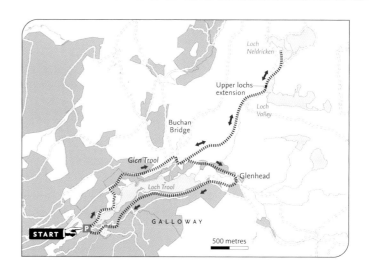

Start & finish Car park at foot of Loch Trool; nearest postcode DG8 6SU (OS ref NX297791)

Walk (5½ miles circuit of Loch Trool, or 10 miles including upper lochs; moderate; OS Explorer 318): Follow woodland path past "green waymarks"/GW sign. NB: GWs are posts with green bands; they carry white waymark arrows (on their reverse sides) for clockwise walkers! In ½ mile enter conifer forest; in 200m, look for GW on left; climb track to road (402799). Right past Bruce's Stone car park (416804); descended rough road to cross Buchan Bridge (418804); fork left and continue (GW/"Gairland Burn"). In 200m, at right bend (420805), Loch Trool Trail continues along road. For Gairland Burn and upper lochs extension, go through gate and up hillside path ("Loch Valley, Gairland Burn"). Follow track to Gairland Burn; continue up left bank. Near top, cross side burns (436818); keep near Gairland Burn to Loch Valley. Keep left of loch, then follow stone wall by burn up to Loch Neldricken. Return to gate near Buchan Bridge; rejoin Loch Trool Trail by turning left along road (GW). In ⅓ mile cross Gairland Burn and continue; go through gate, and in 150m bear right off road (430801; "National Cycle Network 7"). Follow path to cross burn (430800); forward up side of forestry ("Southern Upland Way/SUW"); left along SUW beside Loch Trool for 1¾ miles, to cross Caldons Burn footbridge and reach T-junction (399789) with SUW post, GW post and a blue post marked "7 Stones". Bear right here to footbridge and car park.

Lunch Picnic; Glentrool Visitor Centre (01671 840302)

More information visitscotland.com

MONADHLIATH MOUNTAINS

It rained cats and dogs in the night, and well on until mid-morning. At last, the sky began to brighten – enough to make a kilt for a wee sailor. I'd been looking forward so much to getting up high and wild into the back country of the Monadhliath Mountains that a little bit of spit wasn't going to put me off.

Today, the River Calder in the flat lower strath of Glen Banchor and its tributary Allt Fionndrigh were rumbling and roaring, rain-swollen torrents shifting boulders and pebbles from their glacial banks by the ton.

I passed the old cattle-raising and raiding settlement of Glenbanchor, now nothing more than mossy stones, and made north up the stony track where Glenbanchor's cattle were driven each spring to sweeter grass high in the mountains. The Allt Fionndrigh came crashing down out of the hills, loud and chaotic over its boulders, and I walked upstream to find a footbridge.

Under the rocky bluffs of Geal Charn I found a flimsy wooden bridge and crossed the river. Sodden and squelchy, a path led up and over a saddle of high moorland. I followed a line of old fence posts, descending a long slope towards the hissing torrent of Allt Ballach. On the far side, the hills rose to humpback peaks – Carn Dearg and Carn Macoul, with a jumble of darkly magnificent mountains to the edge of sight beyond.

Down by the River Calder again, I turned for home. A frantic squealing in the upper air drew my binoculars. A pair of slate-grey peregrines swooped down from the clouds and circled me, driving the intruder on and out of their private wilderness.

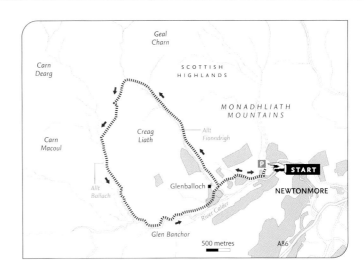

Start & finish Shepherd's Bridge car park, Glen Road, Newtonmore; nearest postcode PH20 1BH (OS ref NN693998)

Walk (8 miles; hard; OS Explorer 402): From car park continue across Shepherd's Bridge; on for ½ mile, passing abandoned cottage. Just before footbridge to Glenballoch (681993) turn right up Allt Fionndrigh river to join track up Fionndrigh glen. In 2 miles, descend left to cross footbridge (659019); follow track up cleft for 500m. At top (657015), more easily visible track swings right, but continue 50m, then bear left up faint grassy 4x4 track, aiming for Creag Liath peak. In 100m, track swings right; in 200m it reaches old fence posts (657012). Follow them to right (tricky underfoot, keep well left of the posts until past peat hags). Follow posts down to Allt Balloch river (652005); left beside river for 1¼ miles to confluence with River Calder (652986). Left by river to Glenballoch and car park.

Lunch Picnic; The Wild Flour, Newtonmore, PH20 1DA (01540 670975)

More information Wildcat Centre, Main Street, Newtonmore PH20 1DD (01540 673131); Aviemore Tourist Information Centre (01479 810930); visitscotland.com; ramblers.org.uk; satmap.com

Mither Tap draws the eye for many miles around. The 1,700ft (518m) peak with its steep flanks and bare granite crown rises high over the low-rolling landscape inland of Aberdeen.

We started up the forest path from Back o' Bennachie on a breezy afternoon, and were soon up above the pines and mossy gullies. A path of crunchy granite led up to the top of Oxen Craig through heather, bilberry and starry white flowers of chickweed wintergreen.

The view encompassed at least 100 miles, from far out across the North Sea in the east to Lochnagar standing tall in the Cairngorm range, and the flanks of Cairngorm mountain itself, blurred and gleaming with snow some 70 miles to the west.

From Oxen Craig we turned eastward across the heathery ridge of Bennachie. Just below the square grey crown of Mither Tap we found the tumbled walls of a Pictish fort 2,500 years old. Looking back to the slopes of Oxen Craig, we pictured the mighty force of 30,000 "Caledonians" who opposed a Roman army of similar size at the Battle of Mons Graupius in AD83. The Caledonians had the high ground, but the Romans wiped the floor with them, slaughtering one in three.

The north-west wind soon blasted us off the peak of Mither Tap. We followed the homeward path to the tors that crown Craigshannoch, and dropped down through Bennachie forest with ravens riding the wind above us like a cohort of ragged black witches.

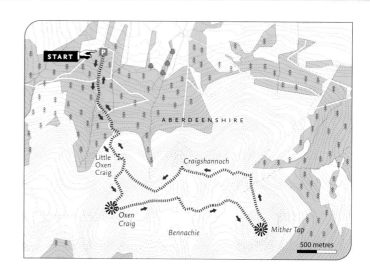

Start & finish Back o' Bennachie car park, near Pitcaple, Inverurie, Aberdeenshire AB52 6RH approx. (OS ref NJ 662246)

Walk (6 miles; strenuous; OS Explorer 421): From pay machine furthest from road, follow "Mither Tap Quarry Trail" (MTQT) signs south on steepening path. Follow MTQT for 3 miles via Little Oxen Craig (663232) and Oxen Craig (663227). Approaching Mither Tap, just beyond "Mither Tap" sign immediately below crags, fork left (682224) and follow path clockwise to summit. Return through fort gateway to path junction (683225). Follow "Bennachie Rowan Tree" (BRT) ahead. In ½ mile, in a hollow, left off BRT path (681231, "Craigshannoch") uphill. Pass cairn on right; at next T-junction, right on MTQT, "Back o' Bennachie" (BB). In 350m, fork right to summit of Craigshannoch (672232). Return to main route, turn right and follow MTQT, then BB, back to car park.

Lunch Picnic

More information Bennachie Visitor Centre, Chapel of Garioch, Inverurie AB51 5HX (01467 681470, bennachievisitorcentre.org.uk); bailiesofbennachie.co.uk; visitscotland.com

Yellow buds of winter aconite were struggling out under the trees at the National Nature Reserve car park. Wrapped up to the eyes, we set out along the coast path above cliffs of volcanic rock so tumbled and jagged that the outcrops resembled shattered castle walls. Grey seals had pupped on the secluded beaches of dusky red sand, and we caught glimpses of the adults offshore as they dived like fat Olympic swimmers after shoals of fish.

The path led into a sheltered green valley for a few minutes' respite before climbing the flank of Kirk Hill and into the wind again. Here on the slope in AD643 Aebbe – a Northumbrian princess in flight from the unwanted attentions of King Penda of Mercia – founded a nunnery. When St Cuthbert of Lindisfarne came visiting, he spent his nights in prayerful immersion, up to his neck in the sea. A hard man for tough times.

Just below the summit stood a lighthouse and the whitewashed cottages where its keepers once lived through wind, sun and wild weather. The walled garden where they grew their greens lay abandoned beyond.

From the viewpoint above a magnificent scene unfolded, west along mudstone cliffs stacked and folded towards the Firth of Forth and the distant hump of North Berwick Law, east over the fishing villages of St Abbs and Eyemouth among their volcanic headlands.

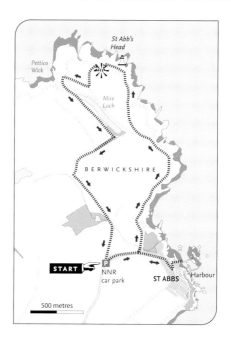

Start & finish St Abb's Head NNR Visitor Centre car park, St Abbs, near Eyemouth TD14 5PL (OS ref NT 913674), £3

Walk (5 miles; moderate; OS Explorer 346): From Visitor Centre follow "Path to St Abb's Head" signs; then "Lighthouse Loop" (purple arrows) to lighthouse (914692) and topograph beyond. Left along road. At northwest end of Mire Loch, left (908690) on Mire Loop (yellow arrows). At lower end of loch, right (913685) up stony track to road (912684). Ahead, following road back to car park. Left along B6438 to St Abbs harbour, and return to car park.

Lunch Old School Café, Ebba Centre, St Abbs (01890 771413, @EbbaCentre) – excellent home cooking and baking, warm welcome all year round. Book ahead if in group of 5+

More information St Abbs Visitor Centre (01890 771672, stabbsvisitorcentre.co.uk)

EOROPIE AND THE BUTT OF LEWIS

It is hard to think of a more beautiful sandy beach than Eoropie Dunes. On a calm spring morning it feels like a foretaste of heaven. But winters can be relentless here, the sea wild, the cliffs and reefs unforgiving.

In a storm on 5 March 1885 two boatloads of fishers from the tiny community of Eoropie were lost just offshore in full view of their families and neighbours who had gathered on the shore. On the clifftop above the beach I passed a memorial to the tragedy. The coast swung north past rugged bays and cliffs where fulmars went planing by, glancing at me with eyes as dark and shiny as blackberry drupelets.

I skirted deep geos or inlets where the waves crashed like cymbals, heading for the talk brick stalk of the lighthouse at the Butt of Lewis. A squadron of gannets flew south in strict line astern a mile out to sea, their sharp black wingtips beating regularly. Far out beyond them fifty of their fellows splashed and plunged soundlessly after an invisible shoal of fish.

At the Butt of Lewis the rocks are of gneiss some two thousand million years old. I sat on the rabbit-nibbled turf and stared my fill. The cliffs and the freestanding sea stacks stood striped, bent, twisted and arched in bands of orange, grey and brown, a remarkable testament to how the heat and pressure of that early subterranean world had bent the solid rock like toffee.

I followed the road back between dozens of narrow fenced croft lands, slim strips that go with each house. Back at Eoropie the only footmarks on the pristine beach were those of an otter, leading out across the sands to vanish in the shallows.

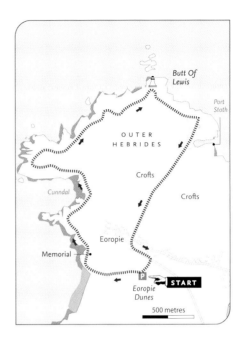

Start & finish Eoropie Dunes car park, near Butt of Lewis HS2 0XH (OS ref NB 517647)

Walk (4 miles; easy; OS Explorer 460): By furthest parking bay, turn right by picnic table on path. Go through gate and on to stone shelter by beach. On; through gate and follow coast path (marker arrows) for two miles, keeping close to cliffs. From Butt of Lewis lighthouse (520664) follow cliffs alongside road, then roadside verge. In ⅔ mile cross B8014 in Eoropie at bus shelter (517650); round left bend; in 250m, right to car park.

Lunch Cross Inn, Cross HS2 0SN (01851 810152, crossinn.com)

More information walkhighlands.co.uk; visitscotland.com

RACKWICK GLEN AND OLD MAN OF HOY

Among the Orkney Islands, Hoy is the odd one out. The other isles of the archipelago lie low and green off the northern tip of mainland Scotland, but Hoy rises in a series of steep dark hills, culminating in the lowering 1,500ft (457m) bulk of Ward Hill.

From the pier at Moaness I bucketed along the rough road to Rackwick aboard the Hoy taxi. Once down there in the sparsely populated old fishing hamlet, I felt a long way from anywhere.

I set off up the grassy hillside track, crossing springs that glinted down over mats of moss and lichens. Turning the corner of the hill of Moor Fea, the sea ahead was a silken blue, the coast a dark red jumble of sandstone cliffs where fulmars planed on stiff wings.

The path ran north above the flat green and purple tableland of Rora Head, the Burn of Stourdale tumbling from the lip of slanted red cliffs in a grey mare's tail of spray.

The Old Man of Hoy is a geological phenomenon, a slender sea stack of sandstone 450ft (137m) high, rising from its footing on the rocky shore to a summit almost level with the cliffs.

The cliff path ran out to a viewing point. As I stood and stared, a horizontal prism formed in the air, bent in an arch and touched its seaward end to the foot of the stack, a once-in-a-lifetime rainbow.

The path from Rackwick back to Moaness led through a wild glen among the hills, a narrow cleft threaded by a boggy old road, as remote as could be. I came down to Moaness Pier as evening fell, the light going out of the day and a green flicker of the northern lights behind the hill of Cuilag to add the final touch of magic to the walk.

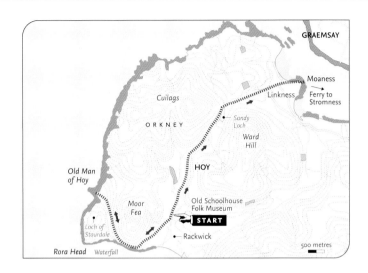

Start Rackwick, Isle of Hoy, Orkney KW16 3NJ (OS ref ND 200997)

Finish Moaness Pier, Isle of Hoy KW16 3NJ (HY 244040)

Walk (8½ miles; rough moorland walking; OS Explorer 461): From Rackwick follow "Old Man of Hoy" signs past schoolhouse, uphill and along track for 2¼ miles to cliff viewpoint opposite Old Man of Hoy (HY 177007). Return to Rackwick. Back up road. In 400m cross Rackwick Burn (202001); follow path ("Moaness 6.5km"). In 2½ miles join road at Sandy Loch (219032); follow it down to Moaness Pier.

Lunch Picnic

More information hoyorkney.com; Orkney International Science Festival (oisf.org); visitorkney.com; ramblers.org.uk

The bonxie surveyed me coldly, raising dark wings and issuing a harsh double croak from its hooked, half open beak. These fierce inhabitants of the Shetland Isles (known as great skuas to the outside world) are not at their sweetest during the chick-rearing season.

The last time I had climbed the Hill of Hermaness – the northernmost point of Unst, the northernmost island in the entire British archipelago – a bonxie had swooped so close that it had parted my hair.

Dodging the bonxies is only one of the many thrills of Hermaness. As you climb the path past the peat-brown lochans there's the chance of spotting snipe and golden plover, and perhaps a rare red throated diver sailing the water. On your right the craggy cliffs of Burra Firth dissolve in and out of the mist. And as you crest the hill and start down the last slope in Britain, ahead are the skerries that close off these islands, a line of canted, gleaming rock stacks with cumbersome, enchanting names: Vesta Skerry and Rumblings, white with nesting gannets; Tipta Skerry; Muckle Flugga with its high perched lighthouse. A little farther off rises the round blob of Out Stack, prosaically named, romantically situated: the end of the end.

I had it all to myself, the whole magical place. Fulmars circled, puffins scurried, gannets wheeled and plunged, the wind blew like a challenge. I dropped to the turf, grinning all over my face, and stared out north to where, 1,000 miles beyond the curve of the sea, the Arctic ice begins.

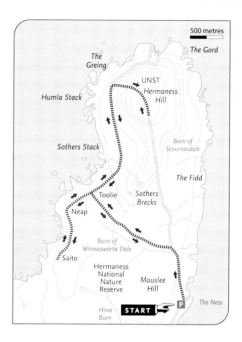

Start & finish The Ness parking place, Burrafirth, Isle of Unst (OS ref HP612147)

Walk (5 miles; moderate; OS Explorer 470): From Ness parking place at end of road, follow marked circular path (green-topped posts) round Hermaness. Allow 2–3 hours. Remote, windy, boggy and slippery underfoot: dress warmly and in waterproofs; walking boots. Take great care on cliff edges. Bring binoculars and a stick. Information leaflets in metal box at start of path.

Lunch Picnic

More information Lerwick Tourist Information Centre (01595 693434), www.shetland.org, visitscotland.com; Hermaness information: Scottish National Heritage, Lerwick (01595 693345); www.snh.org.uk

COIRE LAGAN, CUILLIN HILLS

From the end of the road in narrow Glenbrittle we started up a broad, steep grass slope towards Skye's most magnificent mountain backdrop. The Cuillin Ridge stood ahead, dark and dramatic, with clouds drifting among its razor-toothed peaks. The view back south was of dark blue waves riding in from Loch Brittle towards a long, sandy beach. Violets were struggling out among the grass clumps, and curlews had already begun their haunting territorial calls.

The well-made path trickled with runnels as the rain-sodden slopes disgorged their surfeit of water. We paused for a breather and a look back over Loch Brittle to where three of the Small Isles had slid into view – flat-backed Canna, mountainous Rum and the volcanic prow of Eigg.

A posse of climbers heading for the ridge swung past us, belts a-clink with multicoloured clips. I felt my customary twinge of envy for their careless athleticism and daring, then bent my efforts once more to the upward climb.

Now the sunshine fell behind and we were forging up the cleft of Coire Lagan in the shadow of the Cuillin Ridge. A short, sharp scramble up a jumbled staircase of rocks with a stream hissing down beside the path. Then the reward at the top of the climb: the still, black pool of Loch Coire Lagan under tremendous upthrusts of black gabbro, with the shark fin of Sgùrr Thearlaich rising dramatically to the 3,254ft (992m) pyramid of Sgùrr Alasdair, the highest peak on Skye.

Descending past Loch an Fhir-bhallaich towards Eas Mòr's horse-tail plume of falling water, we stopped for a last look at the high, black rock spires of the Cuillin Ridge. The clouds were already drifting back, and against their grey backdrop a magnificent golden eagle, monarch of the range, was slowly wheeling away.

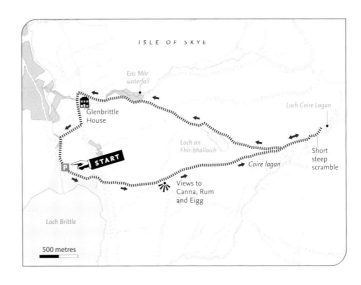

Start & finish Car parking area near Glen Brittle campsite IV47 8TA (OS ref NG 410205)

Walk (5¼ miles; strenuous; OS Explorer 411): From car park area at end of road, continue along track. Pass to left of campsite toilet block (pitched corrugated roof); through kissing gate; up path. In a few metres fork left on path. In 600m ignore path that heads to right (421203) across small burn and waterfall; keep ahead uphill here. In ¾ mile ignore a left fork (434206), and another in 400m with a big cairn (438206), both these paths leading past Loch an Fhir-bhallaich; instead keep ahead up main path. In another 200m path steepens beside Coire Lagan burn on your right, leading up a rocky "staircase" to Loch Coire Lagan (444209). Return down same path; in ½ mile, near large boulder on right (438206), fork right at big cairn on path for 2 miles, passing Loch an Fhir-bhallaich (432208) and later Eas Mòr waterfall (420214) to descend to road at Glenbrittle House (412214). Left along road for ⅔ mile to car park.

Lunch Picnic

More information walkhighlands.co.uk; visitscotland.com; mwis.org.uk

Giant's Causeway, Northern Ireland

DOWNHILL AND BENONE STRAND

Frederick Hervey, 4th Earl of Bristol, Bishop of Londonderry from 1768–1803, was a remarkably broad-minded man. In that intolerant era of Penal Laws against Catholics, the bishop allowed the local priest to celebrate Mass in the Mussenden Temple, one of the follies that he erected around his preposterously extravagant Downhill Estate on the cliffs outside Castlerock.

Jane and I entered Downhill on a brisk windy morning under the knowing grins of the mythic lynx-like beasts that guard the estate's so-called Lion Gate. Beyond lay the Bishop's enormous Palace of Downhill in poignant ruin, its grand fire places hollow and stark, its windows blank, state rooms carpeted with grass and open to the sky.

Down on the brink of the basalt cliffs beside the domed Mussenden Temple, we looked out on a most sensational view: the sea shallows creaming on seven clear miles of sand that ran west in a gentle curve towards the mouth of Lough Foyle, with the clouded hills of "dark Inishowen" beckoning from far-off Donegal. That proved an irresistible call. Down on the strand we pushed into the wind. Waves hissed on the tideline, sand particles scudded by. The black and green rampart of the cliffs was cut vertically by white strings of waterfalls, the falling cascades blown to rags in mid-plummet.

All this vigour and movement whipped us onwards to where the preserved sand dunes of Umbra rose between strand and cliff foot. It was a complete change of tempo here, sheltered among the sandhills, down on our hands and knees amid pyramidal orchids of blazing crimson, yellow kidney vetch, lady's bedstraw sacred to the Virgin Mary, and tall spikes of common spotted orchids.

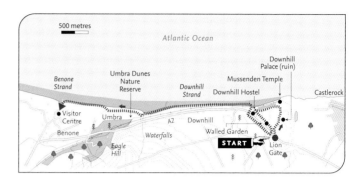

Start & finish Lion Gate car park, Downhill Estate, Castlerock BT51 4RP (OSNI ref C757357)

Walk (6 miles; easy; OSNI Discoverer 04): From Lion Gate car park explore Downhill Palace ruin, then Mussenden Temple (758362). Return anticlockwise along cliff and take in the Walled Garden. From Lion Gate cross A2 (take care!); right downhill beside road on pavement. Short stretch with no pavement leads to foot of hill. Right under railway; left along Downhill Strand. After 1¼ miles, where river leaves dunes, look left for Ulster Wildlife Trust's Umbra Dunes notice (732359). Follow fence through dunes to descend on Benone Strand. Continue to Benone (717362, lavatories, Visitor Centre). Return along beach and A2 to Lion Gate car park.

Lunch Picnic or seasonal café at Benone Bistro, Benone Tourist Complex (028 7775 0555)

More information Downhill (NT) (02870 848728; www.nationaltrust.org.uk); Coleraine Tourist Information Centre (02870 344723); discovernorthernireland.com

GIANT'S CAUSEWAY

A balmy day on Bushfoot Strand, a day of sun and smoky autumn light. Atlantic breakers curved inshore in three lines of creamy foam, and surfers were defying the "Don't Swim" notices. Runkerry House sprawled under the far headland with outflung wings and twin towers, its hedges thick with gleaming scarlet rosehips.

At the outer tip of Runkerry Point, where a welter of black basalt lay at the feet of the cliffs, we looked back round the pristine arc of Bushfoot Strand and on along the jutting green cliffs. Then we turned east and followed the clifftops through drifts of harebells and the white rococo trumpets of convolvulus. The path skirted Leckilroy Cove, with its dark slit of a cave, and led across the flatgrass-grown roof of the futuristic Giant's Causeway Visitor Centre.

The Giant's Causeway, so heavily promoted in tourist literature, is a bird's beak of basalt dipping into the sea. It can seem an awful disappointment if you come on it from the wrong angle.

The best way to see it is to walk beyond the crowded Causeway and on along the mountain path round the next bay. From there, looking back, it is a natural wonder to make you gasp – mighty basalt columns 50ft (15m) high, packed together like organ pipes and, from this steep cliffside path, revealed in all its proper grandeur, backed by a Dante-esque headland.

We couldn't resist a ride in the rattletrap old Causeway tram, trundling "tick-tack, tick-tack" through the dunes to Bushmills at not many miles an hour, emitting banshee wails as it went. A crunchy return path beside the track, a saunter through the dunes and we were back on the broad sands of Bushfoot Strand.

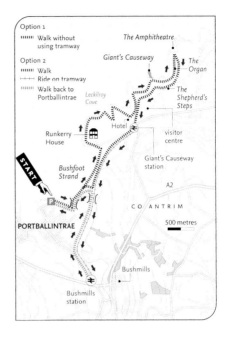

Start & finish Beach Road car park (free), Portballintrae, Co. Antrim BT57 8RT (OSNI ref C929424)

Walk (6½ miles; easy/moderate; OSNI Discoverer 1:50,000 Sheet 4; "Portballintrae Causeway Loop"): Path to beach; cross footbridge; along beach to path below Runkerry House and on to Causeway Hotel and Visitor Centre (944438). Down steps; road to Giant's Causeway (947447). Follow Blue Trail past Causeway, under "The Organ" formation (952449), round next corner to path's end in The Amphitheatre (952452). Back to fingerpost; fork left uphill ("Red Trail"). Up steep Shepherd's Steps to top (951445). Return to Visitor Centre and tramway station below. Option 1: follow path beside tramway; fork right just before river bridge (937426) on dunes boardwalk back to Portballintrae. Option 2: ride the tram from Giant's Causeway station to Bushmills; path returns beside tramway for 1 mile to cross river (937425); in 100m, left on dunes boardwalk to Portballintrae.

Lunch Picnic; Causeway Hotel (028 2073 1210, thecausewayhotel. com); Giant's Causeway Visitor Centre

More information Instructions/map at walkni.com; Giant's Causeway Visitor Centre (028 2073 1855, nationaltrust.org.uk/ giants-causeway); Giant's Causeway and Bushmills Railway (028 2073 2844, freewebs.com/giantscausewayrailway, £5 fare, weekends, bank holidays, April–June; daily, July–August; weekends September–October); discovernorthernireland.com; satmap.com

GLENARIFF

The nine Glens of Antrim are harsh country. Glenariff, the largest and deepest of all, is no exception. Ice Age glaciers gouged Glenariff deep and narrow, and tumbling waterfalls and cataracts continue the scouring process today.

Blue tits gave out a thin, clockwork "pzzit! pzzit!" as we descended the path towards the faint roar of the Glenariff River. Down there in the half-light we crossed Rainbow Bridge to explore the damp cleft beyond, every crevice packed and dripping with luxuriant moss cushions, jointed horsetails and creamy fungi sucking moisture from rotting logs.

The Waterfall Walk led us down wooden stairs and along teetery walkways, winding deeper into the gorge cut by the river. At one moment the path ran beside the water, the next it had leapt 50ft (15m) above it and was catwalking along the wall of the cleft. Zigzagging back down, we crossed a bridge and turned to enjoy a spectacular sight: the double cascade of Ess-na-Larach, the Mare's Fall, tumbling like a swishing horse's tail 50ft (15m) into a smoking pool.

Just above the confluence of the Glenariff and Inver rivers is the second of the glen's breathtaking waterfalls, Ess-na-Crub, the Fall of the Hooves – another equine inspiration, perhaps drawn from the thunderous noise of the water.

A long back-and-forth climb led us up through the forest to the rim of the glen, where the moorland lay silent under strong sunlight. The upper falls of the Inver River came crashing over a basalt lip high on the skyline. Turning down the homeward path, we saw the whole of Glenariff stretched out ahead, wooded slopes sweeping down to a far-off glimpse of the sea in Red Bay, where a solitary fishing boat rocked at ease in the hazy afternoon light.

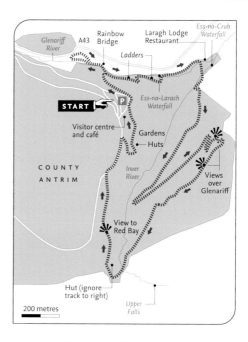

Start & finish Glenariff Forest Park car park, BT44 0QX approx. (OSNI ref D210202)

Walk (5 miles; moderate; OSNI discoverer map 9): From Glenariff Forest Park car park, follow Waterfall Walk/WW signs. At foot of slope, by WW signboard, bear left down path to cross Rainbow Bridge. Track soon doubles back to re-cross bridge and continue along WW. Follow WW to Laragh Lodge tearoom. Cross Glenariff River and start up track; detour left to see Ess-na-Crub waterfall, then on up track. In 100m fork left to cross Inver River, following Scenic Trail/ST upwards through zigzags and up steps and slopes for 1½ miles to cross upper waters of Inver River. Soon a track marked by a signboard branches sharply right past hut; ignore this. In 800m, where ST crosses downward-sloping track opposite old quarry hopper, bear right off ST down track. Right by building at bottom to reach wooden huts in gardens. Steps behind huts lead up into gardens; bear right ("Viewpoint Walk") to car park.

Lunch Glenariff Forest Park café; Laragh Lodge restaurant (028 2175 8221, laraghlodge.co.uk)

More information Download map at walkni.com/walks/234/glenariff-forest-park-scenic-trail; Ballymena Tourist Office (028 2563 5900, discovernorthernireland.com); satmap.com

SLIEVE BINNIAN, MOURNE MOUNTAINS

A cool, blowy morning on the coast of Co. Down, with the clouds rolling off the Mourne Mountains and skylarks beginning to sing their claims to territory in the stony fields at the foot of Slieve Binnian. From an ancient droving route in the Annalong Valley, bounded by walls of giant granite stones, we looked up to see Binnian's rocky head outlined against a dark sky.

The old track forged north to its crossing place through the granite barrier of the Mourne Wall. The climb soon steepened and there were plenty of pauses to look back around the bowl of hills that centres on the rocky-faced Slievelamagan and the tall cone of Slieve Donard, the king of the Mourne range at 2,789ft (850m).

Up ahead a line of granite tors crowned Slieve Binnian's ridge, black and jagged like the turrets of an evil castle. The view that burst on us from the top was worth climbing the tors for – the long steel-blue triangle of Silent Valley reservoir 2,000ft (600m) below, the coires of Slieve Muck beyond, and in the distance the hills of the Cooley Peninsula and the broad spread of Dublin Bay towards the distant Wicklow Mountains.

A path of skiddy granite rubble led us north past the Back Castle's wind-smoothed tors of elephantine grey, to drop steeply to a saddle of ground under Slievelamagan. A last look across Ben Crom Reservoir's dark waters, northwards to the steeples of rock that crown Slieve Bernagh.

Then we followed the rubbly old drove road back down the Annalong Valley, past the shores of Blue Lough, where whitecaps ruffled the water, on down to Carrick Cottage Café and a thoroughly earned pot of tea to toast St Patrick's Day.

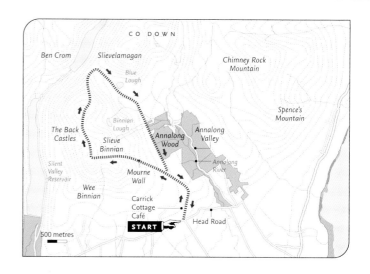

Start & finish Carrick Little car park, Head Road, near Annalong, BT34 4RW approx. (OS ref 345259)

Walk (7 miles; strenuous, OSN1 1:25,000 Activity Map "The Mournes"): From car park, left up stony lane. In 900m, go through gate (345228); in 300m, fork left and climb path with Mourne Wall on left, soon steepening. Near top, pass but don't cross ladder stile on left at wall; aim a little right between two tors to reach ridge (321235) and Slieve Binnian summit. Right on ridge path past the Back Castles for ¾ mile to pass to left of the North Tor (319246). Path descends, soon steeply, for ⅔ mile to path crossing on saddle between North Tor and Slievelamagan (321256). Right on rubbly path for 3¼ miles, passing Blue Lough, then along right side of Annalong Wood, back to car park.

Lunch Carrick Cottage Café, near car park (07595 929307); Brunels Restaurant, Newcastle (028 4372 3951, brunelsrestaurant.co.uk)

More information Newcastle Tourist Information Centre (028 4372 2222, visitmournemountains.co.uk); walkni.com; discovernorthernireland.com

VINEGAR HILL

Martin McGuigan is exactly the man you want with you in the Sperrins Hills of Northern Ireland. This wild range of fells, straddling the waist of Co. Tyrone, is his native ground. "We would never have had this view if it wasn't for the Ice Age," Martin says, pointing out the landscape features of the Sperrins from the heights of the narrow Barnes Gap. "The glaciers scraped and shaped all the hills that you can see; and then, when they were melting, they formed a huge lake. When that overflowed it simply burst through a weak spot in the rock and formed the Gap itself."

A landscape with dynamic origins, and an exceptionally beautiful one. An old stony road, part of the new Vinegar Hill Loop walk that we are following, winds like a scarf around the upper shoulders of Gorticashel Glen.

On Vinegar Hill stands a tumbledown cottage, its rafters half-smothered with fuchsia and Himalayan balsam. Martin fingers the balsam, ruminating: "These flowers were a big thing in my childhood. The bees would go crazy for them, and we'd see how many we could catch in a jam jar before we got stung."

At Scotch Town we find the crossroads guarded by a handsome rooster in a tippet of gleaming ginger feathers. Near Garvagh, as we turn for our homeward step, a great roadside shed stands provisioned for the winter with dried sods of turf.

This whole glen speaks eloquently of the life and work of family farms, present and past. Now, with the opening of the Vinegar Hill Loop, cheerful voices will be heard around the abandoned steadings and boots will tread the forgotten green roads of Gorticashel once more.

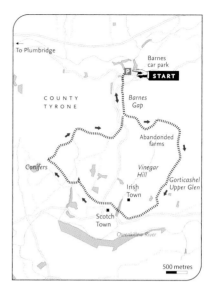

Start & finish Barnes Gap car park/toilet/picnic area at foot of Mullaghbane Road (OSNI ref H551905)

Walk (7 miles; moderate; OSNI 1:50 000 Discoverer 13; purple arrow way marks): Walk up the higher of the two Barnes Gap roads ("Craignamaddy Circuit"/CC, "Ulster Way" sign) past farm (barking dogs!). Right along Magherbrack Road for ⅓ mile; left (552896; CC) along dirt road. Follow it round Gorticashel Glen for 2 miles to road near Irish Town (558873). Right for ⅔ mile to crossroads in Scotch Town (548875; "Gortin" left, "Plumbridge" right). Straight across here and over next two crossroads (544875 and 538880) for 1 mile, to pass turning on left (536883 – tarmac stops here). Ahead for 300m; at stand of conifers, right (534885; "Vinegar Hill Loop") on stony lane. Follow it for just over 1 mile to road (550892). Forward to Barnes Gap road; left to car park.

Lunch Picnic

More information Omagh Tourist Information Centre, Strule Arts Centre, Omagh (02882 247831); walkni.com; discovernorthernireland.com; ramblers.org.uk; satmap.com; sperrinstourism.com

INDEX

ACKNOWLEDGEMENTS

Image Credits

P8–9 © Alamy
P13 © Shutterstock
P17 © Shutterstock
P21© Alamy
P25 © Alamy
P29 © Alamy
P33 © Jane Somerville
P37 © Alamy
P42–43 © Shutterstock
P47 © Shutterstock
P53 © Jane Somerville
P57 © Shutterstock
P63 © Alamy
P68–69 © Alamy
P73 (top) © Jane Somerville
P73 (bottom) © Shutterstock
P79 © Alamy
P83 © Shutterstock
P89 © Shutterstock
P94–95 © Alamy
P99 © Alamy
P105 © Alamy
P109 © Alamy
P113 © Jane Somerville
P117 © Alamy
P120–121 © Alamy
P125 © Shutterstock
P131 © Jane Somerville
P135 © Alamy
P140–141 © Alamy
P145 © Alamy
P149 © Alamy
P153 © Alamy
P157 © Jane Somerville

P159 © Alamy
P162–163 © Alamy
P167 © Alamy
P171 © Alamy
P175 © Alamy
P181 © Shutterstock
P185 © Alamy
P190–191 © Alamy
P195 © Shutterstock
P199 © Alamy
P201 © Jane Somerville
P205 © Alamy
P209 © Alamy
P212–213 © Alamy
P217 © Alamy
P221 © Alamy
P227 © Alamy
P232–233 © Alamy
P237 © Alamy
P241 © Jane Somerville
P245 © Alamy
P247 © Alamy
P249 © Alamy
P254–255 © Jane Somerville
P259 © Alamy
P263 © Alamy
P265 © Alamy
P269 © Alamy
P273 © Jane Somerville
P276–277 © Alamy
P281 © Alamy
P283 © Jane Somerville
P285 © Alamy